Drugs, Alcohol, and Social Problems

Understanding Social Problems:
An SSSP Presidential Series

Understanding Social Problems is a textbook series published in collaboration with the Society for the Study of Social Problems, under the direction of the SSSP Editorial and Publications Committee. The anthologies introduce students to the principles for assessing social problems and to exemplary research studies in the field. Articles selected from the society's leading journal, *Social Problems*, are chosen for their coverage, their relevance, and their accessibility to students. Introductions written by each book's editors situate the issues raised by the articles into a broader sociological perspective.

All royalties from this series go to support the SSSP and its activities.

Social Problems across the Life Course

> Edited by Helena Z. Lopata and
> Judith A. Levy

Drugs, Alcohol, and Social Problems

> Edited by James D. Orcutt and
> David R. Rudy

Health and Health Care as Social Problems

> Edited by Peter Conrad and Valerie Leiter

Drugs, Alcohol, and Social Problems

EDITED BY JAMES D. ORCUTT
AND DAVID R. RUDY

ROWMAN & LITTLEFIELD PUBLISHERS, INC.
Lanham • Boulder • New York • Toronto • Oxford

ROWMAN & LITTLEFIELD PUBLISHERS, INC.

Published in the United States of America
by Rowman & Littlefield Publishers, Inc.
A wholly owned subsidary of the Rowman & Littlefield Publishing Group
4501 Forbes Boulevard, Suite 200, Lanham, Maryland 20706
www.rowmanlittlefield.com

PO Box 317, Oxford OX2 9RU, United Kingdom

British Library Cataloguing in Publication Information Available

Library of Congress Cataloging-in-Publication Data

Drugs, alcohol, and social problems / edited by James D. Orcutt and
David R. Rudy.
    p. cm.
Includes bibliographical references and index.
   ISBN 0-7425-2844-8 (cloth : alk. paper)—ISBN 0-7425-2845-6 (pbk. :
alk. paper)
  1. Drug abuse—United States. 2. Drug abuse—Social aspects—United
States. 3. Alcoholism—United States. 4. Alcoholism—Social
aspects—United States. 5. Substance abuse—Social aspects—United
States. I. Orcutt, James D. II. Rudy, David R.
  HV5825.D7798 2003
  362.29'0973—dc21

                                        2003004918

Printed in the United States of America

Contents

Acknowledgments

The chapters in this volume originally appeared in *Social Problems* and are copyrighted by the Society for the Study of Social Problems. We thank the publisher and authors for permission to reprint the following works:

1. Gusfield, Joseph R. "Constructing the Ownership of Social Problems: Fun and Profit in the Welfare State." *Social Problems* 36 (1989):431–441.
2. Schneider, Joseph W. "Deviant Drinking as Disease: Alcoholism as a Social Accomplishment." *Social Problems* 25 (1978):361–372.
3. Orcutt, James D., and J. Blake Turner. "Shocking Numbers and Graphic Accounts: Quantified Images of Drug Problems in the Print Media." *Social Problems* 40 (1993):190–206.
4. Rouse, Timothy P., and Prabha N. Unnithan. "Comparative Ideologies and Alcoholism: The Protestant and Proletarian Ethics." *Social Problems* 40 (1993):213–227.
5. Beckett, Katherine. "Setting the Public Agenda: 'Street Crime' and Drug Use in American Politics." *Social Problems* 41 (1994):425-447 (Note: Figures 9–14, pp. 438–440 have been omitted).
6. Wysong, Earl, Richard Aniskiewicz, and David Wright. "Truth and DARE: Tracking Drug Education to Graduation and as Symbolic Politics." *Social Problems* 41 (1994):448–472.
7. Wallace, John M., Jr., and Jerald G. Bachman. "Explaining Racial/Ethnic Differences in Adolescent Drug Use: The Impact of Background and Lifestyle." *Social Problems* 38 (1991):333–357.
8. Herd, Denise. "Drinking by Black and White Women: Results from a National Survey." *Social Problems* 35 (1988):493–505.
9. Barr, Kellie E. M., Michael P. Farrell, Grace M. Barnes, and John W. Welte. "Race, Class, and Gender Differences in Substance Abuse: Evidence of Middle-Class/Underclass Polarization among Black Males." *Social Problems* 40 (1993):314–327.
10. Zimmerman, Don H., and D. Lawrence Weider. "You Can't Help but Get Stoned: Notes on the Social Organization of Marijuana Smoking." *Social Problems* 25 (1977):198–207.

11. Adler, Patricia A., and Peter Adler. "Shifts and Oscillations in Deviant Careers: The Case of Upper-Level Drug Dealers and Smugglers." *Social Problems* 31 (1983): 195–207.
12. Kantor, Glenda Kaufman, and Murray A. Straus. "The 'Drunken Bum' Theory of Wife Beating." *Social Problems* 34 (1987):213–230.
13. Faupel, Charles E., and Carl B. Klockars. "Drugs-Crime Connections: Elaborations from the Life Histories of Hard-Core Heroin Addicts." *Social Problems* 34 (1987):54–68.
14. Bourgois, Philippe, Mark Lettiere, and James Quesada. "Social Misery and the Sanctions of Substance Abuse: Confronting HIV Risk Among Homeless Heroin Addicts in San Francisco." *Social Problems* 44 (1997):155–173.

Introduction

The studies of drug and alcohol problems in this book originally appeared in *Social Problems*, a journal of sociological inquiry into major social issues that divide and trouble modern societies. The use of mood- and mind-altering substances is a source of great conflict in North American society. Whereas millions of people view drinking and drug use as pleasurable activities that enhance sociability and personal well-being, millions of others condemn these practices as immoral behavior that threatens the social order and poses serious risks to individuals. Of course, many people embrace both positions, seeing little wrong with "appropriate" uses of certain substances and little good in the "abuse" of these or other drugs. The conflict and ambivalence that surround the use of drugs and alcohol are among the reasons why many sociologists find it a fascinating and fruitful area for research into social problems. In this book, we present some of the best sociological work on these controversial issues—work that will encourage you to reexamine your own views about drugs, alcohol, and social problems.

The fourteen chapters we selected for this volume cover a broad range of drug- and alcohol-related problems and use a variety of theoretical and methodological strategies to examine those problems. However, these studies all have something in common: They examine drinking and drug problems as products of socially organized activity and shared understandings. Whereas many other disciplines view these problems as manifestations of individual disorder or pathology, the sociological perspective that pervades the works in this book emphasizes the fundamental importance of institutionalized social relationships and cultural meanings in the emergence, patterning, and consequences of drug and alcohol problems. As shown by the three "social constructionist" analyses in part I, the activity of organized "claims-making" groups—social movements, treatment professions, the mass media—shapes the way we think about problems such as alcoholism, drunk driving, and cocaine epidemics. By making claims about the threats and costs of alleged conditions, by attaching names like "disease" or "epidemic" to these purported troubles, and by calling for some kind of societal response such as medical treatment or a "War on Drugs," claims-making groups construct social definitions of drug and alcohol problems.

The chapters in part II, "Political and Ideological Contexts," employ three differ-ent analytical strategies to gain insight into the political organization of societal re-sponses to drug and alcohol problems. The first study in this part uses a comparative approach by examining parallels among alcohol policies in the United States and in the former Soviet Union, whereas the second presents a longitudinal analysis of political influences on changes in public opinion about the seriousness of street crime and drug problems. The final article in part II draws upon quasi-experimental evidence from an evaluation project to raise questions about the effectiveness and ideological underpin-nings of DARE, a popular program designed to prevent drug abuse among young peo-ple. Despite these differences in research method, the common constructionist aim of these studies is to show how the claims-making activities of powerful political actors, institutions, and interest groups profoundly influence public support for particular views of social problems and potential solutions to those problems.

Part III turns from the constructionist approach to the "objectivist" standpoint of social epidemiology—the study of the rate and distribution of drug use and drinking behavior in various populations. The three chapters in this part continue the concern for problems of social organization by focusing on systematic patterns of social in-equality and problematic uses of mood-altering substances. There is a long tradition of epidemiological research on social inequality and rates of deviant behavior in the United States. During the 1930s Robert Merton (1938) argued that "normal" features of American society—a strong cultural emphasis on the goal of material success, a be-lief that anyone can potentially obtain this goal, and a class structure that blocks legit-imate opportunities for success among a substantial segment of the population—promote high rates of norm-violating behavior such as crime, chronic drunkenness, and drug addiction in the lower class. In line with Merton's interest in rates of deviant behavior, the three studies in part III use survey data from large population samples to examine the likelihood that people in different class, gender, and race-ethnic locations engage in the use of illegal drugs or drink heavily. As you will see, the results of these epidemiological investigations show that these patterns of behavior are complex and, in some respects, run contrary to theoretical arguments and common-sense stereotypes about the concentration of drug and alcohol problems in lower-class and minority populations.

No line of sociological research better illustrates the importance of social organiza-tion and shared meanings in understanding drug and alcohol problems than does the qualitative work featured in part IV, "Social Worlds." Ethnographic studies of social problems based on direct observation and in-depth interviews also have a long history in American sociology. Starting in the 1920s, sociologists at the University of Chicago went into urban neighborhoods to examine first hand the organization and diversity of community life in "natural areas" of the city such as ghettos, slums, and hobo camps (Bulmer 1984; Faris 1970). The two studies in part IV fall squarely in this tradition. Based on field observation and in-depth interviews with marijuana users and drug deal-ers, these chapters provide richly documented portraits of the daily routines and situa-tional expectations that sustain illegal practices. In so doing, qualitative studies such as these offer a close-up view of the social organization of drug-using communities—the meaningful personal choices, interactional rituals, and subcultural understandings—

that are only indirectly reflected in quantitative data on rates of drug and alcohol use. These studies also provide insight into why outsiders, including many social scientists, often misunderstand the meanings that participants in these social worlds attach to their decisions and experiences with drug-related activity.

As the chapters in part V amply demonstrate, considerable misunderstanding surrounds scientific and public conceptions of linkages between substance use and other social problems. Over the past hundred years in the United States, claims-making groups such as Prohibitionist organizations and drug-control agencies have actively promoted definitions of drug and alcohol use as "root causes" of a variety of public problems and personal pathologies. These socially constructed images attribute social evils like the break-up of families, epidemics of crime, and widespread violence to the power of drugs and alcohol to dissolve moral constraints and unleash antisocial behavior. Given this legacy of claims about the profound influence of mood-altering substances on social disorder, it is not surprising that social scientists have devoted considerable attention to linkages among drugs, alcohol, and other social problems. The investigations in part V use quantitative and qualitative methods to examine three troubling conditions—spouse abuse, criminal behavior, and HIV infection. Each study raises serious questions about simplistic conceptions of substance use as a root cause of these troubles. Instead, the evidence points, once again, to the pervasive influence of social organization and the need for prevention efforts that give greater attention to cultural definitions of violence, the patterning of criminal careers, and the oppressive consequences of social inequality.

The chapters in this volume provide a representative sample of the wide range of issues that fall within the scope of the sociology of drugs and alcohol, and they illustrate many of the theoretical and empirical tools sociologists use in their work on social problems. These studies also offer numerous examples of the critical function of sociological inquiry, in which conventional views and "normal" social arrangements may be treated as analytically problematic and, in some cases, as underlying sources of problematic conditions. The sociological perspective is a valuable resource for understanding the complex problems and controversies of contemporary social life. After reading this book, we think you will agree that the study of drug and alcohol problems offers especially exciting opportunities to make full use of the power of sociological analysis.

References

Bulmer, Martin. 1984. *The Chicago School of Sociology: Institutionalization, Diversity, and the Rise of Sociological Research*. Chicago: University of Chicago Press.

Faris, Robert E. L. 1970. *Chicago Sociology: 1920–1932*. Chicago: University of Chicago Press.

Merton, Robert K. 1938. "Social structure and anomie." *American Sociological Review* 3:672–682.

Part I

THE SOCIAL CONSTRUCTION OF DRUG AND ALCOHOL PROBLEMS

How do activities such as drunk driving or the use of crack cocaine become social problems? For many people the answer is obvious: These are inherently harmful acts whose growing incidence in modern societies poses serious threats to human life, health, and productivity. From this conventional "objectivist" viewpoint, drug and alcohol problems are objective conditions—they are "out there in the real world." However, the three chapters in this part adopt an alternative view of the origin and nature of drug and alcohol problems. Using a "constructionist" perspective, these works focus on how the social reality of public problems is created and maintained by social movements, journalists, treatment professionals, and other claims-making groups. Constructionist researchers have shown that the potential harms or costs of various forms of drug and alcohol use often fail to correspond to public conceptions of the seriousness or threat of such behaviors. Any condition—whether real or imaginary, harmful or not—only becomes a "problem" when claims-making groups succeed in defining it as a problem. Thus, for constructionists such as Gusfield, Schneider, and Orcutt and Turner, the key to understanding how drinking and drug use become social problems is to study how various groups go about the work of constructing social definitions of public threats such as "killer drunks" on the highways, the "disease" of alcoholism, and "epidemics" of drug use in the nation's schools.

We begin this part with an overview of the constructionist approach by one of its foremost practitioners, Joseph Gusfield. In his 1989 presidential address to the Society for the Study of Social Problems, Gusfield shows how socially constructed conceptions of alcohol and other public problems serve as a source of "fun and profit" in the contemporary welfare state. First, he examines how the "troubled-persons" professions—treatment specialists, social workers, operators of institutions, and researchers—benefit from the growing tendency in modern societies to define personal troubles as public issues. For instance, increasing concern about "killer drunks" as a public threat has opened up numerous opportunities for treatment centers, alcohol rehabilitation and education programs, and many other public and private agencies that promote this definition of drunk driving and benefit from it. Turning to public problems as a source of "fun," Gusfield highlights the news and entertainment value of dramatized images of drinkers, drug users, and other troubled (or troublesome) people constructed by the "image-making industries," especially the mass media. His analysis provides excellent examples of how this "mass constructed reality" fundamentally shapes the language we use to talk and think about problems, and, consequently, our moral and political responses to public issues.

In the next chapter, Joseph Schneider traces the historical development of an especially influential definition of alcohol-related problems: the disease conception of "alcoholism." Schneider shows how a number of groups (such as the Temperance Movement, the Yale Research Center, and Alcoholics Anonymous) and individuals (Benjamin Rush, E. M. Jellinek, and Mark Keller) contributed to the transformation of deviant drinking from "sin" to "crime" to "sickness" over a period of two centuries. As he points out, various elements of the modern conception of alcoholism as a disease—that it is an addiction or allergy marked by a loss of control over drinking—emerged through the claims-making activities of medical and nonmedical interest groups rather than from the findings of scientific inquiry. Schneider concludes that the popular definition of "alcoholism" is a socially constructed conception of deviant drinking that reflects a general trend toward the "medicalization" of the definition and control of deviance in the United States and other societies.

Finally, James Orcutt and Blake Turner examine the recent construction of a "drug epidemic" by journalists and other claims-making groups. Following a decade of increasing drug use in the United States, national surveys in the early 1980s began to show steady declines in adolescents' use of many illegal drugs. Yet, in 1986, the national news media devoted unprecedented coverage to drug problems, portraying cocaine use in particular as a growing "epidemic." Orcutt and Turner present a detailed analysis of how media workers—reporters, graphic artists, and editors—used the tools of their trade to construct selective and often distorted accounts of statistical trends in drug use. In some instances, media workers literally built claims about an epidemic "from scratch" by transforming non-significant changes or trivial fluctuations in drug statistics into dramatic verbal and visual images of "plagues" threatening the youth of America. As this study and the chapters by Gusfield and Schneider demonstrate, we can only understand how activities like drinking and drug use become social problems by examining how the definitional activities of claims-making groups create public conceptions of them as "threats," "diseases," and "crises."

CHAPTER 1

Constructing the Ownership of Social Problems

FUN AND PROFIT IN THE WELFARE STATE

Joseph R. Gusfield

The "Social Problems" Culture and the Welfare State

A cultural perspective toward social problems begins at the beginning; with the concept of our study itself, with "social problems," not as an abstract tool of scientific analysis but as a way of interpreting experience. It is not sociologists and their students alone who live in the shadow and sunlight of "social problems." As an object of attention, social problems are a part of modern societies. They have to be seen in an historical context and in a structural dimension interacting with cultural interpretations of experience.

The idea of "social problems" is unique to modern societies. I do not mean that modern societies generate conditions which are problem-laden and cry for reform and alleviation while primitive and pre-industrial ones do not. I do mean that modern societies, including the United States, display a culture of public problems. It is a part of how we think and how we interpret the world around us, that we perceive many conditions as not only deplorable but as capable of being relieved by and as requiring public action, most often by the state. The concept of "social problem" is a category of thought, a way of seeing certain conditions as providing a claim to change through public actions.

All human problems are not public ones. Unrequited love, disappointed friendships, frustrated ambitions, parent-child disputes, biological aging are among the most searing experiences of life, but they have not yet been construed as matters requiring public policy or even capable of being affected by public actions. Much that in primitive and non-industrial societies has been either resignedly accepted or coped with in the confines of the family is now construed as the responsibility of public institutions.

In his recent book, *Total Justice,* the legal historian Lawrence Friedman (1985) has described many new legal rights that have emerged in American justice in the past fifty years. These have created legal entitlements to government aid toward resolving grievances for which, in the past, the only response was "lump it." A small but instructive example makes the point: the special ramps and parking spaces to which physically handicapped people are now legally entitled in the United States. Add to these the vast proliferation of others: civil rights, women's rights, prisoner's rights, children's rights, gay rights, and an etcetera much too lengthy to unpack. There is an inflationary trend that expands the areas described as "social problems," that spawns new movements for new rights and the recognition of new problems.

The concept of "social problems" is not something abstract and separate from social institutions. The late Ian Weinberg (1974) used the term "referral agencies" to describe the institutions and professions to which people turned to cope with public problems, a term I prefer to "social problems." To give a name to a problem is to recognize or suggest a structure developed to deal with it. Child abuse, juvenile delinquency, mental illness, alcoholism all have developed occupations and facilities that specialize in treatment, prevention and reform; for instance: shelters for runaway adolescents and battered women; alcohol and drug counselors and recovery centers; community services for the aged; legal aid for the indigent; community mental health counseling, and centers for the homeless. There is even a national organization called the Society for the Study of Social Problems.

New professions and new rights are continuously emerging, almost in a symbiotic relationship. As sexual therapy becomes a recognized field requiring training, and medical insurance is extended to it, we may find that sexual satisfaction is becoming a social responsibility and a citizen's right. But I promised you an historical rose garden as well as a structural one. Both as a feature of contemporary culture and as a matter of social structure, the conceptualization of situations as "social problems" is embedded in the development of the welfare state. When I speak of "the welfare state" I have in mind the long-run drift in modern societies toward a greater commitment to use public facilities to directly enhance the welfare of citizens (Ehrenreich 1985). This disposition to turn private and familial problems into public ones is a characteristic of most modern societies. It reflects both a higher gross national product and a democratized politics that insures a floor to the grosser inequities of life and the free market (Briggs 1961; Heilbroner 1989). Underlying both of these is the optimism of a sense of progress according to which most of life's difficulties are inherently remediable. The concept of "social problems" does more than point to deplorable situations. It suggests a social responsibility for resolving the resolvable.

The "Troubled Persons" Professions: Profit in Social Problems

Here, I want to discuss two significant parts of social structure: the occupations that serve "social problems"—what I call the "troubled persons professions"; and the occupations and institutions that inform and entertain—the image-making industries, including schools as well as the mass media. They are significant parts of the process by which publics experience social problems, interpret and imbue them with meaning, and create and administer public policies.

Most of us who read this journal, as well as many others in this service economy, live *off* social problems as well as *for* them. There is no adequate census of the social problems profession. In my county of San Diego there are ninety-nine separate organizations and their personnel that owe their existence and livelihood to alcohol problems. This includes the staffs of treatment agencies, such as detoxification and recovery centers, special clinics, lobbying organizations, legally mandated classes for drinking-driver offenders and the staff of the County Alcohol Services Office, one arm of the Substance Abuse Programs. The aphorism about the American missionaries who went to Hawaii three generations ago is an overstatement but it captures some of the process. "They came to do good. They stayed and did well."

The development of professions dedicated to benevolence, the so-called "helping professions," depend upon and accentuate the definition of problem populations as "sick," as objects of medical and quasi-medical attention. The "troubled persons" industries, as I like to call them, consist of the professions that bestow benevolence on people defined as in need. Such occupations include counselors, social workers, clinical psychologists, foundation administrators, operators of asylum-like centers, alcohol rehabilitation specialists, researchers, and the many jobs where the task is to bring people who are seen as trouble to themselves or to others into the stream of "adjusted" citizens. Alvin Gouldner (1970:77) captured this when he wrote: "Increasingly, the Welfare State's strategy is to transform the sick, the deviant, and the unskilled into 'useless citizens,' and to return them to 'society' only after periods of hospitalization, treatment, counseling, training, or retraining."

The key term here is "treatment" ("rehabilitation" is analogous). An example is the disease concept of alcoholism. "Seeing" alcohol problems as primarily those of persons suffering from a condition akin to other diseases did two things. First, it weakened the onus of responsibility on the chronic drunk for his condition. In that sense it marshaled attitudes of commiseration and benevolence. The alcoholic was someone to be helped and not merely condemned. Second, it made it reasonable to develop a body of knowledge and a corps of people who could be trained in the skills and knowledge needed to help the alcoholics. (To a significant degree, it also provided employment for recovering alcoholics who now had capital in their past troubles.) The same logic exists in the development of juvenile delinquency and the rehabilitative orientation toward criminals.

If deviants and troubled people are to be "returned" to society, it requires a special group of workers trained to accomplish the task and to administer the institutions that accomplish it. If, however, the difficulties are understood to be those of moral diversity, of contested meanings, then the problem is a political issue and no system of training can provide help. If the condition is perceived as that of individual illness or deficiency, then there can be a social technology, a form of knowledge and skill, that can be effectively learned. That knowledge is the mandate for a profession's license to "own" their social problem. Insofar as it is accepted it constitutes the source of ownership of a problem.

To "own" a problem (Gusfield 1981) is to be obligated to claim recognition of a problem and to have information and ideas about it given a high degree of attention and credibility, to the exclusion of others. To "own" a social problem is to possess the authority to name that condition a "problem" and to suggest what might be done about it. It is the power to influence the marshalling of public facilities—laws, enforcement abilities, opinion, goods and services—to help resolve the problem. To disown a problem is to claim that one has no such responsibility. In the nineteenth and early twentieth centuries the Protestant churches were the dominant "owners" of the alcohol problem, a status that has since been lost to medical, governmental, and academic institutions.

Patricia Morgan (1980) has suggested that the definition of social problems as those of "troubled persons" is a form of depoliticizing problems. There is much merit in this view. The psychologizing or medicalizing of phenomena, as a way of seeing, draws attention away from the institutional or structural aspects. The slogan of the alcohol industry, "The fault is in the man and not in the bottle," suggests this disowning. An interpretation of a social problem as one of the individual's deficiencies and the emergence of professions based on such assumptions limits the perception of institutional features at work.

The Image-Making Industries:
Social Problems as Fun

For many in this mass society, social problems are also an object of attention, a source of news interest and mass entertainment, a form of fun. Specific social problems are experienced directly by only a small segment of the population. Modern life is experienced both close-at-hand and far away. We know at first hand and face-to-face only a small portion of the stuff that makes up our perception of the "society." Verbal and visual images, the stuff of newspapers, magazines, books and education, of radio, movies, and television, make up the sources by which the larger world is mediated to us (Ericson, Baranek, and Chan 1987). They help to form our image of "society."

As part of this mass construction of reality, society is itself a spectacle, an object played before an audience. They may find it dull or exciting; informative or mysterious. It may be conveyed as a series of separate events or as a patterned sequence of activities. In this whirligig of acts, "social problems" constitute a constant and recurrent source of interest and, in popular culture, a basis for entertainment and even vicarious identification with evil. Crime, delinquency, drug addiction, child abuse, poverty, family violence, sexual deviance, prostitution, alcoholism make up a considerable part of news and popular drama. These provide much of the imagery with which social problems are perceived and acted upon. The criminal, the prostitute, the drug addict and the other objects of problems may be seen as deplorable, as troubled, as dangerous, but they are endlessly dramatic and interesting. Joel Best (1987) has shown how the problem of missing children was conveyed to the general public as the dramatic one of molested and mistreated children. His closer look found most of the cases to be those of children "kidnapped" by ex-husbands or ex-wives in disputes over custody, a much less interesting or lurid story.

In the content of much of popular culture we can find a great deal of the mythology of modern life (Cawelti 1976). The television presentation of the death of Candy

Lightner's child in an auto accident dramatized the drinking-driving problem as a major cause of auto accidents. It portrayed the experience of auto accidents as a morality play; as a contest between villains and victims. It created an image opposite to that of the "troubled person," namely, the image of the "troublesome person"—the myth of the "killer-drunk," as a standard, mythologized "type" through which to see each event (Gusfield 1981).

Such modern myths serve to symbolize complex events, as ways to understand social problems in personal terms. As such they redirect attention from structural and institutional aspects and support a theory of social behavior, and the policies related to it, that sees social policy as geared to remake the person. They make the world a more interesting place, a place where bad people are responsible for evil (Stivers 1988). To build excitement and narrative around such subjects as safety belts, auto design, alcohol availability, and user friendly roads may be possible but seems to lack the possibilities of villainy that the drinking-driver drama contains.

Consensus and Conflict:
The Public Status of Social Problems

The language and rhetoric of "social problems" is a language that assumes and points toward a basic consensus about the problematic character of the condition deplored, in the same fashion that a physician can assume that his/her patient wants to be cured. Child abuse, alcoholism, mental illness, prostitution, gender and racial discrimination, crime, drug addiction are just a few among many which are imbued with an aura of consensus. To challenge their status as social conditions requiring reform is unthinkable in the contemporary public arenas. The point is illustrated in one of my favorite comic strips, *Miss Peach*. The first-grade teacher has told her class that next week they will have a speaker on the topic of juvenile delinquency. "Oh, goody," says one of her young pupils, "Will he be for it or against it?"

Miss Peach's student made a profound utterance about most of the situations sociologists customarily study under the rubric of "social problem." They involve an assumed public consensus from which the behavior targeted for change or reform is perceived as outside the norm, as opposed to societally shared values. It is not publicly acceptable for anyone to be "for" mental illness, alcoholism, gender or racial discrimination, poverty, drinking-driving, air pollution, drug addiction, homelessness, or almost all the titles of chapters in the various texts in the field. To see a situation as a social problem is to set in motion a particular form of discourse and to channel policies in a particular direction.

Conventional language supports a psychologistic perspective. The concept of "substance abuse" locates the problem of alcohol in the abuser rather than the substance—its nature, availability and the conditions that make insobriety dangerous. "Mental illness" locates the phenomena in medical institutions and hospitals.

A point made by Murray Edelman (1977) in his analyses of the language of social problems is instructive. Aid to farmers, he pointed out, is called "parity," aid to business in the form of tax cuts is simply called aid to the general economy; aid to people at the poverty level is called "welfare" or "help." Differing language frames mean differing assessments and evaluations.

Edelman's discussion is pertinent. We use words like "welfare" and "helping" and "social problem" to emphasize the temporary and uncommitted nature of benevolence or control, rather than using the language of rights, which creates a different meaning. To use the language of "social problem" is to portray its subjects as "sick" or as "troublesome." We do not use a language of personal deficiencies to talk about economic concerns or to describe recession as the problem of sick businessmen, nor do we describe investment counselors as "market therapists." The income of the client affects the language of the profession. Subsidies to the auto industry are not called "aid to dependent factories."

Nor is the consensus illustrated by Miss Peach something inherent in the objects attended to. It is a social construction in which an assumed consensus is not contested. It can be contrasted with issues such as abortion or gun control or vivisection where the existence of diversity, of conflict, is so evident that the claim to represent a consensus falls on its face. In these areas a claim to represent the "society" appears patently unacceptable.

Claims to use public resources for reform posit a "society" that is homogeneous, against which the problem situation can be contrasted. In this the nature of "social problems" has not changed much since 1943 when C. Wright Mills (1943) published his justly classic paper, "The Professional Ideology of Social Pathologists." In his critical examination of the field, Mills (1943:531–32) described the method of defining social problems by sociologists as "in terms of *deviation from norms*. The 'norms' so used are usually held to be the standards of the society."

Consider the following claims to benevolent action, 77 years apart. In each the speaker claims to be representing public interests and social standards. In Milwaukee, in 1912, the city council considered legislation restricting the use of premises connected with saloons for purposes of dance halls. Opponents of the ordinance, especially the labor unions, charged class legislation, since the dance halls were a major form of young working class recreation. A social worker replied to this, saying:

> This is not a fight against the Germans or the Poles. It is not a fight against the pleasures of the working class. All we want to do is lift the moral standards of the city. Give our working girls the liberty of a pure city, pure enjoyment, rather than this personal liberty the opposition speaks of. (Harring 1983:185)

In 1989 the California State Supreme Court affirmed a lower court decision that prohibits staff members of mental hospitals from administering antipsychotic drugs against the wishes of patients committed for at least three-day to fourteen-day periods. An attorney for one of the hospitals, in commenting on the case, objected to the decision, saying: "This decision may satisfy someone's notion of an abstract principle but the patients who supposedly would benefit are going to be denied effective treatment" *(Los Angeles Times* 1989).

The speakers assert a claim to be recognized among those who "own" a part of the problems of alcohol use and of mental disorder. In the process of presenting themselves the speakers do more than state a personal opinion. They make a claim to represent more than themselves, to speak for the interests of the public and the interests of those they are acting toward. Not what the "working girls" or the patients want, but what the speakers claim that they need. The speaker asserts that the condition of the dance halls is to be considered a problem even though others—the opposition—do not see it as such. The speaker represents herself to speak for a consensus—a "society," a "true public interest." The situation, as she presents it, is not one of divergent standards but of a consensual society and a deviant minority, a presumed normality and an abnormal condition. It is not a political issue between differing points-of-view and interests. It is a social problem and a united societal consensus affirms it.

Contested and Uncontested Meanings: Benevolence and Social Control

Writing about the state as parent, David Rothman (1981) has recently traced the history of "doing good" as an organized public endeavor. It was part of the legacy of the progressive movement—a legacy that lasted to the mid-1960s. The belief persisted that the problems of the dependent, the disadvantaged, the deviant, and the delinquent could be resolved through a top-down benevolence, "with the better off doing for the worse off" (Rothman 1981:xiii) and, importantly, with a minimum of alteration of the existing institutional structure.

In recent years the claims to benevolence as legitimating the authority of ownership have seemed to sociologists and others to be thin and unsubstantial. The critiques of the medicalization of social problems have stressed the social control aspects of welfare institutions, just as the critiques of poverty programs have stressed the political uses of welfare (Conrad and Schneider 1980; Szasz 1961; Goffman 1961; Piven and Cloward 1977). A stream of studies have documented the primacy of institutional self-preservation in the conduct of social problems organizations. In the very definition of situations as problems the social control elements emerge, whether or not the practitioners are aware of them. These studies have critiqued the claims of the "helping" professions to be helping "troubled persons" (Gusfield 1984).

The idea that there is a unity of concern or interest between those at the top who bestow their benevolence and those at the bottom who receive it is open to doubt. It cannot be maintained without the smirks and winks of skeptical critics. In the California case dealing with anti-psychotic drugs, the successful attorney for the mental patient, when interviewed by the press, said: "What this case essentially does is give the mentally ill the same rights as the mentally healthy. . . . Too often these drugs are used as a substitute for adequate staffing in the hospitals" (*Los Angeles Times* 1989).

The Transformation of Meanings and Problems

As a matter of rhetoric, a form of persuasion, the designation of a situation as a "social problem" involves the claim that a societal consensus exists. It has the effect of limiting or ignoring adversarial elements and turning the problem into a technical or legal one in which alternative frameworks are simply not thought about, not only in Miss Peach's class but in public arenas. The case of "child abuse" will make the point.

What Stephen Pfohl (1977) has called "the discovery of child abuse" occurred in the 1950s with the interpretation by radiologists that bruises and broken bones seen on X-rays of children could be interpreted as results of beatings by parents and guardians. When a prominent pediatrician reported these findings in an important medical journal, monitored regularly by the press, child abuse became a matter of public notice. The activities of the Children's Bureau and the mass media helped place it high on the public agenda (Nelson 1984). Between 1963 and 1967 every state passed some form of law requiring the reporting of child abuse incidents and providing for criminal charges.

"Child abuse" was defined as physical or sexual "abuse" by parents or guardians and consensus about it as a problem was close to complete. Systems of reporting, enforcement agencies, counseling for children and for abusing parents have developed a structure accommodated to the definition of the nature and deplorable character of "child abuse." The meaning of "child abuse" was clear. The problem was located within the family, as a matter of parental misbehavior.

In her study of child abuse and the making of a public agenda, the political scientist Barbara Nelson (1984) distinguished between "valence issues" and "position issues." She writes: "A valence issue such as child abuse elicits a single, strong, fairly uniform emotional response and does not have an adversarial quality. 'Position issues,' on the other hand, do not elicit a single response but instead engender alternative and sometimes highly conflictful responses" (Nelson 1984:27). This is similar to the distinction now being made in social movements literature between conflict movements and consensual movements (Lofland 1989; McCarthy 1988) or to that made by political scientists between consensus issues and conflict issues (Hayes 1981; Crenson 1971). Abortion is a conflict issue; pro-life and pro-choice are conflict movements and counter-movements. It was the absence of controversy, of adversaries, that made the child abuse legislation develop so rapidly, according to Nelson.

Yet Nelson's analysis of child abuse as a valence issue presumes that its character results from its content. Pfohl's description of the earlier child abuse movement of the late nineteenth century indicates the possibility that children might well be experienced as the subjects of a more politicized framework. The similar conception of "child neglect" in that period emphasized the homelessness and malnutrition of children of poverty and threw the onus on the social structure and public institutions which associated poverty with child neglect. This is a much more adversarial, more political definition of the "child abuse" problem. It touches on the institutional arrangements of social and political organization. It cannot be "handled" through reforming persons or law enforcement. There have been some efforts to counter the current emphasis on the problems of parental abuse of children with alternative conceptions or to emphasize the rights of parents against state intervention. However, these have not been mobilized to a point of converting the dominant definition of child abuse from an apolitical to a political one. It now is experienced through the concrete image of good people and bad people; villains and victims.

To be experienced as a "social problem" rather than a "political issue" is a significant step in the construction of phenomena in the public sphere. In his 1977 Presidential address for the Society for the Study of Social Problems, "The Politics of Speaking in the Name of Society," Bernard Beck (1978:357) pointed out that under the guise of a social problem many interests can be served: "working politicians have discovered the usefulness of conducting politics under the guise of treating social problems." Beck used the example of the deinstitutionalization of custodial organizations such as mental asylums. There, as in the case of the decriminalization of public drunkenness, action taken with an eye toward state budgets is justified as benevolence toward people with troubles. Politicians shun the conflicts that embitter and divide their electorates. They are happy when they can "turn over" issues to technicians or into legal decisions.

It is evident, just from the two cases described above—the 1912 dance hall and the 1989 mental patient decision—that the efforts to define situations as "social problems" are far from always successful. Some groups are capable of mobilizing to bring about change or to resist controlling definitions. The gay rights movement is perhaps the most salient example of how the ability to mobilize has enabled a subject group to transform its status. During this century, homosexuals have been thought of as sinful and as sick, objects of condemnation or of medical benevolence. What the gay rights movement did was to resist the public designation of deviance, of abnormality, by attacking the presumed norms and denying that homosexuality constituted a social problem. In the process the phenomenon of homosexuality lost its status as a "social problem" and became a matter of political and cultural conflict over the recognition of alternative sexual styles. What had been an uncontested meaning has been transformed into a political contest.

Again and again sociologists have pointed out how the conditions said to define the social problem are socially constructed, are only one of several possible "realities." The attempt to pose as the arbiters of standards is less and less taken for granted and more and more seen as an accompaniment to social control, to the quest for hegemony. Rothman (1981:87) writes, "As to any effort to define what constitutes normal sexual behavior—one has only to raise this point to recognize immediately how absurd any such attempt would be." The same is true of other areas that are becoming more adversarial, such as mental illness or juvenile delinquency as well as homosexuality. Perhaps George Bernard Shaw said it well when he wrote: "Do not do unto others what you would have others do unto you. Their tastes may be different."

The disposition to deny an adversarial quality to a social problem spills over into research as well. In the corpus of studies of alcohol I find very few that have studied the benefits of drinking and drunkenness. The standard study of the economic costs of alcohol makes little attempt to state the value of benefits of alcohol as well as its costs

(Berry and Boland 1977; Weiner 1981:183-90). More importantly, there is no room for appreciation of the carnival point of view expressed by Omar Khayyám in the Rubaiyat:

> I often wonder what the vintner buys
> One-half so precious as the stuff he sells.

Mobilization for and the Transformation of Social Problems

I referred earlier to the gay rights movement as a striking example of how a mobilized social group has been able to bring about a change in the status of a social problem. The adversarial aspects of the alcohol problem are largely represented by the beer, whiskey, and wine industries. As a body, consumers are not well mobilized. The National Rifle Association is a distinct and powerful exception. The alcohol question has emerged as either a matter of voluntary persuasion, as the alcoholism movement defined it, or, more recently, as a unilateral protection against "troublesome people" whose styles of leisure take on connotations of deviance and consequently need not be given much consideration.

I have been asserting the de-politicizing effects of professionalization and mass culture. Yet the situation is not as simple as a quick generalization might lead us to believe. Shifting interpretations of conditions are not at all inconsistent with some aspects of the professionalization process. The disease concept of alcoholism was both a shift in the character of the alcohol problem and a new interpretation of alcoholism. In the early 1970s this emphasis on "troubled persons" and medicalization underwent a transformation. The problems connected with alcohol were expanded and the drinker described as a "troublesome person."

This shift resulted both from the professions developed by the alcoholism movement and the appearance of new movements, such as Mothers Against Drunk Driving (MADD). The very existence of professionals and clients presents the facilities and occasions for mobilizing the clientele. The development of the National Institute on Alcohol Abuse and Alcoholism emerged out of the efforts of recovering alcoholics, organized in the National Council on Alcoholism, as well as the organization of alcohol treatment professionals. As champions of their clients they were able to mobilize them to achieve entitlements to treatment, to legislative protections, and to medical insurance. A similar process has been at work in the movements for the rights of mental patients and of prison inmates. Stigma becomes the basis of mobilization and entitlements in a manner we need to assess in understanding deviance in the modern society (Gusfield 1982). The entitlements associated with deviance suggest a power and a societal integration that clashes with conventional theory in sociology. In the welfare society deviance is a social status that obtains rights as well as obligations.

A clear instance of how these elements operated politically is evident in the raising of the minimum age of sale of alcohol to twenty-one. After the voting age was dropped to 18, most states lowered the minimum age of sale of alcohol to 18 or 19.

Researchers concluded that the age group, 18 to 21, was a source of many deaths involving drinking-driving. The researchers also concluded that the 21–25 age group was even more "responsible" for such deaths, but no state even seriously considered extending the restriction to this fearfully more responsive group. Federal aid to highway construction was tied to state legislation raising the minimum age to twenty-one, and all 50 states passed such laws. The 18–21 group, the age group with lowest voting or political participation record, produced almost no opposition to the movement.

All of these movements are well within the meanings of an individualistic interpretation of social problems. They gloss over the possible role of institutional and structural features and, in this sense, depoliticize social problems. Yet any simple generalization should be resisted. The same movements and professions have played a key role in the emergence of what some are now calling "the new Temperance movement."

The more recent turn toward preventive policies that constitute considerations of industrial policy, of sales availability, of legal restrictions and liabilities, of automobile design, are products of the same movements that brought about the turn to criminalization. These do bring the problem into arenas of political conflict as they turn the alcohol problem away from medicalization and criminalization and towards a public health perspective (Beauchamp 1988). At the Surgeon-General's recent Workshop on Drunk Driving, advertisers and television networks, upset by the recommendation to restrict advertising, brought suit in an attempt to prevent the workshop from occurring.

In a way this chapter, like most presidential addresses, is a sermon. The moral is not contained in any summative sentence but it is a plea to move the study of social problems closer to the study of how social movements and institutions affect and are affected by the interpretations, the language, and the symbols that constitute seeing a situation as a social problem. At the same time, we need to take care not to separate the study of meanings from the study of their historical and institutional settings.

As interpreters of social problems we earn our livings by other people's troubles. One person's poison is another's mead (not George Herbert or Margaret). What we can best contribute to assuage our guilt is to cast an ironical eye on the passing scene so as to make us all more aware of the possibilities and opportunities that the veils of cultural meanings and institutional arrangements hide from us. It is out of this humanistic self-awareness that societies may yet achieve some control over their own destinies.

Note

This paper is a revised version of the presidential address presented to the Society for the Study of Social Problems, Berkeley, California, August 1989. Correspondence to: Gusfield, Department of Sociology, University of California-San Diego, La Jolla, CA 92093.

References

Beauchamp, Daniel. 1988. *The Health of the Republic*. Philadelphia: Temple University Press.
Beck, Bernard. 1978 ."The politics of speaking in the name of society." *Social Problems* 25:353–60.

Berry, Ralph and James Boland. 1977. *The Economic Costs of Alcohol Abuse*. New York: The Free Press.

Best, Joel. 1987. "Rhetoric in claims-making." *Social Problems* 34:101–21.

Briggs, Asa. 1961. "The welfare state in historical perspective." *Archives of European Sociology* 11:221–58.

Cawelti, John G. 1976. *Adventure, Mystery and Romance*. Chicago: University of Chicago Press.

Conrad, Peter and Joseph W. Schneider. 1980. *Deviance and Medicalization*. St. Louis: C.V. Mosby.

Crenson, Matthew. 1971. *The Un-Politics of Air Pollution*. Baltimore: The Johns Hopkins University Press.

Edelman, Murray. 1977. *Political Language*. New York: Academic Press.

Ehrenreich, John H. 1985. *The Altruistic Imagination*. Ithaca, N.Y.: Cornell University Press.

Ericson, Richard, Patricia Baranek, and Janet Chan. 1987. *Visualizing Deviance*. Toronto: University of Toronto Press.

Friedman, Lawrence. 1985. *Total Justice*. New York: Russell Sage.

Goffman, Erving. 1961. *Asylums*. Garden City, N.Y.: Doubleday.

Gouldner, Alvin. 1970. *The Coming Crisis of Western Sociology*. New York: Basic Books.

Gusfield, Joseph R. 1981. *The Culture of Public Problems*. Chicago: University of Chicago Press.

———. 1982. "Deviance in the welfare state." In *Research in Social Problems and Public Policy*, vol. 2, ed. Michael Lewis, 1–20. New York: JAI Press.

———. 1984. "On the side: practical action and social constructivism in social problems theory." In *Studies in the Sociology of Social Problems*, ed. Joseph W. Schneider and John I. Kitsuse, 31–51. Norwood, N.J.: Ablex.

Harring, Sidney. 1983. *Policing a Class Society: The Experience of American Cities*, 1865–1915. New Brunswick, N.J.: Rutgers University Press.

Hayes, Michael. 1981. *Lobbyists and Legislators*. New Brunswick, N.J.: Rutgers University Press.

Heilbroner, Robert. 1989. "Reflections on capitalism." *The New Yorker Magazine,* January 23:98–109.

Lofland, John. 1989. "Consensus movements: city twinning and derailed dissent in the American eighties." In *Research in Social Movements, Conflict and Change*, ed. Louis Kreisberg, 163–96. New York: JAI Press.

Los Angeles Times. 1989. "Mental patients allowed to refuse drugs." June 24.

McCarthy, John D. 1988. "Exploring sources of rapid social movement growth." (Unpublished manuscript).

Mills, C. Wright. 1943. "The professional ideology of social pathologists." *American Journal of Sociology* 49:16580. Reprinted in *Power, Politics and People: The Collected Essays of C. Wright Mills*, ed. Irving Horowitz, 525–52. New York: Ballantine Books, 1963.

Morgan, Patricia. 1980. "The state as mediator: alcohol problem management in the postwar world." *Contemporary Drug Problems* 9:107–36.

Nelson, Barbara. 1984. *Making an Issue of Child Abuse*. Chicago: University of Chicago Press.

Pfohl, Stephen. 1977. "The discovery of child abuse." *Social Problems* 24:310–23.

Piven, Frances Fox and Richard Cloward. 1977. *Poor People's Movements*. New York: Vintage Books.

Rothman, David. 1981. "The state as parent." In *Doing Good*, ed. Willard Gaylin, Ira Glasser, Steven Marcus, and David J. Rothman, 69–96. New York: Pantheon Books.

Stivers, Richard. 1988. "The concealed rhetoric of sociology: social problems as a symbol of evil" (unpublished manuscript).

Szasz, Thomas. 1961. *The Myth of Mental Illness*. New York: Harper.

Weinberg, Ian. 1974. "Social problems that are no more." In *Handbook of the Study of Social Problems*, ed. Erwin Smigel, 637–72. Chicago: Rand McNally.

Weiner, Carolyn. 1981. *The Politics of Alcoholism*. New Brunswick, N.J.: Transaction Books.

CHAPTER 2

Deviant Drinking as Disease
ALCOHOLISM AS A SOCIAL ACCOMPLISHMENT

Joseph W. Schneider

This chapter presents a brief social history of the idea that certain kinds of deviant drinking behavior should be identified by the label "disease." The historical location is the United States since roughly the end of the eighteenth century. I define the claim that such behavior is a disease as a social and political construction, warranting study in its own right (Berger and Luckmann, 1966; MacAndrew, 1969; Mulford, 1969; Freidson, 1970; Spector and Kitsuse, 1977). Whether such drinking "really" is a disease and, as such, what its causes might be, are not at issue. The analysis will trace the connection between ideas and social structures which appear to support or "own" them (Gusfield, 1975). This study is an investigation of the social bases of an assertion about a drinking behavior. More generally, this discussion is a case example of the medicalization of deviance and social control (Pitts, 1968, Szasz, 1970; Freidson, 1970: 244–277; Kittrie, 1971; Zola, 1972; Conrad, 1976) wherein a form of non-normative behavior is labeled first a "sin," then a "crime," and finally a "sickness."[1]

Clarification of the Problem

To those who treat problems caused by alcohol, debates about the definition of alcoholism as a disease are tedious and academic. After all, if one is employed in a hospital clinic treating alcoholics, then alcoholism must be a disease. However, whether something is a disease depends on significant portions of the medical community accepting the definition or not opposing its use by those in other fields. Because physicians represent the dominant healing profession in most industrialized societies, they have control over the use of the labels "sickness," "illness," and "disease," even if they are sometimes unable to treat those conditions effectively (Freidson, 1970:251). As such, these designations become political rather than scientific achievements (Spector and Kitsuse, 1977). Zola (1972) captures the expansive quality of medical jurisdiction clearly:

> My contention is that if anything can be shown in some way to effect the inner workings of the body and to a lesser extent the mind, then it can be labeled an "illness" or jurisdictionally a "medical problem."

19

This becomes particularly likely when the effects Zola describes are defined as negative rather than positive. The label "sick," although free from the opprobrium and implied culpability of "criminal," nevertheless involves a clearly disvalued moral condition, a deviation from "health, and a threat to the on-going network of interaction (Parsons, 1951). This common moral dimension provides the foundation for the historical shift from one system of social control (the church and state) increasingly to another (science and medicine).

Although it is clear that what is usually called "deviant drinking" fits Zola's description, I am here concerned with only a small segment of the medical model of alcohol: I focus on the idea that a particular pattern of repetitive, usually heavy, and always consequential drinking behavior should, of itself, be considered an instance of disease. A closely related yet distinct issue is the belief that some prior condition, usually identified as "pathological," causes the drinking which is seen as a "symptom" of this prior, and analytically distinct, pathology. Nor am I concerned with medicine's jurisdiction over the pharmacological, physiological, or psychological effects on the body, although this jurisdiction is, nonetheless, political.[2] I am concerned with the assertion that there is a disease called alcoholism that is identifiable independent of the specification of any conditions believed to be causes or effects of it.

Colonial Foundations and Origins of the Disease Concept

Drinking in seventeenth and eighteenth century America was normative and although disapproved, drunkenness was far from rare (Lender, 1978; Levine, 1978; Paredes, 1976; Keller, 1976). If anything was "bad" about drinking it was not drink itself, which even prominent clergy called a "good creature of God." Churches and drinking houses, as social centers of the community, were often close together. Concern about public drunkenness was expressed by a small few scholarly, aristocratic church leaders who warned against the sin of drunken excess, sometimes attributed to the work of the Devil. Punishment was initially a clerical admonition, followed by the extreme sanction of suspension, and finally by excommunication as the ultimate, although probably infrequently used, religious control. Civil authorities affirmed the church's judgment and meted out various forms of public degradation: fines, ostracism, whippings, and imprisonment (Lender, 1973).

The colonists, like their ancestors and descendents, distinguished between being drunk and habitual drunkenness. The latter not only made the drinker a public spectacle but had deleterious effects on health, family, and the larger community. Historically, it is this puzzling and apparently irrational pattern of repeated, highly consequential drinking that calls for an explanation (MacAndrew, 1969). The proposed solution reflects the interests and ideologies of the time as well as the "world views" of specialists charged with providing such answers (Holzner, 1968: 122–162). The religious heritage of the colonies defined such behavior as due to the drinker's will, freely operating in terms of a rational, hedonistic calculus. This kind of drinking, if repeated was often taken as an indicator of moral degeneration. The "ownership" of the problem of drunkenness during this period fell to leading clergy and civil authorities, joined occasionally by prominent citizens concerned about the use of spirituous liquors among workers, farmhands, and other persons of lesser station.

The idea that extended drunkenness might be the joint result of the drink and qualities of the drinker that might be beyond his control was first synthesized by the highly respected physician, Benjamin Rush, in his *An Inquiry of the Effects of Ardent Spirits Upon the Human Body and Mind,* published originally in 1784 (Levine, 1978; Wilkerson, 1966:42–50). Rush studied the bodily effects of various forms of alcoholic drink and provided what is probably the first systematic, clinical picture of intoxication. Most significant in Rush's description of inebriety was the connection between drinker and drink defined as an "addiction" to distilled liquors. He believed the disease developed gradually and was progressive, ultimately producing "loss of control" over drinking. He called inebriety a "disease of the will," assuming that one's will and desire were independent of each other and that the former became weakened and ultimately debilitated by excessive drink. The first step in treatment was abstinence from alcohol.

Although Rush did not specify the mechanisms by which this disease of the will developed, his ideas provided an alternative to the traditional morality of the church. In trying to solve the puzzle of habitual drunkenness, some physicians began to employ science as a framework in which new solutions might be found. They avoided the traditional description of the drinker's "love" of drink and supplied new terms, such as "craving," and "insatiable desire" to describe the link between the individual and alcohol. Important for questions of individual responsibility, this conceptualization implied that since such persons are not willful in their chronic drunkenness, punishment is not an appropriate strategy of control. Treatment and therapy, allegedly employed in the individual's and the community's interest, became the "reasonable" and humanitarian solution. The historical trend whereby persons deemed incapable of willful criminal or wrong intent have been subjected to "treatment" rather than punishment has been called the "divestment" of the criminal justice system and the rise of the "therapeutic state" (Kittrie, 1971; Szasz, 1970). Rush's concept of alcohol addiction represents the beginning of this divestment process for habitual deviant drinking behavior in America.

The Disease Concept and the American Temperance Movement

Rush and his fellow "temperance physicians" provided two themes that became particularly important in the nineteenth century temperance movement. First, they established that alcohol causes both deviant physiology and deviant behavior. Their descriptions became grist for the temperance mill. Facing arguments on both physical and social grounds, the "social drinker" found it more difficult to resist the temperance call. The second theme was the statement that inebriety is a disease, which quickly became a slogan of the movement (Levine, 1978).

The plausibility of Rush's interpretation depended on the decline of the philosophy of free will and the rise of the idea that one's behavior could be determined by forces beyond one's control; that one's will and desire were distinct (Levine, 1978). Demonic possession was an unacceptable solution. The apparently irrational nature of repetitive drunkenness remained a puzzle. However, science slowly provided some solutions. Although crude by contemporary standards, medical explanations referred to natural laws in an "objective," non-mystical fashion. Loss of control was increasingly assumed to be the result of an unknown but natural disease process, an idea that supplied at least the borders of the habitual drunkenness puzzle.

Such a characterization allowed temperance leaders to draw on a cultural universal. Disease, however defined, is undesirable. It should be opposed, controlled, and if possible, eradicated, and by logical extension, so should all known or suspected causes of disease. The physicians who called inebriety a disease provided the movement with an evil more pervasive than sin itself. Rush's prescription of abstinence was also turned to use as "the" temperance solution for any problem drinking. An important consequence of the use, politically, of the disease concept was that the idea was not examined as an intellectual or scientific claim during most of the nineteenth century. As a moral slogan it allowed advocates both to pity the sick inebriate who required treatment and to rail against "Demon Rum" and even moderate drinking as something that demanded control.

An intellectually noteworthy but politically inconsequential exception did occur toward the end of the century. Trying to succeed where traditional institutions such as prisons and mental asylums had failed, a small group of physicians founded the inebriate asylum: a special place to provide physical and moral care to regenerate inebriates's diseased wills. The first was open in Binghamton, New York, in 1867, although the Washingtonian Home for inebriates in Boston had begun operation about two decades before. By 1900, there were more than fifty such institutions operating in the United States (Wilkerson, 1966:142–151). They were regarded skeptically by both the temperance movement and the medical community; the general public was even more hostile because of the use of public monies (Jellinek, 1960). It was not until 1872, when the superintendent physicians formed an association to study and combat the problem of inebriety as a disease caused by sinful indulgence, that the National Temperance Society issued its reserved endorsement:

> The Temperance press has always regarded drunkenness as a sin and a disease—a sin first, then a disease; and we rejoice that the Inebriate Association are now substantially on the same platform. (Quoted in Levine, 1978)

The physician-superintendents and a number of interested colleagues, mostly psychiatrists, began to publish a journal devoted to the belief that inebriety is a disease. The *Journal of Inebriety* was first published in 1876, and continued, on a precarious basis, until 1914. Its approach was distinctly psychiatric. It reinforced the idea that inebriety was a special kind of mental illness. Neither the *Journal* nor the association received the support of the psychiatric community or medical profession. Although one explanation of this reception might be the poor quality of research reported in the journal, it is more insightful to consider: the relatively low status of psychiatry or alienism in American medicine; the moral stigma attached to working with and in support of inebriates; the political controversy surrounding the inebriate hospital coupled with the weak position of the medical profession in the public consciousness. Regardless of the scientific quality of the disease-advocates' work, these conditions would preclude professional and popular support.

The Post-Prohibition Rediscovery: The Yale Center, Alcoholics Anonymous, and the Jellinek Model

As Gusfield (1975) has suggested, there was virtually no organized interest in the disease concept from the end of the nineteenth century until after prohibition. There was considerable interests, however, in science and the professionalization of scientific research in American universities (Ben-David, 1971:139–168). As the moral crusade against alcohol waned, science and scientific work became established. This trend had a great impact on the solutions Americans would pose for a variety of problems. It was not likely that alcohol, popular and again legal after 1933, would be seen as the source of deviant drinking. Intoxication and drunkenness, when requiring control, were problems assigned to civil authorities or the state. But with the rise and achievements of science, the apparent irrationality of chronic drunkenness became a more intriguing and less tolerable mystery.

In this context even more than during Rush's time, science and medicine seemed to hold promise Three developments, all beginning within a decade after repeal, provided the foundation on which a "new" conceptualization of chronic deviant drinking was to rise in the twentieth century: The Yale research center; the self-help group, Alcoholics Anonymous; and a more careful, largely non-psychiatric, specification of the claim "alcoholism is a disease," referred to here the Jellinek model. These developments provided the moral and political foundation for the subsequent rise of the more than two hundred million dollar federal bureaucracy, the National Institute on Alcohol Abuse and Alcoholism (NIAAA), and an "alcoholism industry" (Trice and Roman, 1972:11–12) of professional and other workers devoted to treating this disease.

THE YALE RESEARCH CENTER

The major body coordinating support for scientific work in the mid-1930s was the Research Council on Problems of Alcohol, organized shortly after repeal (Keller, 1976). This council was composed disproportionately of physicians and natural scientists interested in finding the causes of alcoholism. One member of the committee was Howard Haggard, the physician-director of the Laboratory of Applied Physiology at Yale University. Although the Council was unsuccessful in raising substantial monies for alcohol research, the prominence of its members gave the work scientific respectability. One grant, however, was consequential. It was for a review of the literature on the biological effects of alcohol on humans. The Council called on E.M. Jellinek, who had been doing research on neuroendocrine schizophrenia, to administer the project.

Haggard and his colleagues at the Yale Laboratory were involved in alcohol metabolism and nutritional research, a study which was gaining attention through the journal he founded in 1940, *The Quarterly Journal of Studies on Alcohol*.[3] As this work became more interdisciplinary within the natural sciences, Haggard came to believe that adequate study required an even more comprehensive approach. He invited E.M. Jellinek to Yale where he became the director of a truly multidisciplinary Yale Center for Alcohol Studies. The Center, the Laboratory, and the *Journal* became the core of American research on alcohol.[4] One of the Center's most significant contributions to the idea that alcoholism is a disease was its Summer School program, begun in 1943. These annual sessions were educational programs for concerned citizens from around the country who were involved in policy formation in their local communities. A common concern was what to do about alcoholism and alcohol-related problems. Straus (1976) and Chafetz and Demone (1962) suggest that the slogan "alcoholism is a disease" was introduced intentionally by Center staff in an attempt to reorient local and state policy and thinking about "alcoholics." These summer sessions were a good opportunity to disseminate the idea and point out its moral and political implications for treatment and cure. Although only a small segment of the summer program was devoted to the disease question, it soon became a topic of interest among the lay audience. Critics of this idea (Seeley, 1962; Pattison, 1969; Room, 1972; Robinson, 1976) suggest that its appeal must be seen in historical perspective and should be understood in terms of its practical, humanitarian, and administrative consequences rather than on the basis of scientific merit.[5]

These sessions also provided an established organizational foundation for the rise of the National Council on Alcoholism, the leading voluntary association in the United States devoted to public education about the disease (Chafetz and Demone, 1962; Paredes, 1976). The National Council, known initially as the National Committee for Education on Alcoholism, was established in 1944 by three women: a former alcoholic, a journalist, and a psychiatrist. Mrs. Marty Mann, a one-time member of Alcoholics Anonymous, saw the National Committee as supplementing the work of A.A. for public education against ignorance about alcoholism's disease status. In the spring of 1944, these women met with Jellinek and determined that the National Committee "plan" be introduced in the Yale Summer School program. At the time of the original incorporation of the National Committee, its close connection with the Yale Center is evidenced by the Committee's officers: Howard Haggard was named President; E.M. Jellinek was Chairman of the Board; Professor Seldon Bacon of Yale was secretary, and Professor Edward Baird, also of Yale, was the Committee's legal counsel (Chafetz and Demone, 1962:141). Although the National Council become organizationally independent of the Yale Center in 1950, the association was propitious for the disease concept, as suggested by Chaftez and Demone (1962:142):

NCA then began to search for a formula, something which would translate the basic facts of alcoholism into easily understood and remembered phrases. This resulted in the well known concepts or credo: Alcoholism is a disease and the alcoholic a sick person. The alcoholic can be helped and is worth helping. This is a public health problem and therefore a public responsibility.

ALCOHOLICS ANONYMOUS

In 1935 Alcoholics Anonymous was founded by two men, one of whom was a physician. Another physician, Dr. W.D. Silkworth, suggested to these founders the idea that alcoholism is an allergy of the body, the result of a physiological reaction to alcohol (Jellinek, 1960:160). Although medical opinion was generally skeptical of this questionable formulation (Jellinek, 1960:86–88), the concept of alcoholism as a mark of physiological sensitivity rather than moral decay was appealing and the allergy concept came to occupy a central although implicit place in A.A. ideology. This theory had an additional advantage over other versions of the disease concept common during the early decades of the century that suggested alcoholism was a mental illness, a notion opposed strongly by A.A. (Trice and Roman, 1970). The appeal of allergy rests precisely in its identity as a bona fide medical or "disease" condition; people with allergies are victimized by, not responsible for, their condition. Trice and Roman (1970) suggest that much of the apparent success of A.A. involves the process of removing a stigmatized label and replacing it with a socially acceptable identity, such as "sick," "repentant," "recovered," or "controlled."

Two themes relevant to A.A.'s implicit disease concept are found in the first and third of the famous "Twelve Steps to recovery," printed originally in *Alcoholics Anonymous* (1939). The first and most important step is, "We admitted, we were powerless over alcohol-that our lives had become unmanageable." This is precisely the concept of "loss of control," a key idea in the early writing on alcoholism as a disease. Step three is "(We) have made a decision to turn our will and our lives over to the care of God as we understood him." Representatives of A.A. are quick to note that although this language sounds traditionally religious, such terms are to be interpreted broadly and on the basis of the individual's own biography. In discussing the interpretation of step three, Norris (1976) says:

> This turning over of self direction is akin perhaps to the acceptance of a regimen prescribed by a physician for a disease. The decision is made to accept reality, to stop trying to run things, and to let the "Power greater than ourselves" take over.

This partial description of the role of A.A. recalls Parsons's (1951) discussion of the sick role. Norris's suggestion that "God" might be interpreted to be a physician is perhaps not an extreme exaggeration given a doctor's control over the legitimacy of sickness and disease designations and admission to treatment.

The success attributed to the A.A. program in helping drinkers "recover" from alcoholism has become part of popular wisdom and is largely unchallenged, despite the lack of systematic empirical evidence. The effect of A.A programs and ideology on thinking about alcoholism has been humanitarian and educational. The generally high regard for the program throughout the country serves to reinforce the disease concept implied in its approach. This pattern of regard is evidenced by recent research showing that a majority of physicians who agreed that alcoholism is a disease felt that referring such cases to A.A. was the best professional strategy (Jones and Helrich, 1972).

THE JELLINEK MODEL

The Yale Center and Alcoholics Anonymous provided important structural vehicles for the spread and popularization of the disease definition. Without the research and writing of Jellinek, and later Mark Keller (neither of whom, incidentally, are physicians), this idea would probably have remained largely undeveloped. By comparison with previous efforts, Jellinek's work on the disease concept was brilliant and stimulated further research and writing. His reputation as a medical researcher, coupled with his being the director of the Yale Center, established his work as worthy of serious consideration. Excluding Howard Haggard, no one of Jellinek's stature since Rush had chosen to address the question at length.

In a series of articles beginning shortly after his arrival in New Haven and subsequently in a comprehensive manuscript, *The Disease Concept of Alcoholism* (1960), Jellinek (1941, 1946, 1952) set out his understanding of what it meant to call alcoholism a disease. In the early paper with psychiatrist Bowman (1941) as first author, Jellinek raised the question of alcoholism as an addiction. Using data obtained from a questionnaire in an issue of the A.A. *Grapevine*,[6] he constructed his well-known phase progression of the disease (Jellinek, 1946). A revision and extension was published in 1952 titled "The Phases of Alcohol Addiction," which appeared initially under the auspices of the Alcoholism Subcommittee of the World Health Organization, of which Jellinek was a member. Five phases of the progressive disease of alcohol addiction[7] were presented in terms of characteristic drinking and drinking-related behaviors. A major purpose of this paper, beyond presenting the phase progression, was to resurrect and clarify a distinction central to the disease concept. Drinking behavior that results in problems of living, or problem drinking, while important in its own right, was to be kept quite distinct from drinking behavior indicative of disease.[8] Such a distinction is important for the viability of the disease view: first because it serves to define the boundaries within which medicine could (and should, according to Jellinek) operate; second, because it suggests that forms of deviant drinking not properly called disease should be "managed only on the level of applied sociology, including law enforcement" (Jellinek, 1952). Non-disease forms of drinking behavior are here defined as moral problems to be met on moral terms; disease forms are, by contrast, medical problems and deserve the attention and treatment of the medical profession. Without defining alcoholism,[9] Jellinek proposes two subcategories of this larger entity: "alcohol addicts" and "habitual symptomatic excessive drinkers." Although both types have "underlying psychological or social pathology" that leads to drinking, only the former, after a number of years, develops a "loss of control," becomes addicted to alcohol, and is therefore diseased.

"Loss of control" as the distinction between the disease and non-disease types of alcoholism is elaborated in Jellinek's major work, *The Disease Concept of Alcoholism* (1960), which provides an exhaustive review of relevant research and a clearer description of the kinds of behaviors typically called "alcoholism." Using Greek letters to designate distinct types, Jellinek describes four major categories: Alpha, Beta, Gamma, and Delta (1960:36–39). The first two, Alpha and Beta, are not distinct disease entities: Alpha is the symptomatic drinking discussed in the 1952 essay; Beta refers specifically to all physical disease conditions resulting from prolonged substantial drinking, for example, polyneuropathy, gastritis, and cirrhosis of the liver. Only the Gamma and Delta types qualify as disease entities and are defined by four key elements, three of which are unambiguously physiological and common to both: 1) acquired increased tissue tolerance to alcohol, 2) adaptive cell metabolism, and 3) withdrawal symptoms. These three conditions lead to "craving" or physical dependence on alcohol. In addition, Gamma alcoholics lose control over how much they drink, which involves a progression from psychological to physiological dependence. Jellinek identified this type as most typical of the United States; as causing the greatest personal and social damage; and as the type of alcoholism recognized by Alcoholics Anonymous. The Delta alcoholic differs from Gamma in losing control not over quantity of intake, but rather over the ability to abstain for a significant period. As a result, this type of alcoholic, while suffering from the disease of alcoholism, rarely experiences the devastating consequences of the Gamma type. Jellinek suggests that the Delta drinking pattern is characteristic in certain European countries, particularly France. Although the disease is seen as a product of drinking, in neither case are the initial causes important in identifying the disease itself.

Jellinek's explicit development of addiction as the defining quality of the disease was a necessary condition for the contemporary medicalization of deviant drinking. Although addiction is itself not a particularly precise concept (See Coleman [1976] and Grinspoon and Bakalar [1976:177–178] for recent critiques), its contemporary association with narcotics and their physiological effects renders it a medicalized condition. Use of the term serves to locate the above forms of alcoholism in the body,[10] thus identifying them as legitimate problems for medical attention and intervention. Medicine reluctantly assumed responsibility. In 1956, the American Medical Association's Committee on Alcoholism (A.M.A., 1956) issued its well known statement encouraging medical personnel and institutions to accept persons presenting the syndrome of alcoholism defined by excessive drinking and "certain signs and symptoms of behavioral, personality, and physical disorder." A key sentence in the statement asserts:

> The Council on Mental Health, its Committee on Alcoholism, and the profession in general recognizes this syndrome of alcoholism as illness which justifiably should have the attention of physicians. (A.M.A., 1956:750)

State and local medical societies soon created their own committees on alcoholism based on this reaffirmation of an idea that had already achieved a certain degree of official recognition. Keller (1976a) notes that "Alcohol Addiction" and "Alcoholism" were included in the first volume of the Standard Classified Nomenclature of Disease issued by the National Conference on Nomenclature of Disease in 1933 and approved by the American Medical Association. The significance of the 1956 statement was to reiterate this and other previous definitions. Regardless of how many American physicians agreed with the A.M.A. statement, the formal re-endorsement of the idea that alcoholics fall properly within medical jurisdiction became compelling "evidence" in support of the disease concept.[11] In this context, Jellinek's (1960:12) comments on whether his Gamma and Delta types are "really" diseases are instructive:

> Physicians know what belongs in their realm.
> . . . a disease is what the medical profession recognizes as such.
> . . . the medical profession has officially accepted alcoholism as an illness, whether a part of the public likes it or not, and even if a minority of the medical profession is disinclined to accept the idea.

Almost impatiently, the concept's leading proponent argues that diseases are what physicians say they are and since physicians, as represented by their major professional organization, have said so, alcoholism is a disease and that should settle the matter!

Since Jellinek's death in 1963, the leading spokesman for the disease concept has been Mark Keller, long time colleague of Jellinek at the Yale Center and editor of the *Journal of Studies on Alcohol,* a position he has held since its inception in 1940.[12] In two early essays, Keller (1958, 1962) attempted to develop a definition of alcoholism consistent with the disease view but useful also in epidemiological and survey research. In the first essay, he defines alcoholism as a "chronic behavioral disorder" in which repeated drinking exceeds "dietary and social uses of the community" and causes harm to the drinker's health and social and economic functioning. The two key and familiar elements are that the drinking is deviant and causes harm. Although ambiguous on the question of disease, Keller agrees with Jellinek's position that persons apparently addicted to alcohol suffer from the disease of alcoholism. In a subsequent essay, Keller (1962) provides a "medical definition" of alcoholism as a "psychogenic dependence on or a physiological addiction to alcohol, the defining characteristic of which is "loss of control." He translates the latter idea in behavioral terms: "Whenever an alcoholic starts to drink it is not certain that he will be able to stop at will." In an attempt to show the links between harm due to drinking, loss of control, and the existence of disease, Keller gives revealing insight into the intellectual core of the idea that chronic drunkenness is a disease:

> The key criterion, for all ill effects, is this: Would the individual be expected to reduce his drinking (or give it up) in order to avoid the injury or its continuance? If the answer is yes and he does not do so, it is assumed—admitting it is only an assumption—that he cannot, hence that he has "lost control over drinking," that he is addicted to or dependent on alcohol. This inference is the heart of the matter. Without evident or at least reasonably inferred loss of control, there is no foundation for the claim that "alcoholism is a disease," except in the medical dictionary sense of diseases . . . caused by alcohol poisoning. (Keller, 1962)

In order to extend the research use of the disease concept, Keller applies canons of reason and medicine to the behavioral puzzle of repeated, highly consequential drinking: (1) If one drinks in an excessive, deviant manner, (2) so as to bring deprivation and harm to self and others, (3) while remaining impervious to pleas and admonitions based on this "obvious" connection, (4) the person is assumed not to be in control of his or her will (regardless of desire); (5) such lack of control is then "explained" by the medical concept disease and the medicalized concept addiction, inherent in which is the presumption of limited or diminished responsibility. Resting on the inference of loss of control in a cultural system in which values of rationality, personal control, science, and medicine are given prominence, the assertion that alcoholism is a disease becomes an affirmation of dominant cultural and institutional values on which empirical data are never brought to bear. Indeed, it is precisely this quality of the question that holds the key to its viability as well as its controversy: it is a statement not for scientific scrutiny but for political debate.

Keller's (1976a) most recent defense of the idea supports this contention. In a style at once more polemical and less cautious than that of his mentor Jellinek, Keller reiterates that alcoholism is a "dysbehaviorism" typified by deviant drinking that causes harm; that "It is the same as alcohol addiction and classified as a chronic disease of uncertain etiology and undetermined site." Wishing to base his argument on logic, Keller defines disease to mean the same as "disablement" of physical or mental functioning, in effect saying that alcoholism is a behavior disorder that impairs typical functioning and is therefore a disease because disease is a disablement. Using this circular and inclusive argument Keller proceeds to defend the disease concept against all detractors, both real and imagined, taking liberty with the critical arguments he chooses to cite.[13] Keller's defense has a particularly *ad hominem* quality illustrated by the following remarks concerning skeptics' motives (1976a):

> It is possible that some people look with envy—unconscious, of course—at those fellows who are having an uproariously good time at everybody else's expense, getting irresponsibly drunk and then demanding to be cared for and coddled—at public cost yet.
>   Another motive is apparent in those who, not being M.D.'s, think they know better than doctors how to treat alcoholism. . . . It is understandable that some people would feel uncomfortable—they might even perceive it to be illegal—to be treating a disease without a license to practice medicine. But if only it is not a disease—why, then they are in business![14]

Not only are the critics' characters under attack, but, as Keller's discussion makes clear, they also run the risk of definition as anti-medical, unhumanitarian and, perhaps worst, modern day moral crusaders. His attempts at "logic" notwithstanding, Keller is primarily a disciple arguing that the disease formulation is revealed truth, and that skeptics and detractors, whether physicians or social scientists, are heretics. Such, of course, is the quality of ideological debate.

Conclusions

The purpose of this chapter has been to develop a social historical overview of the major structural and cultural supports of the idea that certain forms of deviant drinking behavior should be considered as instances of disease. I have not attempted to defend the empirical validity of this idea. Indeed, such an attempt would produce a tautological discussion. The question of whether or not a given condition constitutes a disease involves issues of politics and ideology—questions of definition, not fact. The disease concept of alcoholism has a long history in America and has been supported both by medical and non-medical people and organizations for a wide variety of reasons. That certain forms of deviant drinking are now or have been for more than one hundred and fifty years medicalized is not due to a medical "hegemony," but reflects the interests of the several groups and organizations assuming, or being given, responsibility for behaviors associated with chronic drunkenness in the United States. The disease concept owes its life to these variously interested parties, rather than to substantive scientific findings. As such, the disease concept of alcoholism is primarily a social rather than a scientific or medical accomplishment.

Notes

Revised version of a paper presented at meetings of the Midwest Sociological Society, Minneapolis, Minnesota, 1977. The author thanks Peter Conrad, Malcolm Spector, Seldon Bacon, and Harry Levine for their critical comments on an earlier draft.

1. The medicalization of a variety of forms of deviance and social control is discussed in Conrad and Schneider (Forthcoming), which contains a considerably expanded version of this chapter.

2. Seldon Bacon has pointed out to me that the recent controversy over alcohol use among pregnant women attests to the political nature of even these "obvious" medical questions.

3. This journal, which in 1975 became *The Journal of Studies on Alcohol* and is issued monthly, is perhaps the key international publication on alcohol research, its tenure of continuous publication being second only to the *British Journal of Addiction,* which began in 1892 as *The British Journal of Inebriety.*

4. In 1962 the Yale Center was moved to Rutgers—the State University, where it remains one of the most prestigious of the few such centers in the world. Straus (1976) provides some insight into the social and political history leading to this move. He suggests that the wide publicity the Yale Center received was an embarrassment to the University because of the substance of the Center's work, and that its interdisciplinary quality was perceived as inappropriate in the context of the traditional departmental structure of the University.

5. Trice and Roman (1968) suggest some unintended consequences of adopting the sick role that may serve to perpetuate and perhaps reinforce the individual's self-definition as one who cannot control his or her drinking.

6. The A.A. *Grapevine* began publication in 1944 and continues as a monthly magazine comprised of items written mainly, although not exclusively, by alcoholics themselves about A.A. and alcoholism (Norris, 1976).

7. Jellinek called these phases the prealcoholic symptomatic phase, the prodromal phase, the crucial phase (wherein loss of control develops), and the chronic phase. The retrospective "dis-

covery" of these phases is not unlike similar discovery processes discussed recently for hyperactivity (Conrad, 1976) and child abuse (Pfohl, 1977). Analysis of such diagnostic categories from a sociology of knowledge perspective suggests that they represent a particular organization of information that serves or reinforces values, assumptions, or beliefs held by the discoverers. Using disease as his guiding assumption, Jellinek decidedly increased the probability of "discovering" phase movement and progression, given the processural, temporal imagery that this concept conveys (Fabrega, 1972; Room, 1974).

8. Recent research by Cahalan and Room (1974) on problem drinking among American men suggests the importance of distinctions between "problem drinkers" and "alcoholics" to be less than once thought and perhaps misleading in terms of the typical history of drinking problems. This and previous research (Trice and Wahl, 1958) also questions the popular notice of the inevitable progression of alcoholism. For a thorough, critical review of these and other disease propositions, see Pattison, et al. (1977).

9. In avoiding a conceptual definition of alcoholism, Jellinek is not unlike many if not most students of the problem (see Bacon, 1976, for a complete and critical discussion of the definitional chaos in this field of study).

10. The medicalization of deviance does not depend solely on the presence of physiological dimensions. Other conditions, such as the availability of relevant and efficacious technology, moral and ethical considerations, and a supportive political context, must be considered (see Conrad, 1976:92–100, for a preliminary discussion).

11. Fingarette (1970) discusses the impact of the disease concept of alcoholism in the law and in key United States Supreme Court rulings based thereon.

12. Keller has recently assumed the position of editor emeritus for the *Journal*.

13. For example: Sociologists, no less humane [than social workers], object to classifying alcoholism as a disease because that involves labeling people. This concern is especially touching in the case of alcoholism and alcoholics, labels that tend to stigmatize (Keller, 1976a). Keller gives no citation to support this allegation and although frequent reference is made to "social scientist" critics, work cited in this regard appears to be by psychiatrists and other physicians, e.g. Thomas Szasz.

14. Keller's (1967a) faith in the disease status of alcoholism and physician's abilities to diagnose it is steadfast: "I have never met a physician who could not diagnose alcoholism if he was willing."

References

Alcoholics Anonymous. 1939. *Alcoholics Anonymous*. New York: A.A. World Services.

The American Medical Association. 1956. "Report of the board of trustees: Hospitalization of patients with alcoholism." *Journal of The American Medical Association* 162 (October 20):750.

Bacon, Selden D. 1976. "Concepts." Pp. 57–134 in W. Filstead, J. Rossi, M. Keller (eds.), *Alcohol and Alcohol Problems*. Cambridge, Mass.: Ballinger.

Ben-David, Joseph. 1971. *The Scientist's Role in Society*. Englewood Cliffs, N.J.: Prentice Hall.

Berger, Peter L., and Thomas Luckmann. 1966. *The Social Construction of Reality*. Garden City, N.Y.: Anchor.

Bowman, K.M., and E.M. Jellinek. 1941. "Alcohol addiction and chronic alcoholism." *Quarterly Journal of Studies on Alcohol* 2:98–176.

Cahalan, Don, and Robin Room. 1974. *Problem Drinking Among American Men: A Monograph*. New Brunswick, N.J.: Rutgers Center for Alcohol Studies.

Chafetz, Morris E., and Harold W. Demone, Jr. 1962. *Alcoholism and Society*. New York: Oxford University Press.

Coleman, James W. 1976. "The myth of addiction." *Journal of Drug Issues* 6 (Spring):135–141.

Conrad, Peter. 1976. *Identifying Hyperactive Children: The Medicalization of Deviant Behavior*. Lexington, Mass.: D. C. Heath.

Conrad, Peter, and Joseph W. Schneider. Forthcoming. *From Badness to Sickness: A Sociology of Deviance and Social Control*. St. Louis: Mosby.

Fabrega, Horacio Jr. 1972. "Concepts of disease: Logical features and social implications." *Perspectives in Biology and Medicine* 15 (Summer):583–616.

Fingarette, Herbert. 1970. "The perils of Powell: In search of a factual foundation for the 'disease concept of alcoholism'." *Harvard Law Review* 83:793–812.

Freidson, Eliot. 1970. *The Profession of Medicine*. New York: Dodd, Mead.

Grinspoon, Lester, and James B. Bakalar. 1976. *Cocaine*. New York: Basic Books.

Gusfield, Joseph. 1975. "Categories of ownership and responsibility in social issues: alcohol use and automobile use." *Journal of Drug Issues* 5 (Fall):285–303.

Holzner, Burkart. 1972. *Reality Construction in Society*. Revised Edition. Cambridge, Mass.: Schenkman.

Jellinek, E.M. 1946. "Phases in the drinking history of alcoholics." *Quarterly Journal of Studies on Alcohol* 7:1–88.

———. 1952. "Phases of alcohol addiction." *Quarterly Journal of Studies on Alcohol* 13:673–684.

———. 1960. *The Disease Concept of Alcoholism*. Highland Park, N.J.: Hillhouse.

Jones, R. W., and A. R. Helrich. 1972. "Treatment of alcoholism by physicians in private practice: a national survey." *Quarterly Journal of Studies on Alcohol* 33:117–131.

Keller, Mark. 1958. "Alcoholism: nature and extent of the problem." *The Annals of the American Academy of Political and Social Science* 315:1–11.

———. 1962. "The definition of alcoholism and the estimation of its prevalence." Pp. 310–329 in D. J. Pittman and C. R. Snyder (eds.), *Society, Culture and Drinking Patterns*. New York: Wiley.

———. 1976. "Problems with alcohol: An historical perspective." Pp. 5–28 in W. Filstead, J. Rossi, M. Keller (eds.), *Alcohol and Alcohol Problems*. Cambridge, Mass.: Ballinger.

———. 1976a. "The disease concept of alcoholism revisited." *Journal of Studies on Alcohol* 37 (September):1694–1717.

Kittrie, Nicholas. 1971. *The Right to Be Different*. Baltimore: Johns Hopkins University Press.

Lender, Mark. 1973. "Drunkenness as an offense in early New England: A study of Puritan attitudes." *Quarterly Journal of Studies on Alcohol* 34:353–366.

Levine, Harry Gene. 1978. "The discovery of addiction: Changing conceptions of habitual drunkenness in America." *Journal of Studies on Alcohol* 39 (January):143–174.

MacAndrew, Craig. 1969. "On the notion that certain persons who are given to frequent drunkenness suffer from a disease called alcoholism." Pp. 483–501 in S. C. Plog and R. B. Edgerton (eds.), *Changing Perspectives in Mental Illness*. New York: Holt, Rinehart and Winston.

Mulford, Harold. 1969. *"Alcoholics," "Alcoholism" and "Problem Drinkers": Social Objects in the Making*. Washington, D.C.: National Center for Health Statistics, Department of Health, Education and Welfare.

National Conference on Nomenclature of Disease. 1933. *A Standard Classified Nomenclaure of Disease*. H.B. Logie (ed.) New York: Commonwealth Fund.

Norris, John L. 1976. "Alcoholics anonymous and other self-help groups." Pp. 735–776 in R. Tarter and A. Sugerman (eds.), *Alcoholism*. Reading, Mass.: Addison-Wesley.

Paredes, Alfonso. 1976. "The history of the concept of alcoholism." Pp. 9–52 in R. Tarter and A. Sugerman (eds.), *Alcoholism*. Reading, Mass.: Addison-Wesley.

Parsons, Talcott. 1951. *The Social System*. New York: The Free Press.

Pattison, E.M. 1969. "Comment on the alcoholic game." *Quarterly Journal of Studies on Alcohol* 30:953.

Pattison, E.M., Mark Sobell, and Linda Sobell. 1977. *Emerging Concepts of Alcohol Dependence*. New York: Springer.

Pfohl, Stephen J. 1977. "The 'discovery' of child abuse." *Social Problems* 24 (February):310–323.

Pitts, Jesse. 1968. "Social control: the concept." *International Encyclopedia of the Social Sciences*. No. 14. New York: Macmillan.

Robinson, David. 1976. *From Drinking to Alcoholism: A Sociological Commentary*. New York: Wiley.

Roman, Paul M., and H. M. Trice. 1968. "The sick role, labelling theory, and the deviant drinker." *International Journal of Social Psychiatry* 14:245–251.

Room, Robin. 1972. "Drinking and disease: Comment on 'the alcohologist's addiction.'" *Quarterly Journal of Studies on Alcohol* 33 (December): 1049–1059.

———. 1974. "Governing images and the prevention of alcohol problems." *Preventive Medicine* 3:11–23.

Seeley, John R. 1962. "Alcoholism is a disease: implications for social policy." Pp. 586–593 in D. J. Pittman and C. R. Snyder (eds.), *Society, Culture and Drinking Patterns*. New York: Wiley.

Spector, Malcolm, and John I. Kitsuse. 1977. *Constructing Social Problems*. Menlo Park, Calif.: Cummings.

Straus, Robert. 1976. "Problem drinking in the perspective of social change 1940–1973." Pp. 29–56 in W. Filstead, J. Rossi, M. Keller (eds.), *Alcohol and Alcohol Problems*. Cambridge, Mass.: Ballinger.

Szasz, Thomas. 1970. *The Manufacture of Madness*. New York: Dell.

Trice, H.M., and Paul Roman. 1972. *Spirits and Demons at Work: Alcohol and Other Drugs on the Job*. Ithaca, N. Y.: New York State School of Industrial and Labor Relations, Cornell University.

———. 1970. "Delabeling, relabeling, and alcoholics anonymous." *Social Problems* 17:538–546.

Trice, H.M., and Richard J. Wahl. 1958. "A rank order analysis of the symptoms of alcoholism."

Wilkerson, A. E. 1966. *A History of the Concept of Alcoholism as a Disease*. Unpublished doctoral dissertation, University of Pennsylvania.

Zola, Irving K. 1972. "Medicine as an institution of social control." *Sociological Review* 20:487–504.

CHAPTER 3

Shocking Numbers and Graphic Accounts

QUANTIFIED IMAGES OF DRUG PROBLEMS IN THE PRINT MEDIA

James D. Orcutt and J. Blake Turner

Since 1975, the Monitoring the Future project at the University of Michigan Institute for Social Research (ISR) has been conducting annual surveys of drug use and attitudes in representative samples of high school seniors in the United States (Johnston, O'Malley, and Bachman 1991). Reports released from this project in 1986, which presented time-series data from 1975 to 1985, received extensive coverage in the mass media. Much of this publicity focused on the "disturbing finding that *cocaine* use increased among seniors in 1985" (Johnston, O'Malley, and Bachman 1986:13) following a period of little or no change in sample estimates of prevalence from 1979 to 1984.

Our purpose here is to show how media workers used this and other findings from the ISR surveys of high school seniors and older cohorts to construct quantified images of a "drug crisis" in 1986. We examine some of the products of journalistic and artistic work—statistical and graphic representations of drug problems which appeared in national print media—to gain insight into the labor process through which raw materials from the ISR reports were crafted into "plagues" and other icons of antidrug crusades. Our constructionist analysis of this historical episode departs from earlier efforts to adjudicate the "objective reality" of the 1986 drug crisis (see Goode 1989; Jensen, Gerber, and Babcock 1991; Reinarman and Levine 1989). Instead, we focus on the empirically verifiable correspondence between numbers contained in the ISR reports—sample estimates of points and trends in the prevalence of drug use—and reproductions of those numbers in the mass media. This strategy allows us to move beyond Best's (1989) analysis and refutation of baseless "statistical claims" about missing children. Given the known statistical properties of the survey data reported by Johnston, O'Malley, and Bachman (1986), we can use quantitative criteria such as tests of significance and measures of distortion to assess the shocking numbers and graphic accounts that media workers constructed from the ISR estimates.

The Media Epidemic of 1986

Media coverage of drug problems generally, and cocaine use specifically, reached epidemic proportions in 1986. Although similar in some ways to earlier "drug crises"

(Musto 1987), an unprecedented and well-documented "feeding frenzy" of drug coverage emerged by the middle of 1986, an election year, as the electronic and print media, the president and Congress, and other claims makers competed for audiences, voters, and ownership of this issue (Diamond, Accosta, and Thornton 1987; Kerr 1986b; Shoemaker 1989).

Merriam (1989:23) provides an especially clear picture of this media epidemic in his descriptive analysis of the National Media Index. Figure 3.1 shows his plot of the proportion of space and time devoted to drug issues by television network news, weekly news magazines, and five major newspapers from 1983 to 1987. Until 1985, coverage of drug issues rarely exceeded 1 percent of the total space and time in the news media. Drug stories, mainly concerned with trafficking and crime, received a greater share of total coverage in 1985; but, as Merriam points out, this was merely a "foothill for the mountain of drug coverage that was to come" (1989:24). Starting from less than 1 percent of total coverage in the first quarter of 1986, coverage of all drug issues eventually consumed nearly 5 percent of the space and time in the national media during July, August, and September. As noted in Merriam's graph, the peak of the media epidemic immediately followed a classic drug "horror story" (Johnson 1989): the death of basketball star Len Bias on 19 June, which was attributed to cocaine ingestion. More specifically, four weeks after Bias's death, coverage of drug abuse issues (apart from trafficking and

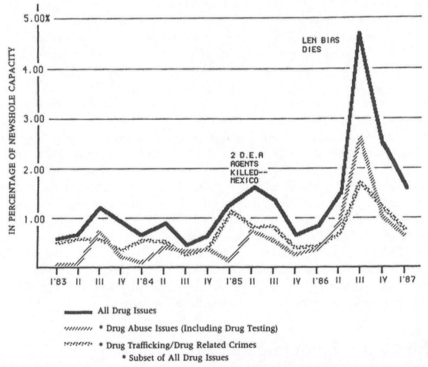

Figure 3.1.   Media Coverage of Drug Issues, 1983–1987. *Source:* Merriam 1989:23. Reprinted by permission of Lawrence Erlbaum Associates. Copyright 1987 by The Conference on Issues & Media, Inc.

crime) accounted for 3.2 percent of total space and time in the national media (Merriam 1989). By the final quarter of 1986, the media epidemic subsided somewhat, but attention to all drug issues still amounted to 2.4 percent of news coverage by network television, news magazines, and major newspapers.

Based on an extensive search of several media data bases, Reese and Danielian (1989) found important differences in the timing and relative contributions of various national news media to coverage of cocaine issues during the 1986 "drug crisis." In contrast to coverage of cocaine issues by network television and *The New York Times,* which peaked during the summer months of 1986, the number of pages in *Newsweek* and *Time* on cocaine and "crack" reached its highest level in March. A large share of this early news magazine coverage came from a seven page cover story in the 17 March issue of *Newsweek,* "Kids and Cocaine: An Epidemic Strikes Middle America." Kerr links this important, precedent-setting article to the concern of Richard M. Smith, the editor-in-chief of *Newsweek,* about the growing "drug crisis" and his feeling of responsibility "as an editor . . . to put the drug problem in a larger context than we had in the past" (1986b:B6).

Following Smith's editorial design, the team of correspondents, feature writers, photographers, and graphic artists who worked on the 17 March issue produced a dramatic account of a frightening epidemic: "In cities and suburbs all across the nation, a generation of American children [is] increasingly at risk to the nightmare of cocaine addiction" (*Newsweek* 1986a:58). For the most part, this story was assembled with conventional journalistic material on the personal troubles of individuals, such as vignettes ("A Cheerleader's Fall—and Rise") and photographs of teenage victims. It cited expert testimony on the psychopharmacological powers of crack cocaine ("almost instantaneous addiction") and pessimistic reports from the front-line of the drug war ("'We have lost the cocaine battle,' Los Angeles police detective Frank Goldberg says flatly" [1986a:60]). However, to lend authority and substance to their epidemiological rendition of the "larger context" of the cocaine problem, senior writer Tom Morganthau, graphic artist Christoph Blumrich, and their co-workers turned to the research of Johnston and his associates at the ISR.

The ISR Time Series, 1975–85

The 1986 annual report of the ISR surveys of high school seniors from 1975 through 1985 was not released until July (Halloran 1986). *Newsweek* "scooped" the other national media with results from this time series and an interview with Johnston in the 17 March article. As the final ISR report would show (and *Newsweek* noted in passing), prevalence estimates for most illicit drugs had steadily declined since the late 1970s—although Johnston, O'Malley, and Bachman (1986:13) pointed out that the downward trend in overall drug use "appears to have halted" in 1985. Nevertheless, the staff of *Newsweek* saw the potential for a "plague" in the ISR estimates of cocaine use.

In Figure 3.2 we use the simple line graph preferred by Johnston, O'Malley, and Bachman (cf. 1986:58) to present the ISR trend results for three measures of cocaine

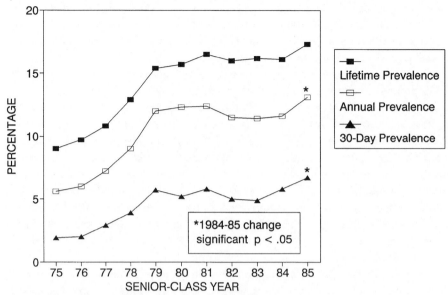

Figure 3.2.   Trends in Lifetime, Annual, and 30-Day Prevalence of Cocaine Use. *Source:* **Johnston, O'Malley, and Bachman 1986.**

prevalence among high school seniors from 1975 to 1985. First, all measures of prevalence reflected "a dramatic and accelerating increase in popularity" of cocaine from 1976 to 1979—followed by a period of "little or no change in any prevalence statistics" from 1979 to 1984 (1986:48). However, from 1984 to 1985, Johnston and his colleagues noted statistically significant and "disturbing" increases in their estimates of 30-day (used in the last 30 days) and annual prevalence (used in the last 12 months). On the other hand, their most inclusive estimate of cocaine use—lifetime prevalence (ever used)—did not show a significant change in 1985, remaining essentially stable since 1979.

The *Newsweek* "Coke Plague"

To align the ISR time series with the master metaphor of the 17 March issue—the national "epidemic" of cocaine use—the media workers at *Newsweek* faced two major dilemmas. First, as Best points out, claims makers and the media "tend to use big numbers when estimating the scope of a social problem" (1989:21). Yet, the statistically significant change in 30-day prevalence or "current use" that Johnston, O'Malley, and Bachman (1986:13) highlighted in their report provided a relatively "little" number: 6.7 percent of high school seniors in 1985. Although the figures for lifetime prevalence offered the biggest numbers, this particular estimate did not yield a statistically significant change from 1984 to 1985. Setting aside this technical difficulty, *Newsweek* followed the claims maker's rule of thumb—"big numbers are better than little numbers" (Best 1989:32)—and focused on lifetime prevalence in the 17 March issue and subsequent articles on the "drug crisis" (*Newsweek* 1986b; Smith 1986).

Second, whereas Johnston, O'Malley, and Bachman documented a dramatic increase in cocaine use from 1976 to 1979, this in itself was hardly newsworthy seven years later. In fact, these early changes dwarfed the yearly fluctuations in prevalence estimates from 1980 to 1985. The staff of *Newsweek* grasped both horns of this dilemma by incorporating the shocking numbers from the 1970s into the text of the 17 March article while using graphic techniques to highlight the threat of more recent changes in lifetime prevalence. Figure 3.3 shows the final product of this work: *Newsweek's* graphic account of "A Coke Plague."

The text immediately adjacent to this graph in the *Newsweek* "Kids and Coke" feature story reads as follows:

> There is simply no question that cocaine in all its forms is seeping into the nation's schools. An annual survey conducted by the Institute of [sic] Social Research at the University of Michigan shows the percentage of high-school seniors who have ever tried cocaine has nearly doubled in the past 10 years, from 9 percent to 17.3 percent (chart). (1986a:63)

The quantified image of "doubling" in the text, where the referent to the full 1975–85 time series is left implicit, reinforces the visual impact of the recent, upturned spike in the "plague." Note also the textual forecast within the graph which projects this spike toward an even bigger number in the near future: "Within the next two years, more than 20 percent of high-school seniors may have tried cocaine." Even the label, "cocaine usage," is put to work, transforming lifetime prevalence into a more active, ongoing condition.

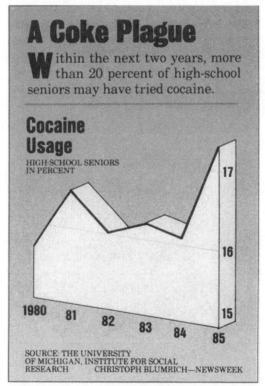

Figure 3.3.   A Coke Plague. *Source: Newsweek* **1986a:63, Christoph Blumrich. Reprinted by permission.**

In Figure 3.4 we reconstruct the "Coke Plague" by tracing the creative steps of Blumrich, *Newsweek*'s graphic artist. Panel A displays the original construction site— the 1975–85 ISR time series for lifetime prevalence of cocaine use. In Panel B we show the heavy "editorial deletions" that Blumrich had to make to prepare the foundation for his graphic account. First, he obliterated the historic increase in lifetime prevalence during the 1970s by censoring the first half of the ISR time series from 1975 to 1980. Then, he cut away over four-fifths of the original foundation for the remaining portion of the time series by truncating the 1980–85 data at the lofty level of 15 percent. In effect, these initial stages of construction removed over 95 percent of the information from the ISR time series on lifetime prevalence.

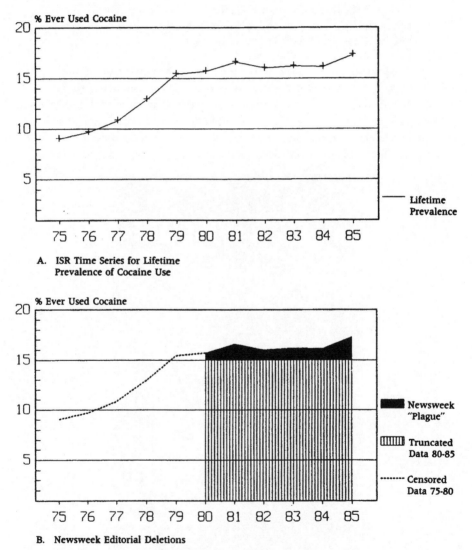

A. ISR Time Series for Lifetime
    Prevalence of Cocaine Use

B. Newsweek Editorial Deletions

Figure 3.4A and B.   Reconstruction of "A Coke Plague." *Source:* **Johnston, O'Malley, and Bachman 1986;** *Newsweek* **1986a:63.**

Panel C illustrates an intermediate stage of construction which increased the intensity of the "Coke Plague." By setting the Y-axis to a finer scale and focusing closely on the residue of his editorial deletions, Blumrich transformed statistically nonsignificant fluctuations in the ISR estimates of lifetime prevalence from 1980 to 1985 into striking peaks and valleys.

We reconstruct some of the final stages of Blumrich's creative labor in Panel D. With the addition of color, the illusion of depth, and the name of an ancient terror, he completed his job of transfiguring a series of six numbers into a tangible and threatening social fact. Through Blumrich's compelling graphic account, *Newsweek* readers could literally *see* the menacing, three-dimensional entity that was "seeping into the nation's schools."

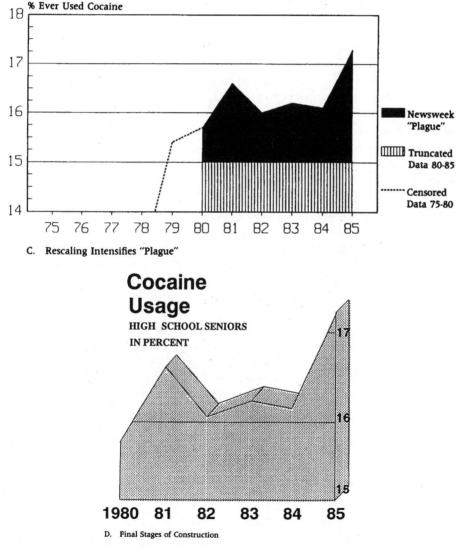

C. Rescaling Intensifies "Plague"

D. Final Stages of Construction

Figure 3.4C and D.   Reconstruction of "A Coke Plague." *Source:* Johnston, O'Malley, and Bachman 1986; *Newsweek* 1986a:63.

Editor-in-chief Smith (1986:15) drew upon this image for the title of a special editorial in the 16 June issue of *Newsweek,* "The Plague Among Us," in which he expressed his pride with the "Kids and Cocaine" issue and his concern with a drug "that 1 of every 6 of our teenage youngsters will have sampled before senior-prom night in high school." This editorial also marked the debut of a thematic logo, "The Drug Crisis," which highlighted coverage of this putative epidemic for several years as *Newsweek* implemented Smith's plan "to cover it as a crisis, reporting it as aggressively . . . as we did the struggle for civil rights, the war in Vietnam and the fall of the Nixon presidency" (1986:15).

Other Images of the ISR Time Series

We searched 1986 issues of *Newsweek, Time,* and *U.S. News & World Report* as well as the *New York Times, Washington Post,* and *Chronicle of Higher Education* for other quantified images of drug problems constructed from the ISR time series. The final 1986 report, which Johnston and his associates released on 7 July at the peak of the media epidemic, included for the first time follow-up data from panels of college students and other young adults. The print media devoted extensive coverage to a limited set of findings contained in an ISR press release, whose headline read: "U-M study indicates cocaine use remains high on American college campuses, while other drug frequency is down" (University of Michigan 1986). To document these trends, the press release presented one table from the 1986 report (Johnston, O'Malley, and Bachman 1986:182) showing 1980–85 estimates of annual prevalence for a variety of drugs from the college panel data. A reasonably faithful reproduction of this table in a 8 July *New York Times* article (Halloran 1986) included an essentially stable series of percentages for the annual prevalence of cocaine use (see table 3.1). Yet, the eye-catching headline over Halloran's article offered a more dynamic interpretation of this flat line of numbers than did the ISR press release: "Student Use of Cocaine Is Up as Use of Most Other Drugs Drops."

Similar versions of the annual prevalence table appeared in the *Washington Post* (Russell 1986) and *Chronicle of Higher Education* (Meyer 1986), but the headlines over these articles highlighted a shocking estimate of lifetime prevalence reported in the 7 July press release: "By the end of their fourth year of college, roughly 30 percent of all students will have tried cocaine" (University of Michigan 1986). This lifetime estimate was rounded up to "One-Third of College Students" in the 8 July *Washington Post* headline and "1 in 3 College Students" above the 16 July *Chronicle of Higher Education* story, and it was mentioned at some point during July or August in virtually all of the print media we examined (Halloran 1986; *Newsweek* 1986b; *U.S. News & World Report* 1986a). In contrast, only one of these articles (Russell 1986) cited the relatively low figure for 30-day prevalence of cocaine use among college students—"one in 14 (7 percent)"—which also appeared in the ISR press release (University of Michigan 1986). Despite the promi-

Table 3.1.   Annual Prevalence of Cocaine Use, 1980–1985

1980	1981	1982	1983	1984	1985
17%	16%	17%	17%	16%	17%

nence of the shocking number of "1 in 3 College Students" in media coverage during the summer of 1986, Johnston, O'Malley, and Bachman did not include separate estimates of lifetime prevalence of cocaine use among college students in their final report (1986:201–232)—only 30-day and annual prevalence.

The surge of shocking numbers during the summer of 1986 reached an apex in August when Kerr incorporated the following claim into his *New York Times* account of the "Rising Concern on Drugs":

> A continuing survey by the University of Michigan Institute for Social Research found that 10 percent of the high school seniors who graduated in 1975 had used cocaine. In 1985, *40 percent of the graduating seniors* had at least tried the drug. (italics added, 1986a: A28)

The 7 July ISR press release did state that "nearly 40 percent of all high school graduates have tried [cocaine] by age 26 or 27" (University of Michigan 1986:1), a finding based on follow-up data from young adults who had graduated in 1976 (cf. Johnston, O'Malley, and Bachman 1986:150). We do not know if Kerr simply misread this statement while preparing his story, but we can be sure that his inference of a ten-year quadrupling of cocaine use among high school seniors created rising concern among many readers of the *New York Times.*

Although the media epidemic continued through September, there were clear signs of change in the nature of this coverage and the quality of quantified images of drug problems. A shift toward a more reflective and occasionally critical posture was signaled by William Safire's 11 September essay in the *New York Times* (1986) on "The Drug Bandwagon," in which he observed that "news magazines have been conducting a circulation-building war on drugs for months." Less than a week later, the cover of *Time* (15 September 1986) featured a special report on "Drugs: The Enemy Within" with a lead article on "America's Crusade." This piece raised the possibility that the "press and politicians may be guilty of hyping the drug crisis"and used Musto's (1987) historical work to show that "the U.S. periodically launches antidrug crusades" (*Time* 1986:61). More to the point of our analysis, the article noted that since 1978 the "percentage of high school seniors [who] smoked marijuana every day . . . has dropped by half" and that "even cocaine use has evened out" (*Time* 1986:62). Finally, we see some revealing differences between the *Newsweek* "Coke Plague" and the graph that Joe Lertola prepared for this issue of *Time* from the ISR time series (figure 3.5).

Although it is certainly arguable whether figures on 30-day prevalence can sustain the title image of "High School Habits," it is noteworthy that this graph neither censors nor truncates the ISR percentage estimates from 1975 to 1985. Lertola's inclusion of marijuana prevalence in this graph not only calls attention to the long-term decline in ISR estimates for this drug, but it also provides a distinct contrast to the much lower and flatter trends for cocaine, hallucinogens, and heroin. Most interesting, perhaps, is Lertola's use of embellishments or "chart junk" (Tufte 1983): The academic scene of a student reading from the flat surface of a blackboard invites us to reflect on *our* act of reading and reminds us that these are "only numbers."

A very similar graph titled "Shifting Habits" appeared just two weeks later in a *U.S. News & World Report* article which raised the question, "War on drugs: More than

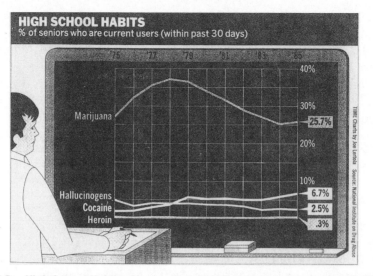

Figure 3.5.   High School Habits. *Source: Time* **1986:64, Joe Lertola. Copyright 1986 Time Inc. Reprinted by permission.**

a 'short-term high'?" (29 September 1986). Using annual prevalence figures from 1975 to 1985, an anonymous graphic artist contrasted incremental changes in cocaine, tranquilizer, and heroin use with a much higher, parabolic trend-line for marijuana use that literally goes "off the chart" in 1979. In addition, the text of this article drove home the following point about the "drug crisis":

> The antidrug frenzy in Washington notwithstanding, there is little evidence
> to support alarmist claims. Indeed, reliable data show some forms of drug
> use declining, while others have remained flat. Only cocaine use . . . is up
> (but] it's barely a blip on the statistical screen. (1986b:28)

In little more than half a year, the quantified image of a "Coke Plague" had shrunk to a mere "Statistical Blip."

Back to the Future: Newsweek's Recycled Crisis

As we noted earlier, the media epidemic declined precipitously during the last three months of 1986, with drug stories virtually disappearing from the major news magazines by the end of that year (Reese and Danielian 1989). Reinarman and Levine (1989:120–21) have already commented on a brief spate of "skewed reporting" in February 1987, when figures from the 1986 ISR high school survey were released to the press. While the familiar estimates of lifetime, annual, and 30-day prevalence of cocaine use all showed slight decreases, the *New York Times* (Kerr 1987) highlighted a similarly slight increase in daily prevalence (i.e., used on 20 or more occasions in the preceding 30 days). Interestingly, in his own commentary on "American's Drug Problem in the Media," Johnston (1989) cites this same prevalence estimate—which entailed only 0.4 percent of approximately 15,200 seniors in the 1986 sample—as evidence of a "real cocaine crisis" during that year.

However, toward the end of 1987, even *Newsweek* seemed ready to make a grudging withdrawal from its aggressive campaign on the "drug crisis" in a brief story written by Mark Miller, "Drug Use: Down, But Not in the Ghetto" (23 November 1987). Miller portrayed the long-term declines in ISR estimates of marijuana prevalence as "preliminary . . . signs of progress among middle-class teens" (1987:33). More importantly, his account of the recent ISR estimates for cocaine provided only a faint echo of the "Coke Plague" and a substantial revision of its two-year forecast of a growing epidemic:

> Cocaine use by high-school seniors rose to 17.3 percent in 1985, a U.S. record, and dropped only slightly in 1986. . . . Lloyd Johnston, a Michigan survey researcher, predicts that the 1987 high school survey will chart a growing disenchantment in cocaine use. (1987:33)

Having touched on this "good news," in which the ISR probability sample is narrowly framed as "middle-class teens," Miller devoted most of his article to the "bad news . . . that crack . . . is now deeply entrenched in the ghetto" (1987:33).

As the "good news" of decreasing cocaine prevalence, including "crack," flowed unrelentingly from the ISR surveys through the late 1980s (e.g., Berke 1989), the print media generally turned to more reliable sources of shocking numbers such as the Drug Abuse Warning Network (DAWN) reports of medical room emergencies or State Department estimates of worldwide cocaine production (e.g., *Newsweek* 1988; *New York Times* 1989; Sciolino 1989, 1990). However, the media's growing disenchantment with the cocaine problem was epitomized by contributing editor Larry Martz's article in the 19 February 1990 issue of *Newsweek:* "A Dirty Drug Secret: Hyping Instant Addiction Doesn't Help." Although Martz did not mention any specific cases, his disclosure of the "dirty little secret about crack" struck close to home.

> As with most other drugs, a lot of people use it without getting addicted. In their zeal to shield young people from the plague of drugs, the media and many drug educators have hyped the very real dangers of crack into a myth of instant and total addiction. (1990:74)

Martz also turned the "big number" strategy against the image of a national epidemic by pointing to a steep decline of "50 percent, from 5.8 million to 2.9 million" in the National Institute on Drug Abuse's household survey estimates of monthly users of cocaine in 1985 and 1988 (NIDA 1989). Even though the editorial staff of *Newsweek* segregated Martz's "Ideas" piece from hard news and buried it in the back pages, it still read like an epitaph for the "Coke Plague" and other spawn of the media epidemic.

Yet, just two years later, *Newsweek* came back with an especially stunning illustration of how the "good news" of declining prevalence estimates can be recycled as "bad news" of a new "drug crisis." The 3 February 1992 issue included a report on "The New Age of Aquarius," whose headline proclaimed that "LSD . . . is turning on a new generation of American teenagers." Lead writer Jean Seligmann reinforced this theme with statistical observations from the ISR surveys:

> Though far more teenagers still resort to liquor or marijuana, the use of LSD is *rising alarmingly.* In 1990 and 1991, for the first time since 1976, annual surveys by the University of Michigan and the National Institute on Drug Abuse found more high-school seniors had used LSD than cocaine in the previous 12 months. (italics added, *Newsweek* 1992:65).

Seligmann's quantified image of a recent and "alarming rise" in LSD relative to the well-known cocaine problem leaves it to the reader's imagination to fill in the missing data from 1976 to 1990. In figure 3.6, we offer a more explicit and uncensored account of the trends in annual prevalence that link the original "Age of Aquarius" with the 1990s.

The critical implications of our graphic account of how *Newsweek* recycled a dying epidemic should be clear. It seems almost gratuitous to add that the decrease from 1989 (6.5 percent) to 1990 (5.3 percent) in the annual prevalence of cocaine use among high school seniors was statistically significant (p < .01), whereas the corresponding increase for LSD from 4.9 percent to 5.4 percent was within the range of sampling error. In his 16 June 1986 editorial, Smith had noted that *Newsweek*'s very first cover story on drugs "dealt with LSD, then the drug of choice of flower children" (1986:15). And so, in fabricating this fantastic image of an emerging "drug crisis," his current staff truly "jumped back to the future."

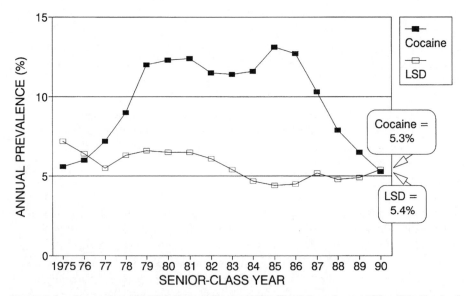

Figure 3.6.   Percentage of High School Seniors Who Used Cocaine or LSD within the Last 12 Months. *Source:* **Johnston, O'Malley, and Bachman 1991.**

Discussion and Conclusion

Consistent with Spector and Kitsuse's (1977:75) occupational approach to the study of claims-making activity, we have examined the journalistic and artistic products of "people who work in . . . the process of creating" drug problems. This exhibition of numerical and graphic reproductions of the ISR time series displays, at least indirectly, the skills, choices, and routine practices of the media workers who constructed these quantified images. In particular, our own archeological reconstruction of the *Newsweek* "Coke Plague" demonstrates the potential complexity and transformative power of this creative process.

Again, our purpose here is not to enter the arena of claims making and the familiar debate over the "reality" of the 1986 "drug crisis"—e.g., "Social construction or objective threat?" (Goode 1989); "Is it real or is it Memorex?" (Johnston 1989). That is, we are not concerned about population parameters estimated by Johnston, O'Malley, and Bachman, but with uses of the ISR statistical estimates per se by media workers. From this standpoint, we might consider another question: Did journalists and graphic artists "lie" about those statistics? Even though Tufte (1983:54) argues that preoccupation with the question of statistical and graphical integrity has stifled intellectual progress in the study of data graphics, this question bears on some broader issues in our study of the claims-making activities of media workers.

We can start with the *Newsweek* "Coke Plague." In truncating the ISR time series at the 15 percent level and rescaling the Y-axis to intensify yearly changes, Blumrich followed the classic blueprint for a "Gee-Whiz Graph" in Huff's *How to Lie with Statistics* (cf. 1954:65). Tufte (1983:56–57) provides a more formal way of assessing how much distortion—how big a "lie"—resulted from these operations in his first principle of graphical integrity and his measure of its violation:

> The representation of numbers, as physically measured on the surface of the graphic itself, should be directly proportional to the numerical quantities represented. . . . Violations of the first principle constitute one form of graphic misrepresentation, measured by the

$$\text{Lie Factor} = \frac{\text{size of effect shown in graphic}}{\text{size of effect in data}}$$

Let us use the crucial (albeit nonsignificant) increase from 16.1 percent in 1984 to 17.3 percent in 1985 to calculate Tufte's Lie Factor for the "Coke Plague." First, when this annual increase of 1.2 percent is divided by the actual 1984 baseline of 16.1 percent, the size of the effect in the ISR data stands at a relatively modest 7.4 percent change. However, the scale in the graph is truncated at the level of 15 percent. Thus, the 1984 baseline shown in the "Coke Plague" is not 16.1 percent but, rather, a much smaller 1.1 percent. In relation to this truncated baseline, an increase of 1.2 percent amounts to a 109.1 percent change from 1984 to 1985. The Lie Factor is simply the ratio of the effect in the graph over the effect in the data:

$$\text{Lie Factor} = \frac{\text{effect in "Coke Plague"}}{\text{effect in ISR data}} = \frac{109.1\% \text{ change}}{7.4\% \text{ change}} = 14.7$$

This result is intriguing because it is virtually identical to the degree of distortion in a *New York Times* graph that Tufte (1983:57–58) selected as an "extreme example" of graphic misrepresentation (Lie Factor = 14.8).

The "Coke Plague" also violates Tufte's second, qualitative principle of graphical integrity: "Clear, detailed, and thorough labeling should be used to defeat graphical distortion and ambiguity" (1983:56). Far from defeating distortion, labels within the graph and the ambiguous reference to "doubling" in the text add conceptual energy to the ominous image of a growing epidemic. Judged against Tufte's principles for "telling the truth about the data," it is evident that Blumrich and his co-workers told the readers of *Newsweek* a story which stretched the "true" numbers in the ISR report considerably.

Yet, if Blumrich's "Coke Plague" lacked graphical integrity, it made a vital contribution to the thematic integrity of *Newsweek*'s coverage of "Kids and Cocaine" with its concrete, visual representation of the social facticity of this national epidemic. As the graphic artist for this major project, Blumrich's job was neither to report—nor to distort—the findings of the ISR surveys, but to make the hard reality behind "abstract statistics" (Smith 1986) more accessible to the readers of *Newsweek*. The numbers from the ISR survey authenticated his work of art; he could in truth say, "I'm not making this up." But, along with the reporters, writers, and photographers who worked on this issue, Blumrich had to edit, polish, and interpret his source material to get at the real story of a growing epidemic. In form and content, his graphic account of "A Coke Plague" was ultimately faithful to this journalistic design.

The "Kids and Cocaine" issue was a well-coordinated and highly successful venture into the journalistic arena of social problem definition (Hilgartner and Bosk 1988). Editor-in-chief Smith's early decision to put the cocaine "problem in a larger context" with a thematic issue on a "national epidemic" was influential in setting the agenda for subsequent coverage of this story in *Newsweek* and among its competitors (Kerr 1986b:B6; Reese and Danielian 1989). From his own account of this project, it appears that Smith (1986) took an unusually strong and active role in the planning and execution of work on the cocaine problem. Although Gans notes that journalists often describe news organizations as "militaristic," he points out that news magazine executives at the level of editor-in-chief rarely exercise their potential control over the story selection and production process (1979:84–85). Yet, Smith's (1986) editorial statement reflected his personal command of drug statistics and of *Newsweek*'s mission to cover "The Plague Among Us"—a title which acknowledged the editor-in-chief's special pride in Blumrich's skillful contribution to this operation. In introducing a distinctive graphic trademark, "The Drug Crisis," Smith staked his organization's proprietary claim to the discovery of an "epidemic . . . as pervasive and as dangerous in its way as the plagues of medieval times" (1986:15).

As other news organizations rushed to cover the epidemic, their fevered pursuit of this story through the summer of 1986 retraced the outline of Blumrich's plague (cf. Figures 3.1 and 3.3) and reproduced on a much grander scale the competitive dynamics which Fishman (1978) found in his analysis of a local media "crime wave." Blumer's (1971) characterization of social problems as collective behavior provides an apt description of the labor process among media workers during this period of focused competition over the drug crisis. As he noted, knowledge about putative conditions—such as the ISR estimates of drug prevalence—"may be ignored, distorted, or smothered by other considerations . . . in the process of collective definition which determines the fate of social problems" (1971:305). Indeed, "other considerations" seemed to prevail during the media "feeding frenzy," and we found ample evidence of media workers snatching at shocking numbers from an ISR press release, smothering reports of stable or decreasing use under more ominous headlines, and distorting the cocaine problem to epidemic proportions as high as 40 percent of high school seniors. In contrast to the more deliberate, thematically integrated quality of Blumrich's work, the heavy-handed and sometimes shoddy images during the summer of 1986 reflect a labor process that was itself distorted by competitive pressures in the journalistic arena.

Our comparison of college panel data contained in the 7 July ISR press release (University of Michigan 1986) with those that Johnston and his associates (1986) chose to include in their final report indicates that these researchers delivered a special order of lifetime prevalence estimates to meet the heavy demand for "big numbers" in the media marketplace. Just as Fishman (1978) observed that media crime waves depend on the supply of thematically relevant incidents from law enforcement agencies, the construction of shocking headlines about "1 in 3 College Students" during the summer of 1986 depended on the provision of numbers that could be used as instances of an "epidemic." It is important to note that media workers largely ignored smaller numbers from the college data that appeared in both the ISR press release and the final report—the annual and 30-day prevalence estimates that Johnston, O'Malley, and Bachman treat as indicators of "active use" (1986:16). Thus, the production of quantified claims at the peak of the media epidemic depended both on a supply of suitable materials by the ISR researchers and on an internal labor process through which the highest estimates were extracted and refined into shocking numbers.

The media epidemic of the "cocaine summer" became the story in September. Taking a new tack, *Time, U.S. News & World Report,* and some newspaper columnists seemed to grant *Newsweek*'s claim to the "drug crisis," and then to show how this claim had been abused through "hype" and political misappropriation. Working under this condition of counterissue competition, graphic artists created images of the ISR time series that conformed fairly well to Tufte's (1983) standards for graphical integrity. But, here too, we should not lose sight of Blumer's (1971) point that the uses and representations of such knowledge are always contingent on other considerations in the process of collective definition. The "honest" design of the graphs of drug "habits" in September 1986 issues of *Time* and *U.S. News & World Report* reinforced textual claims that the cocaine epidemic was only a "statistical blip" and that the "real story" behind the crisis was yet another U.S. crusade against drugs.

In the meantime, Smith and his staff were clearly reluctant to relinquish their claim to the "drug crisis." Miller's (1987) article placed the declines in the ISR time series within a middle-class ghetto, and directed attention to the plague that was still roaming freely in the streets of the inner city. Even Martz's (1990) belated entry into the counterissue market had less to say about the role of the media in "hyping" the cocaine problem than about limitations in the survey data that had betrayed predictions of a growing epidemic. Above all, the recent image of an "alarming rise" in LSD which was erected on the eroding foundation of the "Coke Plague" shows that the prospectors at *Newsweek* are still at work. We suspect that Seligmann and her colleagues were put on the trail of the "New Age of Aquarius" by advance information of a flat trend that was announced in a 27 January 1992 press release from the ISR (University of Michigan 1992). After commenting on dramatic declines in prevalence estimates for cocaine and other drugs, Johnston noted that "one drug which bears watching is LSD, since use of it has not declined among seniors since the early 1980s" (University of Michigan 1992:4). Rather than waiting and watching, the staff of *Newsweek* went to work on the numbers and, in virtually no time at all, produced a new and "alarming" drug problem.

Media distortion of research findings may not be fresh news in the field of social problems. However, we question whether analysts who dispose of this material by debunking statistical claims or reducing media coverage to political propaganda have fully explored its sociological potential. We find ample grounds for the claim that media workers "lie"; but we have also tried to understand the creative choices and skills that are entailed in the fabrication of these distorted images of drug problems. Moreover, by attending to systematic variations in the nature and degree of distortion in media workers' products, we have attempted to gain insight into organizational and competitive conditions that affect this labor process. Although our work sheds no light on what "really" happened to drug use in 1986, we think it offers a sociologically pertinent account of how media workers used drug data to construct the social reality of a national epidemic.

Note

This is a revised version of a paper presented at the 1992 annual meeting of the Society for the Study of Social Problems, Pittsburgh. We are grateful to John Galliher, Larry Hazelrigg, and the anonymous *Social Problems* reviewers for their helpful comments. Correspondence to: Orcutt, Department of Sociology, Florida State University, Tallahassee, FL 32306-2011.

References

Berke, Richard L. 1989. "Student survey detects decline in use of crack." *New York Times* 1 March: A16.

Best, Joel. 1989. "Dark figures and child victims: Statistical claims about missing children." In *Images of Issues: Typifying Contemporary Social Problems*, ed. Joel Best, 21–37. New York: Aldine de Gruyter.

Blumer, Herbert. 1971. "Social problems as collective behavior." *Social Problems* 18:298–306.

Diamond, Edwin, Frank Accosta, and Leslie-Jean Thornton. 1987. "Is TV news hyping America's cocaine problem?" *TV Guide* 7 February: 4–10.

Fishman, Mark. 1978 . "Crime waves as ideology." *Social Problems* 25:531–543.

Gans, Herbert J. 1979. *Deciding What's News*. New York: Pantheon.

Goode, Erich. 1989. "The American drug panic of the 1980s: Social construction or objective threat?" *Violence, Aggression and Terrorism* 3:327–348.

Halloran, Richard. 1986. "Student use of cocaine is up as use of most other drugs drops." *New York Times* 8 July: A12.

Hilgartner, Stephen, and Charles L. Bosk. 1988. "The rise and fall of social problems: A public arenas model." *American Journal of Sociology* 94:53–78.

Huff, Darrell. 1954. *How to Lie with Statistics*. New York: W.W. Norton.

Jensen, Erich L., Jerg Gerber, and Ginna M. Babcock. 1991. "The new war on drugs: Grassroots movement or political construction?" *Journal of Drug Issues* 21:651–667.

Johnson, John M. 1989. "Horror stories and the construction of child abuse." In *Images of Issues: Typifying Contemporary Social Problems*, ed. Joel Best, 5–19. New York: Aldine de Gruyter.

Johnston, Lloyd D. 1989. "America's drug problem in the media: Is it real or is it Memorex?" In *Communication Campaigns About Drugs: Government, Media, and the Public*, ed. Pamela J. Shoemaker, 97–111. Hillsdale, N.J.: Lawrence Erlbaum.

Johnston, Lloyd D., Patrick M. O'Malley, and Jerald G. Bachman. 1986. *Drug Use Among American High School Students, College Students, and Other Young Adults: National Trends through 1985*. Rockville, Md.: National Institute on Drug Abuse.

———. 1991. *Drug Use Among American High School Seniors, College Students and Young Adults, 1975–1990*. Volume I: High School Seniors. Rockville, Md.: National Institute on Drug Abuse.

Kerr, Peter. 1986a. "Rising concern on drugs stirs public to activism." *New York Times* 10 August: Al, 28.

———. 1986b. "Anatomy of the drug issue: How, after years, it erupted." *New York Times* 17 November: Al, B6.

———. 1987. "High-school marijuana use still declining, U.S. survey shows." *New York Times* 24 February: A21.

Martz, Larry. 1990. "A dirty drug secret: Hyping instant addiction doesn't help." *Newsweek* 19 February: 74–77.

Merriam, John E. 1989. "National media coverage of drug issues, 1983–1987." In *Communication Campaigns About Drugs: Government, Media, and the Public*, ed. Pamela J. Shoemaker, 21–28. Hillsdale, N.J.: Lawrence Erlbaum.

Meyer, Thomas J. 1986. "1 in 3 college students tries cocaine, study finds." *Chronicle of Higher Education* 16 July: 1, 30.

Miller, Mark. 1987. "Drug use: Down, but not in the ghetto." *Newsweek* 23 November: 33.

Musto, David F. 1987. *The American Disease: Origins of Narcotic Control*. Expanded Edition. New York: Oxford University Press.

National Institute on Drug Abuse (NIDA). 1989. *National Household Survey on Drug Abuse: Population Estimates 1988*. Rockville, Md.: National Institute on Drug Abuse.

Newsweek. 1986a. "Kids and cocaine." 17 March: 58–65.

———. 1986b. "Trying to say 'no.'" 11 August: 14–19.

———. 1988. "Crack, hour by hour." 28 November: 64–75.

———. 1992. "The new age of Aquarius." 3 February: 65–67.

New York Times. 1989 . "Crack: A disaster of historic dimension, still growing." 28 May: E14.

Reese, Stephen D., and Lucig H. Danielian. 1989. "Intermedia influence on the drug issue: Converging on cocaine." In *Communication Campaigns About Drugs: Government, Media, and the Public*, ed. Pamela J. Shoemaker, 29–45. Hillsdale, N.J.: Lawrence Erlbaum.

Reinarman, Craig, and Harry G. Levine. 1989. "The crack attack: Politics and media in America's latest drug scare." In *Images of Issues: Typifying Contemporary Social Problems*, ed. Joel Best, 115–37. New York: Aldine de Gruyter.

Russell, Cristine. 1986. "One-third of college students try cocaine, survey finds." *Washington Post* 8 July: A3.

Safire, William. 1986. "The drug bandwagon." *New York Times* 11 September: A27.

Sciolino, Elaine. 1989. "Drug production rising worldwide, State Dept. says." *New York Times* 2 March: Al, 12.

———. 1990. "World drug crop up sharply in 1989 despite U.S. effort." *New York Times* 2 March: Al2.

Shoemaker, Pamela J., ed. 1989. *Communication Campaigns About Drugs: Government, Media, and the Public*. Hillsdale, N.J.: Lawrence Erlbaum.

Smith, Richard M. 1986. "The plague among us." *Newsweek* 16 June: 15.

Spector, Malcolm, and John I. Kitsuse. 1977. *Constructing Social Problems*. Menlo Park, Calif.: Cummings.

Time. 1986. "America's crusade." 15 September: 60–68.

Tufte, Edward R. 1983. *The Visual Display of Quantitative Information*. Cheshire, Conn.: Graphics Press.

University of Michigan. 1986. "U-M study indicates cocaine use remains high on American college campuses, while other drug frequency is down." Press Release, 7 July. Ann Arbor: News and Information Services.

———. 1992. "Most forms of drug use decline among American high school and college students, U-M survey reports." Press Release, 25 January. Ann Arbor: News and Information Services.

U.S. News & World Report. 1986a. "America on drugs." 28 July: 48–54.

———. 1986b. "War on drugs: More than a 'short-term high'?" 29 September: 28–29.

Part II

POLITICAL AND IDEOLOGICAL CONTEXTS

In the conclusion of his historical analysis of the disease conception of alcoholism, Schneider observes that the "question of whether or not a given condition constitutes a disease involves issues of politics and ideology—questions of definition, not fact" (1978:370). The three chapters featured in this part expand on this theme by examining the political and ideological foundations of contemporary definitions of alcohol and drug problems.

We begin with a work by Timothy Rouse and Prabha Unnithan that compares the "disease" conception of alcoholism in the United States with medical definitions and treatment of deviant drinking in the former Soviet Union. The central question in their analysis is this: How did two societies with such different political ideologies and economic systems develop similar approaches to alcohol-related problems? Rouse and Unnithan propose two answers. First, in spite of numerous differences, the ideological frameworks of capitalism and communism also shared some commonalities. Both the Protestant Ethic in the United States and the Proletarian Ethic during the Soviet regime stressed the moral value of dedication to hard work and productivity over and above the immediate material rewards of labor. Consequently, in each society, excessive drinking was defined as morally "unethical," as a failure to honor the strong value placed on work and as a threat to harmonious relations in the workplace. Second, Rouse and Unnithan argue that parallels in the modern industrial development of the United States and the Soviet Union provided a common structural basis for the emergence of the medical definition and treatment of alcoholism. That is, policies designed to "cure" alcoholics and return them to work were driven by an expanding need for a sober and productive labor force in both of these complex industrial societies. More generally, Rouse and Unnithan's analysis demonstrates how a cross-national comparative perspective can shed light on basic societal conditions that have affected the development of moral and medical approaches to alcohol problems throughout the twentieth century.

The next chapter by Katherine Beckett employs a longitudinal perspective to examine alternative explanatory models of change in public concern about the problems of drug use and street crime. On the one hand, the "objectivist model" proposes that changes in the actual incidence of drug use and crime have a direct impact on shifts in public concern about these problems. On the other hand, the "constructionist model" argues that the views of the public are shaped, instead, by claims-making activity—i.e., media stories and political initiatives about drugs and crime. Beckett uses quantitative evidence such as FBI crime statistics, measures of media coverage, and data from public opinion surveys to determine which of these models best accounts for variations over the past several decades in the public's ratings of the "most important problem facing the nation." Her analysis reveals that media attention and political initiatives are much better predictors of levels of public concern than are actual rates of crime and drug use. More specifically, she finds that public concern about drugs and crime tends to peak immediately after intense periods of political claims-making activity (e.g., the "War on Drugs" in the late 1980s). As Beckett concludes, her results indicate that the politicization of drug- and crime-related issues in recent years by elite claimsmakers and the media has profoundly influenced public conceptions of the seriousness of these social problems.

In the final chapter, Wysong, Aniskiewicz, and Wright present an evaluation and critique of one of the most widely used weapons in the "War on Drugs"—Drug Abuse Resistance Education, or DARE. Aimed at early prevention of drug use and abuse among youth, DARE programs have been introduced in thousands of schools in the United States during the 1980s and 1990s. In the first part of their analysis, Wysong and associates use a quasi-experimental approach to examine the long-term impact of DARE on student drug use and other outcomes. That is, they compared a group of high school seniors who participated in DARE as seventh graders with a "control group" of seniors who were never exposed to the program. The results of this comparative analysis are quite clear: After five years, there were virtually no differences between the two groups in levels of drug use or other outcomes (e.g., self-esteem) that advocates of DARE claim as benefits of the program. If DARE doesn't work, then what accounts for its popularity? Wysong et al. go on to provide a constructionist analysis of DARE's enormous *symbolic* benefits for a variety of stakeholders—politicians, corporate sponsors, school officials, and law-enforcement agencies that have gained legitimacy and public support by promoting this drug prevention initiative. Even though impact evaluations find little evidence that this program actually reduces drug use, DARE continues to thrive nationwide because of its powerful ideological appeal to a society at war with drugs. Few programs better illustrate how political and ideological forces shape the course of social problem interventions.

Reference

Schneider, Joseph W. 1978. "Deviant drinking as disease: Alcoholism as a social accomplishment." *Social Problems* 40:361–372.

CHAPTER 4

Comparative Ideologies and Alcoholism

THE PROTESTANT AND PROLETARIAN ETHICS

Timothy P. Rouse and Prabha N. Unnithan

Exemplifying how conceptions of habitual drunkenness are linked to prevailing ideologies, Levine attributes the importance attached to individual responsibility in the U.S. "addiction" (medical) model to its "Protestant and Puritan heritage" (1978:164). Similarly, the negative response to alcoholism in the United States can be traced to the alcoholic's culturally unacceptable loss of control over his or her own behavior, which is "incompatible with the dominant Protestant ethic" (Ames 1985:26). This line of reasoning suggests that if another country did not share the same heritage and was guided by another ideology, its conceptions of alcoholism and alcohol-related problems would be different. Although this perspective makes sense, the issue has never been explored empirically using comparative information about alcoholism in two countries.

The ideological underpinnings of the former Soviet Union,[1] and its political and economic arrangements, have often been characterized in opposition to those of the United States. However, in both the United States and the former Soviet Union (where attention has most often focused on politically dominant Russia; see Treml 1982) alcoholism has been considered a major social problem (Connor 1972; Fishbein 1991; Gallup 1985; Treml 1982; Trice 1984).[2] At the same time, in both countries a good deal of debate has taken place on the etiology, epidemiology, and treatment of alcoholism. In this chapter we compare, the ideological underpinnings of "definitions" of alcohol-related problems in the United States and the former Soviet Union. Wiseman declares that ideology, "can set the parameters of policymaking, [and] the approach to treatment of substance abuse" (1985:248, see also Tournier 1985).

Our major focus is on each society's definitions of alcoholism, alcoholics, and what should be done about the problem. In developing the analysis, we "take care not to separate the study of meanings from the study of their historical and institutional settings" (Gusfield 1989:439). We attempt to gauge similarities in the ideologies underlying each country's definitions of alcohol-related problems by comparing and contrasting their strategies for managing alcoholism and alcoholics. Although there are many differences in the definitions and strategies adopted, we suggest that these stem from models and ideologies with some commonalties. In the United States, the relevant ideology is the Protestant ethic (Weber [1904–05] 1958) and in the Soviet Union it was the proletarian ethic (Luke 1983).

We employ a case-oriented approach (Ragin 1987) which allows us to interpret descriptive details about each country in the light of its underlying ideology and other relevant conditions. Using evidence from previously published sources, we delineate each society's ideological framework and then describe how each defined the alcoholism problem and its strategies for dealing with it. The linkages between ideological frameworks, alcohol-problem definitions, and treatment strategies are explored in our concluding discussion with a view to explaining similarities and differences. Our approach is inductive in that we describe the ideologies, definitions, and strategies of each nation so that common themes and patterns can be identified, summarized, and explained.

Ideological Frameworks

THE PROTESTANT ETHIC

Weber's classic text, *The Protestant Ethic and the Spirit of Capitalism* ([1904–05] 1958), was a historical account of the significance of religion in social change, in this instance, the development of a unique political-economy: capitalism as it related to the industrialization of Europe. There are three fundamental elements of the Protestant ethic in Weber's observations of Calvinism and the Reformation.

The first element of the Protestant ethic is the notion of a *calling*. Calvinists believed that not only the clergy were called to do God's work, but any and all were called to God's cause. The Protestant calling was "the fulfillment of duty in worldly affairs as the highest form which the moral activity of the individual could assume" (Weber [1904–5] 1958:80). Thus, one could be a good "godly" baker, butcher, or banker. The significance of such a calling is that one works in a way that makes God happy and proud. Instructions come from the church for living on a path which leads toward salvation.

The second element, the *work ethic,* is related to the calling in that the individual works for the "glory of God" in all of his or her labors. The Puritan notion of "the covenant of works" indicated that humankind would be eternally destined to hardship and toil as punishment for Adam's behavior in Eden (Erikson 1966:83–84). The individual was expected to work and not to have too much idle or leisure time. Saving the fruits of labor, money, and investing it to make more money provides an assurance that God is happy with one's labors. Work is profitable.

The final element, predestination, is related to the first two. Reformation thinkers posited that God offered humanity *a* second covenant: a covenant of grace. This doctrine maintained that God determined salvation for humanity by randomly selecting a few souls who would escape eternal damnation; here good works did not matter since one's destiny in the hereafter was predetermined before birth (Erikson 1966:83). Therefore, to relieve anxiety concerning eternal life, it became essential to work hard in the hope that one could "disperse religious doubts and [find] the certainty of grace" (Weber 1958:112). Consequently, the idea of fulfilling one's calling in a "godly" manner, working hard and investing wisely, became a way to "hope" that God had smiled favorably on one's soul. Poverty could be interpreted as little more than a frown, suggesting where one might exist in the hereafter. To the elect, destiny might be comprehended by evaluating an individual's work ethic. Hard work is necessary but not sufficient for salvation; if a person is successful in his or her work an assumption of God's blessings may be made.

The Protestant ethic provides a basis for working, being productive, and contributing to the economy. In secular terms, a conscientious hardworking citizen answers a moral calling and is morally superior.

THE PROLETARIAN ETHIC

Luke (1983) describes the proletarian ethic as a work ethic inspired by Lenin and growing out of the Bolshevik revolution. Leninism as a form of "correct consciousness of Marxist thought"[3] is as crucial to a proletarian understanding of labor as Protestantism is to Christianity. For the committed, there is a high level of zeal and vigor (see Luke 1983:595–596).

Luke (1983) outlines three principles of the proletarian ethic. First, is the notion of a *socialist calling*. If Bolshevism is conceived as a civil religion, then the calling was from the party. Only the party could save the Bolshevik from boredom and lethargy by providing disciplined meaningful labor in service to the country. "Socialism was his faith, the people—his God" (Luke 1983:593). The calling for a socialist revolution would bring the final reward—a classless society.

A second element of the ethic is the idea of *consciousness*. Correct socialist consciousness was the goal. In the proletarian world, consciousness was materially based, and according to the intelligentsia it included a call for revolution (Luke 1983:597). Answering the call and developing consciousness was a skill for the elect and enlightened few; it became an ascetic profession. The proper consciousness meant having the right theories of scientific socialism (Luke cites Szamuely 1974:169). They were the "magic" which would transform society and create a new future. The intelligentsia were not the only ones capable of orchestrating and retaining such consciousness; workers were encouraged to strive for consciousness as well, whether they were activists in the state or factory.

"Consciousness was also propagated through mass educational offensives, like the literacy campaigns, the Time League, and Soviet Taylorism" (Luke 1983:597). It gave rise to increased labor productivity and literacy rates. Increased labor productivity was a critical variable in Lenin's prescriptions for communist society. Lenin was strongly committed to the party's efforts in waging a cultural war against "slovenliness, carelessness, untidiness, unpunctuality, nervous haste, the inclination to substitute discussion for action" (Lenin [1917] 1964:412). Workers were also cautioned by Lenin: "keep regular and honest accounts of money, manage economically, do not be lazy, do not steal, observe the strictest labour discipline" (Lenin [1917] 1980a:405). Lenin himself attempted to model this behavior in his own ascetic lifestyle (Luke 1983:595).

The third element is the *proletarian ethic* itself as a guide to action. Answering a calling to the party through hard work and consciousness is the heart of the proletarian ethic. The proletarian ethic is about the sacredness of labor and putting group needs before individual desires.[4] Further, it was to be the epitome of the new Soviet man/woman. The new Soviet persona takes on mythic proportions, emerging as "a man of steel, a builder who overcomes all obstacles, practicing the self-denial of a saint and the ruthlessness of a soldier in battle" (Wiseman 1985:253). Soviet citizens were to be "'thinking realists,' who, by mortifying self-discipline, rigorous living, and decisive dedication at the revolutionary profession, voluntarily committed themselves to Russia's transformation" (Luke 1983:594). Lenin concentrated his efforts on making Marxism "a 'profession' in both senses of the word, a profession by which and through which one lived and made one's living, and a profession of one's faith" (Wolfe 1960:60; also see Luke 1983:594). For Lenin, work was a heroic duty (see Lenin [1918] 1980b:456–467).

Alcoholism in the United States and the Soviet Union

International statistics are unclear concerning the seriousness of alcohol-related problems in the United States and Soviet Union. There is evidence to support the conclusion that in both the United States and the former Soviet Union, serious alcohol-related problems exist. The estimated number of alcoholics in the United States is 4 percent of the general population or eight million people (Akers 1992; Royce 1989; see also Williams et al. 1987). Officials in the Soviet Union put the estimate at 10 percent of the total population or 28 million (Kirn 1987b). Among other indicators of the perceived seriousness of the problem is the death rate from alcohol poisoning (Treml 1982). Based on official reports, Treml concludes that "compared with the 1976 U.S.S.R. rate of death from all poisons of 25.7 per 100,000 of population, and deaths from alcohol poisoning of 15.9 per 1000,000, the rate in the USA in the same year was 2.94 for deaths from all poisons, and 0.18 for alcohol poisonings" (1982:489). Treml also notes that for 19 countries in 1969, World Health Organization statistics reveal the mean rate for *all* poisoning (including alcohol) deaths was 5.68. Finland was the only other country, with a rate of 6.04 for alcohol poisoning, that approached the high Soviet figure. Treml (1982) also suggests the historical continuity of high alcohol poisoning death rates experienced in Russia, and later the U.S.S.R. Comparable rates for the United States have historically shown upward and downward trends, but generally have been lower (Hyman et al. 1980).

There is considerable controversy over cultural perceptions regarding alcohol-related problems and alcoholism (Levine 1984; Peele 1989; Ward 1985; Weiner 1981), and "few people agree on what it [alcoholism] is" (Ames' 1985:23). Thus, "figures published about the number of alcoholics . . . often represent the propaganda intent of the agency or institute issuing the data" (Fingarette 1988:5). However, we can say that both the United States and the Soviet Union defined themselves as having serious alcohol-related problems. In the United States, the Secretary of Health and Human Services, Louis W. Sullivan, described alcoholism and alcohol abuse as one of America's "most pervasive public health problems" (*Alcohol and Health* 1990:vii). Eduard Drozdov, Moscow's chief specialist in chemical dependency treatment described the problem of alcoholism as "a very serious one" (*Soviet Life* 1990b:55).

The alarm created by official self-definitions has impelled politicians and health officials in both countries to develop prevention and treatment efforts. For example, from 1985 to 1988, the Soviet Union conducted a major campaign to reduce drunkenness and alcoholism in the workplace (*The Economist* 1989; Heath 1989; Partanen 1987). Around the same time, a similar initiative in the U.S. corporate sector began to deal with a variety of substance abuse issues, including alcoholism in the workplace, with emphasis placed on loss of productivity and accidents (Wagner 1987).[5] To aid governmental efforts, the Soviet Union created an agency called the All-Union Voluntary Temperance Promotion Society (TPS) whose functions were equivalent to the National Institute on Alcoholism and Alcohol Abuse (NIAAA) in the United States. The main preventive activities common to both countries have been raising the price of beverage alcohol, emphasizing nonalcoholic leisure time pursuits, raising the drinking age from 18 to 21, and limiting the hours of purchase (*The Economist* 1989; Kirn 1987b, 1987c). One major difference was that in the Soviet Union, the state was able to control and reduce the official production, distribution, and sale of alcohol (although illicit and home brewing increased in response, see *The Economist* 1989). Such a policy was not possible in the *laissez-faire* political economy of the United States.

Alcoholism Treatment in the United States and Soviet Union

In the United States and the Soviet Union, two views have dominated efforts aimed at dealing with or treating alcoholism—the medical model and the morality model (Fingarette 1988; Gusfield 1963; Schneider 1978; Ward 1985; Wiseman 1985).

THE MEDICAL MODEL

In the United States, the notion of excessive alcohol use as an illness was first conceived of in the late eighteenth century by the physician Benjamin Rush. Rush's early lectures and writings about alcohol use (especially his 1784 essay, "An Inquiry into the Effects of Spirituous Liquors Upon the Human Body and Mind" [1814] 1934), provided the rhetoric necessary to conceptualize drunkenness as a health problem for which the natural caretaker was the physician. Not only did his early writings and lectures lend credence to the cause of temperance, but they assisted in developing a new paradigm of addiction, which has had serious adherents since the nineteenth century (Alexander 1987:47; Levine 1978:152–53).

The new paradigm shifted the focus from the object of deviance—alcohol—to the host site—the body (Levine 1978:143). Deviance came to be situated in the individual (Ward 1985). Individuals were thought to have a genetic predisposition to addiction or faulty upbringing which made them susceptible to addiction (Alexander 1987:48–49). In this framework, alcoholism is defined as a chronic, progressive, terminal disease primarily characterized by the individual's loss of control over when, where, and how to drink (Johnson 1973; Levine 1978; Ward 1985). In the early to mid-twentieth century this model was extended by the founding of Alcoholics Anonymous in 1935 (Alcoholics Anonymous 1957; Kurtz 1979), the Yale School of Alcohol Studies (Conrad and Schneider 1980), and the works of E.M. Jellinek (1960).

Tournier (1985) has summarized the growth of the disease concept through the use of disease terminology beginning in the nineteenth century. Tournier relies on Keller (1976) in noting:

> Trotter's 1804 *An Essay, Mental, Philosophical, and Chemical on Drunkenness* and Kain's 1828 "On Intemperance Considered as a Disease" opened the century; in 1866 the French physician Gabriel first used the term alcoholism in its modern sense: *The Journal of Inebriety*, founded in 1876, championed an "alcoholism as illness" perspective, and from its founding until it ceased publication in 1913, published more than eighty papers and editorials on a disease concept of alcoholism (Keller 1976). (Tournier 1985:39)

Jellinek's *Disease Concept of Alcoholism* (1960) was a landmark publication that furthered acceptance of the disease model after the disease rhetoric lost ground to the view of alcohol abuse in moralistic and criminal terms in the early part of the twentieth century (i.e., Prohibition). A series of official events prepared the way for a return to the disease concept.

> In 1946, the General Assembly of the Presbyterian Church accepted the notion that alcoholism was a disease (Roueche 1960); in 1956, the Board of the American Medical Association passed a resolution urging hospitals to admit alcoholics on the basis of clinical indications alone (American Medical Association 1968), a resolution seconded in 1957 by the American Hospital Association. (Toumier 1985:40)

Since the 1950s, much work has attempted to disprove or support and improve this model in the disciplines of both physiology and psychology (Alexander 1987; Bacon 1973; Johnson 1973; Keller 1976; Mello 1983).

This model suggests that the afflicted suffer from an irreversible disorder for which they are not responsible; it places the onus of treatment on endogenous factors. The first requirement of treatment is total abstinence followed by a restructuring of the patient's basic lifestyle.

Recent research has focused on scientific investigation of genetic and chemical factors leading to alcoholism. Fingarette (1988) has surveyed the scientific community's opinions and concludes the view of alcoholism as a disease is based largely on myth. Yet, the disease concept reigns as the accepted treatment model in the United States (Tournier 1985).

In the Soviet Union, where the disease concept was based on Pavlovian notions of human behavior (Kim 1987c), the focus was on aversion conditioning. While physicians are the primary caretakers in the Soviet Union, in the United States alcoholism counselors predominate (Kim 1987c:2634). Many alcoholism counselors in the United States are former alcohol abusers who work in a network sustaining hegemonic definitions of alcohol recovery. Sobriety is often viewed as a "reward" and intoxication (or any alcohol use) as a "punishment."

Wiseman (1985) has noted that Pavlovian psychiatry in the Soviet Union has not been the only treatment perspective. Earlier, prescription tranquilizers were shunned by Soviet psychiatrists as palliatives for the jobless and homeless in capitalist societies, though more recently, these drugs have been clinically prescribed to alleviate worry, depression, and tension (Wiseman 1985:252). Similarly, Freudian psychotherapy is now also practiced to a greater extent than in the past (Kim 1987c).

Treatment in the United States often refers to a "continuum of care." Elaborate employee assistance programs (EAP) have been set up in many of the nation's major corporations (e.g., Honeywell, 3M, IBM, Hewlett-Packard, and Burlington-Northern). Intervention is followed by outpatient, inpatient, and aftercare treatment, including group therapy, individual therapy, and family therapy. Treatment for the codependent (individuals in relationships with alcoholics) is the latest trend in the United States (Gomberg 1989). The most common treatment regime, however, is that developed by Alcoholics Anonymous (Peele 1989).

In the former Soviet Union, medical treatment was a three phase procedure established on a twin model approach (Fishbein 1991; Kim 1987c). The first approach was medical and holistic. The subject was given an opportunity for treatment. If he or she failed to follow the treatment regimen, criminal procedures could be invoked (Wiseman 1985). The second approach was behavioristic in its orientation, though both cognitive and behavioral matters were addressed. In this second approach, aversion therapy along with the drug disulfiram (Antabuse) and mild shock treatments were common. In this medical model, a series of counseling sessions coupled with hypnosis and insulin shock therapy might also be prescribed. The major emphasis was apparently on "aversive treatment protocols" (Fishbein 1991:1212) using drugs, with a secondary focus on psychotherapy and counseling. In addition, the USSR also had several "sobering stations" which were similar to detoxification centers in the United States (*Mother Jones* 1991).

In the United States, when treatment regimes fail, subjects can be sanctioned in various ways. An indigent person can be returned to the streets, and an employed person can be fired. In the Soviet Union, the alternative for many when treatment failed was "another form of aversion treatment-deportation to the eastern frontier work camps and enterprise farms" (Wiseman 1985:257).

Finally, Kim (1987c) reports that of the Soviet Union's 1.2 million physicians, 7,000 were narcologists—specialists in the study of alcoholism and drug addiction. The government attempted to attract new physicians to this specialty and treatment was paid for by the state. Similarly, in the United States, physicians specialize in the alcoholism field, though typically they direct treatment programs. Their presence serves to associate alcoholism with notions of disease and medical treatment and to legitimate payment of health insurance benefits (Peele 1989). Direct treatment work is often left to nonmedical personnel, usually paraprofessionals from the fields of psychology and social work, and often others who have experienced alcohol and/or drug problems themselves (Weisner 1983).

The Soviet Union began incorporating both the medical and moral imagery used by Alcoholics Anonymous (cf. Maxwell 1984; Rudy 1986). Twice in 1987, emissaries from the United States traveled to the Soviet Union to spread the message of AA, and Moscow's first AA chapter was formed in 1989 (*Time* 1989:30–34; Alcoholics Anonymous 1988:28–35).

THE MORALITY MODEL

In the Soviet Union, as in the United States, drinking was linked to numerous social problems ranging from auto accidents, crime rates, impaired work performance, and divorce rates. Wiseman summarized a study by Willis (1981) noting that "drunkenness lacks the social stigma in Russia that it carries in most western societies, but the current regime seems determined to create such a stigma with its continued campaign against any form of substance abuse" (Wiseman 1985:252). More pointedly, Partanen states, "on the level of symbols, the emphasis on alcoholism differentiates the present regime from the previous one and affirms its *moral* superiority" (italics added, Partanen 1987:5–11).

The morality model is based on prescriptions of what constitutes "right" conduct or the "right" principles to live by. Moral judgements are often issued and propagated by moral entrepreneurs who attempt to impose their brand of morality on others (Becker 1963:147–163). The moral entrepreneur implicitly assumes that the poor ignorant other is not only unaware of the "right" brand of morality, but, perhaps, actually craves enlightenment. The U.S. Prohibition movement has often been understood in such terms.

In the United States, the roots of Prohibition can be found in the efforts of eighteenth-century temperance workers. The moral crusade to eradicate alcohol from society reached its zenith during the early part of the twentieth century when moral entrepreneurs (Gusfield 1963) along with economic elites (Levine 1983; Rouse 1991;1992; Rumbarger 1989) were able to impose coercive reforms on U.S. society which lasted from 1919 to 1933 (Kobler 1973; Sinclair 1962; Timberlake 1963; Unnithan 1985). Economic elites concerned with labor problems and urban progressives (Levine 1985; Rumbarger 1989:123–151) exerted political clout in conjunction with pressure from Methodists and Baptists (Blumberg and Pittman 1991) on key members of the U.S. Congress. In addition, a vigorous barrage of press propaganda (Rouse 1992) and school education about alcohol problems (Gusfield 1963), all combined to pave the road for the Eighteenth Amendment to be pushed through Congress in December 1917.

The Reagan administration's "Just Say No" campaign (1985–1988), which focused on controlling alcohol and drug use, also included *moral* judgments as to the causes of such behavior (Morgan, Wallack, and Buchanan 1989).[6] Where earlier in U.S. history, such behavior was "of the devil" (cf. Erikson 1966:157–159, also Szasz 1985:142, 172), the Reagan administration's campaign depicted rampant drug and alcohol use as a reflection of liberal social policies resulting in indulgent and permissive values. Wiseman summarized the argument as: liberals create policies that scoff at the "work ethic," hand out welfare to everyone, and encourage individuals to experiment with "new lifestyle values" that destroy the traditional family and marriage (1985:249). Substance abuse is thus culturally symbolic of the loosening of the moral order (Peele 1987).

In the former Soviet Union, the alcoholic was morally defined as a "parasite" (Connor 1972, 1973; Field 1955; Wiseman 1985) or evil (Zaigraev 1988). The alcoholic was seen as not living up to the correct notion of the "New Soviet Man or Woman" (Medish 1985; Wiseman 1985) and as incompatible with a "socialist way of life" (Zaigraev 1988). Lenin set the example for the life of the "true socialist." Alcoholics were a population understood at a moral level as "free riders." They took more than they gave and refused to join in the pains of proletarian labor. They stood as remnants of capitalist decadence (Connor 1972; Field 1955; Wiseman 1985).

The moralist's view of substance abuse as a dreadful sinful act or an egregious habit has been modified in the United States by Alcoholics Anonymous, followed by the Yale Center for Alcohol Studies (now Rutgers School of Alcohol Studies), and the works of E.M. Jellinek (Conrad and Schneider 1980). The transition from the moral to medical model was officially endorsed by Congress in enacting the Alcoholic Rehabilitation Act (PL 90–574) in 1968, which declared alcoholism a health problem in need of early detection, prevention, treatment, and rehabilitation (see introduction in *Alcohol and Health* 1983). However, the rhetoric of the morality model was never completely abandoned, as the "Just Say No" campaign indicates. Similarly, though the Soviet Union gave greater credence to the medical model, the moral model persisted.

Discussion

Both the Protestant ethic, which permeates U.S. society, and the proletarian ethic, the driving ideology of the former Soviet Union, have affected the definition and treatment of alcoholism. There were differences in each society's ability to officially control alcohol production and in specific treatment methods. However, there are several similarities. Prominent authorities have defined alcohol and alcoholism as serious and have utilized policies drawn from the medical and moral models. There is an underlying similarity in definitions of alcoholism and attempts to deal with alcoholics. Both society's strategies have emphasized alcoholics' failure to contribute to work and the economy, and their "unethical behavior."

In the United States, the alcoholic fails to answer the moral calling of work and "honest" effort and his or her moral destiny is clearly negative. The alcoholic violates the sense of the centrality of work as a way of life in the United States by substituting heavy drinking as the preferred "central activity" (Fingarette 1988:101).

In the Soviet Union, the alcoholic failed to answer the socialist calling, failed to develop the requisite socialist consciousness which takes labor seriously, and failed to act in line with these principles. The key problem the 1985 Soviet campaign attempted to deal with was "how to effectuate a rapid rise in work, productivity" (Partanen 1987:517). Thus Gorshkov and Shergei declare approvingly that the 1985 campaign against drunkenness and alcoholism yielded, "a noticeable improvement in the *moral climate of many work collectives* and families, an improvement in discipline and organization, and an *increase in labor productivity"* (italics added, 1987:92; see Smith 1990 for a similar discussion).

In both countries, alcoholics do exhibit problems in the work setting. For example, in the United States, Cahalan identifies problems such as "reduced productivity and lost employment . . . and remedial welfare programs" (1989:169). In the Soviet Union, Zaigraev reports that "drunks had a negative judgment about their work collectives three times more frequently than did [other] respondents" (1988:43). Alcoholics have become "eligible for management as deviant [because] they disturb, hinder or call into question" the economic arrangements of their society (Spitzer 1975:642). Alcoholism becomes "a social anomaly clashing with the development of civilization. Society has a right to eradicate it with any means available" (Shergei 1988:25). The adversarial quality of official judgments leave no room for discussion of what Gusfield characterizes as "the benefits of drinking and drunkenness . . . [particularly] . . . the carnival point of view" (1989:435). The intensity of rhetorical self-definition as countries with serious alcohol problems is matched by the equally intense negative characterization of alcoholics themselves. Though the degree of coercion and control varied in the United States and the Soviet Union, in both countries alcoholism and alcoholics posed a fundamental threat to economic arrangements and the ideologies justifying those arrangements.

Two explanations help us to understand how the United States and the Soviet Union, rival societies with opposing ideological objectives and varying cultural heritages, came to define and deal with alcohol-related problems in essentially similar ways. First, Levine's (1978) conclusion that conceptions of alcoholism reflect prevailing ideology leads to a focus on ideological frameworks themselves. The goals of the Protestant ethic (deciphering clues to religious salvation) and the proletarian ethic (contributing to establishment of a communist society) are different, yet our analysis has shown that the two ethics share important commonalities. Both emphasize, for example, the value of work and labor beyond their immediate rewards. The alcoholic appears to hold this greater calling in contempt. Marcuse noted that the values proclaimed by Leninism were "in every respect [part of] a *competitive work morality"* similar to Calvinism and "not too far from Puritan exhortations to good business" (1958:233, 242). In particular, Marcuse found that "what the Calvinist work morale achieved through strengthening irrational anxiety about forever-hidden divine decisions, is here accomplished through more rational means: a more satisfying human existence is to be the reward for the growing productivity of labor" (1958:239).

Consequently, similar methods for dealing with alcohol-related problems developed in both countries. The morality model predominated in the United States because of its religious and ideological framework, and the medical model predominated in the Soviet Union because of its secular (and professed antireligious) ideological antecedents. The Soviet authorities' willingness to allow quasi-spiritual groups such as AA to operate, and that group's continued popularity in the United States can be traced to its skillful rhetorical weaving of medical and moral imagery. AA's rhetoric does not contradict, and may even have incorporated, components of both the Protestant and proletarian ethics. For example, although the word "God" is often used in the organization, there are no sectarian or denominational overtones to the "higher power" that AA members rely on (for Soviet purposes it could be translated into the "principles of socialism"). A spirit of camaraderie and mutual help, which could be regarded as socialistic, as well as capitalistic individualism, are part of the AA approach.

Alcoholics Anonymous has long claimed to be neither medicine nor religion (Alcoholics Anonymous 1957; Kurtz 1979). One of its cofounders, William Wilson, was adamant about not alienating the religious or medical communities; rather, he wished to "cooperate" with them, not replace them (Alcoholics Anonymous 1957). This approach may be acceptable as a treatment modality because it is both quasi-medical and quasi-religious. There are no paid professional AA physicians or clerics. Many members speak of sobriety and character building as steps necessary to living a healthy and contented life. Members also speak of the three choices left them—death, insanity, or sobriety—by the time they are willing to follow AA's prescribed steps. The camaraderie that AA members experience may result from a "fellowship" not unlike the functional equivalents of religion that Durkheim ([1915] 1965) illustrated. The social solidarity among alcoholics appears to transcend even national boundaries. Its existentialist elements have been elaborated by Kurtz.

> Guided by AA, alcoholics come to understand finitude, to discern the existential meaning of "nothingness," in two ways. Some, confronted with the dire choice of abstinence, insanity or death, by reflecting on those possibilities become aware of the reality of the fact that some absolute limitation has become absolutely inevitable. They thus attain the consciousness described by Sartre: "Consciousness is a being, the nature of which is to be conscious of the nothingness of its being." (1982:44)

A second explanation relates to earlier sociological debates about whether communism and capitalism are "two alternate forms of a single complex industrial society (see Hollander 1969b). This structural explanation suggests both societies were driven by the logic of economic industrialization, both required the active participation of citizens in productive labor, and therefore both discouraged heavy drinking. As a result, the two societies experienced "convergence" (Hollander 1969b; Smith 1985, 1990) on the methods for dealing with alcoholics and alcohol problems. The Protestant ethic in the United States led to methods initially based on a religious and moral model (prohibition of alcohol because it was evil). Those efforts were supplemented and later largely replaced by a medical model that sought to intervene and arrest the development of the "disease of alcoholism" in citizens who might otherwise be productive employees. In the Soviet Union, given its secular proletarian ethic, methods for dealing with alcohol problems were drawn mostly from the medical model (Pavlovian psychiatry, narcology) along with socialistic moral opprobrium.

Industrial development has led to similar solutions to the alcohol problem. Both societies tapped into the prestige of physicians (through the medical model) by expanding disease treatment programs (often centered in the workplace) to "cure" alcoholics and to return them to work. They also utilized the convictions of moral entrepreneurs (through the morality model) to reform heavy drinkers, and to persuade others to resist; for example, Nancy Reagan's involvement in the "Just Say No" campaign (Morgan et al. 1989) and Mikhail Gorbachev's 1985 temperance campaign in the U.S.S.R. (Smith 1990; Zaigraev 1988).

We have presented "ideological commonalities" and "industrial convergence" as two separate explanations for similarities in the United States and the Soviet Union in the treatment of alcoholics. The definitions of and responses to alcohol-related problems in these two countries suggest that societies will find means consistent with their ideological and economic contexts to label and treat those who do not conform to central expectations.

Notes

An earlier version of this paper was presented at the 1990 annual meetings of the Academy of Criminal Justice Sciences in Denver, CO. Our thanks to David Freeman and anonymous Social Problems reviewers for useful comments. The order of authorship is alphabetical. Correspondence to: Rouse, Department of Sociology, Anthropology, and Social Work, Middle Tennessee State University, Murfreesboro, TN 37132.

1. Although the Soviet Union has disintegrated, there are a number of reasons for examining Soviet society. First, by comparing rival societies, we are better able to appreciate their commonalties in dealing with alcohol-related issues. Second, the relatively closed nature of Soviet society previously limited systematic information gathering (Connor 1972; Dmytryshn 1977; Field 1955; Hollander 1969b; Inkeles and Bauer 1961). Only recently has more information and the detailed descriptions needed for making comparisons became available (Darialova 1991; The Economist 1989; Fishbein 1991; Herlihy 1991; Kirn 1987a, 1987b, 1987c; Medish 1985; Quinn-Judge 1990; Soviet Life 1990a, 1990b, 1990c; Treml 1982). Finally, the former Soviet Union was dominated by the culture of Russia. Thus, in the short-term, we can expect some degree of continuity in Russia's handling of its alcohol-related problems.

2. Hollander (1969a) made the first brief and speculative attempt to compare drunkenness in the Soviet Union and the United States.

3. Smith writes, "it is the Leninist creed on which rests the infallibility of the Communist Party and its leaders. . . . Marx is strictly secondary" (1985:280). The Soviet interpretation of Marxism in terms of Leninism is not necessarily acceptable to others in the same ideological tradition. For example, Chinese leader Deng Xiaoping has defined Marxism as the principles of "seeking truth from facts" (Butterfield 1982:301).

4. The ethic's seriousness is captured in Kennan's description of the early Soviet leadership as "men who had a burning social faith, and were relentless and incorruptible in the pursuit of it . . . [they] knew what they wanted; they worked day and night to carry it into effect; they gave no thought to themselves. They demanded discipline from others: they accepted it for themselves" (1961:61).

5. Both the Soviet and American campaigns relating to alcohol consumption were the latest in a long series of similar efforts dating back to the formative years of both nations. For information about earlier campaigns, see Moore and Gerstein (1981) and Lender and Martin (1987) regarding the United States; and The Economist (1989) regarding the Soviet Union.

6. While some might question our analysis of alcohol and drug control, particularly with regard to the "Just Say No" campaign, we are emphasizing the use of *moral* judgments in *moral crusades* by *moralizing* opinion leaders. The "Just Say No" campaign was able to capture a good deal of media attention just as various moral entrepreneurs captured the media before and during Prohibition (cf. Rouse 1992). Not only bootleggers and smugglers were regarded as criminals, but alcohol users also became criminals through the very act of drinking. Similarly, the "Just Say No" campaign made an implicit character judgment not only about the kind of people who

"abused" drugs (including alcohol) but also people who "used" them. This is reflected in both alcohol and other drug treatment programs which contend that "use is abuse," "abusing is losing," and "users are losers," Thus, saying "no," or yes to total abstinence, is the first step to "winning," "being a winner," or becoming a productive, responsible, and contributing member of society.

References

Akers, Ronald L. 1992. *Drugs, Alcohol and Society: Social Structure, Process and Policy.* Belmont, Calif.: Wadsworth.

Alcoholics Anonymous. 1957. *Alcoholics Anonymous Comes of Age: A Brief History of A.A.* New York: Alcoholics Anonymous World Services, Inc.

———. 1988. "Experience, strength, and hope—visit to the Soviet Union." *AA Grapevine* July: 29–35.

Alcohol and Health. 1983. *Alcohol and Health: Fifth Special Report to the U.S. Congress from the Secretary of Health and Human Services.* Rockville, Md.: National Institute on Alcohol Abuse and Alcoholism.

———. 1990. *Alcohol and Health: Seventh Special Report to the U.S. Congress from the Secretary of Health and Human Services.* Rockville, Md.: National Institute on Alcohol Abuse and Alcoholism.

Alexander, Bruce K. 1987. "The disease and adaptive models of addiction: A framework evaluation." *Journal of Drug Issues* 17:47–66.

American Medical Association. 1968. *Manual on Alcoholism.* Chicago, Ill.: American Medical Association.

Ames, Genevieve M. 1985. "American beliefs about alcoholism: Historical perspectives on the medical-moral controversy." In *The American Experience with Alcohol,* ed. Linda A. Bennett and Genevieve M. Ames, 23–39. New York: Plenum.

Bacon, Seldon. 1973. "The process of addiction." *Quarterly Journal of Studies on Alcohol* 34:1–27.

Becker, Howard. 1963. *Outsiders.* New York: Free Press.

Blumberg, Leonard U., and William L. Pittman. 1991. *Beware the First Drink!* Seattle, Wash.: Glenn-Abbey.

Butterfield, Fox. 1982. *China: Alive in the Bitter Sea.* New York: Times Books.

Cahalan, Don. 1989. "Public policy on alcohol and illicit drugs." *Drugs and Society* 3:169–186.

Connor, Walter D. 1972. *Deviance in Soviet Society: Crime, Delinquency, and Alcoholism.* New York: Columbia University Press.

———. 1973. "Criminal homicide, U.S.S.R./U.S.A.: Reflections on Soviet data in a comparative framework." *Journal of Criminal Law and Criminology* 64:111–117.

Conrad, Peter, and Joseph W. Schneider. 1980. *Deviance and Medicalization: From Badness to Sickness.* St. Louis, Mo.: C.V. Mosby.

Darialova, Natalia. 1991. "Vodka: The opiate of the masses." *Forbes* 147:96–98.

Dmytryshyn, Basil. 1977. *A History of Russia.* Englewood Cliffs, N.J.: Prentice-Hall.

Durkheim, Emile. [1915]. 1965. *The Elementary Forms of Religious Life.* New York: Free Press.

The Economist. 1989. "Russia's anti-drink campaign: Vendi, vidi, vodka." *The Economist.* 313:50–54.

Erikson, Kai T. 1966. *Wayward Puritans.* New York: John Wiley & Sons, Inc.

Field, Mark G. 1955. "Alcoholism, crime, and delinquency in Soviet society." *Social Problems* 3:100–109.

Fingarette, Herbert. 1988. *Heavy Drinking: The Myth of Alcoholism as a Disease*. Los Angeles, Calif.: University of California Press.

Fishbein, David Joel. 1991. "Do Dna: Alcoholism in the Soviet Union." *Journal of the American Medical Association* 266:1211–1212.

Gallup, George. 1985. "Attitudes toward drinking/alcoholism." *Gallup Report* 1985/Report No. 242:23–48.

Gomberg, Edith S.L. 1989. "On terms used and abused: The concept of codependency."' *Drugs and Society* 3:113–132.

Gorshkov, Mikhail K., and Frants E. Shergei. 1987. "Public opinion and the battle against drunkenness and alcoholism." *Soviet Sociology* 26:92–104.

Gusfield, Joseph R. 1963. *Symbolic Crusade: Status Politics and the American Temperance Movement*. Urbana, Ill.: University of Illinois Press.

———. 1989. "Constructing the ownership of social problems: Fun and profit in the welfare state." *Social Problems* 36:431–441.

Heath, Dwight B. 1989. "The new temperance movement through the looking glass." *Drugs and Society* 3:143–168.

Herlihy, Patricia. 1991. "'Joy of the Rus': Rites and rituals in Russian drinking." *The Russian Review* 50:131–147.

Hollander, Paul. 1969a. "The effects of alcohol." In *American and Soviet Society: A Reader in Comparative Sociology and Perception*, ed. Paul Hollander, 351–352. Englewood Cliffs, N.J.: Prentice-Hall.

———. 1969b. "Are the two societies becoming alike." In *American and Soviet Society: A Reader in Comparative Sociology and Perception*, ed. Paul Hollander, 559–560. Englewood Cliffs, N.J.: Prentice-Hall.

Hyman, Merton M., Marilyn A. Zimmerman, Carol Guriolio, and Alice Hedrich. 1980. *Drinkers, Drinking, and Alcohol-Related Mortality and Hospitalizations: A Statistical Compendium*. New Brunswick, N.J.: Journal of Studies on Alcohol, Inc.

Inkeles, Alex, and Raymond Bauer. 1961. *The Soviet Citizen: Daily Life in a Totalitarian Society*. Boston, Mass.: Harvard University Press.

Jellinek, E.M. 1960. *The Disease Concept of Alcoholism*. New Haven, Conn.: Hillhouse.

Johnson, Vern E. 1973. *I'll Quit Tomorrow*. New York: Harper and Row.

Keller, Mark. 1976. "The disease concept of alcoholism revisited." *Quarterly Journal of Studies on Alcohol* 37:1694–1717.

Kennan, George F. 1961. *Russia and the West Under Lenin and Stalin*. Boston, Mass.: Little, Brown and Co.

Kim, Timothy F. 1987a. "Soviets attack alcohol problems anew, this time armed with 'perestroika.'" *Journal of the American Medical Association* 258:2341–2348.

———. 1987b. "Soviets, Americans allied in new war; common foe this time: Alcohol abuse." *Journal of the American Medical Association* 258:2480–2485.

———. 1987c. "Prevention important in Soviet antialcohol efforts, but medical treatment also emphasized." *Journal of the American Medical Association* 258:2634–2635.

Kobler, John. 1973. *Ardent Spirits*. New York: Putnam.

Kurtz, Ernest. 1979. *Not-God: A History of Alcoholics Anonymous*. Center City, Minn.: Hazelden.

———. 1982. "Why A.A. works: The intellectual significance of Alcoholics Anonymous." *Journal of Studies on Alcohol* 43:38–80.

Lender, Mark Edward, and James Kirby Martin. 1987. *Drinking in America: A History*. New York: Free Press.

Lenin, V.I. [1917]. 1964. "How to organize competition." In *Collected Works*, vol. 26. Moscow: International Publishers.

———. [1917]. 1980a. "The immediate tasks of the Soviet government." In *Lenin: Selected Works*. New York: International Publishers.

———. [1918]. 1980b. "Letter to American workers." In *Lenin: Selected Works*. New York: International Publishers.

Levine, Harry Gene. 1978. "The discovery of addiction: Changing conceptions of habitual drunkenness in America." *Journal of Studies on Alcohol* 39:143–174.

———. 1983. "The Committee of Fifty and the origins of alcohol control." *Journal of Drug Issues* 13:95–116.

———. 1984. "What is an alcohol-related problem? (Or, what are people talking about when they refer to alcohol problems?)." *Journal of Drug Issues* 14:45–62.

———. 1985. "The birth of American alcohol control: Prohibition, the power elite, and the problem of lawlessness." *Contemporary Drug Problems* 12:63–115.

Luke, Timothy W. 1983. "The proletarian ethic and Soviet industrialization." *American Political Science Review* 77:588–601.

Marcuse, Herbert. 1958. *Soviet Marxism*. New York: Columbia University Press.

Maxwell, Milton. 1984. *The Alcoholics Anonymous Experience: A Close-up View for Professionals*. New York: McGraw-Hill.

Medish, Vadim. 1985. *The Soviet Union*. Englewood Cliffs, N.J.: Prentice-Hall.

Mello, Nancy K. 1983. "A behavioral analysis for the reinforcing properties of alcohol and other drugs in man." In *The Biology of Alcoholism*, vol. 7., "Biological Factors," ed. Benjamin Kissin and Henri Begleiter, 133–198. New York: Plenum.

Moore, Mark H., and Dean R. Gerstein, eds. 1981. *Alcohol and Public Policy: Beyond the Shadow of Prohibition*. Washington, D.C.: National Academy Press.

Morgan, Patricia, Lawrence Wallack, and David Buchanan. 1989. "Waging drug wars: Prevention strategy or politics as usual." *Drugs and Society* 3:99–124.

Mother Jones. 1991. "Sobering up." *Mother Jones* 16:52.57.

Partanen, Juha. 1987. "Serious drinking, serious alcohol policy: The case of the Soviet Union." *Contemporary Drug Problems* 14:507–538.

Peele, Stanton. 1987. "A moral vision of addiction: How people's values determine whether they become and remain addicts." *Journal of Drug Issues* 17:187–215.

———. 1989. *Diseasing of America: Addiction Treatment Out of Control*. Lexington, Mass.: Lexington Books.

Quinn-Judge, Paul. 1990. "Absolut hell." *The New Republic* 203:12–13.

Ragin, Charles C. 1987. *The Comparative Method: Moving Beyond Qualitative and Quantitative Strategies*. Los Angeles, Calif.: University of California Press.

Roueche, B. 1960. *The Neutral Spirit: A Portrait of Alcohol*. Boston, Mass.: Little, Brown and Co.

Rouse, Timothy P. 1991. "Sociologists and American prohibition: A study of early works in The American Journal of Sociology 1895–1935." *The American Sociologist* 22:232–242.

———. 1992. *The media and moral reform: The* New York Times *and American Prohibition*. Ph.D. diss., Colorado State University.

Royce, James E. 1989. *Alcohol Problems and Alcoholism*. New York: Free Press.

Rudy, David R. 1986. *Becoming Alcoholic: Alcoholics Anonymous and the Reality of Alcoholism*. Carbondale, Ill.: Southern Illinois University Press.

Rumbarger, John J. 1989. *Profits, Power and Prohibition: Alcohol Reform and the Industrializing of America 1800–1930*. Albany, N.Y.: SUNY Press.

Rush, Benjamin. [1814 8th ed.]. 1934. "An inquiry into the effect of ardent spirits upon the human body and mind." In *A New Deal for Liquor: A Plea for Dilution*, ed. Y.A. Henderson, 185–221. New York: Doubleday.

Schneider, Joseph W. 1978. "Deviant drinking as a disease: Alcoholism as a social accomplishment." *Social Problems* 25:361–372.

Shergei, Frants E. 1988. "The causes and social consequences of drunkenness." *Soviet Sociology* 27:13–25.

Sinclair, Andrew. 1962. *Prohibition: The Era of Excess*. Boston, Mass.: Little, Brown and Co.

Smith, Hedrick. 1985. *The Russians*. New York: Times Books.

———. 1990. *The New Russians*. New York: Avon Books.

Soviet Life. 1990a. "Alcoholism: The hidden disease." *Soviet Life* 401:51–52.

———. 1990b. "Back from bondage." *Soviet Life* 401:53–54.

———. 1990c. "Toward a sober society." *Soviet Life* 401:55.

Spitzer, Steven. 1975. "Toward a Marxian theory of deviance." *Social Problems* 22:638–651.

Szamuely, Tibor. 1974. *The Russian Tradition*. New York: McGraw-Hill.

Szasz, Thomas. 1985. *Ceremonial Chemistry*. Holmes Beach, Fla.: Learning Publications, Inc.

Timberlake, James H. 1963. *Prohibition and the Progressive Movement 1900–1920*. Cambridge, Mass.: Harvard University Press.

Time. 1989. "Where slava starts over again."10 April: 30–34.

Tournier, Robert E. 1985. "The medicalization of alcoholism: Discontinuities in ideologies of deviance." *Journal of Drug Issues* 15:39–49.

Treml, Vladimir G. 1982. "Death from alcohol poisoning in the USSR." *Soviet Studies* 34:487–505.

Trice, Harrison. 1984. "Alcoholism in America revisited." *Journal of Drug Issues* 14:109–123.

Unnithan, N. Prabha. 1985. "A cross-national perspective on the evolution of alcohol prohibition." *International Journal of The Addictions* 20:591–604.

Wagner, David. 1987. "The new temperance movement and social control in the workplace." *Contemporary Drug Problems* 14:539–556.

Ward, David A. 1985. "Conceptions of the nature and treatment of alcoholism." *Journal of Drug Issues* 15:3–16.

Weber, Max. [1904–5]. 1958. *The Protestant Ethic and the Spirit of Capitalism*. New York: Charles Scribners Sons.

Weiner, Carolyn. 1981. *The Politics of Alcoholism: Building an Arena around a Social Problem*. New Brunswick, N.J.: Transaction.

Weisner, Constance M. 1983. "The alcohol treatment system and social control: A study in institutional change." *Journal of Drug Issues* 13:117–133.

Williams, Gerald D., Frederick S. Stinson, Douglas A. Parker, Thomas C. Harford, and John Noble. 1987. "Demographic trends, alcohol abuse and alcoholism." *Alcohol Health & Research World* 91:80–83.

Willis, David K. 1981. "From politburo to peasant: Five ranks of society and privilege." *Christian Science Monitor* 14 January: 12–14.

Wiseman, Stanley Frederic. 1985. "Communist ideology and the substance abuser: A peripatetic look at the use of the medical paradigm to oppress political deviants." *Journal of Drug Issues* 15:247–261.

Wolfe, Bertram D. 1960. *An Ideology in Power: Reflections on the Russian Revolution*. New York: Thomas Y. Crowell.

Zaigraev, Grigori G. 1985. "The alcohol situation: A target for preventive action." *Soviet Sociology* 27:39–49.

CHAPTER 5

Setting the Public Agenda

"STREET CRIME" AND DRUG USE
IN AMERICAN POLITICS

Katherine Beckett

Crime and drug use have received unprecedented levels of political and public attention in recent decades. For example, the percentage of Americans identifying crime-related problems as the nation's most important increased from 5.6 percent in 1957 to 37.9 percent in 1971 (Stinchcombe et al. 1980). Similarly, the percentage reporting that drug abuse was the nation's most important problem jumped from 3 percent in 1986 to 64 percent in 1989 (Berke 1989). The increased visibility of these issues has had dramatic consequences, as the federal government and many state legislatures have adopted and implemented increasingly punitive crime and drug policies. As of 1989, the rate of incarceration in the United States was the highest in the world, and nearly half of those in federal prisons had been convicted of drug law violations (Mauer 1991).

How can the growth of public concern regarding these problems be explained? What accounts for the emergence of these issues on the political agenda? To many observers, the causal relationship between the increasing crime rate, growing public concern about crime, and the importance of "street crime" in national politics during the 1960s and early '70s seemed obvious (see Mayer 1992; Niemi, Mueller, and Smith 1989; Wilson 1975). In contrast, the reported incidence of drug use declined while the drug issue in national politics and public concern increased during the 1980s (see Jensen, Gerber, and Babcock 1991; Reinarman and Levine 1989). These two case studies therefore provide a unique opportunity to examine the relative impact of the reported incidence of crime and drug use and state and media initiative on public concern about crime and drugs. Was growing concern about crime in the 1960s and drugs in the 1980s a response to increases in the reported incidence of crime and drug use? Or were the claimsmaking activities of state actors and the media more important in setting the public agenda?

My focus, then, is on the process by which some members of the public came to define crime and drugs as the most important problems facing the nation. The data presented here, derived primarily from OLS regression techniques, suggest that increased public concern around "street crime" and drug use cannot be explained in terms of the reported incidence of those phenomena. Instead, the definitional activities of state actors and the mass media have played a crucial role in generating public concern about "street crime" and drug use.

71

These findings are consistent with a substantial body of research that suggests that state elites and the mass media play a prominent role in the construction of social issues, and, as a result, in the generation and shaping of public concern around those issues (Bennett 1980; Edelman 1988; Hall et al. 1978; Iyengar and Kinder 1987; Jensen, Gerber, and Babcock 1991; Nelson 1984; Reinarman and Levine 1989). Social actors attempt to place issues on the public agenda by calling attention to them and defining them as subject to political action. Furthermore, as advocates of particular kinds of political arrangements and policies, state actors and others represent social issues in ways that imply the need for desired policy outcomes (Edelman 1988). As Lukes (1974) and others have pointed out, the ability to politicize issues in this way represents an important component of the exercise of power: the selection, omission, and framing of issues and events are crucial in shaping not only public opinion, but political debate and policy as well.

While other researchers have suggested that campaigns against crime and drug use are not explicable solely in terms of the incidence of those phenomena (Dickson 1968; Epstein 1973; Fishman 1978; Gordon 1990; Hall et al. 1978; Helmer 1975; Himmelstein 1973; Jensen, Gerber, and Babcock 1991; Klein 1983; Mark 1975; Morgan 1978; Reinarman and Levine 1989; Rosch 1985; Scheingold 1986, 1990), the importance of specifically state and media activity in shaping public concern has not been demonstrated using quantitative methods. The findings presented here provide support for these "constructionist" arguments by demonstrating that public concern about "street crime" and drug use is not determined by the reported incidence of those phenomena. Furthermore, the results presented here suggest that public concern about crime and drugs is strongly associated with state initiative on those issues, and thus highlight the importance of the role of the state in the construction of social problems.

Historical Background

The control of crime, with the exception of a limited number of federal crimes (including most narcotics law violations), has been largely the responsibility of local law enforcement throughout U.S. history (Epstein 1977; McWilliams 1991). Bureaucratic efforts to create and enlarge the scope of the FBI during the 1920s and '30s played on widespread concern about crime and immigration, and the federal government's responsibility for crime increased somewhat during this period (Fogleson 1977; Walker 1977). After its initial appearance on the national political scene, however, the salience of the crime issue attenuated. Crime did not re-emerge as a major political issue at the national level until the 1960s.

"Law and order" rhetoric first re-emerged in the South in the late 1950s as southern politicians called for a crackdown on "hoodlums" and "agitators" who challenged segregation and black disenfranchisement. The issue of crime was subsequently seized and given a place on the national political agenda by Barry Goldwater in his 1964 presidential campaign (Caplan 1973). Goldwater and other conservatives focused on "street crime" in particular and linked such crime to social unrest, permissive courts, and declining moral standards (Matusow 1974). "Street crime" is not a legal category, and as a result its precise meaning is ambiguous. This category was generally used to refer to crimes of violence committed by strangers. The discourse of "law and order" conflated political protest and ordinary crime, and resonated most with those most opposed to racial and social reform (Cohn, Barkan, and Halteman 1991; Corbett 1981; Furstenberg 1971; Stinchcombe et al.. 1980). The emergence of the Watergate scandal in 1974 relegated the issue of "street crime" to the back pages, and public concern about crime subsequently dropped.

Conservative analyses of crime since the early 1970s have not deviated from Goldwater's early approach. The Reagan and Bush administrations' "get tough" agenda also focused on "street crime" rather than organized, white-collar or domestic crime. In addition, these administrations defined "street crime" as the consequence of declining moral standards (linked in turn to the expansion of the welfare state). But the Reagan administration gradually focused on drugs as the most important component and cause of "street crime." Indeed, drug use, a minor political issue in the late 1970s, was declared by President Bush to be "the most pressing problem facing the nation" by the late 1980s (Berke 1989). Later that same month a *New York Times*/CBS News Poll found that 64 percent of those polled identified drugs as the most significant problem in the United States. This percentage had risen from 3 percent in April of 1986, and was the highest recorded percentage since the poll began in 1976 (Berke 1989).

The Reagan and Bush administrations not only paid an unusual amount of attention to "the drug problem," but defined it in a particular way—as a criminal rather than a public health or social problem. This definition is important, as it implies that a certain kind of "solution" (increased law enforcement rather than job creation, drug treatment, or educational programs) is appropriate. The public, too, came to support increased law enforcement efforts, harsher sentences, and the contraction of civil rights for alleged drug offenders as the appropriate solution to the drug problem. For example, the percentage of Americans who felt that "testing workers in general" for drug use would be an unfair invasion of privacy declined from 44 percent in 1986 to 24 percent in 1989 (Berke 1989). Similarly, the percentage of Americans who felt that possession of small amounts of marijuana should be treated as a criminal offense increased from 43 percent in 1980 to 74 percent in 1988 (Gallup 1988).

How did the issues of "street crime" and drug use assume such a central place in the public agenda? What accounts for increased public concern regarding these issues? I outline two main theoretical approaches to this question below.

The Politicization of "Street Crime" and Drug Use: Two Contending Models

Two main explanations of the politicization of "street crime" can be identified in the existing literature. These models can also be applied to the more contemporary "War on Drugs."[2] Each approach specifies a different relationship between reported rates of crime/ drug use, state and media initiative, and public concern about crime and drugs.

THE OBJECTIVIST MODEL

According to the objectivist model, knowledge of objective conditions is a necessary and largely sufficient condition for the identification of a social problem: social problems are those phenomena which are problematic for social well-being (Manis 1974). While most objectivists recognize the definitional component of social problems (see, for example, Merton and Nisbet 1971), their emphasis is nonetheless on the nature and extent of those social conditions that are defined as problematic.

Specifically, objectivists argue that the increased incidence of "street crime" and drug use has led to increased public concern about those issues. In this view, the Nixon, Reagan, and Bush administrations' "get tough" approach to crime has been a response to public concern, itself a consequence of the increased incidence of crime. For example, one major analysis of trends in public opinion concludes that increased fear of crime and support for punitive measures "have been shaped largely by objective shifts in the level of criminal activity" (Niemi, Mueller, and Smith 1989:133). Similarly, Mayer (1992:274) claims that "rising crime rates led to growing public support for the death penalty and a tougher criminal justice system." The argument that there has been "an objective shift in criminal activity" is based on official crime statistics that suggest such a trend. Thus, while the theoretical premise of objectivism does not necessarily imply an acceptance of official statistics as an accurate reflection of the actual incidence of social phenomena, objectivists rely on such statistics for their information about social conditions. As a result, objectivists anticipate that these measures will be associated with public concern[3] (see Morganthau and Miller 1986; Niemi, Mueller, and Smith 1989).

Objectivist accounts of the crime and drug issues also tend to conflate objectivism with the pluralist assumption that state actors primarily react to, rather than attempt to shape, public opinion. For example, Wilson (1975:xvi) argues that "public opinion was well ahead of political opinion in calling attention to the rising problem of crime." This approach thus presumes that state initiative on the crime issue was a response to a prior increase in public concern about crime.

The following hypotheses can be derived from this model: first, the objectivist hypothesis (HI) anticipates a positive relationship between the reported incidence of crime/drug use and subsequent levels of public concern regarding these issues; second, the pluralist hypothesis (112) predicts that shifts in the level of public concern *precede* corresponding shifts in the level of state anti-crime and anti-drug activity.

THE CONSTRUCTIONIST MODEL

The constructionist model emphasizes the social nature of assessments of those phenomena that are defined as social problems. For constructionists reality is not known directly, but must be comprehended through "maps of meaning" or "frames" which select, order, and interpret that reality (Hall et al. 1978). These "frames" give meaning and coherence to events and phenomena (Gamson et al. 1992), including social problems. Because each issue frame has a different set of political implications, a variety of social actors may compete in sponsoring their preferred frames[4] (Edelman 1988; Gamson et al. 1992). In sum, constructionists emphasize the subjective, social, and political dimension of social problems.

A constructionist account of the crime and drug issues anticipates that the public's assessment of the nature of those problems will be shaped by their popular representation. This approach therefore rejects the objectivist hypothesis (Hl) that levels of public concern will necessarily correspond to the reported incidence of crime/drug use. Instead, the constructionist hypothesis (H3) anticipates a strong association between media and state claimsmaking activities on the one hand and levels of public concern on the other. However, there is some disagreement among constructionists about the nature of the relationship between public opinion and state initiative on social problems such as crime and drug use.

CULTURAL VERSUS ELITE CONSTRUCTIONISM

Culturalist constructionists argue that the tendency to focus on the most terrifying types of "predatory crime" and the desire for a "quick fix" to complex social problems lead the public to become concerned about crime and to embrace a punitive approach toward it (Rosch 1985; Scheingold 1986). This tendency is exacerbated by "amorphous stress" which intensifies in times of perceived social crisis. According to these theorists, "law and order" politics do not emanate from politicians or the media. Instead, such policies are a response to public concern and orientation: the implementation of punitive policies by the state primarily reflects the public's desire for scapegoats against whom "free-floating anger" and anxiety can be directed (Rosch 1985; Scheingold 1990). The politicization of crime and drugs, then, is largely the consequence of social, economic, and political forces which cause insecurity among Americans.

In sum, culturalists reject the objectivist hypothesis (H1) that public concern about crime/drugs necessarily corresponds to the reported incidence of "street crime" or drug use (Gordon 1990; Rosch 1985; Scheingold 1986, 1990). However, like the objectivist model, culturalists anticipate that shifts in public concern will precede shifts in levels of state initiative (H2), as state initiative is assumed to be a response to public sentiments.[5]

Others working within the constructionist paradigm (e.g., Bennett 1980; Edelman 1988; Hall et al. 1978), however, reject this pluralist hypothesis. According to these theorists, public opinion is more accurately conceptualized as fluid and variegated than as fixed and monolithic (Bennett 1980; Edelman 1964). This fluidity of public opinion, combined with the "ambiguity of events" and the unequal distribution of motivation, organizational capacity, and resources, means that most public issues are brought into being by political elites (Bennett 1980). This inequality is exacerbated by the reliance of the media on "institutional" sources, which ensures that political elites enjoy a high degree of access to the media (Gans 1980; Hall et al. 1978; Hertsgaard 1988; Whitney et al. 1989). Thus, while the capacity of political elites to mobilize public opinion is not unlimited, "the general public is most often called on by interest groups and elites to participate in the debate about issues that have already been defined" (Bennett 1980:57).

The relationship between elite definitional activities and public concern is undoubtedly a reciprocal one; it is unlikely that state actors and other elites would persist in these activities if the public did not appear to be receptive to them. Public receptivity, however, is not the same thing as public initiative, and it may be possible to determine whether shifts in the level of public concern about crime or drugs precede or follow shifts in the level of state activity. Elite theorists' agenda-setting hypothesis (H4) predicts that shifts in the level of state initiative will precede shifts in the level of public concern.

In sum, two sets of competing hypotheses may be derived from these models. First, the objectivist hypothesis (H1) predicts that the reported incidence of crime/drug use will be strongly related to subsequent levels of public concern, while the constructionist hypothesis (H3) suggests that state initiative and media coverage shape public opinion. Second, the pluralist hypothesis (H2) anticipates that shifts in the degree of public concern precede corresponding shifts in levels of state activity, while the agenda-setting hypothesis (H4) predicts that state initiative drives public concern.

Research Design

DATA AND VARIABLES

Information regarding the crime rate was taken from the FBI's Uniform Crime Index (1964-1974) (victimization surveys were not administered nationally until 1972).[6] The rate of "violent crimes" (per 100,000 persons) as reported by the FBI was utilized as an indicator of the incidence of "street crime."

Data regarding the incidence of drug use were taken from the National Institute on Drug Abuse survey, "The Household Survey on Drug Abuse." The percentage of survey respondents age twelve and over reporting drug use in the past month was used as an indicator of the incidence of drug use. While DAWN (Drug Abuse Warning Network) data report the number of drug-related emergency room visits and therefore better capture the intensity of the drug problem (rather than the incidence of drug use), these data were not collected throughout the period studied here. In addition, methodological changes in NIDA's estimation procedures means that the DAWN data collected before and after 1990 are not comparable. These data will, however, be considered in the discussion.

The level of media initiative was derived from the Television News Index and Abstracts[7] for the drug case and the New York Times Index for the crime case.[8] The number of stories indexed under "crime in the U.S." for the crime case and "drug abuse" and "drug trafficking" for the case of drug use served as an indicator of the level of media initiative. Only those stories in which federal state actors were not quoted or cited as sources were included in this category. "Media initiative" thus includes the number of stories which did not cite state actors as their source of information.[9]

In contrast, the number of speeches, statements, and other crime- or drug-related activities undertaken by federal state actors and reported in the mass media *(New York*

Times for the crime case; network television news for the drug case) was utilized as an indicator of state initiative.[10] The use of this indicator rests in part on the assumption that federal state actors have a relatively constant degree of access to the mass media, and that fluctuations in the reported level of state initiative therefore reflect variation in state rather than media practices. Empirical studies that demonstrate that the media tend to consistently rely on institutional sources provide support for this assumption (see Gans 1980; Hall et al. 1978; Hertsgaard 1988; Whitney et al. 1989). Furthermore, I assume that in order for state definitional activities to have an impact on public opinion, they must be made public by the mass media.

This indicator of state initiative was the best available option for other more practical reasons. First, no alternative indicator which simultaneously reflects the activities of the various groups which comprise the federal state—administration officials, legislators, and bureaucrats—exists. Second, while budget outlays have been used as indicators of state activity in historical analysis (see Mann 1986), government expenditures generally increase or decrease annually. In contrast, dramatic shifts in public opinion frequently occurred in less than a month. The association between shifts in annual expenditures and the more short-term fluctuations in public opinion, therefore, is weak. Last, legislative activity varies dramatically depending on whether it is an election year or not, and is therefore a less desirable indicator of state activity.

Information regarding the dependent variable—public concern—was derived from the Gallup Poll and the *New York Times*/CBS News Polls. Both of these are national public opinion polls which ask the open-ended question "What do you think is the most important problem facing the nation?" on a fairly regular basis. The percentage of respondents identifying "crime," "juvenile delinquency" or "the breakdown of law and order" in the crime case, and "drugs" or "drug use" in the drug case as the "most important problem facing the nation" served as the indicator of public concern.

In the drug case (1985–1992), there were 25 polls taken in which this question was asked (n=25). Twenty-nine such polls were taken in the crime case (1964–1974) (n=29). These polls were taken at three- to five-month intervals. The periodization of these case studies was designed to capture the rise and fall of public concern around each issue: these cases could not be extended without including lengthy periods in which the dependent variable (public concern) remained at or close to zero.

ANALYSIS

To test the objectivist hypothesis (H1) that public opinion is associated with the reported incidence of crime/drug use, and the constructionist hypothesis (H3) that such concern is associated with state and media initiative, the effects of the explanatory variables were estimated using OLS regression techniques for each of the two cases.[11] These explanatory variables were measured in terms of their average rate in the three- to five-month period preceding the public opinion poll; the (non-lagged) regression results thus indicate the level of association between these variables and *subsequent* levels of public concern. I also estimated these regressions with a lag of 1 (6–10 months) and 2 (9–12 months) in order to assess the extent to which the explanatory variables were associated with delayed shifts in the level of public concern.[12] Given the uncertainty associated with small samples such as those analyzed here, I employed bootstrap resampling techniques and used the distribution of these bootstrap replications to determine the significance of the original coefficients.[13]

The time series of each of the variables are depicted in Figures 5.1–5.8 below, and indicate that short-term fluctuations in all the variables except crime/drug use were quite pronounced. Because I am primarily interested in identifying those factors associated with short-term fluctuations in public concern, the regression results presented here are based on an analysis of the differenced data. Differencing is a technique used to remove the linear trend from the data. With the linear trend removed, the regression coefficients estimate the association between short-term fluctuations in the explanatory and dependent variables.

Adjudication between the pluralist (H2) and agenda-setting (H4) hypotheses requires that the relationship between public concern and state initiative be more dearly discerned. The existence of simultaneity bias between these two variables indicates that their relationship is a reciprocal one: state initiative and public concern are largely mutually reinforcing. Statistical techniques designed to estimate the effects of reciprocal causal relationships make an elaborate set of assumptions about the data, and as a result may introduce significant specification errors. Furthermore, the statistical properties of the techniques which propose to estimate reciprocal causal effects in small samples are unknown. Given these difficulties, I utilize a more straightforward case study method to explore the relationship between shifts in the level of public opinion and state initiative over time.

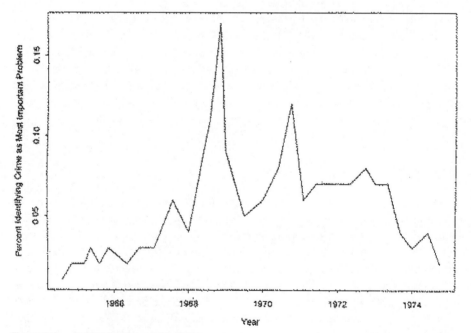

Figure 5.1.   Public Concern about Crime

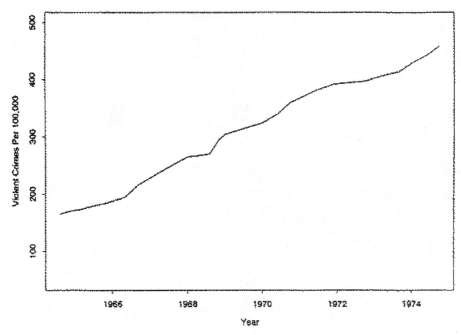

Figure 5.2.   Crime Rate

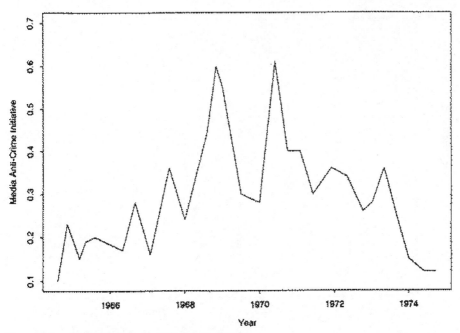

Figure 5.3.   Media Coverage of the Crime Issue

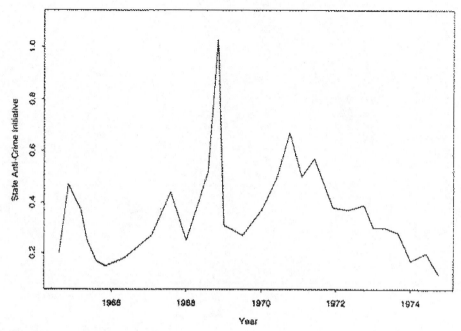

Figure 5.4.   Anti-Crime Initiative

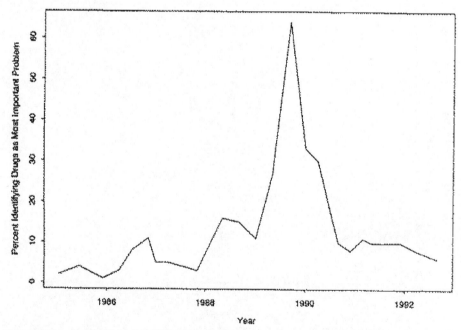

Figure 5.5.   Public Concern about Drugs

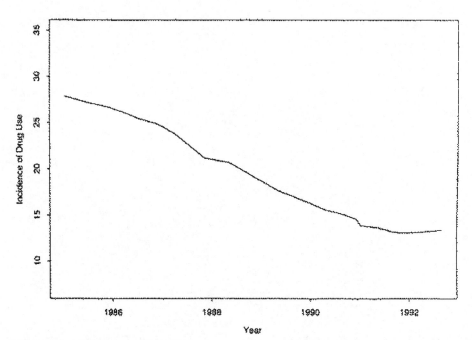

Figure 5.6.   Incidence of Drug Use

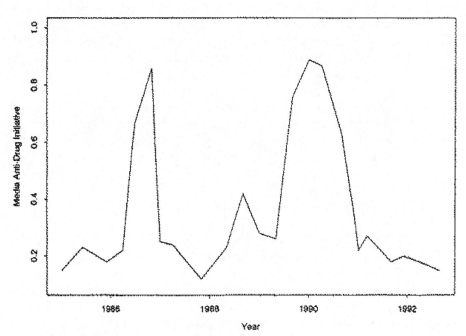

Figure 5.7.   Media Coverage of the Drug Issue

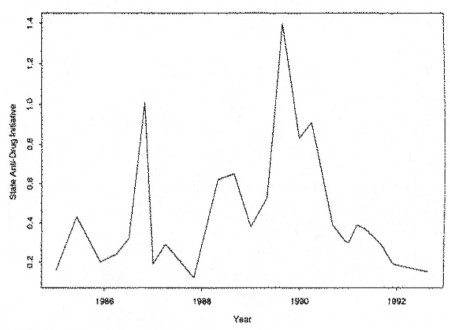

Figure 5.8.   State Anti-Drug Initiative

Results

The regression results provide significant support for the constructionist hypothesis (H3). In the crime case, both state and media initiative are significantly associated with public concern about crime, while in the drug case only state initiative is significantly associated with public concern. The reported incidence of crime/drug use is not significantly associated with subsequent public concern about those phenomena. In addition, the analysis of the case studies indicates that shifts in the level of state initiative precede rather than follow corresponding shifts in public opinion, and thus provide support for the agenda-setting hypothesis (H4) rather than the pluralist hypothesis (H2). In general, the results provide support for the view that state and media definitional activities play a crucial role in shaping public opinion.

THE OBJECTIVIST AND CONSTRUCTIONIST HYPOTHESES

The results of the OLS regressions are presented in tables 5.1 and 5.2. The unstandardized coefficient for each variable is shown, and the standard error appears beneath it in parentheses.

The results of the OLS analysis of the crime case indicate that media and state initiative are associated with subsequent levels of public concern about crime. These relationships are consistent over time: state and media continue to be significantly and positively associated with public concern when an extended time period is analyzed.

Table 5.1.   Crime Rate, Media and State Initiative, and Public Concern about Crime, 1964–1974

Variables	Lag=0 (3–5 months)	Lag=1 (6–10 months)	Lag=2 (9–15 months)
Intercept	−.1090	.111	.1079
	(.1322)	(.1301)	(.129)
Crime rate	−.0077	−.0067	−.005
	(.011)	(.013)	(.022)
Media initiative	1.2504*	1.3103**	1.2107*
	(.5547)	(.497)	(.5372)
State initiative	1.3711**	1.3511**	1.2721**
	(.3509)	(.3364)	(.3409)
Adjusted R^2	.5649	.5866	.5712

Notes:
*p < .05   **p < .01   ***p < .001

The regression coefficients may be interpreted in the following manner. The coefficient for the crime rate (in Column 1) is -.0077: for every unit increase in the crime rate, the odds that a person would identify crime as the nation's most important problem would decrease $e^{-.0077}$ or 1.007 times. A unit increase in media and state initiative, according to the regression coefficients, means that respondents would be $e^{1.25}$ and $e^{1.37}$, or 3.49 and 3.94 (respectively) times more likely to identify crime as the nation's most important problem.

In the drug case, the results indicate that neither the incidence of drug use nor media initiative on the drug issue are significantly related to subsequent public concern about drug use. State initiative on this issue, however, is positively and significantly related to subsequent increases in public concern about drugs. The regression coefficients may be interpreted in the following manner. According to the results presented in Column 1, a single unit increase in the rate of drug use would lead to an increase of $e^{.0152}$ (1.015) in the odds that a respondent would identify drugs as the nation's most important problem. A

Table 5.2.   Rates of Drug Use, Media and State Initiative, and Public Concern about Drugs, 1985–1992

Variables	Lag=0 (3–5 months)	Lag=1 (6–10 months)	Lag=2 (9–15 months)
Intercept	.0541	.0622	.0619
	(.1736)	(.1811)	(.179)
Drug use	.0096	.0082	.014
	(.2178)	(.1917)	(.2077)
Media initiative	.0594	.0781	.0999
	(.7459)	(.699)	(.6781)
State initiative	1.8393***	1.762***	1.1221**
	(.4551)	(.446)	(.4997)
Adjusted R^2	.6337	.6291	.6009

Notes:
*p < .05   **p < .01   ***p < .001

unit increase in media and state initiative would increase the odds that a person would respond in this manner by e^{0295} and $e^{1.861}$ (1.29 and 6.43) times respectively.

Although diagnostics indicate that the residuals are normally distributed in both cases, the sample sizes are relatively small. In order to assess the uncertainty that may therefore be associated with these coefficients, I generated 500 bootstrap replications of these coefficients.

For the crime case, the state and media regression coefficients as predicted by the null hypothesis (0) fall outside the range of the 95 percent confidence interval, and the regression coefficient can therefore be considered statistically significant. In contrast, the regression coefficient for the crime rate as predicted by the null hypothesis falls within the 95 percent confidence interval for the bootstrap replications, and therefore cannot be rejected. The bootstrap replications thus confirm the original results indicating that state and media initiative (but not the reported incidence of crime) are associated with subsequent levels of public concern about crime.

In the drug case, only the regression coefficient for state initiative predicted by the null hypotheses falls outside the 95 percent confidence interval and can therefore be considered statistically significant. The bootstrap results thus indicate that the uncertainty associated with the original regression model is minimal, and confirm that state and media initiative in the crime case and state initiative in the drug case are positively and significantly associated with subsequent public concern about crime and drugs.

THE PLURALIST AND AGENDA-SETTING HYPOTHESES

Last, to evaluate the relationship between public concern and state initiative, I analyze several cases in which public opinion grew dramatically to determine whether shifts in state initiative followed or preceded changes in the level of public concern. While the existence of simultaneity bias in the regression results indicates that state initiative and public concern are mutually reinforcing, this case study method allows us to adjudicate between the pluralist hypothesis (H2), which predicts that the changing nature of public concern shapes the level of state activity, and the agenda-setting hypothesis (H4), which predicts that level of state activity shapes public concern. Four cases are presented in diagram form in table 5.3.[14]

In each of the cases, public concern and state initiative move largely in parallel directions. However, in each of the cases, a drop in the level of state initiative towards the end of the cycle is not explicable in terms of a preceding drop in public concern. For example, in Case 1, the level of state initiative drops from 1.03 to .31 initiatives per day, despite the fact that the most recent public opinion poll indicated that public concern about crime had increased. This drop in the level of state initiative is followed by a decline in the level of public concern about crime. The same pattern can be discerned in each of the four cases. Thus, while public concern and state initiative tend to move in parallel directions and are generally mutually reinforcing, dramatic drops in state initiative cannot be explained in terms of declining levels of public concern. These drops in state initiative are, however, *followed* by declining levels of public concern.

Table 5.3.   State Initiative and Public Concern about Crime and Drugs

Case 1:	Public Concern and State Initiative on Crime, January 1968–January 1969			
State initiative	.25	.52	1.03	.31
	1/68------- >4/68------- >7/68------- >10/68------ >1/69			
Public concern	3% 4% 11% 17% 9%			

Case 2:	Public Concern and State Initiative on Crime, May 1969–January 1971			
State initiative	.37	.50	.77	.50
	5/69------- >1/70-------- >5/70------- >10/70------ >1/71			
Public concern	5% 6% 8% 13% 6%			

Case 3:	Public Concern and State Initiative on Drugs, January 1986–January 1987			
State initiative	.24	.42	1.01	.19
	1/86------- >4/86------- >7/86 ------- >10/86------->1/87			
Public concern	1% 3% 8% 11% 5%			

Case 4:	Public Concern and State Initiative on Drugs, September 1988–December 1989			
State initiative	.38	.53	1.4	.83
	9/88------- >1/89------- >5/89------- >9/89------->1/90			
Public concern	15% 11% 27% 64% 33%			

Discussion

THE OBJECTIVIST AND CONSTRUCTIONIST HYPOTHESES

The results presented in tables 5.1 and 5.2 lend greatest support to the constructionist hypothesis (H3); very little is found for support for the objectivist hypothesis (H1). In particular, the results indicate that levels of public concern are not strongly correlated with the incidence of crime/drug use, but that media and especially state initiative play an important role in generating subsequent public concern. In the crime case, the regression results indicate that media and state initiative are positively associated with increased public concern about crime, while the crime rate does not appear to have had such an impact. These results thus provide support for the constructionist hypothesis (H3).

In the drug case, the regression results suggest that only state initiative is associated with concern about drugs. One possible explanation for the absence of significant association between drug use and concern about drugs is that it is not the reported incidence of drug *use* but the reported severity of drug *abuse* (and particularly abuse of cocaine and crack) which has contributed to the definition of drug use as the nation's most important problem. If this hypothesis were correct, we would expect the number of cocaine-related emergency room visits to correspond to rates of public concern about drugs. In fact, DAWN (Drug Abuse Warning Network) data indicate that the number of cocaine-related emergency room visits increased between 1986 and 1989, as did public concern (although the increase in concern was, again, much more un-even). After a brief drop in 1990, however, the number of cocaine (and heroin) related emergency room visits enumerated by DAWN began to increase. By 1992, the number of all drug emergency room visits, including those involving cocaine and heroin, had reached record levels (Treaster 1992, 1993). In contrast, public concern dropped dramatically between 1990 and 1992.

In sum, it does not appear that either the reported incidence of drug use or the severity of drug abuse is consistently related to levels of public concern about drugs. Instead, the significant positive effect of state initiative on public concern provides support for the constructionist hypothesis (H3), which predicts that the construction of the crime and drug issues is crucial in shaping public opinion. State actors appear to play a particularly important role in this process of signification.

The indeterminant nature of the relationship between the reported rate of crime/drug use and public concern around those issues found in this analysis does not appear to be unique to the two time periods selected for analysis. During the 1970s, reported rates of crime and drug use both increased dramatically: official statistics indicate that the crime rate peaked in 1981, while general drug use reached its zenith in 1979 and declined consistently thereafter (Federal Bureau of Investigation 1988; National Institute on Drug Abuse 1988). Despite this, the percentage of respondents indicating that crime/drugs were the nation's most important problem remained quite low (Gallup 1980). Thus, it does not appear that the public identifies crime/drugs as the nation's most important problem on the basis of the reported prevalence of those phenomena. Instead, the degree to which state actors and the mass media focus on those issues is crucial.

THE PLURALIST AND AGENDA-SETTING HYPOTHESES

The results presented in table 5.3 provide support for the agenda-setting (H4) rather than the pluralist (H2) hypothesis: while public concern and state initiative generally move in parallel directions and tend to be mutually reinforcing, drops in the level of state initiative are followed rather than preceded by declines in the level of public concern. In other words, state initiative on crime and drugs is not consistently explicable in terms of public concern around those issues, but plays a consistent role in shaping that opinion.

A more detailed examination of these cases strengthens our confidence in these findings. Public concern about crime reached its zenith (17 percent) in October 1968, near the end of an election campaign in which "street crime" was a central issue. State initiative was at an all-time high of 1.03 initiatives per day in the period preceding this poll, while media initiative reached its peak at .6 stories per day. Post-election drops in state and media initiative on the crime issue were followed by corresponding drops in public concern (despite the ever-increasing crime rate).

Similarly, the percentage of poll respondents reporting that drugs were the most important problem facing the nation reached its peak at the end of a period characterized by unprecedented media and state anti-drug activity. In the first year after his election,

President George H. W. Bush increasingly focused on drugs as the central domestic issue. In late August and early September of that year, Bush made several special speeches
on "the drug crisis" and unveiled his program for fighting drugs: the average number of
state initiatives increased from .53 to 1.4 per day during this period. Media initiative also
increased from .26 to .76 stories per day devoted to the drug issue. A subsequent public
opinion poll indicated that 64 percent of the American public, the highest percentage
ever recorded, felt that drugs were the most important problem facing the nation.

Furthermore, there is no evidence that state actors' initial involvement in the
crime and drug issues was a response to public concern. For example, in 1964 when
Goldwater declared that "crime is a major issue in this election—at least I'm going to
make it one, because the responsibility has to start someplace," no public opinion research indicated that public concern about crime had increased. Similarly, when Reagan first declared a "national war on drugs" in 1982, and in 1986 when he called for
a renewal of this "all-out effort," national opinion polls indicated that less than 3 percent of poll respondents were most concerned about drugs. In sum, it does not appear
that either increases or decreases in the level of state initiative around crime and drugs
are consistently explicable in terms of corresponding shifts in public concern.

Conclusion

The results of this analysis provide greatest support for the constructionist (H3) and
agenda-setting (H4) hypotheses, and therefore for elite rather than cultural constructionism or objectivism. The elite constructionist approach emphasizes the social and
political nature of the "street crime" and drug issues, as well as the role of the media
and especially the state in shaping public concern around those issues.

Each of the contending models, however, makes an important contribution to our
understanding of the politicization of crime and drug use and, more generally, the
formation of the public agenda. The support found here for the constructionist hypothesis does not mean that "objective" factors and their indicators are irrelevant, but
that their interpretation by social and political actors is crucial. For example, while the
incidence of general drug use declined in the 1980s, and while only a very small proportion of the population has ever tried crack cocaine, it is true that heavy use of cocaine and its derivative, crack, appears to have increased throughout the 1980s (Goode
1989). The spread of crack, combined with its association with minorities, violent
crime, and urban blight, undoubtedly facilitated the construction of drug use as "the
gravest domestic challenge we've faced in decades" (Bush, quoted in Nelson 1989). As
noted earlier, however, the reported increases in crack use have not been associated
with high levels of public concern before 1986 or since 1990. Thus, it appears that the
downward mobility of smokeable cocaine facilitated but did not determine the politicization of drug use in the 1980s.[15]

Similarly, it is true that public opinion plays an important role in the politicization
of social problems. It does not follow from the agenda-setting hypothesis that the state's
ability to influence public opinion is unlimited. State actors' success in mobilizing public concern around these particular issues was not inevitable, and must be explained in

terms of the resonance of the construction of the crime and drug issues with particular themes in American political culture. Furthermore, claims about some types of issues may be more likely than others to generate high levels of public concern. For example, "valence issues" (see Nelson 1984) provoke a fairly uniform emotional response and, unlike "position issues," do not have supporters and opponents.[16] Similarly, the existence of a variety of interest groups making claims around a particular issue will likely diminish the capacity of a single group of claimsmakers to define that issue (Burstein 1991; May 1991). Thus, claimsmakers may be more successful in shaping public concern when there are fewer participants in the struggle to frame an issue, or when that issue provokes a fairly uniform emotional response. Further research is needed to assess the role of cultural and historical context and issue characteristics in shaping public receptivity to state and media claimsmaking activities.

In sum, the findings presented in this chapter suggest that the politicization of the crime and drug issues has been the result of their social construction by the mass media and especially state actors. While a complete explanation for the involvement of these actors is beyond the scope of this chapter, I suggest that state initiative on these issues may be seen as part of a "hegemonic project" (Omi 1987) aimed at rebuilding political consensus around opposition to the reform movements of the 1960s and to the subsequent expansion of the welfare state. Racially charged "social issues" such as "street crime" and drug use have played a central role in this project. The support found here for the constructionist and agenda-setting hypotheses are consistent with this interpretation and may serve as a useful starting point for further research.

Notes

I would like to thank Bruce Weston, whose generosity, patience and expertise made this project possible. I am also grateful to Franklin Gilliam, Steve Herbert, William Roy, and Ivan Szelenyi for their instructive comments and suggestions. Correspondence to: Beckett, University of California Los Angeles, Department of Sociology, 405 Hilgard Ave., Los Angeles, CA 90024-1551.

1. Jensen, Gerber, and Babcock (1991) use some quantitative measures (but not regression techniques) to support their argument that state actors provided the impetus for the institutionalization of drug use as a social problem.

2. While many social scientists have attempted to account for the emergence of "drug scares" in U.S. history (see Dickson 1986; Epstein 1977; Helmer 1975; Himmelstein 1973; Mark 1975: Morgan 1978; Musto 1973), the Reagan/Bush "War on Drugs," because it is so recent, is relatively untheorized (some exceptions: Jensen, Gerber, and Babcock 1991; Reinarman and Levine 1989; Scheingold 1990).

3. I therefore use these statistics to test the objectivist hypothesis that the reported rate of crime/drug use shapes public concern around those issues.

4. The construction of meaning and the struggle to imbue public discourse around events and issues with this meaning is an ongoing political process. For this reason, media discourse may be fruitfully conceptualized as an independent rather than dependent variable (Gamson et al. 1992:385).

5. Mauss's (1975) argument that social problems may be conceptualized as a particular type of social movement is also based on this pluralist assumption.

6. The FBI Uniform Crime index is based on the number of crimes reported to the police, and is therefore considered by some to be less reliable than the national victimization surveys. While the FBI's Uniform Crime index indicated that the incidence of crime was increasing, evidence suggests that the increased reporting of crime accounts for at least a substantial portion of this increase (see O'Brien 1985; President's Commission on Law Enforcement and the Administration of Justice 1968). In addition, the degree of professionalization of police departments and political factors may influence police reporting to the FBI (O'Brien 1985). These data, then, probably overestimate the extent to which crime was increasing in the '60s and early '70s, and may reflect in part increased public awareness of crime. The fact that the crime rate may be endogenous to public concern about crime may upwardly bias statistical estimates of the association between the two.

7. To ensure consistency, I enumerated only those stories which appeared on the early weeknight broadcast of the network television news.

8. Because the Vandenderbilt Television News Abstracts began in 1968, it was not possible to analyze television news coverage of the crime issue.

9. Because I analyzed newspaper stories indexed under "crime in the U.S." and national television news broadcasts, less than 2 percent of the stories analyzed focused on the activities of the police and local state actors. These stories were therefore eliminated from the analysis.

10. Because indexing procedures may vary from year to year, indexes are an imperfect measure of media coverage. Furthermore, because the abstracts offered for each story are incomplete, it is possible that some stories which covered state initiatives were included in the category "media initiative." However, it is unlikely that the abstracts for items in which state initiative figured prominently failed to mention that state activity. (To the extent that less prominent state initiatives were omitted in the indexing process, the association between state initiative and subsequent public concern may be underestimated.)

11. Although the data analyzed are longitudinal, the residuals are not serially correlated. Time series techniques are therefore unnecessary.

12. The single equation models used here assume a one-way causal relationship between the explanatory and dependent variables. It is likely, however, that the dependent variable also influences the independent variables. These models thus tend to overestimate the effects of the independent variable; the results should be interpreted with this upward bias in mind.

13. In regression models, the bootstrap technique involves resampling rows from a matrix of regression coefficients in order to assess the significance of these coefficients. This technique provides a means by which the uncertainty associated with statistical estimates may be assessed, and is particularly useful where the sampling distribution is not normal or sample sizes are small.

14. These cases were selected in the following manner. First, for each issue, I identified the poll in which the level of public concern reached its highest point. The three polls preceding and one following this poll represent a "case." The same procedure was used to identify a second case wherein public concern reached its second highest level. The number corresponding to "state initiative" indicates the average number of state initiatives per day in the period between the two polls.

15. This argument is consistent with Fishman's (1980) argument that reports of a "wave" of crime against the elderly in the 1970s did not require that there was an actual increase in such incidents. Instead, the occurrence of this crime "wave" required only that some of these incidents occurred and that important news sources called attention to these incidents.

16. While there may be some debate about how to best respond to "valence issues" such as crime and child abuse, there is no "pro-crime" or "pro-child abuse" lobby.

References

Bennett, W. Lance. 1980. *Public Opinion in American Politics.* New York: Harcourt Brace Jovanovich, Inc.

Berger, Peter, and Thomas Luckmann. 1966. *The Social Construction of Reality.* New York: Doubleday.

Berke, Richard L. 1989. "Poll finds most in U.S. back Bush strategy on drugs." *New York Times,* September 12:B8.

Burstein, Paul. 1991. "Policy domains: Organization, culture and policy outcomes." *Annual Review of Sociology* 17:327–350.

Caplan, Gerald. 1973. "Reflections on the nationalization of crime, 1964–8." *Law and the Social Order* 1973:583–638.

Cohn, Steven F., Steven E. Barkan, and William A. Halteman. 1991. "Punitive attitudes toward criminals: Racial consensus or racial conflict?" *Social Problems* 38:287–296.

Corbett, Michael. 1981. "Public support for 'law and order': Interrelationships with system affirmation and attitudes toward minorities." *Criminology* 19:328–343.

Department of Justice. 1988. "Criminal victimization in the United States, 1988." Office of Justice Programs, Bureau of Justice Statistics Bulletin.

Dickson, Donald. 1968. "Bureaucracy and morality: An organizational perspective on a moral crusade." *Social Problems* 16:143–157.

Edelman, Murray. 1964. *The Symbolic Uses of Politics.* Chicago: University of Illinois Press.

———. 1988. *Constructing the Political Spectacle.* Chicago: University of Chicago Press.

Epstein, Edward. 1977. *Agency of Fear: Opiates and Political Power in America.* New York: Verso Press.

Federal Bureau of Investigation. 1961. "The U.S. F.B.I. crime reports." Washington, D.C.: Department of Justice, 88.

Fishman, Mark. 1980. *Manufacturing the News.* Austin: University of Texas Press.

Fogelson, Robert. 1977. *Big City Police.* Cambridge, Mass.: Harvard University Press.

Furstenberg, Frank. 1971. "Public reaction to crime in the streets." *The American Scholar* 40:601–610.

Gallup, George. 1964. *The Gallup Poll.* Wilmington, Del.: Scholarly Resources, 90.

Gans, Herbert. 1980. *Deciding What's News.* New York: Vintage Books.

Garrison, William, David Croteau, William Hoynes, and Theodore Sasson. 1992. "Media images and the social construction of reality." *Annual Review of Sociology* 18:373–393.

Goode, Eric. 1989. 'The American drug panic of the 1980's: Social construction or objective threat?' *Violence, Aggression and Terrorism* 3:327–348.

Gordon, Diana R. 1990. *The Justice Juggernaut: Fighting Street Crime, Controlling Citizens.* New Brunswick: Rutgers University Press.

Hall, Stuart, Chas Critcher, Tony Jefferson, John Clarke, and Brian Roberts. 1978. *Policing the Crisis: Mugging, the State and Law and Order.* London: Macmillan Press.

Helmer, John. 1975. *Drugs and Minority Oppression.* New York: Seabury Press.

Hertsgaard, Mark. 1988. *On Bended Knee: The Press and the Reagan Presidency.* New York: Schocken Books.

Himmlestein, Jerome. 1973. "Drug politics theory: Analysis and critique." *Journal of Drug Issues* 8:37–52.

Iyengar, Shanto, and Donald Kinder. 1987. *News That Matters.* Chicago: University of Chicago Press.

Jensen, Eric L., Jurg Gerber, and Ginna M. Babcock. 1991. "The new war on drugs: Grass-roots movement or political construction?" *Journal of Drug Issues* 3:651–667.

Kitsuse, John, and Malcolm Spector. 1987. *Constructing Social Problems*. New York: Aldine De Gruyter.

Klein, Dorie. 1983. "111 and against the law: The social and medical control of heroin users." *Journal of Drug Issues* 1983:31–54.

Lukes, Steven. 1974. *Power: A Radical View*. London: Macmillan Press.

Manis, Jerome. 1976. "The concept of social problems: Vox populi and sociological analysis." *Social Problems* 21:305–315.

Mann, Michael. 1986. *The Sources of Social Power*. Oxford: Oxford University Press.

Mark, Gregory Yee. 1975. "Racial, economic and political factors in the development of America's drug laws." *Issues in Criminology* 10:49–72.

Matusow, Allen J. 1984. *The Unraveling of America: A History of Liberalism in the 1960's*. New York: Harper Torchbooks.

Mauer, Marc. 1991. "Americans behind bars: A comparison of international rates of incarceration." The Sentencing Project.

Mauss, Armand L. 1975. *Social Problems as Social Movements*. New York: J.B. Lippincott Co.

May, Peter J. 1991. "Reconsidering policy design: Policies and publics." *Journal of Public Policy* 11:187–206.

Mayer, William G. 1992. *The Changing American Mind: How and Why American Public Opinion Changed Between 1960 and 1988*. Ann Arbor: University of Michigan Press.

McWilliams, John C. 1991. "Through the past darkly: The politics and policies of America's drug war." *In Drug Control Policy: Essays in Historical and Comparative Perspective,* ed. William O. Walker III, 5–41. State College: Pennsylvania State University.

Merton, Robert K., and Robert Nisbet. 1971. *Contemporary Social Problems*. New York: Harcourt, Brace and World.

Morgan, Patricia. 1978. "The legislation of drug laws: Economic crisis and social control." *Journal of Drug Issues* 8:53–62.

Morganthau, Tom, and Mark Miller. 1986. "Crack and crime." *Newsweek,* June 16:16–22.

Musto, David. 1973. *The American Disease: Origins of Narcotic Control*. New York: Oxford University Press.

National Institute on Drug Abuse. 1979–88. "National household survey on drug abuse: Main findings." Rockville, Md.: National Institute on Drug Abuse.

Nelson, Barbara J. 1984. *Making an Issue of Child Abuse: Political Agenda Setting for Social Problems*. Chicago: University of Chicago Press.

Nelson, Jack. 1989. "Bush tells plan to combat drugs." *New York Times,* September 6:A1.

New York Times/CBS News Polls. 1989. August Survey:2–4. New York: New York Times Poll.

Niemi, Richard G., John Mueller, and Tom W. Smith. 1989. *Trends in Public Opinion: A Compendium of Survey Data*. New York: Greenwood Press.

O'Brien, Robert M. 1985. *Crime and Victimization Data. Law and Criminal Justice Series, Vol. 4*. Beverly Hills: Sage Publications.

Office of the Federal Register. 1981–91. Public Papers of the President. Washington, D.C.: U.S. Government Printing Office.

Omi, Michael Allen. 1987. "We shall overturn: Race and the contemporary American right." Dissertation, University of California, Santa Cruz.

President's Commission on Law Enforcement and the Administration of Justice. 1968. *The Challenge of Crime in a Free Society*. New York: Dutton Books.

Reinarman, Craig, and Harry Levine. 1989. "Crack in context: Politics and media in the making of a drug scare." *Contemporary Drug Problems* 16:535–577.

Rosch, Joel. 1985. "Crime as an issue in American politics." In *The Politics of Crime and Criminal Justice,* eds. E. Fairchild and E. Webb. Beverly Hills: Sage Publication.

Scheingold, Stuart. 1986. *The Politics of Law and Order: Street Crime and Public Policy.* Philadelphia: Temple University Press.

———. 1990. "The war on drugs in context: Crisis politics and social control." Paper presented at the 1990 Annual Meeting of the Law and Society Association, May.

Stinchcombe, Arthur L., Rebecca Adams, Carol A. Helmer, Kim Lane Scheppele, Tom W. Smith, and D. Garth Taylor. 1980. *Crime and Punishment in America: Changing Attitudes in America.* San Francisco: Jossey Bass Publishers.

Treaster, Joseph. 1992. "Emergency room cocaine cases rise." *New York Times,* October 24:A6.

———. 1993. "Emergency hospital visits rise among drug abusers." *New York Times,* April 24:A8.

U.S. Office of the National Drug Control Policy. 1989. National Drug Control Strategy. Washington, D.C.: Executive Office of the President.

Vandenderbilt Television News Archive. 1980–90. *The Television News Index and Abstracts.* Nashville, Tenn.: Vandenderbilt Television News Archive.

Walker, Samuel. 1977. *A Critical History of Police Reform: The Emergence of Professionalism.* Lexington, Mass.: Lexington Books.

Whitney, Charles, Marilyn Fritzler, Steven Jones, Sharon Mazzarella, and Lana Rakow. 1989. "Source and geographic bias in television news 1982–4." *Journal of Electronic Broadcasting and Electronic Media* 33:159–174.

Wilson, William J. 1975. *Thinking About Crime.* New York: Basic Books, Inc.

CHAPTER 6

Truth *and* DARE

TRACKING DRUG EDUCATION TO GRADUATION AND AS SYMBOLIC POLITICS

Earl Wysong, Richard Aniskiewicz, and David Wright

The period following former President Reagan's 1986 "War on Drugs" campaign witnessed a rapid expansion of anti-drug programs at federal, state, and local levels with active support from corporations, the mass media, and community agencies (Jensen et al. 1991; Males 1992). Federal drug-related expenditures for law enforcement, treatment, and education rose from $2.6 billion in 1985 to nearly $13 billion in 1993 (U.S. Office of Management and Budget 1990, 1992). To coordinate public and corporate policies aimed at reducing both the supply of and demand for drugs, a "National Drug Control Strategy" was initiated by former President Bush (*National Drug Control Strategy* 1990). The "demand reduction" dimension of this strategy aimed at preventing drug use through drug education programs, mass media campaigns, and policy directives. The latter two approaches are illustrated by the well-known "This Is Your Brain On Drugs" media campaign (sponsored by the privately-funded Partnership for a Drug-Free America) and the 1989 Drug Free Schools and Community Act which outlaws drug possession and use in schools *(Understanding Drug Prevention* 1992; *National Drug Control Strategy* 1991). While the educational aspect of drug prevention encompasses numerous activities, schools quickly became the focus of such efforts due in part to the requirement that schools receiving federal funds include drug education programs in their curricula *(National Drug Control Strategy* 1992). As a result, by 1990 more than 100 school-based drug education programs were being promoted (Miley 1992; Pereira 1992) with wide variations reported in their approaches, duration, costs, and reputed effectiveness (Ambtman et al. 1990; Bangert-Drowns 1988; Pellow and Jengeleski 1991; Tobler 1986).

Within the diverse array of drug prevention curricula, DARE (Drug Abuse Resistance Education) has become the largest and best known school-based drug education program in the United States (Harmon 1993; Rosenbaum et al. 1994). In 1990 DARE programs were in place in more than 3,000 communities in all 50 states and were reaching an estimated 20 million students (U.S. Congress: House 1990). The DARE curriculum involves the presentation of anti-drug lessons by uniformed police officers who have undergone 80 hours of specialized training (U.S. Department of Justice 1991). With training costs of more than $2,000 per officer and program costs reaching as much as $90,600 per year for each full-time officer-instructor, DARE is expensive to implement and maintain (Miley 1992; Pope 1992). In 1993 total nationwide expenditures for DARE programs from all sources were estimated to be $700 million (Cauchon 1993). The costs to schools adopting DARE are typically covered by federal, state, and foundation grants as well as by corporate support and local education and law enforcement agencies (U.S. Department of Justice 1991). However, at this time no institutionalized funding base exists to sustain the program on a permanent basis (U.S. Congress: House 1990; *Congressional Record* 1992a).

Despite its high cost and the absence of laws or formal policies mandating its implementation in the schools, DARE has gained widespread acceptance and support. One indicator of DARE's growing political popularity has been the emergence of Congressional proposals for direct federal funding of DARE. In 1990 $15 million of the Drug Free Schools fund was specifically targeted for DARE (U.S. Congress: House 1990) and in 1992 $50 million was proposed for increased operational funding of DARE (*Congressional Record* 1992b). DARE received further national recognition and political support when the U.S. Congress and former President Bush designated September 10, 1992, as "National DARE Day" (*Congressional Record* 1992a, 1992b, 1992c).

Political popularity not withstanding, DARE's size, claims, and expense have made it the focus of a number of questions concerning its effectiveness. Short-term evaluations conducted within weeks or months following completion of the DARE program indicate it does produce "anti-drug" effects among students, especially in terms of creating and/or reinforcing anti-drug attitudes and drug-resistant coping skills (Aniskiewicz and Wysong 1990; Clayton et al. 1991a; DeJong 1987; Faine and Bohlander 1989; Harmon 1993; Ringwalt et al. 1991). However, claims for the program extend beyond the short-term. DARE is now being represented as "a long term solution" to the problem of drug use (U.S. Department of Justice 1991J), but studies of the program's long-term effectiveness are virtually nonexistent.[1] Longitudinal studies are under way at DARE Regional Training Centers (U.S. Department of Justice 1991) and DARE AMERICA (a nonprofit organization in Los Angeles) is funding an eight-year study in six U.S. cities (DARE AMERICA 1991), but it will not be completed until near the end of this century. In addition to the efficacy issue are less frequently addressed, but equally important, questions concerning DARE's emergence as a potent political force and the implications of this reality for program evaluations.

Assessment Framework

We view the issues of DARE's efficacy and political potency as interrelated. Thus, our investigation links both psychosocial and political-economy considerations to develop a more complete understanding of the power of DARE (i.e., its long-term effects), DARE as a program of power (its political potency), and the links between these two dimensions. The magnitude of the program and the claims made for DARE make it important to begin assessing the long-term effects issue as information becomes available. The present study advances this objective with an analysis of data collected from 1987 through 1992 as part of a multi-year assessment of DARE in Kokomo, Indiana (a medium-sized midwestern city). We explore DARE's effects on high school seniors five years after their initial exposure to the program through a two-track assessment framework utilizing both impact and process evaluation procedures (Chelimsky 1985; Deutscher and Beattie 1988; Nachmias 1980; Patton 1987). The former approach is used as the principal means for assessing, by quantitative measures, whether and/or the extent to which students' exposure to DARE produces lasting effects related to the program's primary and secondary objectives. At the micro-level, the latter approach uses qualitative data from a focus group interview (Morgan 1988) with former DARE participants to explicate program dynamics and interpret outcomes.

As an extension of our previous work (Aniskiewicz and Wysong 1990), we also utilize a macro-level process perspective to explore DARE's political potency, organizational support structure, and the implications of these factors for program evaluation and implementation. This approach views DARE as a socially constructed (Snow et al. 1986; Benford and Hunt 1992; Buechler 1993) form of symbolic politics (Edelman 1964, 1979, 1988) growing out of and embedded within the larger Drug War of the late 1980s and early 1990s. It calls attention to the role played by stakeholders (Shadish 1987) in developing, legitimating, and expanding the program as well as the nature and extent of DARE's organizational support structure. It also provides a macro-level framework for considering the links between DARE as a program of power, program evaluation, and implementation dynamics including "external factors that help anticipate and explain success, failures, and changes in the program" (Roberts-Gray and Scheirer 1988:65).

Project DARE

DARE originated in 1983 as a joint venture between the Los Angeles Police Department (LAPD) and the Los Angeles Unified School District (LAUSD) and is the best known of the "new generation" of drug prevention programs.[2] It uses uniformed officers to teach a standardized anti-drug curriculum that primarily targets elementary school students. DARE attempts to shape students' attitudes and social skills so they will be able to resist peer and media pressures to try drugs including tobacco and alcohol.[3]

The DARE "core" curriculum is designed for fifth and sixth graders and consists of 17 weekly lessons approximately 45 to 60 minutes each in length. All classroom activities are scheduled during the regular school day and emphasize active student involvement in exercises such as "question and answer [sessions], group discussions, and role-play[ing] activities" (U.S. Department of Justice 1991:7). The curriculum can also be extended down to earlier grades as well as up to the middle and high school levels. In addition to classroom instruction, several other activities have been developed to enhance the program's effectiveness including informal officer/student contacts, teacher orientation, parental education, and community presentations.

Evaluating DARE: Background and Procedures

Kokomo was the first city in Indiana to implement the DARE program[4] (Miley 1992). During 1987-1988, all Kokomo fifth graders received the full DARE core curriculum while all seventh graders received a shortened 11-week version. We conducted short-term program assessments for the fifth and seventh grade groups utilizing the "DARE SCALE" developed in Los Angeles (Nyre 1984, 1985) which supposedly provides a general measure of DARE's effectiveness in the areas of drug-related attitudes, knowledge, and anti-drug coping skills. In a pre- and post-test design, we found significant increases in post-DARE scores for fifth graders, but not for seventh graders. While both groups are part of a larger study, the former seventh graders (as 1992 seniors) are used as the basis for evaluating DARE's long-term effectiveness in this inquiry.

IMPACT EVALUATION: OBJECTIVES, SAMPLE, DESIGN

The impact dimension of the study uses data from a multi-part questionnaire completed by Kokomo High School (KHS) seniors in 1991 (non-DARE group, no DARE exposure) and in 1992 (DARE group, exposed to DARE as seventh graders). Several comparisons are made to assess whether and/or the extent to which DARE exposure is associated five years later with effects in four areas. The first two areas are directly linked to DARE's primary objectives of preventing/reducing/delaying drug use and include measures of (1) self-reported drug use rates and (2) drug attitudes, drug knowledge, and drug-resistant coping skills. If DARE exposure in the seventh grade produces lasting anti-drug effects, then measures of the DARE group's characteristics in these two areas should be significantly different from the non-DARE group.

The other two areas are related to DARE's secondary objectives of enhancing self-worth and decision-making skills. They are assessed by measures of self-esteem (Rosenberg 1965) and locus of control (Rotter 1966). The former concept refers to the evaluative feature of the self with self-esteem levels ranging from high to low (Penny and Robinson 1986). The latter term refers to a cognitive style which may trend in either an "internal" or "external" direction. "People who believe they have some control over their destinies are called internals. . . . 'Externals,' on the other hand, believe their outcomes are determined by agents or factors external to themselves" (MacDonald 1973:169). Previous research and the nature of the DARE curriculum indicate that self-esteem and locus of control may act as mechanisms for mediating and facilitating the program's primary effects. Studies of the linkages between both factors and adolescent drug use suggest higher levels of self-esteem and internal cognitive styles tend to be associated with lower rates of drug use (Olton 1985; Penny and Robinson 1986). If DARE has long-term effects in these areas, then DARE group scores on these factors should be significantly different from the non-DARE group.[5]

The questionnaire was completed by samples of 1991 and 1992 KHS seniors nearly evenly divided by gender. Subjects were chosen through a random selection of classes (e.g., English, science etc.) with students participating on a voluntary basis. Using ballot-box style procedures to ensure confidentiality and anonymity, responses were obtained for 331 1991 seniors (class size=511) and 334 1992 seniors (class size=474). Of the latter group, 288 were identified as having completed DARE as seventh graders. This sub-population is referred to as the 1992 "DARE group" in the comparisons developed throughout the study.

The questionnaire included four scales:(1) DRUG USE SCALE, (2) DARE SCALE, (3) SELF-ESTEEM SCALE, and (4) LOCUS OF CONTROL SCALE.

The DRUG USE SCALE[6] is used to compare the 1991 and 1992 KHS senior groups on five measures of drug use:

(1) Lifetime Prevalence. Percentages of students reporting use (any amount) of each type/category of drug during their entire lives.

(2) Recency of Use (Past Year). Percentages of students reporting use (any amount) of each type/ category of drug during the past 12 months.

(3) Recency of Use (Past Month). Percentages of students reporting use (any amount) of each type/category of drug during the past 30 days.

(4) Grade Level at First Drug Use. The mean grade at first use for each type/category of drug.

(5) Frequency of Use. Percentages of students reporting drug use by number of occasions for three time periods-lifetime, past year, and past 30 days.

The DARE SCALE is a slightly modified version of the instrument developed in Los Angeles. It consists of 19 questions with five response choices for each item ranging from strongly agree to strongly disagree. Scores were computed according to the procedures used in Los Angeles whereby the percentage of students responding with "Appropriate" answers (disagree or strongly disagree) to each item was calculated along with the overall mean percentage of "Appropriate" responses for all 19 items. According to this coding and scoring approach, the higher the individual item percentages and overall mean scores, the more the results are supposedly indicative of anti-drug attitudes, greater drug knowledge, and enhanced drug-resistant coping skills.

The SELF-ESTEEM SCALE (Rosenberg 1965) provides a global measure of self-esteem. It consists of 10 statements with five possible responses (strongly agree to strongly disagree) for each item. Scores range from 10 to 40 with higher scores presumably indicative of higher levels of self-esteem. The LOCUS OF CONTROL SCALE (Rotter 1966) measures the extent to which individuals view their behavior as controlled by their own actions and choices versus outside forces over which they have little control. It consists of 23 paired items (and 6 fillers). For each pair a score of 1 applies when the "external" control statement is selected and 0 when the "internal" control statement is chosen. Scores range from 0 to 23 with higher scores presumably reflecting external orientations and lower scores reflecting internal orientations. "The most recognized cut-off point differentiating one kind of control from the other is a score of eight" (Natera et al. 1988:183).

MICRO-LEVEL PROCESS EVALUATION: OBJECTIVES AND DESIGN

The micro-level process portion of the study is based on a focus group interview with six KHS seniors who completed the DARE program as seventh graders with the same DARE officer and remained in the Kokomo schools through graduation. Group members were recruited from informal community contacts and were evenly divided by gender. The interview consisted of a one-hour session divided into two segments. The first portion focused on students' recollections of their DARE experiences as seventh graders *(DARE in the Past)*. The second part addressed students' views regarding DARE's long-term impact upon their peers' drug-related behaviors and attitudes and the general issue of drug education *(DARE in the Present)*. Responses were evoked through five open-ended questions (and follow-up probes) in each segment. The interview was taped with the subjects' knowledge and consent and their anonymity was assured. This qualitative dimension was included because focus groups are especially well suited for accessing how and why individuals feel as they do about particular experiences/issues which they have personally encountered that are of direct concern to them (Bertrand et al. 1992; Krueger 1988; Morgan 1988; Stewart and Shamdasani 1990).

Results: Impact Evaluation

DRUG USE SCALE

Comparisons of data from the DRUG USE SCALE for 1991 non-DARE and 1992 DARE seniors reveal that self-reported drug use rates among both groups are very similar for (1) Lifetime Prevalence (figure 6.1), (2) Recency of Use (figures 6.2 and 6.3), (3) Grade Level at First Drug Use (figure 6.4), and (4) Frequency of Use (data not shown). For some drugs and periods, drug use rates are *higher* for the 1992 DARE group than for the 1991 non-DARE group. However, for other drugs and periods, the rates are reversed.

Figure 6.4 illustrates the similarities between the two groups regarding Mean Grade Levels at First Drug Use.[7] A separate set of eight t-tests revealed no significant differences between the two groups on this measure for each drug type/category. Finally, Frequency of Use measures (though not reported here) revealed the same similarities and mixed patterns of use illustrated in figures 6.1–6.4.[8]

Prevalence, Recency, and Frequency data were further analyzed via several chi-square tests comparing drug use among DARE and non-DARE seniors for all drug types/categories, time periods, and use levels. While too lengthy to report in detail here, the results reveal no significant differences in drug use rates or patterns between the two groups in each area (prevalence, recency, frequency) for each drug type/category—with two exceptions. The results were significant for comparisons of the 1991 and 1992 groups' hallucinogen use over the last 30 days in terms of use/no use response categories (sig.=.0004) and levels of use (sig.=.02). Interestingly, in both instances *higher* use rates were recorded for the 1992 DARE group.[9]

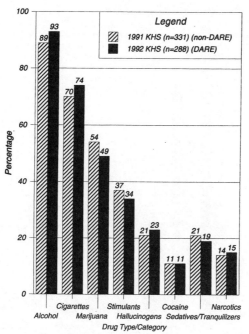

Figure 6.1.   Drug Use Scale: Lifetime Prevalence

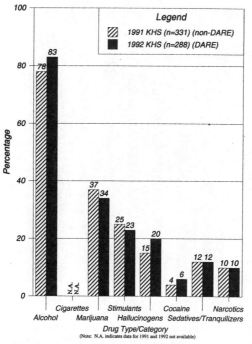

(Note: N.A. indicates data for 1991 and 1992 not available)

Figure 6.2.   Drug Use Scale: Recency of Use (Last Year)

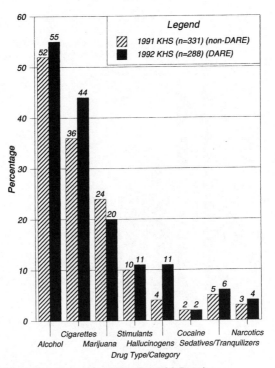

Figure 6.3. Drug Use Scale: Recency of Use (Last 30 Days)

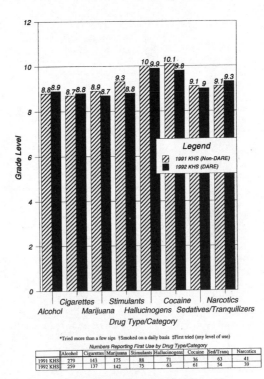

*Tried more than a few sips †Smoked on a daily basis ‡First tried (any level of use)

Numbers Reporting First Use by Drug Type/Category

	Alcohol	Cigarettes	Marijuana	Stimulants	Hallucinogens	Cocaine	Sed/Tranq	Narcotics
1991 KHS	279	143	175	88	71	36	63	41
1992 KHS	259	137	142	75	63	61	54	39

Figure 6.4. Drug Use Scale: Mean Grade Level at First Drug Use

DARE SCALE

Table 6.1 summarizes the DARE SCALE results and reinforces the basic findings of the previous section, that: DARE exposure appears to produce no significant long-term effects in areas related to the program's primary objectives. As the table indicates, the mean percentages of "Appropriate" responses for all 19 scale items were similar for all three groups with no statistically significant differences apparent in the groups' mean scores.[10]

Despite the similarities, some interesting differences on individual items were discovered. For example, there was a sharp decline in positive attitudes towards the police, and a growing unwillingness to condemn peer's consumption of alcohol. However, on the other items the 'Appropriate' response results were higher for the 1992 DARE seniors than they recorded as seventh graders. Despite these potentially confusing trends, the DARE and non-DARE senior groups had virtually identical response percentages for all 19 items indicating that differences between students' responses as seventh graders and later as seniors were not due to DARE exposure.

Finally, it is important to note that comparisons of results on the DARE SCALE with those from the DRUG USE SCALE call into question the utility of the DARE SCALE as a meaningful predictor of drug use. For example, despite the fact that high percentages of both senior groups gave "Appropriate" responses for most items on the scale, substantial majorities in these groups reported using various drugs (especially alcohol and cigarettes). These results are consistent with a number of findings in the drug education literature showing that while anti-drug information is easily imparted, producing changes in drug-related attitudes and behaviors is much more difficult and problematic (Bangert-Drowns 1988; Pellow and Jengeleski 1991). Moreover, the results suggest that rather than measuring any meaningful attitudinal or behavioral changes, the DARE SCALE simply assesses the extent to which DARE encourages students to uncritically recall and repeat information. In this sense the scale appears to be a very self-serving measure which by the design of its questions and coding procedures elicits the *appearance* of positive results thereby overstating the impact and efficacy of the DARE program.

Table 6.1.   DARE SCALE Results: ANOVA of "Appropriate" Response Means (1991 Seniors, 1992 Seniors and 1992 Seniors as 7th Graders)

DARE SCALE	1991 KHS (Non-DARE Group)	1992 KHS (DARE GROUP)	1992 KHS (as 7th Graders)	F-value	Sig. F
"Appropriate" Response Means:	82	82	79		
Std. Dev.:	12.86	12.21	11.10	.313	.732*
Cases:	n=331	n=288	n=596		

Note:
* = non-significant

Table 6.2.   Self-Esteem Results: Means and T-Test (Non-DARE and DARE Seniors)

DARE SCALE	1991 KHS (Non-DARE Group)	1992 KHS (DARE GROUP)	T-value	2-Tail Probability
Means:	29.72	29.81		
Std. Dev.:	5.06	4.54	−0.23	0.821*
Cases:	n=331	n=288		

Note:
* = non-significant

Table 6.3.   Locus of Control Results: Means and T-Test (Non-DARE and DARE Seniors)

DARE SCALE	1991 KHS (Non-DARE Group)	1992 KHS (DARE GROUP)	T-value	2-Tail Probability
Means:	11.04	11.42		
Std. Dev.:	3.79	3.73	−1.25	0.213*
Cases:	n=331	n=288		

Note:
* = non-significant

SELF-ESTEEM AND LOCUS OF CONTROL SCALES

Tables 6.2 and 6.3 report the SELF-ESTEEM SCALE and LOCUS OF CONTROL results for the DARE and non-DARE groups. As the tables illustrate, the mean scores on each scale are very similar for both groups. Moreover, the t-tests indicate no significant differences in the means of the DARE and non-DARE seniors. Since these scales are viewed as measures of DARE's secondary objectives, the results are indicative of two more areas where we see no long-term effects resulting from DARE exposure.

Results: Micro-level Process Evaluation

The focus group interview reinforced the quantitative findings and provided insights into students' views on a number of issues related to DARE and drug education. It also revealed a general shared resentment toward adult authorities related to the students' perception that their views about DARE had been ignored. For example, despite completing DARE evaluation questionnaires, group members noted that no one had ever asked them directly what they thought about DARE. One student's remarks elicited group approval on this issue:

> It's like nobody cares what we think. . . . The DARE cops just wanted us to do what they told us and our teachers never talked about DARE. . . . It seems like a lot of adults and teachers can't bring themselves down to talk to students . . . so you don't care what they think either.

Student perspectives on their DARE experience evoked positive and negative recollections, disagreements over lesson content, and a consensus on DARE's isolation from other school activities. Students' perceptions of the DARE officer and of DARE's interactive nature emerged as especially relevant to the tone of their recollections. Those who recalled DARE in positive terms emphasized how the warm and friendly style of the DARE officer created legitimacy, credibility, and acceptance. These students described the officer as "a pretty cool guy" and as "someone who cared about us and liked talking to us." They also recalled looking forward to "workbook activities and group projects [that] were fun." By contrast, students with negative recollections perceived the DARE officer as having stern, judgmental, and moralistic qualities which undermined his credibility and legitimacy. To illustrate, three group members recalled the officer insisted that rock music (especially "heavy metal") led to Satan worship and drug use and that his views were widely ridiculed by students. As one put it: "We mostly made fun of him; especially what he said about rock music." These students also recalled DARE more as an imposed set of lectures rather than an interactive program.

Lesson content was another area of disagreement. Most students recalled DARE as dealing only with illicit drugs. However, one student disagreed and said the DARE officer "wrote definitions on the board about alcohol, cigarettes, amphetamines or whatever and then he'd go over each one with us in class." Regarding DARE's isolation from other school activities, group members were unable to recall classroom teachers making more than passing remarks about it. Also, no one recalled any involvement in DARE-related activities outside of their DARE classes. As one student put it, "Our teachers never talked about DARE and we didn't hear about it except on the days we had it in class."

DARE was judged by all group members as having no lasting influence on students' drug-related attitudes or behaviors. The prevailing group view was captured by one student who said: "Nobody cared about DARE in high school. They didn't care what you told them in the seventh grade. They just didn't think about it any more." To account for this perceived outcome group members cited the influence of competing opinions (e.g., advertising) and peer pressure. Regarding the former factor, group members agreed with one student who said that as students got older:

> They started hearing more opinions other than just like in the seventh grade or someone coming in and talking about drugs. As you got older you kept hearing more opinions from different people and seeing like ads for like alcohol and cigarettes. And it looked more like fun or maybe like what you wanted to decide for yourself.

Another group member emphasized the influence of advertising in stimulating students' curiosity—especially about alcohol and cigarettes: "I think it makes them wonder what this beer tastes like or smokin' a Marlboro or compared to whatever. I think they think about that. I know I did." (Ironically, the influence of advertising is an area directly targeted by DARE lessons.)

On the issue of peer pressure, many group members made statements similar to what one student said:

> If your friends say 'Let's go out and get drunk,' you don't say 'Oh my gosh, well DARE teaches me not to.' You don't stop and think about it. You just go and do what your friends do. Does DARE help you deal with peer pressure? No! You're just going to follow your friends.

Another peer pressure-related theme involved the perceived existence of a widely shared norm of acceptance towards the use of various drugs (especially alcohol). Students said this norm increased peer pressure to use drugs–as evidenced in the remarks of two students who said:

> An overwhelming majority of kids drink and if you don't then you're not cool or whatever. So most kids go along so they can be part of the like popular group or at least so they won't be dorks.

> If somebody came up to you and said they were going drinkin' this weekend and there's gonna be a keg or whatever, nobody would say 'Hey that's not right.' Everybody your age, your peers just accepted it. Nobody really said anything.

Group members agreed that drug education should be part of the curriculum at all grade levels. However, there was also a consensus *against* DARE-style programs and *in favor* of "shock treatment" and counseling programs at the high school level. The former approach was exemplified by one student's view that teenagers need to be taken to hospitals and courts "to see 'crack babies' and addicts [and] to see how many years in prison people get for using drugs.[11] The latter approach with adults interacting with students as equals was also widely favored. As one student said:

> They need to get to know the kids personally and find out why they're using drugs or whatever. You need to know the kids and find out why they're doing something before you can do anything about it. That's one reason DARE wouldn't work [in the high school]. Kids don't respect or trust cops.

Despite their negative views on DARE, most group members didn't see it as a waste of time *in the lower grades* for two reasons. First, DARE was viewed as having some positive short-term effects. As one student said, "It did good for some people and kept them off drugs for awhile. It did help the younger kids." Second, although they didn't use the term, group members appeared to see DARE as an important symbol exemplifying official concern with the drug issue and sending the message that adults cared about students. As one student put it, "They're tryin' to do something positive. They're trying to do something good. You can't discourage it."

While recollections of events occurring five years earlier are likely to be less than complete and these students' views on DARE are not necessarily representative, the focus group accounts do provide a sense of the lasting impressions DARE makes upon students. Also, variations in students' reactions to DARE are indicative of a need for greater sensitivity to several factors which influence the dynamic relationship between program design, implementation, and how students actually experience the program. These issues are revisited later in the "Alternative Interpretations" section.

Macro-level Process Perspective

A macro-level process perspective reminds us that programs are never implemented in a vacuum nor under ideal conditions (Weisheit 1983). As noted earlier, it is an approach grounded in the social constructionist theoretical tradition which views social problems and related public policies as linked to political, social, and cultural processes[12] (Burstein 1991; Gamson et al. 1992; Snow et al. 1986). In the case of DARE, this theoretical orientation directs our attention to three interrelated lines of inquiry regarding DARE's development as a nation-wide program. First, it explores the links between the media and politically constructed Drug War and DARE's emergence as a reassuring form of symbolic politics. Second, it highlights the role of various stakeholders in promoting the program and in creating an organizational base to undergird DARE's legitimation and expansion. Third, it serves as the basis for considering the implications of DARE's evolution into a major political force for program evaluation and implementation.

DARE: SYMBOLIC POLITICS AND
ORGANIZATIONAL SUPPORT STRUCTURE

Edelman's (1964) concepts of "symbolic politics/action" are useful in understanding the links between the Drug War and DARE's emergence as a popular programmatic policy response in two respects. First, combined with the constructionist view, they help focus attention on the role and interests of political elites and the media in constructing the Drug War and in promoting popular anti-drug policies to deal with it. Second, they alert us to the importance of the symbolic dimensions of ameliorative social programs in generating political and public support. The latter point refers to the idea that the public reassurance features of such programs are likely to be more important in generating political and public support than their actual substantive effects. Furthermore, the reassurance value of such programs can be viewed as linked to the extent to which they are grounded in widely respected and legitimate institutions and cultural traditions. Thus, ameliorative programs which are imbued with these potent symbolic qualities (like DARE's links to schools and police) are virtually assured widespread public acceptance (regardless of actual effectiveness) which in turn advances the interests of political leaders who benefit from being associated with highly visible, popular symbolic programs.

The mid-1980s witnessed a substantial increase in attention by the mass media and national political leaders to illicit drug use resulting in the "social construction" of the "drug crisis" as a major national social problem (Reese and Danielian 1989; Jensen et al. 1991). Research on media reports of drug issues indicate such accounts "reached epidemic proportions in 1986" (Orcutt and Turner 1993:191) with extensive coverage continuing into the early 1990s (Jensen et al. 1991; Orcutt and Turner 1993). Parallel with expanding media coverage was growing political attention to the drug problem among both Democrats and Republicans throughout the same period (Jensen et al. 1991). The political nature of the drug issue was underscored in September 1986 by the nationally-televised joint address of former President Reagan and his wife Nancy wherein the President officially declared a national "War on Drugs" (Boyd 1986; *New York Times* 1986). As the 1980s ended, the Drug War was extended and systematized under the Bush administration in the form of the previously noted "National Drug Control Strategy."

With the Drug War shifting public attitudes in a direction more supportive of anti-drug programs, political interest in drug education quickly increased. DARE was well positioned to take advantage of this emerging context by offering a convenient, individual-level programmatic "solution" to the drug threat. By 1986, DARE had already established a positive track record in Los Angeles and was rapidly acquiring an expanding circle of enthusiastic promoters including (now former) LAPD Chief Daryl Gates (Pope 1992). While promoted as an ameliorative program, DARE also represented a high profile, powerful symbolic affirmation of traditional values and institutions on the highly charged drug issue. This point is illustrated in the testimony of DARE officials at Congressional hearings on drugs and drug education. For example, the Arizona Project DARE coordinator called attention to DARE's effects in reinforcing respect for authority:

> Police chiefs report that there is a higher respect for police officers . . . [and] school administrators and teachers report there's a higher degree of respect for authority in general among the students that have received DARE. (U.S. Congress: Senate 1988a:199)

The director of DARE in Washington state echoed this sentiment while directly commenting on DARE as a symbol and its linkages to traditional community centers of authority:

> DARE provides . . . a rallying symbol to do something positive about the drug abuse problem. . . . It combines . . . the parents and the community, the schools and the law enforcement agency. (U.S. Congress: House 1990:36)

The politically constructed nature of the drug threat combined with the symbolic dimensions of DARE's popular appeal highlight the utility of considering it as a form of symbolic politics. As Edelman (1964) has pointed out, politically constructed threats lead to politically-motivated interest in creating and/or expanding popular solutions imbued with symbolic appeal. Since expanding the DARE program offered public reassurance in the face of the constructed drug threat, DARE can be seen as a clear example of symbolic politics and action.

As political support for DARE increased, the program shifted from being a local success story to that of national symbol in the war on drugs. Drug War–driven public sentiment helped create popular and political support for individuals, officials, and organizations directly and indirectly associated with DARE. The result was an arrangement of mutual support and reinforcement among *direct* DARE stakeholders (its support staff and directly supportive organizations) and *indirect* stakeholders (e.g., political supporters and organizations contributing to the program). Both stakeholder groups benefited from the reflected approval, legitimacy, and widespread public support associated with a program linking a popular cause with traditional authority structures symbolized by the involvement of schools and law enforcement agencies. While we are not suggesting that every individual or organization affiliated with DARE was or is motivated by self-serving reasons, it is difficult to imagine that the many stakeholders are unaware of the potential material and/or ideological gains likely to accrue to them and/or their organizations as a result of their association with a popular program infused with potent symbolism. For example, little imagination is required to envision the "National DARE Day" proclamation as a political gesture on the part of indirect stakeholders. By linking themselves to DARE, national political candidates clearly stood to gain in terms of boosting their own popularity. At the same time, their political support helped to further legitimize the DARE program and increase its funding prospects benefiting individuals and organizations directly involved with its operation and/or expansion.

The "DARE Day" episode represents the tip of an iceberg of links between national, state, and local politicians and the DARE program. For example, at the national level some members of Congress have closely aligned themselves with the program by sponsoring hearings to provide a national forum for publicizing DARE and by lobbying for increased federal funding. In the House, Congresswoman Jolene Unsoeld's (D-Washington) involvement with DARE illustrates the publicity angle. She conducted DARE hearings to "build . . . momentum . . . so that we can go back to Congress to give that extra push to promote this very worthwhile effort" (U.S. Congress: House 1990:1). As Congressman Kildee (D-Michigan) observed, "Congresswoman Jolene Unsoeld is Ms. DARE in Washington. . . . I do not recall a meeting in which she has not mentioned DARE and what a great program this is" (U.S. Congress: House 1990:7). In the Senate, Senator Kasten (R-Wisconsin) illustrates the funding angle. He was instrumental in providing an extra $500,000 in federal funds for DARE officer training in 1991 and introduced S.2678 in 1992 to provide $50 million in federal operating funds for DARE (*Congressional Record* 1992b).

DARE's direct and indirect stakeholders have also collaborated to embed the program within a complex organizational support structure to ensure its continued existence and growth. An important feature of this structure is DARE AMERICA, a nonprofit corporation organized in 1987 as an I.R.S. 501(c) (3) tax-exempt organization. With an annual budget of $1.3 million in 1990 (Pope 1992), DARE AMERICA has become an effective organizational advocate for DARE with goals that include: "the adoption of DARE in all States and communities. . . . Support [for] a national DARE instructor training program . . . [and] Coordinat[ing] national fundraising for DARE" (U.S. Department of Justice 1991:11). The organization has actively recruited corporate sponsors as well as numerous corporate, political, and entertainment elites to serve as DARE spokespersons and fund raisers. For example, its Board of Directors "consists of prominent national business, political, law enforcement, and educational leaders" (U.S. Department of Justice 1991:11) and over the years has included philanthropist Armand Hammer, singer Michael Jackson, Daryl Gates, Diane Disney Miller, and former Virginia Governor Gerald L. Baliles (U.S. Congress: House 1990; Pope 1992).

Another dimension of DARE's support structure consists of an interrelated network of organizational ties linking DARE programs to various federal, state, and local government agencies as well as to private corporations. For example, the Bureau of Justice Assistance (BJA—an agency within the U.S. Department of Justice) serves as a major organizational link tying DARE programs to the federal government. This connection dates to 1986 when Daryl Gates succeeded in arranging a BJA grant of $140,000 to the LAPD "to share [the] unique DARE Program with other communities throughout the United States" (U.S. Congress: Senate 1988b:198). BJA involvement with DARE expanded in the late 1980s and led to agency funding of five regional DARE training centers. The BJA also appoints five of the 15 members comprising the DARE Training Center Policy Advisory Board (TCPAB) responsible for overseeing the training of DARE officers (U.S. Department of Justice 1991). Other federal agencies with ties to DARE include the National Institute on Drug Abuse (NIDA), which has funded DARE evaluation research (Clayton et al. 1991a), and the U.S. Department of Education, which provides some program funding through the 1989 Drug Free Schools and Communities Act (U.S. Congress: House 1990). Government linkages also extend to the state and local levels and involve law enforcement agencies, schools, and community groups (U.S. Congress: House 1990; Rogers 1990).

Beyond the public sector are numerous links tying DARE to corporate sponsors at the national, state, and local levels. DARE AMERICA has been especially instrumental in recruiting national corporate sponsors such as McDonald's, Security Pacific National Bank (SPNB), and Kentucky Fried Chicken to help fund the program (U.S. Congress: House 1990; Pope 1992). For example, SPNB contributed $500,000 in 1989 and pledged another $1 million over five years (Rogers 1990). Corporate support at the state and local levels involves hundreds of large and small firms contributing to the program (U.S. Congress: House 1990).

Implications for Program Evaluation

The implications of DARE's existence as a potent form of symbolic politics for the evaluation process are twofold: (1) It increases the prospects for tension as negative evaluation findings threaten the interests of powerful stakeholders. (2) It underscores the importance of framing results in a process perspective offering alternative interpretations for observed outcomes.

TENSION BETWEEN RESULTS AND STAKEHOLDER INTERESTS

While our negative results create the potential for conflict with DARE stakeholders, this prospect is further magnified by three other recent developments concerning

DARE. First, the program has received some negative national publicity as a kind of "Big Brother" spy operation resulting from cases where DARE students reported their drug-using parents to the police (Pereira 1992). Second, increasing concerns over the expense of the program have grown and as national, state, and local budgets find it more difficult to cover existing program costs, DARE has been targeted for budget cuts (Hughes-Lazzell 1993; Miley 1992; Pope 1992). Third, looming ominously for continued DARE funding (for stakeholders) are recent reports suggesting the Clinton administration has reduced the Drug War from "one of three top [national] priorities to Number 29 on a list of 29" (Schneider 1993:1). Also, journalistic reports on DARE's ineffectiveness could tarnish the program's appeal and affect its funding prospects (Cauchon 1993).

Our negative evaluation results could strengthen DARE's critics and make the case for cutting the program's budgets even stronger. Thus, our findings constitute a potential threat to program stakeholders and are likely to elicit their wrath. In fact, we have already witnessed an early skirmish along these lines. A local official associated with DARE has made negative comments about our findings to community groups saying: "They must not know how to measure things . . . if they could just see the kids' faces they'd know how much good its doing." This reaction is suggestive of what is likely to happen when negative evaluation results call into question the efficacy of a program laced with symbolic politics and supported by numerous powerful stakeholders.

Although our findings increase the prospects for tension with powerful stakeholders, framing the results within a macro-level process approach provides a means for considering alternative interpretations of outcomes, thereby tempering the hard edge of one-dimensional statistical results. This does not mean evaluators should anticipate stakeholder pressures by discounting the validity or importance of their results. However, when the issue under consideration is important and the stakes are high, program evaluators must be the first to call attention to the complex and inexact nature of the evaluation process. In the present case, our obligation is to provide the DARE program and its supporters with not only our findings, but also with an interpretive understanding of factors that may have influenced those results. However, it must also be pointed out that interpretive explanations are based largely on informed speculation and are capable of cutting both ways. That is, interpretations which appear to account for our findings could, in some cases, be reversed and presented in ways that would cause the program to be seen as even more ineffective than our data indicate.

ALTERNATIVE INTERPRETATIONS OF RESULTS

Alternative interpretations of our "no effects" findings involve a number of considerations but essentially cluster around three main issues: (1) the influence of contextual factors, (2) disjunctions between key DARE program assumptions/ideals and the manner in which the program was implemented, and (3) program design limitations.

Contextual factors and results. As noted earlier, the National Drug Control Strategy was built around the complementary goals of reducing both the demand for and supply of drugs *(National Drug Control Strategy* 1990). By the early 1990s, the political, social, and cultural contexts were increasingly pervaded by numerous anti-drug messages, policies, and programs stemming from this strategy. However, the exposure of the local seventh grade group to DARE in 1987-1988 occurred *before* the implementation of several important facets of the 1989 National Strategy. These included (for example) the organization (in 1987) of the privately-funded Partnership for a Drug-Free America *(Understanding Drug Prevention* 1992) and the passage of two major federal anti-drug laws: (1) the Anti-Drug Abuse Act of 1988 (*National Drug Control Strategy* 1990) and (2) the 1989 Drug Free Schools and Communities Act of 1989 (*National Drug Control Strategy* 1991). This meant the seventh-grade group was exposed to DARE *without* the reinforcing effects of coordinated mass media campaigns, community programs, and federally mandated anti-drug school policies. Although these additional features of the Drug War eventually became part of these students' experiences, their absence during the initial exposure of the group to DARE *could* have diminished both the immediate and long-term effects of the program for them.

While the preceding scenario appears plausible, the focus group narratives suggest an alternative explanation regarding the context-results linkage. Interview comments revealed the apparent effects of multiple macro-level cultural contexts containing contradictory messages that influence students' drug-related behaviors and attitudes. For example, adolescent subcultural norms and experiences appeared to encourage drug experimentation and negative attitudes toward adult authority structures. At the same time, the wider, Drug War–driven cultural context (including media messages infused with DARE's potent symbolic imagery and appeal) encouraged anti-drug and pro-drug education attitudes among students.

At the subcultural level, focus group comments suggest that student drug use reflects conformity to peer-enforced norms that are part of the adolescent subcultural context. Viewed in these terms, drug use serves as a means of validating membership in and allegiance to the adolescent subculture while at the same time demonstrating a rejection of remote and alienating adult authority structures. This perspective illuminates how the subcultural context increases the likelihood of adolescent drug use and at the same time provides students, *based on their own experiences,* with evidence of DARE's ineffectiveness over the long-term (as noted by the focus group members).

However, despite the potential of the peer-based subcultural context for encouraging drug use, focus group members also expressed *positive attitudes* towards drug education in the schools, including DARE programs in the lower grades. Such attitudes, at least in part, can be interpreted as reflective of students' membership and experiences in the wider cultural context imbued with anti-drug messages encouraging shared perceptions of drugs as bad and DARE as a sincere effort to protect vulnerable children from the drug threat. Viewed in these terms, we can see how the Drug War and the related promotion of DARE represent potent features of the wider cultural context and how these messages influence students' attitudes towards drugs and DARE.

An interpretative approach grounded in the effects of membership in multiple contexts provides a means of resolving the paradoxical mix of adolescents' anti-drug attitudes combined with tendencies towards drug experimentation. It reminds us of the existence and power of multiple "lifeworld" contexts (Mishler 1984; Waitzkin 1989) composed of contrasting and even conflicting themes and messages which become woven into the fabric of adolescents' lives. This view is very different from the notion that context represents a kind of unitary social reality subject to conscious policy manipulation so as to reinforce the effects of drug programs aimed at altering adolescents' attitudes and behaviors.

Disjunction: Program assumptions, implementation, and results. A central assumption guiding national drug prevention policy is the view that "drug [use] reflects bad decisions by individuals with free wills" (*National Drug Control Policy* 1992:2). However, the "user accountability" principle associated with this view is tempered by a recognition that "actions can be taken to encourage [individuals] to make the right choices" (*National Drug Control Policy* 1992:3). The DARE program reflects a similar philosophy and views drug use as an individual decision, but it is also seen as a choice that is heavily dependent upon knowledge, attitudes, and social skills. Consequently, DARE assumes it is possible to intervene in these areas via systematically organized anti-drug lessons that will produce effective and long-lasting attitudinal and behavioral effects. Two related program assumptions associated with DARE's implementation include the ideas that anti-drug effects will be maximized by (1) early intervention and (2) the uniform presentation of a standardized curriculum.

A comparison of the preceding assumptions with the realities attendant to DARE's implementation among Kokomo seventh graders in 1987-88 reveals three important disjunctions relevant to our findings. First, this group was exposed to the program two years later than recommended for optimal results. Second, the seventh graders did not receive the full 17 sessions of the DARE "core" curriculum, but an abbreviated 11-week version. (Although DARE includes a 10-session middle/junior high curriculum, it is designed "to reinforce the lessons of the elementary curriculum" [U.S. Department of Justice 1991:7] and is not intended as a "stand alone" program.) Third, our qualitative data suggests that departures from the objectives of uniform presentation and "curriculum fidelity" (Clayton et al. 1991a:310) occurred in at least some sessions for some students. It is important to recall that the purpose of the 80-hour DARE-officer training requirement is to ensure that instructors will "go by the book." The focus group interview identified lesson content and classroom interaction as at least two areas of departure from standardized lesson plans and program format.

While these disjunctions appear to represent potential threats to DARE's long-term effectiveness, a sociologically informed alternative interpretation suggests that they may be rather trivial and perhaps even inconsequential factors. As we note in the next section, an important design limitation of all school-based drug prevention programs, including DARE, is the failure of such programs to address the role of structural factors in the etiology of drug use. This problem may represent not simply a limitation, but rather may constitute a fatal flaw ensuring the long-term ineffectiveness of such programs.

Program design limitations and results. Prior research suggests that DARE's effectiveness may be inhibited by program design limitations related to three areas not explicitly considered by the DARE curriculum. These include: the unexamined impact of DARE's mandatory nature in schools adopting the program combined with wide variations in student receptiveness to DARE; the role of classroom factors in shaping such variations; and the influence of structural factors upon students' drug use. Regarding the first issue, we have shown elsewhere that student receptiveness to DARE exists on a continuum of interest ranging from enthusiastic involvement to active resistance (Aniskiewicz and Wysong 1990). The presence of students with the latter orientation in DARE classes presents problems for a mandated curriculum designed to reach groups with pre-existing neutral or positive attitudes towards drug education. Imposing DARE upon divided student audiences produces outcomes likely to diminish the program's effectiveness, especially among resistant students. Other studies confirm this prospect and demonstrate that "when socially deviant youths are required to participate in the school setting in peer-led denunciation of activities they value, they are more likely to become alienated than converted" (Baumrind 1987:32). Thus, for students resistant to the DARE message, the program's credibility, legitimacy, and effectiveness will continue to be problematic as long as the curriculum is both routinely mandated and not more closely connected to students' life experiences.

The factor of "classroom climate" has also been shown to be influential in conditioning student receptiveness to DARE (Aniskiewicz and Wysong 1990:737-738). This means that varying pedagogical styles and levels of enthusiasm for DARE among regular classroom teachers act as factors capable, at least in part, of facilitating or inhibiting student enthusiasm for the program. The absence of explicit attention by the DARE curriculum to such factors and their impact upon student receptiveness to DARE illustrates another area where program design limitations are likely to inhibit the program's effectiveness.

The third and most important limitation of the program stems from DARE's implicit embrace of "free will/user accountability" principles. This orientation contributes to a kind of one-dimensional program focus with DARE's scope and emphasis strictly limited to the interactional context within which students' choices are made. While drawing attention to social-psychological dynamics, this kind of orientation is an important, but not sufficient basis for understanding the etiology of drug use. Such a sharply limited view restricts DARE's prevention efforts to manipulating a narrow range of psychosocial factors while ignoring and excluding important structural factors such as students' socio-economic backgrounds, family influences, and employment prospects. As we note in the discussion section, the effectiveness of drug prevention efforts can benefit by paying greater attention to such structural factors given their role in conditioning adolescents' behavioral choices and perceptions of options (Lohrmann and Fors 1986). Approaching drug education from this perspective calls attention to how DARE's limitation inhibits its effectiveness (and thus helps us understand our results), and also to the limitations of school-based drug education programs generally in preventing adolescent drug use (Lohrmann and Fors 1986; van de Wijngaart 1990). From Durkheim to the present, sociological approaches to understanding social behavior have recognized the deterministic impact of social structures upon social behavior. In the face of extensive sociological research supporting such a view, DARE's assumption that drug-related attitudes and behavior can be significantly influenced over the long-term by a relatively brief exposure to a persuasive communication program appears to be rather naive.

Discussion

After tracking DARE for five years, our quantitative and qualitative data both point in the direction of no long-term effects for the program in preventing or reducing adolescent drug use. Despite the massive scope of the Drug War, the existence of powerful DARE stakeholders, and the potential controversies that our findings might generate, we believe our evaluation of DARE represents a fair and accurate assessment of the program's long-term effects *for the group we studied.* Of course, for reasons noted earlier, we also believe our conclusions must be viewed as suggestive rather than definitive. We explicitly recognize the limitations of our findings given the local nature of our sample and the complexities of conducting longitudinal evaluation research on a popular program addressing adolescent drug use. However, it is precisely because our efforts have gone far beyond a one-dimension impact evaluation approach that we believe the study is important and deserves widespread attention.

Our findings will help stimulate a reconsideration of several issues related to the etiology of drug use and related assumptions concerning programs aimed at preventing and/or delaying drug use among young adults. For example, should drug prevention efforts be expanded beyond those programs aimed at changing attitudes or improving social skills through sophisticated persuasive communication programs? Raising such questions underscores the need for a more complete consideration of the appropriate balance between prevention approaches focusing primarily on the psychosocial dimension of drug use versus policies addressing cultural and structural factors related to drug use (e.g., Waldorf et al. 1991).

Programs linked to the latter approach might include changes in structural factors contributing to inequalities, alienation, and social isolation among adolescents. For example, programs ensuring that adolescents and young adults have access to diverse, high-quality educational programs and later to meaningful job opportunities that would allow them to be economically self-supporting could be usefully tied to more traditional education-based prevention approaches. To the extent that our evaluation results help stimulate a more multifaceted discourse on the nature and merits of various psychosocial and structural drug prevention policies and programs, then the DARE program, regardless of its long-term efficacy, will have made a positive contribution to addressing the continuing problem of drug use.

Notes

An earlier version of this chapter was presented at the 1993 meetings of the North Central Sociological Association. Support for this project was provided in part by Faculty Fellowship Grants from Indiana University Kokomo. However, the views expressed in this chapter are solely those of the authors. We are indebted to *Social Problems'* anonymous reviewers and to the Editor for their constructive comments that helped slip the project through the razorwire and into print. Direct all correspondence to: Earl Wysong, Indiana University Kokomo, Department of Social and Behavioral Sciences, 2300 South Washington Street, Kokomo, IN 46902.

1. Three studies have been completed that track DARE over intermediate periods of time. A one-year follow-up study has been reported by Rosenbaum et al. (1994) and a two-year study (as part of a five-year investigation) has been completed by Clayton et al. (1991b). A summary of a three-year (unpublished) study of DARE in the LAUSD by a private evaluation company (Evaluation and Training Institute) commissioned by the Los Angeles Board of Police Commissioners was included in recent Congressional hearings on DARE (U.S. Congress: House 1990).

2. DARE combines factual/informational, cognitive/affective decision-making, and psychosocial life skills approaches to drug education. Research from the late 1970s and early 1980s demonstrates greater efficacy for programs combining features from these three approaches (Ambtman et al. 1990; Battjes 1985; Clayton et al. 1991a; Johnson et al. 1990; Pellow and Jengeleski 1991; Ringwalt et al. 1991).

3. DARE's objectives regarding student drug use embrace the same "zero tolerance/no-use/drug free" orientations that have guided national drug policies for the past several years (U.S. Congress: House 1991:160–164). This means that DARE makes no distinctions between legal and illegal drugs and advocates total abstinence as the only acceptable approach to all types and categories of drugs. The program appears to assume that drug experimentation (with any drug at any level) either equals drug abuse or will inevitably lead to drug abuse. Despite evidence that drug experimentation among adolescents is fairly common (e.g., Johnston et al. 1981, 1992), but seldom leads to "problem drug use" (Shedler and Block 1990), DARE equates these two phenomena. As a result of attempting to prevent all drug experimentation and/or use, DARE's objectives are not only unrealistic but also possibly counter-productive because they are obviously unattainable.

4. Kokomo's 1990 population of 45,000 consisted largely of white, working-class families with nonwhites (primarily African Americans) making up only 7 percent of the total (Slater and Hall 1992). In some respects the community is similar to Muncie, Indiana (of "Middletown" fame—cf. Lynd and Lynd 1929; Caplow et al. 1982), with cultural and political value orientations trending in a conservative direction. The Kokomo Center School Corporation serves 7,722 students (1991, grades K-12) with a much smaller number (about 700) enrolled at all grade levels in five private religious schools (two Catholic and three fundamentalist Christian schools).

5. Although some studies indicate linkages between selected personality attributes and adolescent drug use which support our line of inquiry, other research in this area has produced mixed results. For example, some studies have found that adolescents who experimented with illicit drugs (especially marijuana) were better adjusted than either abstainers or frequent users (Shedler and Block 1990) and were more socially skilled with higher levels of self-esteem than abstainers (Hogan et al. 1970; Bender 1987). While these findings are intriguing, resolving the personality traits drug use issue is well beyond the scope of this project. Our purpose here is simply to explore whether DARE exposure produces lasting effects in two psychosocial areas related to DARE's explicit and/or implicit program objectives.

6. The DRUG USE SCALE categories of hallucinogens, cocaine, sedatives/tranquilizers, and narcotics are used to report use rates among KHS seniors for combinations of specific drugs reported separately in the national senior survey. For example, our questions on hallucinogens asked students to respond within that category if they had used any related drugs (such as LSD, PCP, etc.). By contrast, the national senior survey asks for and reports use rates on each specific drug (Johnston et al. 1981, 1989, 1991, 1992).

7. The "Numbers Reporting First Use' sub-figure illustrates that aside from alcohol, the mean grade level figures reflect drug use among relatively small groups of students compared to the total samples.

8. The details regarding Frequency of Use comparisons between the DARE and non-DARE groups are too lengthy to report in this study. A table summarizing these results is available from the authors.

9. The finding of significantly higher hallucinogen use among the DARE group raises the *possibility* that drug education programs may increase student curiosity about drugs and lead to earlier and greater drug experimentation. In fact, there is some support for this prospect in the drug education literature (Goodstadt 1980; Olton 1985; Whiddon and Halpin 1977). However, in the present case the hallucinogen finding stands alone and is not part of an overall pattern of higher drug use among the DARE group. It *could* be an indicator of DARE exposure piquing student interest in drugs, but absent a pattern of increased use of other drugs as compared with the non-DARE group, it appears to represent more of an unexplained anomaly than a trend.

10. In a separate analysis of "Appropriate" mean response percentages for each DARE Scale question by each of the three groups identified in table 6.1, we found similar results for most of the 19 items. The DARE Scale results for each of the 19 items are too lengthy to report in detail in this chapter. A table summarizing the results for all 19 items is available from the authors.

11. Ironically, despite student support for "scared straight" approaches, these are among the kinds of programs cited by the Office of National Drug Control Policy as examples of drug prevention programs that *don't work (Understanding Drug Prevention* 1992).

12. See Beckett (this issue) for a detailed discussion of various social constructionist models and the characteristics of each type.

References

Ambtman, Rudy, Paul Madak, Denise Koss, and Mark J. Strople. 1990. "Evaluation of a comprehensive elementary school curriculum-based drug education program." *Journal of Drug Education* 20:199–225.

Aniskiewicz, Richard, and Earl Wysong. 1990. "Evaluating DARE: Drug education and the multiple meanings of success." *Policy Studies Review* 9:727–747.

Bangert-Drowns, Robert L. 1988. "The effects of school-based substance abuse education—A meta-analysis." *Journal of Drug Education* 18:243–264.

Battjes, Robert J. 1985. "Prevention of adolescent drug use." *International Journal of the Addictions* 20:1113–1134.

Baumrind, Diana. 1987. "Familial antecedents of adolescent drug use: A developmental perspective." In *Etiology of Drug Abuse: Implications for Prevention,* eds. Coryl L. Jones and Robert J. Battjes, 13–44. Rockville, Md.: National Institute of Drug Abuse.

Beckett, Katherine. 1994. "Setting the public agenda: 'Street crime' and drug use in American politics." *Social Problems* 41:425–447.

Benford, Robert D., and Scott A. Hunt. 1992. "Dramaturgy and social movements: The social construction and communication' of power." *Sociological Inquiry* 62:36–55.

Bentler, Peter M. 1987. "Drug use and personality in adolescence and young adulthood: Structural models with nonnormal variables." *Child Development* 58:65–79.

Bertrand, Jane T., Judith E. Brown, and Victoria M. Ward. 1992. "Techniques for analyzing focus group data." *Evaluation Review* 16:198–209.

Boyd, Gerald M. 1986. "Reagans advocate 'crusade' on drugs." *New York Times,* September 15:A1, B10.

Buechler, Steven M. 1993. "Beyond resource mobilization? Emerging trends in social movement theory." *Sociological Quarterly* 34:217–235.

Burstein, Paul. 1991. "Policy domains: Organization, culture, and policy outcomes." In *Annual Review of Sociology,* eds. W. Richard Scott and Judith Blake, 327–350. Palo Alto, Calif.: Annual Reviews.

Caplow, Theodore, Howard M. Bahr, Bruce A. Chadwick, Reuben Hill, and Margaret H. Williamson. 1982. *Middletown Families.* Minneapolis: University of Minnesota Press.

Cauchon, Dennis. 1993. "Studies find drug program not effective." *USA Today,* October 11:1–2.

Chelimsky, Eleanor. 1985. "Old patterns and new directions in program evaluation." In *Program Evaluation: Patterns and Directions,* ed. Eleanor Chelimsky, 1–35. Washington, D.C.: American Society for Public Administration.

Clayton, Richard R., Anne Cattarello, L. Edward Day, and Katherine P. Walden. 1991a. "Persuasive communication and drug prevention: An evaluation of the DARE Program." In *Persuasive Communication and Drug Abuse Prevention,* eds. Lewis Donohew, Howard E. Sypher, and William J. Bukowski, 295–313. Hillsdale, N.J.: Lawrence Erlbaum.

Clayton, Richard R., Anne Cattarello, and Katherine P. Walden. 1991b. "Sensation seeking as a potential mediating variable for school-based prevention intervention: A two-year follow-up of DARE." *Health Communication* 3(4):229–239.

Congressional Record. 1992a. "Senate Joint Resolution 295. Joint Resolution Designating September 10, 1992, as National D.A.R.E. Day." April 30:S5915-S5916.

———. 1992b. "National DARE Day." September 10:S13299.

———. 1992c. "National DARE Day." July 21:H6333-S6334.

D.A.R.E. AMERICA. 1991. Request for Proposal. D.A.R.E. America, Inc. 606 South Olive, Suite 1206, Los Angeles, California.

DeJong, William. 1987. "A short-term evaluation of Project DARE (Drug Abuse Resistance Education): Preliminary indications of effectiveness." *Journal of Drug Education* 17:279–294.

Deutscher, Irwin, and Martha Beattie. 1988. "Success and failure: Static concepts in a dynamic society." *Evaluation Review* 12:607–623.

Edelman, Murray. 1964. *The Symbolic Uses of Politics.* Chicago: University of Illinois Press.

———. 1979. *Political Language: Words That Succeed and Policies That Fail.* New York: Academic Press.

———. 1988. *Constructing The Political Spectacle.* Chicago: University of Chicago Press.

Faine, John R., and Edward Bohlander. 1989. "DARE in Kentucky schools, 1988–89: An evaluation of the Drug Abuse Resistance Education Program." Annual Report from the Social Research Laboratory, Western Kentucky University, Bowling Green, Ky.

Gamson, William, David Croteau, William Hoynes, and Theodore Sasson. 1992. "Media images and the social construction of reality." In *Annual Review of Sociology,* eds. Judith Blake and John Hagan, 373–393. Palo Alto, Calif.: Annual Reviews.

Goodstadt, Michael S. 1980. "Drug education: A turn on or a turn off?" *Journal of Drug Education* 10:89–99.

Harmon, Michele A. 1993. "Reducing the risk of drug involvement among early adolescents." *Evaluation Review* 17:221–239.

Hogan, R., D. Mankin, J. Conway, and S. Fox. 1970. "Personality correlates of undergraduate marijuana use." *Journal of Consulting and Clinical Psychology* 35:58–63.

Hughes-Lazzell, Terri. 1993. "Appealing to the community." *Kokomo Tribune,* January 5:2.

Jensen, Eric J., Jurg Gerber, and Ginna M. Babcock. 1991. "The new war on drugs: Grass roots movement or political construction?" *Journal of Drug Issues* 21:651–667.

Johnson, C. Anderson, Mary A. Pentz, Mark D. Weber, James H. Dwyer, Neal Baer, David P. Mackinnon, William B. Hansen, and Brian R. Flay. 1990. "Relative effectiveness of comprehensive community programming for drug abuse prevention with high-risk and low-risk adolescents." *Journal of Consulting and Clinical Psychology* 58:447–456.

Johnston, Lloyd D., Patrick M. O'Malley, and Jerald G. Bachman. 1981. *Monitoring the Future: Student Drug Use in America 1975–1981.* Rockville, Md.: National Institute on Drug Abuse.

———. 1989. *Drug Use, Drinking, and Smoking: National Survey Results from High School, College, and Young Adult Populations 1975–1988.* Rockville; Md.: National Institute on Drug Abuse.

———. 1991. *Drug Use Among American High School Seniors, College Students and Young Adults, 1975–1990.* Volume I. Rockville, Md.: National Institute on Drug Abuse.

———. 1992. *Smoking, Drinking, and Illicit Drug Use Among American Secondary School Students, College Students, and Young Adults, 1975–1991.* Volume I. Rockville, Md.: National Institute on Drug Abuse.

Krueger, Richard A. 1988. Focus *Groups: A Practical Guide for Applied Research.* Newbury Park, Calif.: Sage.

Lohrmann, David K., and Stuart W. Fors. 1986. "Can school-based educational programs really be expected to solve the adolescent drug abuse problem?" Jour*nal of Drug Education* 16:327–339.

Lynd, Robert S., and Helen M. Lynd. 1929. *Middletown.* New York: Harcourt, Brace Jovanovich.

MacDonald, A.P. 1973. "Internal-external locus of control." In *Measures of Social Psychological Attitudes,* eds. John P. Robinson and Phillip R. Shaver, 169–211. Ann Arbor, Mich.: Institute for Social Research, University of Michigan.

Males, Mike. 1992. "Drug deaths rise as the war continues." In *These Times,* May 20–26:17.

Miley, Scott L. 1992. "DARE beats drugs; truth is, funding's in a 'crisis.'" *Indianapolis Star,* May 18:D-1.

Mishler, Elliot G. 1984. *The Discourse of Medicine: Dialectics of Medical Interviews.* Norwood, N.J.: Ablex.

Morgan, David L. 1988. *Focus Groups As Qualitative Research.* Newbury Park, Calif.: Sage.

Nachmias, David. 1980. "Public policy evaluation: An overview." In *The Practice of Policy Evaluation,* ed. David Nachmias, 1–22. New York: St. Martin's Press.

Natera, G., M.E. Herrejon, and M. Casco. 1988. "Locus of control in couples with different patterns of alcohol consumption." *Drug and Alcohol Dependence* 22:179–186.

National Drug Control Strategy. 1990. The White House, January 1990. Washington, D.C.: U.S. Government Printing Office.

———. 1991. The White House, February 1991. Washington, D.C.: U.S. Government Printing Office.

———. 1992. The White House, January 1992. Washington, D.C.: U.S. Government Printing Office.

New York Times. 1986. "Excerpts from speech on halting drug abuse." September 15:B 10.

Nyre, Glenn F. 1984. "An evaluation of project DARE (Drug Abuse Resistance Education)." Los Angeles: Evaluation and Training Institute.

———. 1985. "Final evaluation report, 1984–1985: Project DARE (Drug Abuse Resistance Education)." Los Angeles. Evaluation and Training Institute.

Olton, Andre L. 1985. "The effect of locus of control and perceptions of school environment on outcome in three school drug abuse prevention programs." *Journal of Drug Education* 15:157–169.

Orcutt, James D., and J. Blake Turner. 1993. "Shocking numbers and graphic accounts: Quantified images of drug problems in the print media." *Social Problems* 40:190–206.

Patton, Michael Q. 1987. *How to Use Qualitative Methods in Evaluation.* Newbury Park, Calif.: Sage.

Pellow, Randall A., and James L. Jengeleski. 1991. "A survey of current research studies on drug education programs in America." *Journal of Drug Education* 21:203–210.

Penny, Gillian N., and James O. Robinson. 1986. "Psychological resources and cigarette smoking in adolescents." *British Journal of Psychology* 77:351–357.

Pereira, Joseph. 1992. "The informants: In a drug program, some kids turn in their own parents." *Wall Street Journal*, April 20:1, A4.

Pope, Lisa. 1992. "DARE-ing program at risk." *Los Angeles Daily News*, September 20:G-6, G-7.

Reese, Stephen D., and Lucig H. Danielian. 1989. "Intermedia influence on the drug issue: Converging on cocaine." In Communication Campaigns About Drugs: Government, Media, and the Public, ed. Pamela J. Shoemaker, 29–45. New York: Aldine de Gruyter.

Ringwalt, Christopher L., Susan T. Ennett, and Kathleen D. Holt. 1991. "An outcome evaluation of Project DARE." *Health Education Research* 6:327–337.

Roberts-Gray, Cynthia, and Mary A. Scheirer. 1988. "Checking the congruence between a program and its organizational environment." In *Evaluating Program Environments,* eds. Kendon J. Conrad and Cynthia Roberts-Gray, 63–81. San Francisco: Jossey-Bass.

Rogers, Everett M. 1990. "Cops, kids, and drugs: Organizational factors in the spontaneous diffusion of Project D.A.R.E." Paper presented at the Conference on Organizational Factors in Drug Abuse Prevention Campaigns. Bethesda, Maryland.

Rosenbaum, Dennis P., Robert L. Flewelling, Susan L. Bailey, Chris L. Ringwalt, and Deanna L. Wilkinson. 1994. "Cops in the classroom: A longitudinal evaluation of Drug Abuse Resistance Education (DARE)." *Journal of Research in Crime and Delinquency* 31:3–31.

Rosenberg, Morris. 1965. *Society and the Adolescent Self-Image.* Princeton, N.J.: Princeton University Press.

Rotter, Julian B. 1966. "Generalized expectancies for internal versus external control of reinforcement." *Psychological Monographs* 80:1–28.

Schneider, Andrew. 1993. "Latin America senses retreat as Clinton muzzles drug war." *Indianapolis Star,* February 13:1.

Shadish, William R. 1987. "Program micro- and macrotheories: A guide for social change." In *Using Program Theory in Evaluation,* ed. Leonard Bickman, 93–108. San Francisco: Jossey-Bass.

Shedler, Jonathan, and Jack Block. 1990. "Adolescent drug use and psychological health: A longitudinal inquiry." *American Psychologist* 45:612–630.

Slater, Courtenay M., and George E. Hall. 1992. *County and City Extra Annual Metro, City and County Data Book.* Lanham, Md.: Bernan Press.

Snow, David A., E. Burke Rochford, Jr., Steven K. Worden, and Robert D. Benford. 1986. "Frame alignment processes, micromobilization, and movement participation." *American Sociological Review* 51:464–481.

Stewart, David W., and Prem N. Shamdasani. 1990. *Focus Groups: Theory and Practice.* Newbury Park, Calif.: Sage.

Tobler, Nancy S. 1986. "Meta-analysis of 143 adolescent drug prevention programs: Quantitative outcome results of program participants compared to a control or comparison group." *Journal of Drug Issues* 16:537–568.

Understanding Drug Prevention. 1992. "An Office of National Drug Control Policy White Paper. " May 1992. Washington, D.C.: U.S. Government Printing Office.

U.S. Congress: House of Representatives. 1990. "Oversight hearing on drug abuse education programs." Committee on Education and Labor. Subcommittee on Elementary, Secondary, and Vocational Education. 101st Congress, 1st session. Serial No. 101–129. Washington, D.C.: U.S. Government Printing Office.

———. 1991. "Field hearing on The Drug Education Program." Committee on Education and Labor. Subcommittee on Select Education. 102nd Congress, 1st session. Serial No. 102–146. Washington, D.C.: U.S. Government Printing Office.

U.S. Congress: Senate 1988a. "The Criminal and Juvenile Justice Partnership Act of 1987." Committee on the Judiciary. 100th Congress, 2nd session. Washington, D.C.: U.S. Government Printing Office.

————. 1988b. "Drug abuse, prevention, and treatment." Committee on Labor and Human Resources. 100th Congress, 2nd session. Washington, D.C.: U.S. Government Printing Office.

U.S. Department of Justice, Bureau of Justice Assistance. 1991. PROGRAM BRIEF: An Introduction to DARE: Drug Abuse Resistance Education. Second Edition. Washington, D.C.: Bureau of Justice Assistance. U.S. Office of Management and Budget.

————. 1990. Budget of the U.S. Government, Fiscal Year 1991. Washington, D.C.: U.S. Government Printing Office.

————. 1992. Budget of the U.S. Government, Fiscal Year 1993. Washington, D.C.: U.S. Government Printing Office.

van de Wijngaart, Govert F. 1990. "The Dutch aproach: Normalization of drug problems." *Journal of Drug Issues* 20:667–678.

Waldorf, Dan, Craig Reinarman, and Sheigla Murphy. 1991. *Cocaine Changes.* Philadelphia: Temple University Press.

Waitzkin, Howard. 1989. "A critical theory of medical discourse: Ideology, social control, and the processing of social context in medical encounters." *Journal of Health and Social Behavior* 30:220–239.

Weisheit, Ralph A. 1983. "The social context of alcohol and drug education: Implications for program evaluations." *Journal of Alcohol and Drug Education* 29:72–81.

Whiddon, Thomas, and Gerald Halpin. 1977. "Relationships between drug knowledge and drug attitudes for students in large, intermediate, and small schools." *Research Quarterly* 48:191–195.

Part III

SOCIAL PATTERNS: EPIDEMIOLOGICAL RESEARCH

Epidemiology, the study of the rate and distribution of problematic conditions in various populations, is one of the oldest and most important approaches to social problems research. Chapters in previous parts by Orcutt and Turner and Beckett included examples of the use (and misuse) of epidemiological data to describe longitudinal trends in the prevalence of drug use and incidence of crime in the United States. The epidemiological studies in this part focus on cross-sectional patterns in drug- and alcohol-related problems—that is, they examine variations in rates of illegal drug use and deviant drinking across different segments of the population at one point or interval of time. These chapters illustrate how epidemiological research serves a valuable descriptive function by identifying population subgroups or social locations associated with both high rates and greater risk of drinking or drug problems. In addition, each of these studies makes a significant theoretical contribution by attempting to explain underlying causes of the social patterning of drug and alcohol problems.

The first study by John Wallace and Jerald Bachman focuses on racial and ethnic differences in cigarette, alcohol, and illegal drug use among U.S. high school seniors. The data for this investigation come from a well-known epidemiological survey, the Monitoring the Future project discussed by Orcutt and Turner in part I. Wallace and Bachman combine several years of data from this annual survey to provide a comprehensive, and sometimes surprising, comparison of the prevalence of drug use and heavy drinking for young men and women in six population subgroups: whites, African Americans, Mexican Americans, Puerto Rican and other Latino Americans, Asian Americans, and Native Americans. The basic descriptive results in table 1 of their chapter show that, with the exception of Native Americans, minority students are generally less likely to smoke, drink heavily, or use illegal drugs than are white students. A major aim of Wallace and Bachman's analysis is to determine the extent to which these epidemiological patterns are due to differences in the social backgrounds (e.g., parents' education, urban or rural residence) and personal lifestyles (e.g., religiosity, dating behavior) of white and minority students. When Wallace and Bachman use multivariate statistical techniques to control or adjust for group differences in background and lifestyle, they find that white students still tend to have higher rates of heavy drinking and drug use than most minority students, including African Americans. Thus, the results of this broad-ranging epidemiological investigation directly contradict the popular notion that adolescent drinking and drug use in the United States is disproportionately a "minority problem."

In the next chapter, Denise Herd examines a similar epidemiological pattern among adult women in the United States. A number of studies have found that black women are far more likely than white women to abstain from alcohol use, although a few studies also find higher rates of alcohol problems among black women who do drink. Herd's descriptive results from a nationally representative household survey show that nearly half of black women (46 percent) versus only a third of white women (34 percent) are abstainers. In addition, she finds somewhat higher rates of heavier and more frequent drinking among white women. Furthermore, as shown in table 3 of her chapter, these basic patterns persist when Herd controls individually for the effects of age, marital status, family income, and employment status. As in Wallace and Bachman's analysis of adolescent drinking and drug use, Herd's multivariate analysis of alcohol use among adult women indicates that racial differences in income, employment, and other social characteristics do not adequately explain why whites are more likely to use alcohol and drink heavily than are African Americans.

However, a rather different picture emerges from the final chapter by Kellie Barr, Michael Farrell, Grace Barnes, and John Welte, which presents epidemiological evidence from a survey of adults in New York State. This study is guided by William Wilson's (1978; 1987) influential theoretical analysis of the black "underclass" and argues that drinking problems, drug use, and other personal consequences of racial segregation and industrial decline in urban areas will be particularly severe among lower-class African American men. Barr and associates' findings provide striking support for their line of argument. As depicted in figures 1 to 6, one race/gender subgroup stands out dramatically in multivariate analyses that include the effects of income or education on alcohol consumption, drinking problems, and illegal drug use. Black men at the lowest income or education level consistently show the highest rates of substance use and alcohol-related problems. In other respects, the descriptive findings of this study are similar to those of Herd's national study of women—that is, black respondents are more likely than whites to abstain from alcohol. However, by including patterns of gender difference in their epidemiological analysis, Barr et al. are able to move toward a sociological explanation of the impact of racial and class inequality on drug and alcohol problems in North American society. They conclude their chapter with interesting speculations about why their results for adults depart from those of other epidemiological studies such as Wallace and Bachman's that find relatively low rates of drinking and drug use among African American youths.

References

Wilson, William J. 1978. *The Declining Significance of Race*. Chicago: University of Chicago Press.

———. 1987. *The Truly Disadvantaged*. Chicago: University of Chicago Press.

CHAPTER 7

Explaining Racial/Ethnic Differences in Adolescent Drug Use

THE IMPACT OF BACKGROUND AND LIFESTYLE
John M. Wallace, Jr., and Jerald G. Bachman

During adolescence many young people initiate behaviors which can negatively affect their development and their future mental, physical, and material well-being. Behaviors which have been shown to be most detrimental to long-term well-being include dropping out of school, early sexual involvement, and the use and abuse of drugs (Hayes 1987; Hofferth and Hayes 1987; Jessor and Jessor 1977; Newcomb and Bentler 1988; see also Dryfoos, 1990, for a review). As noted by Newcomb and Bender (1989), "substance use and abuse during adolescence are strongly associated with other problem behaviors such as delinquency, precocious sexual behavior, deviant attitudes, or school dropout" (243). Young people who use and abuse drugs, who drop out of school, and/or who engage in early sexual activity have been found to have greater than average marital instability and interpersonal problems later in life, to have diminished lifetime earnings and limited future job prospects, to have poor mental and physical health as adults, to be at increased risk to contract sexually transmitted diseases and experience reproductive difficulties, and to become dependent on welfare (Dryfoos 1990; Hayes 1987; Hofferth and Hayes 1987; Jessor and Jessor 1977; Newcomb and Bentler 1988). Clearly, these various "problem behaviors" all have long term impact on the lives of young people; additionally, they appear to be linked together into what has been called a "problem behavior syndrome" (Dryfoos 1990; Jessor and Jessor 1977).

The extent to which young people exhibit various problem behaviors differs along a number of sociological dimensions including gender, region of residence, socioeconomic status, and racial/ethnic group membership (Bachman et al. 1991; Dryfoos 1990; Furstenberg et al. 1987; Rumberger 1983). In spite of fairly consistent findings of racial/ethnic differences in problem behaviors, and in drug use specifically, relatively little research has been done to explain why these differences exist.

The present study uses recent (1985–1989) large, nationally representative samples to examine one of the most prevalent problem behaviors among young people—the use and abuse of drugs. We investigate drug use among white, black, Mexican American, Puerto Rican and other Latino American, Asian American, and Native American youth. Our purpose is to explore whether the often large racial/ethnic differences in drug use may be attributable to racial/ethnic differences in background and in other important

123

lifestyle factors. The present study replicates and extends earlier research on adolescent drug use based on the senior class of 1979 (see Bachman, Johnston, and O'Malley 1981). Subsequent to the earlier study (which provided race data for only black and white youth), there have been significant changes in adolescent drug use and a growing concern with racial/ethnic differences in drug use (Bachman et al. 1990; Johnston, O'-Malley, and Bachman 1989). The nation's minority population has increased appreciably and is expected to continue to do so in the future (Dryfoos 1990). Because the minority population is disproportionately young and drug use is disproportionately concentrated among the young, research on drug use within these segments of the population has increasingly important implications for the nation as a whole.

Adolescent Problem Behavior

A variety of sociological and social-psychological theories have been developed to account for "deviant" or problem behavior among young people; these include social control theory (Hirshi 1969), differential association theory (Akers 1977), problem behavior theory (Jessor and Jessor 1977), self-derogation theory (Kaplan, Martin, and Robbins 1982), and socialization theory (Kandel 1980). Though often implicit rather than explicit, several similarities exist among theoretical models which undergird much of the research on problem behaviors.

The basic theoretical structure of much present research can be subsumed under the "problem behavior" model posited by the Jessors (1977). The Jessors' model is a comprehensive framework comprised of antecedent background variables and three systems of social-psychological and behavioral variables—the personality system, the perceived environment system, and the behavior system. The variables in the three primary systems interrelate to produce within the individual a greater or lesser proneness to become involved in problem behaviors. More specifically, the theory hypothesizes that young people who are less invested in traditional versus deviant behaviors, who are more strongly tied to peers than to parents, who are alienated from society, who have low self-esteem, and who hold unconventional beliefs, values, and attitudes are prone to become involved in problem behavior. The Jessors and their colleagues used their longitudinal database to test the theoretical model and found it to be quite successful in explaining adolescent problem behavior—particularly drug use (see Jessor 1987; Jessor and Jessor 1977).

The various background and lifestyle factors identified by the Jessors consistently have been found to influence adolescent problem behavior—including the use and abuse of drugs (see Bachman et al. 1981; Kandel 1980; Radosevich et al. 1980). Accordingly, research on individual and racial/ethnic differences in problem behavior typically considers background characteristics antecedent to problem behavior, such as age (Hayes 1987; Newcomb et al. 1987; Segal 1986), gender (Bachman et al. 1990; Bachman et al. 1991; Furstenburg et al. 1987; Kandel 1980; Rumberger 1983), parental education and employment status, and family income (Bachman et al. 1981; Kandel 1980; Rumberger 1983; Furstenburg et al. 1987), and region (Bachman et al. 1981; Dryfoos 1990; Johnston, O'Malley, and Bachman 1989; National Institute on

Drug Abuse 1990). The key background variable of concern in studies of subgroup differences is, of course, racial/ethnic group membership.

The lifestyle factors that researchers investigate in relation to drug use and other problem behaviors include variables that are both "distally" and "proximally" related to the behavior in question (cf. Jessor and Jessor 1977). According to Jessor and Jessor, distal variables are "relatively more remote in the logic of the causal chain, variables that do not directly or necessarily implicate problem behavior but can be linked to its occurrence by reliance on theory and the mediation of other variables" (27). Conversely, proximal variables are those which are "rather directly or obviously related to the occurrence of problem behavior" (28). The variables conceptually most proximal to a particular problem behavior include attitudes, beliefs, and interpersonal relationships specific to that behavior. In the case of drug use, drug use by close friends and parents, easy access to drugs, positive attitudes toward drug use, and the perception that there is little risk associated with the use of drugs are all very proximal and thus strongly related to adolescent drug use (Bachman, Johnston, O'Malley 1990; Bachman et al., 1988; Kandel 1980; Maddahian, Newcomb, and Bender 1986). More distally related lifestyle variables that past research has investigated include religious affiliation and commitment, school performance, truancy, attitudes toward school, college plans, dating, participation in extracurricular activities, employment, and political orientation (Bachman, et al. 1981; Barro and Kolstad 1987; Dryfoos 1990; Furstenberg et al. 1987; Jessor and Jessor 1977; Kandel 1980; Radosevich et al. 1980).

Racial/Ethnic Differences in Problem Behavior

In recent years there has been an increasing amount of research on the impact of background and lifestyle variables on racial/ethnic differences in a number of problem behaviors, including dropping out of school, sexual activity, and drug use. Barro and Kolstad (1987) found that black and Hispanic youth are more likely than white youth to drop out of school. However, when background (parental occupation and education, family income, family structure, number of siblings, and mother working) and lifestyle variables (religious affiliation and religiosity) are controlled, black youths' dropout rate is actually lower than that of white youth, and the difference in drop out rates of white youth and Hispanic youth is significantly reduced (National Center for Educational Statistics 1989). Similarly, adjusting for subgroup differences on background variables (gender, mother's education, racial composition of school) and a proximal lifestyle measure (proportion of peers sexually active) significantly attenuates racial/ethnic differences in sexual activity (Furstenberg et al. 1987).

Like other problem behaviors, the use of drugs in America is often perceived as a behavior found disproportionately among racial and ethnic minority group members. Contrary to popular belief, however, recent surveys of drinking and drug use patterns indicate that drug use is often more prevalent among white Americans than among people of color, and that such differences are especially large among adolescents (Austin 1988; Austin and Gilbert 1989; Austin, Prendergast, and Lee 1989; Bachman et al. 1990; Bachman et al. 1991; National Institute on Drug Abuse 1990; Prendergast et al. 1989).

SURVEYS OF DRUG USE

In a large representative sample of New York state 7–12th grade students, Kandel and her colleagues found that black and Hispanic students were less likely than white students to report any lifetime use of hard liquor, beer or wine, or marijuana (Kandel, Single, and Kessle 1976). Although black and Hispanic students also reported less lifetime use of most illicit drugs (e.g., LSD, barbiturates, amphetamines, and tranquilizers) than white students, they reported slightly higher lifetime use of cocaine and heroin. Similar percentages of black and white youth smoked cigarettes, but cigarette use was somewhat lower among Hispanic youth. The Kandel, Single, and Kessler (1976) sample also included small numbers of Asian American and Native American students. The Asian American youth reported the lowest use of hard liquor, wine or beer, cigarettes, and most illicit drugs, while the Native American youth reported the highest use of most drugs.

More recent studies tend to confirm most of the earlier findings reported by Kandel, Single, and Kessler. A 1983 study of a representative sample of 27,335 New York state 7–12th graders compared patterns of alcohol and drug use among white, black, West Indian, Hispanic, Asian, and Native American students (Welte and Barnes 1987). The black and West Indian students reported the lowest mean ounces of absolute alcohol consumed per day, the lowest percentage of heavy drinkers, and the fewest times drunk per month. Generally, the Hispanic students reported higher levels of alcohol and drug use than black students, but lower levels than white students. The Asian American students showed fairly low rates of alcohol use; however, those who did drink tended to drink heavily, particularly males. Asian American males also reported relatively high mean levels of illicit drug use. Native America youth in the sample reported the highest rates of heavy drinking and illicit drug use.

Using data from the Monitoring the Future study, Table 7.1 presents means and proportions on selected drug use measures for a number of racial and ethnic subgroups by sex (see Bachman et al. 1990). The information in the table is consistent with past research which shows that drug use is not disproportionately high among youth in most racial/ethnic minority groups. Relative to white seniors, the proportions who use any alcohol or cigarettes are significantly lower among black, Puerto Rican, Asian American, and Mexican American seniors (particularly females). Mean amounts of cigarette and alcohol use among these group are also generally lower than those of white seniors. On average, current cigarette use among Native American youth exceeds that among white youth, but 30 day alcohol use is comparable within the two groups. Heavy alcohol use (5 or more drinks in a single sitting) is quite similar among white and Native American youth, and Mexican American males, but distinctly lower among the other groups. Annual marijuana use does not significantly differ among white, Mexican, and Native American males. Among females, however, Mexican Americans' use is significantly lower than average while Native Americans' is significantly higher. Although annual cocaine use is distinctly lower than average among black and Asian American youth, prevalence and means for white, Mexican, Puerto Rican, and Native American youth are comparable. It should be noted that the patterns of subgroup difference shown in table 7.1 were based on seniors in the classes of 1985–1989; however, similar differences also were evident for most drugs from 1976 through 1984 (Bachman et al. 1990; Bachman et al. 1991).

Table 7.1. Racial/Ethnic Differences in Selected Types of Drug Use Among High School Seniors (1985–1989): Percentages and State Means for Males (M) and Females (F)

Drug Category[1]			White	Black	Mexican	Puerto Rican	Asian	Native American
30 Day Cigarette	M	%	29.8	15.6*	23.8*	22.0*	16.8*	36.8*
		X	1.70	1.29*	1.44*	1.45*	1.33*	1.94*
	F	%	34.0	13.3*	18.7*	24.7*	14.3*	43.6*
		X	1.78	1.24*	1.31*	1.44*	1.32*	2.18*
30 Day Alcohol	M	%	72.3	49.2*	65.0*	55.4*	43.7*	69.0
		X	2.82	2.10*	2.67*	2.23*	1.87*	2.90
	F	%	66.6	32.8*	50.5*	43.0*	34.2*	60.2
		X	2.42	1.52*	2.01*	1.73*	1.60*	2.35
Heavy Alcohol	M	%	48.1	24.0*	45.3	31.4*	19.4*	48.1
		X	2.15	1.58*	2.13	1.72*	1.38*	2.28
	F	%	31.3	9.3*	23.6*	14.5*	10.7*	33.7
		X	1.64	1.18*	1.50*	1.27*	1.21*	1.74
Annual Marijuana	M	%	40.2	29.8*	37.3	30.6*	19.6*	42.0
		X	2.32	1.90*	2.16	1.97*	1.57*	2.45
	F	%	36.0	18.4*	26.0*	21.3*	17.1*	44.0*
		X	2.01	1.44*	1.68*	1.50*	1.40*	2.30*
Annual Cocaine	M	%	11.9	6.1*	14.7	15.6	5.8*	14.2
		X	1.29	1.13*	1.37	1.44*	1.15*	1.39
	F	%	9.3	2.6*	7.6	8.2	5.7*	15.5*
		X	1.22	1.06*	1.17	1.17	1.12	1.35

Notes:
Asterisks (*) indicate that values are significantly (p ≤ .05) different from those for White youth.
% = Percent of seniors reporting any use.
X = Mean scale value on drug use measure.
1. Exact wording of measures are presented in Appendix A.

The studies cited above are based on samples of students. Although student samples may accurately represent the drug use of young people in school (see Johnston and O'Malley 1985) they do not include the drug use of young people who have dropped out. Because drug use is higher among adolescents who drop out of school (Dryfoos 1990) and because national drop out rates have been higher for black (22 percent), Hispanic (28 percent) and Native American youth (36 percent) than for white youth (15 percent) (National Center for Educational Statistics 1989:26), student samples may be a misleading basis for conclusions about the total population of youth. Household surveys include dropouts and absentees; such surveys thus provide one potential way to determine if, in the general population, minority youth use alcohol and other drugs less than their white counterparts.

Data from the National Household Survey on Drug Abuse indicate that black youth (ages 12–17) are less likely than white or Hispanic youth ever to have used or to be current users of cigarettes, alcohol, marijuana, cocaine, and most other illicit drugs (National Institute on Drug Abuse 1990). With the exception of cocaine, the Hispanic youth are also less likely than white youth ever to have used or to be current users of these drugs. Unfortunately, because of their small numbers in the general population, no national household data have been published on Asian American and Native American youth.

As noted by Adlaf, Smart, and Tan (1989), "A basic limitation of the literature on racial/ethnic differences in drug use is that it emphasizes differential rates of use between subgroups rather than looking for intervening or causally prior variables which may account for the observed differences" (2). A number of researchers suggest that racial and ethnic differences in adolescent drug use are heavily confounded by racial/ethnic differences in background variables and lifestyle factors (Gordon and McAlister 1982; Harper 1988). This might be taken to imply that the observed racial/ethnic differences in drug use can be "explained" if these various background and lifestyle "confounders" are statistically controlled.

Controlling for racial/ethnic group differences in background and lifestyle helps to explain the higher prevalence of sexual activity and dropping out among minority youth. However, since drug use is, generally, less prevalent among most categories of minority youth than among white youth, adjusting for factors such as family background might actually heighten rather than reduce some racial/ethnic group differences in adolescent drug use.

The Present Focus on Background and Lifestyle

Existing research has not fully resolved whether racial/ethnic differences in drug use result from differences in background and lifestyle factors. For example, Barnes and Welte (1986) found that black, West Indian, Hispanic, Asian American, and Native American youth were less likely than white youth to use alcohol, after controlling a number of background variables (sex and age), distal lifestyle variables (school misconduct and grades), and some very important proximal lifestyle variables (parental attitudes about children drinking, age of first drunkenness, and the proportion of friends that got drunk weekly). On the other hand, a longitudinal study of Los Angeles County youth found that when background (income) and key proximal lifestyle variables (availability from friends, ease of acquisition, and initial drug use) were controlled, drug use among black, Asian, and Hispanic youth was not significantly different from that of white youth (Maddahian, Newcomb, and Bentler 1986).

The Jessors note that despite the stronger empirical relationship between proximal variables and problem behaviors, the linkage between the distal variables and the problem behavior may be of greater theoretical interest (Jessor and Jessor 1977:28). Past research which attempted to explain racial/ethnic differences in drug use (and in other problem behaviors) typically controlled for background and both distal and very proximal lifestyle factors simultaneously. In all likelihood, the relationship between the most proximal variables and drug use are so strong (e.g., Bachman et al. 1988, table 4, reported a correlation of -.68 between disapproval of marijuana use and self-reported use of the drug) that they "wash out" the impact of the theoretically more interesting (and distal) variables on racial/ethnic differences.

Although controlling for proximal measures such as disapproval and peer use probably can "explain" the racial/ethnic differences in drug use, they provide little insight into the theoretically interesting mechanisms which may underlie the subgroup differences. For example, controlling for the proportion of friends who drink may cause the difference between the alcohol use of Native American and white youth to disappear. Nevertheless, it is still not clear why Native American youth *as a group* are more likely to drink than are white youth. If, however, controlling for less proximal variables such as socioeconomic status, religiosity, and educational factors causes the racial/ethnic differences in drug use to disappear, considerably more theoretical insight is gained. Several examples may help to make this point more clear.

A significant proportion of Native American families and youth are socioeconomically disadvantaged (Secretary's Task Force 1985). Drug use among Native American youth is also disproportionately high (Austin 1988). If differences between the drug use of Native American youth and that of other youth are eliminated when socioeconomic status is controlled, it strongly suggests that the subgroup differences in socioeconomic status underlie the subgroup differences in drug use.

As a second example, it has been noted that the historically fundamentalist orientation of the black church may have a profound impact on community norms regarding the use of drugs, particularly alcohol (Herd, 1985). Relative to the majority of American youth, black youth have been found to be more committed to religion (Bachman, Johnston, and O'Malley, 1987). Because religious commitment negatively relates to drug use, controlling for the strong religious orientation and fundamentalist affiliations of many black youth may help to account for their relatively low drug use.

A final example pertains to educational commitment. Past research indicates that young people who are strongly committed to educational endeavors are considerably less likely than their uncommitted counterparts to use drugs (e.g., Bachman et al. 1981; Barnes and Welte 1986; Kandel 1980; Schulenburg et al. 1990). As a group, Asian Americans' academic performance exceeds that of other groups and their drug use is, on average, less than that among other groups (Bachman et al. 1991; Sue and Okazaki 1990). When the academic success and strong commitment to educational pursuits among Asian American youth are taken into account, differences in their drug use and that of other groups may be sizably reduced if not completely eliminated.

We acknowledge the strong relationships between the conceptually most proximal variables (e.g., peer drug use) and drug use. We also acknowledge the potential of these variables to "explain" racial/ethnic differences in drug use, but consistent with the Jessors' (1977:28) we take the position that the relationship between the more distally related variables and drug use are of greater theoretical interest. Accordingly, our primary concern is to investigate the extent to which a number of variables, less proximal than drug-specific perceptions and attitudes, are able to account for racial/ethnic differences in adolescent drug use.

Methods

SAMPLE

The data used in this study are drawn from the Monitoring the Future project, which involves large, nationally representative samples of high school seniors surveyed annually by the University of Michigan's Survey Research Center. Detailed information on the samples, instruments, and validity of the measures are available elsewhere (Bachman and Johnston 1978; Bachman, Johnston, and O'Malley 1987; Johnston and O'-Malley 1985).

The study uses a multi-stage sampling procedure, which results in samples representative of high school seniors in the 48 coterminous states. First, particular geographic areas are selected. Next, schools are selected—approximately 135 schools participate each year. Finally, up to 400 seniors are selected in each school. In schools with fewer than 400 seniors, the entire senior class is typically included in the data collection. In schools with more than 400 students, the students are obtained by randomly selecting classrooms or some other unbiased method. The students complete machine readable, self-administered questionnaires during a normal class period.

Response rates average about 83 percent. Absence on the day of data collection is the primary reason that students are missed; additionally, about one percent refuse to complete the questionnaire. Obtained samples number about 16,000–17,000 each year. The total number of cases used in this analysis is approximately 77,500. The racial/ethnic distribution of the sample is as follows: 77.5 percent white (n = 60,062), 11.9 percent black (n = 9,223), 4.4 percent Mexican American (n = 3,410), 2.0 percent Puerto Rican and other Latin American (n = 1,550), 2.6 percent Asian American (n = 2015), 1.6 percent Native American (n = 1,240). Youth who did not indicate any racial/ethnic affiliation (approximately two percent of the sample) are omitted from the analyses; also omitted are those with missing data on the drug use measures (see Bachman et al. 1990). In light of past research which suggests race by gender interactions in drug use (e.g., Austin and Gilbert 1989; Prendergast et al. 1989; see also table 7.1), the data are analyzed separately for males and females.

Some of the racial/ethnic groups in the sample are rather small proportions of the nation's total population and are clustered in particular regions and schools. Since small sample sizes and clustered groupings may result in sizeable sampling errors for data from any single year, we combine data from 1985–1989. Additionally, design effects have been estimated and significance tests have been adjusted to account for error introduced by the multistage sampling procedure (see Bachman et al. 1990 and Bachman, Johnston, and O'Malley 1987, for a discussion of design effects for these samples).[1]

MEASURES

The analysis presented here focuses upon racial/ethnic differences in the use of tobacco, alcohol, marijuana, and cocaine. Brief descriptions of the measures are presented below. Complete wording of the dependent and independent measures is presented in appendix A. The tobacco use measure indicates how frequently the respondent has smoked cigarettes during the last thirty days. The alcohol measure indicates how often the respondent has had 5 or more drinks, in a row in the last two weeks. The marijuana and cocaine measures each indicate on how many occasions the respondent has used the drug in the last year. The annual versus thirty day measures of marijuana and cocaine were chosen to provide adequate variance.

The key independent variable in this study is the students' racial/ethnic group identification. The race/ethnicity groups are white, black, Mexican American, Puerto Rican and other Latino American, Asian American, and Native American. In addition to racial/ethnic group membership, the independent measures include background and lifestyle variables that past research (Bachman et al. 1981; Jessor and Jessor 1977; Kandel 1980) has identified as important correlates of adolescent drug use. The background variables include a mean of father's and mother's education (as a measure of socioeconomic status), number of parents in the home, region, and urbanicity. The lifestyle variables include (1) educational experiences and behaviors—high school curriculum (college preparatory or not), college plans (will attend a four year college versus will not), high school grades, and truancy (number of days skipped school in the last thirty days); (2) occupational experiences and behaviors—hours worked per week during the school year, and average weekly income; and (3) other lifestyle orientations—religious commitment (average of church attendance and importance of religion), political views (very conservative to radical), frequency of evenings out for fun and recreation, and frequency of dating.

Analyses and Results

The purpose of the present study is to determine if racial/ethnic differences in high school seniors' drug use result largely from variation in family background and lifestyle behaviors and experiences. In order to investigate this question, we estimate a series of dummy variable multiple regression equations, first controlling only for background, then controlling for both background and lifestyle.

If racial/ethnic subgroup differences in drug use are indeed attributable to differences in background and lifestyle, there should be no significant differences in the groups' mean levels of drug use after these variables are statistically controlled (i.e., the regression coefficients for the race dummy variable should approach zero, thus indicating that the racial/ethnic difference is "explained"). The regression models tested here estimate the levels of drug use which would occur among the various subgroups if they were all "average"—if they were distributed the same way as the total sample in terms of family background and lifestyle traits. Because white youth comprise the vast majority (77.5 percent) of the sample, this is tantamount to asking how the mean levels of drug use among the other subgroups would be affected if their background and lifestyle characteristics were much the same as those of white seniors.

Tables 7.2–7.5 present the results of the regression analyses for level of 30 day cigarette use, heavy alcohol use (five or more drinks in a single sitting), annual marijuana use, and annual cocaine use, respectively. In order to assess the independent impact of background factors on racial/ethnic differences in drug use and to examine the idea presented above that controlling for background alone may actually *increase* some racial/ethnic differences in drug use, the analysis proceeds in two stages. The first stage (the left half of each table, columns 1–4) presents the unstandardized (b) and standardized (β) regression coefficients (for males and females separately), when only background is controlled. The second stage of the analysis (the right half of each table, columns 5–8) presents the unstandardized and standardized regression coefficients, for males and females, when both background and lifestyle variables are controlled.

Figure 7.1 (Parts A–D) presents a more readily interpretable version of these findings, showing percentages of drug users in each racial/ethnic subgroup under three conditions: first unadjusted, then adjusted for background, and finally adjusted for both background and lifestyle.

RACIAL/ETHNIC DIFFERENCES IN DRUG USE:
THE IMPACT OF BACKGROUND

Past research indicates that drug use is generally lower than average among black and Asian youth, at intermediate levels among white and Hispanic youth, and higher than average among Native American youth. In this section we explore the question: Are these often large differences in drug use the result of variations in background characteristics, such as parents' education, family structure, urbanicity, and region of residence?

For most racial/ethnic subgroups and most drugs, the answer is no. For example, table 7.2 indicates that controlling for background factors alone does little to attenuate subgroup differences in 30 day cigarette use. Net of the background factors, black, Mexican, Puerto Rican, and Asian youth still smoke significantly less than white youth. In fact, if black youth were as likely as white youth to live in two-parent households, to have highly educated parents, and so forth, their average cigarette use might be even lower than reported. The same is true for Puerto Rican females. This information can be garnered from figure 7.1 (part A) and by comparing the unstandardized bivariate correlation coefficients (r) (see appendix B) with the multivariate beta coefficients (β) between racial/ethnic subgroup membership and cigarette use. For example,

Table 7.2. 30 Day Cigarette Use Controlling for Background and Background and Lifestyle Factors, by Sex (1985–1989): Unstandardized (b) and Standardized (β) Regression Coefficients

Variables	b M	b F	β M	β F	b M	b F	β M	β F
RACE								
Black	-.518	-.648	-.132***	-.176***	-.469	-.513	-.119***	-.139***
Mexican	-.308	-.486	-.051***	-.081***	-.242	-.363	-.040***	-.060***
Puerto Rican	-.346	-.546	-.039***	-.062***	-.282	-.383	-.032**	-.043***
Asian	-.304	-.431	-.041***	-.055***	-.028	-.196	-.004	-.025**
Native Am.	.132	.330	.013	.033**	.011	.208	.001	.021**
White	—	—	—	—	—	—	—	—
BACKGROUND								
Parents' Educ	-.008	-.008	-.072***	-.081***	.002	.001	.017	.006
# of Parents	-.197	-.203	-.092***	-.096***	-.109	-.106	-.051***	-.050***
Urbanicity	-.019	.049	-.015	-.039***	-.024	.009	-.020*	.007
Region								
South	-.086	-.123	-.032**	-.047***	-.042	-.034	-.016	-.013
Northeast	-.008	.155	-.003	.051***	-.036	.121	-.012	.040***
West	-.202	-.234	-.064***	-.073***	-.264	-.319	-.083***	-.100***
North Central	—	—	—	—	—	—	—	—
LIFESTYLE								
Educational								
Clg. Prep					-.118	-.175	-.047***	-.071***
College Plans					-.138	-.108	-.126***	-.102***
Grades					-.059	-.073	-.093***	-.112***
Truancy					.016	.018	.131***	.132***
Employment								
Hrs work/wk					.022	.022	.043**	.041**
Weekly Income					.013	.017	.024*	.030**
Other								
Religiosity					-.009	-.014	-.067***	-.106***
Political Views					.068	.066	.064***	.051***
Eves out					.097	.125	.103***	.132***
Dating					.030	.022	.037***	.031**
Constant	2.48	2.40			1.90	2.02		
Adj. Multiple R	.178	.241			.388	.442		
Adj. R-squared	.032	.058			.151	.196		

Notes:
*** p ≤ .001
** p ≤ .05
* p ≤ .10

Table 7.3. 5 + Drinks in a Row in the Last Two Weeks, Controlling for Background and Background Lifestyle Factors, by Sex (1985–1989): Unstandardized (b) and Standardized (β) Regression Coefficients

	b		β		b		β	
Variables	M	F	M	F	M	F	M	F
RACE								
Black	-.604	-.453	-.133***	-.141***	-.512	-.320	-.113***	-.099***
Mexican	-.027	-.101	-.004	-.019*	.049	-.001	.007	-.000
Puerto Rican	-.441	-.395	-.043***	-.051***	-.345	-.259	-.034***	-.033***
Asian	-.720	-.408	-.083***	-.059***	-.389	-.223	-.045***	-.032***
Native Am.	.053	.091	.005	.010	-.014	.051	-.001	.006
White	—	—	—	—	—	—	—	—
BACKGROUND								
Parents' Educ	-.003	-.001	-.025**	-.013	.003	.002	.022**	.019*
# of Parents	-.162	-.065	-.066***	-.035***	-.073	-.012	-.029***	-.007
Urbanicity	-.041	.007	-.029**	.006	-.076	-.039	-.053***	-.036***
Region								
South	-.166	-.193	-.054***	-.085***	-.110	-.122	-.036**	-.054***
Northeast	-.083	-.086	-.024*	.033***	-.130	-.120	-.037***	.046***
West	-.162	-.200	-.044***	-.072***	-.255	-.284	-.070***	-.120***
North Central	—	—	—	—	—	—	—	—
LIFESTYLE								
Educational								
Clg. Prep					-.067	-.039	-.023**	-.018
College Plans					-.041	-.012	-.033**	-.013
Grades					-.054	-.045	-.073***	-.080***
Truancy					.031	.024	.218***	.194***
Employment								
Hrs work/wk					.005	.005	.009	.010
Weekly Income					.024	.019	.038**	.040**
Other								
Religiosity					-.011	-.009	-.068***	-.078***
Political Views					.057	.041	.047***	.036***
Eves out					.225	.168	.206***	.204***
Dating					.049	.005	.054***	.007
Constant	2.81	1.88			1.43	1.23		
Adj. Multiple R	.172	.174			.444	.406		
Adj. R-squared	.030	.030			.197	.165		

Notes:
*** $p \leq .001$
** $p \leq .05$
* $p \leq .10$

Table 7.4. 5 + Annual Marijuana Use Controlling for Background and Background Lifestyle Factors, by Sex (1985–1989): Unstandardized (b) and Standardized (β) Regression Coefficients

Variables	b M	b F	β M	β F	b M	b F	β M	β F
RACE								
Black	-.488	-.617	-.077***	-.125***	-.371	-.354	-.059***	-.072***
Mexican	-.221	-.325	-.023**	-.040***	-.125	-.142	-.013	-.018*
Puerto Rican	-.527	-.701	-.037***	-.059***	-.423	-.454	-.030**	-.038***
Asian	-.897	-.708	-.075***	-.067***	-.496	-.435	-.041***	-.041***
Native Am.	.119	.279	.007	.021**	.009	.194	.001	.014
White	—	—	—	—	—	—	—	—
BACKGROUND								
Parents' Educ	-.001	-.000	-.004	-.002	.007	.006	.044***	.041***
# of Parents	-.275	-.248	-.080***	-.087***	-.133	-.130	-.039***	-.046***
Urbanicity	.100	.099	.050***	.059***	.050	.021	.025**	.013
Region								
South	-.155	-.160	-.036**	-.046***	-.046	-.025	-.011	-.007
Northeast	-.128	.204	.027**	.050***	.041	.120	.009	.030**
West	.131	.043	.026**	.010	-.016	-.125	-.003	-.029**
North Central	—	—	—	—	—	—	—	—
LIFESTYLE								
Educational								
Clg. Prep					-.025	-.068	-.006	-.021*
College Plans					-.058	-.041	-.033**	-.029**
Grades					-.105	-.075	-.103***	-.086***
Truancy					.042	.042	.212***	.227***
Employment								
Hrs work/wk					.001	.017	.001	.023*
Weekly Income					.021	.020	.024*	.027***
Other								
Religiosity					-.024	-.026	-.113***	-.143***
Political Views					.164	.117	.097***	.068***
Eves out					.245	.220	.162***	.174***
Dating					.036	.026	.028**	.027**
Constant	2.44	2.07			1.11	1.22		
Adj. Multiple R	.142	.189	.142		.427	.458	.427	.458
Adj. R-squared	.020	.036	.020	.036	.182	.210	.182	.210

Notes:
*** p ≤ .001
** p ≤ .05
* p ≤ .10

Table 7.5. Annual Cocaine Use Controlling for Background and Background Lifestyle Factors, by Sex (1985–1989): Unstandardized (b) and Standardized (β) Regression Coefficients

Variables	b M	b F	β M	β F	b M	b F	β M	β F
RACE								
Black	-.188	-.181	-.062***	-.076***	-.144	-.110	-.048***	-.046***
Mexican	-.014	-.103	-.003	-.026**	.010	-.056	.002	-.014
Puerto Rican	.027	-.144	.004	-.025**	.060	-.080	.009	-.014
Asian	-.248	-.174	-.043***	-.034**	-.116	-.095	.020**	-.019*
Native Am.	.088	.123	.012	.019*	.051	.089	.007	.014
White	—	—	—	—	—	—	—	—
BACKGROUND								
Parents' Educ	-.002	-.001	-.023**	-.014	.001	.001	.009	.019*
# of Parents	-.108	-.092	-.066***	-.067***	-.060	-.054	-.037***	-.039***
Urbanicity	.059	.050	.062***	.061***	.041	.028	.043***	.035**
Region								
South	.019	.007	.009	.004	.042	.039	.021	.023*
Northeast	.169	.164	.073***	.084***	.137	.140	.060***	.072***
West	.236	.201	.097***	.097***	.174	.143	.072***	.069***
North Central	—	—	—	—	—	—	—	—
LIFESTYLE								
Educational								
Clg. Prep					-.037	-.052	-.020	-.033**
College Plans					-.021	-.023	-.025**	-.034**
Grades					-.019	-.013	-.039***	-.032**
Truancy					.017	.015	.181***	.162***
Employment								
Hrs work/wk					-.009	.000	-.022	.001
Weekly Income					.024	.012	.058***	.034**
Other								
Religiosity					-.006	-.006	-.060***	-.068***
Political Views					.049	.041	.060***	.050***
Eves out					.070	.046	.097***	.076***
Dating					.020	.019	.033**	.040***
Constant	1.24	1.15			.605	.778		
Adj. Multiple R	.150	.161			.326	.306		
Adj. R-squared	.023	.026			.106	.094		

Notes:

*** p ≤ .001

** p ≤ .05

* p ≤ .10

figure 7.1 shows an unadjusted difference of 9 percent between white and Puerto Rican females' 30 day cigarette use. Controlling for background increases this difference to 13 percent. In correlational terms, the 30 day cigarette use correlation for Puerto Rican females is -.028. Controlling for background increases the strength of this relationship to = -.062.

Table 7.3 presents dummy variable regression results for racial/ethnic differences in heavy alcohol use. Table 7.1 showed that rates of 30 day and heavy alcohol use among Native American and white seniors are quite similar, followed by Mexican, Puerto Rican, black, and Asian seniors. Controlling for background factors reduces the relatively small differences in alcohol use between Mexican American and white seniors (see table 7.3; also part B of figure 7.1). Overall, controlling for background fails to reduce the differences in heavy alcohol use between white seniors and seniors in the other racial/ethnic groups.[2]

Table 7.4 presents regression results for annual marijuana use. The findings are much the same as those for cigarette and alcohol use—i.e., adjusting for background factors does not reduce most of the racial/ethnic differences. If anything, a number of the differences become larger when background is controlled (comparing bivariate r's to multivariate β's; see also part C of figure 7.1). Net of racial/ethnic group membership, living with both parents and living in a non-urban area both relate to low marijuana use.

The final drug use category examined is annual use of cocaine. Table 7.1 and part D of figure 7.1 indicate that annual cocaine use among Mexican and Puerto Rican males is slightly higher than average. Among females, use among Native Americans is especially pronounced. Controlling for differences in background reduces the relatively high levels of cocaine use among Mexican and Puerto Rican males. On the other hand, if Mexican and Puerto Rican *females* were more similar to the sample mean on the background variables, their levels of cocaine use, along with those of Asian and black females, would perhaps be even lower than those among white and Native American females.

Thus far we have determined that the often sizeable racial/ethnic differences in high school seniors' drug use are not largely the result of racial/ethnic differences in socioeconomic status (parental education), family structure, urbanicity, or region of residence. In fact, the data suggest that if black and Hispanic youth were as likely as white youth to have highly educated parents, to live with both parents, and to live outside of large urban areas, then their levels of use for a number of drugs would be even lower than reported. Moreover, the data suggest that the higher than average level of drug use reported by Native American youth may be linked to their relatively disadvantaged socioeconomic status. Once background differences are adjusted, the white versus Native American differences in drug use are virtually eliminated among male seniors and reduced or eliminated among female seniors.

RACIAL/ETHNIC DIFFERENCES IN DRUG USE:
THE IMPACT OF BACKGROUND AND LIFESTYLE

In light of the information presented above, the next question to be addressed is: After controlling for background differences, to what extent are reported racial/ethnic

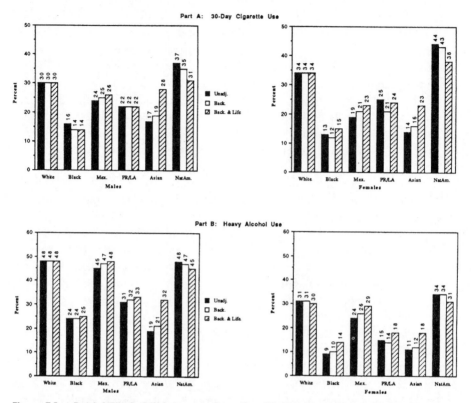

Figure 7.1.   Racial/Ethnic Differences in Drug Use (%). Unadjusted by Controlling for Background, and Adjusted by Controlling for Background and Lifestyle (1985–1989)

differences in licit and illicit drug use the result of different lifestyle beliefs, behaviors, and orientations such as educational and religious commitment, employment characteristics, political views, and time spent interacting with friends? The right-hand portions of tables 7.2–7.5 (and figure 7.1) present the data that address this question.

Table 7.2 indicates that after controlling for lifestyle factors some groups are more changed than others. On the one hand, black, Mexican, and Puerto Rican seniors still smoke at lower levels than their white counterparts. On the other hand, after these controls, Native American females smoke at only slightly higher levels than white females, and the mean differences in 30 day cigarette use between white and Asian American seniors are completely "explained" for males and substantially reduced for females (see figure 7.1, part A).

An examination of the correlation matrices in table 7.B shows that racial/ethnic differences in region, in the educationally related variables, and in the amount of peer interaction seem to be particularly important in accounting for the difference in level of 30 day cigarette use between white and Asian seniors. Cigarette use is relatively low in the West, where the Asian American seniors disproportionately reside. Asian American seniors also are more likely than average to be enrolled in college preparatory classes, to plan to graduate from a four-year college, and to have good grades. Because these variables all negatively relate to cigarette use and because Asian American youth

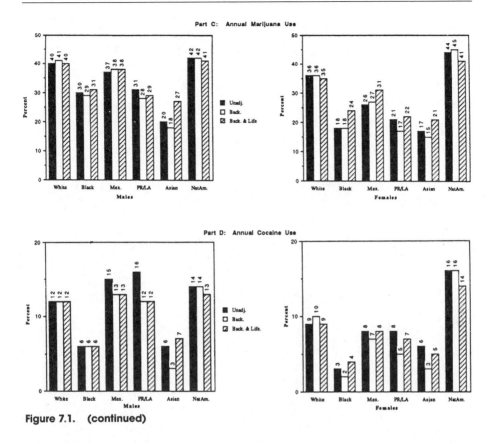

Figure 7.1.   (continued)

score higher than average on them, controlling for their influence reduces the Asian-white difference. Asian American seniors also report fewer than average evenings out for fun and recreation and dating. Since these behaviors positively relate to cigarette use, controlling these variables further reduces the Asian-white difference in current cigarette use.

Although some of the multivariate coefficients are weak, all of the lifestyle factors significantly relate to seniors' current cigarette use. Young people who are in college preparatory classes, who plan to graduate from college, who have good grades, and who are not truant smoke less than youth who are not as educationally involved and committed. Like truancy, increased hours working and increased income also relate to increased cigarette use. Among the other lifestyle factors, being committed to religion deters cigarette use, but having radical political views and spending a significant amount of time outside of the home for recreation and dating result in increased levels of cigarette use. The full model explains 15 percent of the variance in 30 day cigarette use among males and almost 20 percent for females.

Alcohol use prevalence rates among white, Mexican, and Native American seniors are fairly similar (see table 7.1). In the presence of the fairly extensive set of background and lifestyle controls, their differences in heavy alcohol use are even smaller and all non-significant (see table 7.3 and figure 7.1, part B). Controlling background and

Table 7.B. Correlation Matrix[1]

			1	2	3	4	5	6	7	8	9	10	11	12
	MALE MEAN	1.64												
	S.D.	1.24												
	MEAN	S.D.	2.07 1.66	2.07 1.43	2.24 1.99	1.28 .95	.78 .42	.11 .32	.05 .21	.02 .14	.03 .17	.02 .12	37.19 11.81	
FEMALE			1.64 1.24	2.07 1.66	2.07 1.43	2.24 1.99	1.28 .95	.78 .42	.11 .32	.05 .21	.02 .14	.03 .17	.02 .12	37.19 11.81
1. 30 day cigs	1.68	1.23		.328	.327	.408	.276	.106	-.097	-.035	-.022	-.042	.031	-.062
2. 30 day alcohol	2.26	1.39	.382		.797	.473	.308	.139	-.125	-.005	-.040	-.085	.015	.004
3. 5+drinks	1.56	1.07	.364	.718		.461	.310	.120	-.115	.009	-.033	-.081	.018	-.024
4. 12 month MJ	1.91	1.64	.486	.500	.438		.518	.075	-.060	-.009	-.019	-.058	.014	.010
5. 12 month coke	1.20	.79	.311	.287	.268	.483		.026	-.053	.021	.025	-.023	.015	-.010
6. White	.77	.42	.150	.214	.136	.119	.056		-.667	-.407	-.269	-.321	-.237	.180
7. Black	.13	.33	-.136	-.195	-.131	-.106	-.067	-.698		-.077	-.051	-.061	-.045	-.083
8. Mexican	.04	.20	-.064	-.038	-.013	-.029	-.006	-.390	-.081		-.031	-.037	-.027	-.212
9. Puerto Rican	.02	.14	-.028	-.053	-.039	-.035	-.004	-.260	-.054	-.030		-.024	-.018	-.063
10. Asian	.03	.16	-.047	-.075	-.053	-.050	-.015	-.292	-.061	-.034	-.023		-.022	.066
11. Native Am.	.02	.12	.050	.007	.020	.029	.024	-.226	-.047	-.026	-.017	-.020		-.063
12. Parent Ed	36.51	11.92	-.052	.068	.005	.022	.006	.198	-.098	-.204	-.071	.052	-.063	
13. #Parents	1.67	.58	-.063	.021	-.001	-.056	-.050	.198	-.214	-.009	-.049	.011	-.044	.107
14. Urbanicity	3.87	.97	.018	.014	-.009	.056	.067	-.106	.055	.039	.093	.078	-.054	.120
15. South	.33	.47	-.068	-.097	-.072	-.093	-.077	-.163	.204	.045	-.020	-.055	.023	-.095
16. NE	.21	.41	.098	.043	.018	.076	.071	.050	-.039	-.104	.099	.008	-.015	.022
17. NCentral	.28	.45	.043	.078	.083	.014	-.051	.135	-.071	-.092	-.048	-.038	-.016	.025
18. West	.18	.39	-.070	-.018	-.027	.018	.079	-.010	-.127	.162	-.023	.104	.006	.063
19. Curriculum	.52	.50	-.173	-.024	-.074	-.090	-.077	.126	-.097	-.077	-.023	.040	-.067	.308
20. College plans	2.96	1.16	-.206	-.036	-.079	-.096	-.075	.027	-.015	-.048	.007	.073	-.072	.359
21. HS grades	5.99	1.88	-.207	-.115	-.138	-.169	-.103	.133	-.130	-.058	-.035	.053	-.039	.192
22. Truancy	15.38	8.85	.217	.295	.265	.320	.227	.003	-.048	.037	.014	.027	.007	.011
23. Hrs. work/wk	3.95	2.26	.129	.117	.086	.106	.072	.099	-.082	-.043	-.015	-.036	.014	-.052
24. Total week $	5.68	2.21	.128	.142	.107	.126	.096	.027	-.001	-.032	.007	-.043	.009	-.011
25. Religiosity	28.05	8.98	-.212	-.209	-.158	-.243	-.147	-.150	.171	.054	.019	-.030	-.021	.009
26. Politics	3.16	.96	.092	.105	.078	.129	.087	-.022	.012	.015	.002	.022	-.014	.047
27. Evenings out	3.36	1.30	.229	.327	.285	.275	.150	.172	-.123	-.058	-.048	-.083	-.001	.031
28. Dates/week	3.61	1.65	.160	.191	.144	.159	.112	.144	-.106	-.055	-.030	-.080	.019	-.018

(continued)

Note:
1. Means, standard deviations, and correlations above the diagonal are for males and below the diagonal are for females.

Table 7.B. Correlation Matrix[1] (Continued)

	13	14	15	16	17	18	19	20	21	22	23	24	25	26	27	28
MALE MEAN	1.68	3.84	.32	.22	.27	.19	.49	2.89	5.45	16.68	4.22	6.09	25.99	3.11	3.63	3.40
S.D.	.58	1.00	.47	.41	.44	.39	.50	1.13	1.96	9.98	2.40	2.27	9.22	1.18	1.31	1.56
FEMALE																
1. 30 day cigs	-.066	-.040	-.017	.023	.047	-.056	-.178	-.224	-.198	.207	.134	.125	-.151	.105	.183	.119
2. 30 day alcohol	-.023	-.036	-.034	.014	.040	-.020	-.095	-.104	-.152	.309	.115	.152	-.167	.103	.304	.190
3. 5+ drinks	-.035	-.049	-.038	-.002	.057	-.019	-.117	-.128	-.160	.301	.099	.126	-.149	.099	.299	.174
4. 12 month MJ	-.060	.047	-.067	.041	.006	.030	-.095	-.109	-.185	.305	.076	.110	-.201	.156	.251	.127
5. 12 month coke	-.055	.070	-.063	.056	-.056	.079	-.076	-.076	-.112	.253	.064	.112	-.132	.104	.167	.102
6. White	.201	-.110	-.127	.042	.136	-.047	.109	.037	.102	-.017	.082	.044	-.123	-.026	.071	.102
7. Black	-.213	.051	.176	-.027	-.060	-.115	-.088	-.039	-.128	-.032	-.072	-.020	.137	.017	-.013	-.064
8. Mexican	-.022	.034	.037	-.110	-.094	.180	-.078	-.050	-.040	.052	-.018	-.019	.049	.017	-.036	-.016
9. Puerto Rican	-.044	.092	-.020	.108	-.067	-.014	-.020	.005	-.032	.021	-.001	.003	.002	.011	-.028	-.014
10. Asian	-.001	.094	-.066	.011	-.050	.125	.064	.098	.082	.011	-.059	-.053	.000	-.005	-.079	-.106
11. Native Am.	-.045	-.049	.025	-.024	-.002	-.003	-.074	-.078	-.030	.008	.020	.005	-.019	.012	-.001	.009
12. Parent Ed	.085	.130	-.096	.041	.011	.059	.314	.359	.200	-.016	-.115	-.045	.016	.004	-.008	.010
13. #Parents		-.002	-.050	.015	.039	.061	.128	.099	-.010	-.062	-.020	-.034	.059	-.047	.001	.004
14. Urbanicity	-.004		-.167	.172	-.024	-.001	.117	.162	.104	.056	-.017	.097	-.072	.016	.024	.005
15. South	-.068	-.167		-.366	-.419	-.333	.099	.033	.018	-.066	-.059	-.015	.160	-.051	.026	.005
16. NE	.013	.172	-.363		-.322	-.256	.005	-.001	.009	.012	.017	.043	-.108	.049	.041	.018
17. NCentral	.044	-.024	-.438	-.317		-.293	-.006	.037	-.024	.004	-.002	-.032	-.014	-.002	-.046	.007
18. West	.019	.051	-.333	-.241	-.291		-.022	.030	-.004	.135	.004	.010	-.062	.012	-.071	-.032
19. Curriculum	.131	.064	-.067	.083	.015	-.022		.531	.389	-.111	-.156	-.104	.069	-.031	-.070	-.064
20. College plans	.107	.129	-.028	.012	-.006	.030	.493		.376	-.090	-.175	-.101	.114	-.023	-.101	-.030
21. HS grades	.166	-.064	.050	-.011	-.024	-.021	.368	.332		-.183	-.117	-.103	.113	-.057	.205	-.036
22. Truancy	-.037	.085	-.109	.017	-.041	.163	-.097	-.056	-.197		.111	.151	-.144	.105	.008	.112
23. Hrs. work/wk	-.029	.061	-.090	.044	.030	.029	-.067	-.073	-.050	.103		.664	-.061	.017	.105	.140
24. Total week $	-.055	.142	-.064	.069	-.007	.016	-.044	-.025	-.059	.127	.664		-.077	.020	.127	.202
25. Religiosity	.065	-.077	.174	-.123	-.006	-.076	.058	.096	.098	-.156	-.095	-.093		-.132	-.085	-.015
26. Politics	-.044	.039	-.063	.059	.003	.014	.010	.020	-.041	.088	.012	.012	-.179		.049	.022
27. Evenings out	.045	.039	-.062	.036	.048	-.018	-.039	-.041	-.065	.201	.038	.127	-.085	.049		.324
28. Dates/week	.003	.005	.005	.018	.007	-.032	-.064	-.104	-.048	.104	.129	.176	-.075	-.004	.394	

Note:
1. Means, standard deviations, and correlations above the diagonal are for males and below the diagonal are for females.

lifestyle factors reduces the magnitude of the differences between white seniors' rates of heavy alcohol use and the rates for black, Puerto Rican, and Asian American seniors; still, significant differences remain.

The beta coefficients (β) indicate that truancy, evenings out, and to a lesser extent low religious commitment, are particularly important correlates of alcohol use. Along with these variables, having educated parents, not living in the West, not living in an urban area, earning poor grades, having a large income, and radical political views all relate to higher levels of current and heavy alcohol use, for both males and females. The model accounts for roughly 20 percent of the variance in males' heavy alcohol use and 17 percent of the variance in females' heavy alcohol use.

The pattern of mean racial/ethnic differences in annual marijuana use is fairly similar to that for differences in cigarette and alcohol use (see table 7.1 and figure 7.1). Native Americans, followed by white males and females, have the highest levels of marijuana use. Use among Mexican youth is slightly lower, followed by even lower levels of use for Puerto Rican, black and Asian seniors. The right-hand columns in table 7.4 present regression results for racial/ethnic differences in annual marijuana use, after introducing the lifestyle controls. After these adjustments, the differences among the white, Native American, and Mexican American youth remain small among the males, whereas among the females the differences are reduced. The differences between white youth and the other groups are also considerably reduced, but remain significant (see also part C of figure 7.1).

Truancy, frequency of evenings out, low religious commitment, poor grades, and level of political radicalism are the variables which relate most strongly to level of annual marijuana use. Having highly educated parents and not living with both parents also relate to increased marijuana use when the other lifestyle factors are controlled. Although the addition of the lifestyle controls does not fully explain all of the racial/ethnic differences in marijuana use, it considerably increases the predictive power of the model, explaining 18 percent of the variance in males' annual marijuana use and 21 percent in females' use.

The final regression model reveals the impact of the lifestyle factors on the relatively small racial/ethnic differences in annual cocaine use which remain after background is controlled. Among Asian males and black, Mexican, Puerto Rican, and Asian females, adjusting for background alone reduces their cocaine use, thus enlarging their differences from white youth. Conversely, incorporating the lifestyle measures increases the levels of annual cocaine use among these groups, thus reducing the differences between them and white seniors (see table 7.5 and part D of figure 7.1). The addition of the lifestyle controls has little impact on the cocaine use of black, Mexican, Puerto Rican, and Native American males. Although truancy is overwhelmingly the most powerful correlate of cocaine use, evenings out, religious commitment, and living in the Northeast or West (relative to North Central) are also important correlates. Though relatively weak, the relationships between family structure, urbanicity, college plans, grades, weekly income, political orientation, dating, and cocaine use also remain significant. The full model explains 11 percent and 9 percent of the variance in annual cocaine use for males and females, respectively.

The information in tables 7.2–7.5 and figure 7.1 suggests that if the subgroups did not differ along the background and lifestyle dimensions examined here, then levels of drug use by Native American, white, and Mexican seniors would be virtually the same. Nevertheless, sizeable differences would remain between these three relatively high use groups and the three relatively low use groups—Puerto Rican, black, and Asian seniors. This distinction exists across drugs except for cocaine, where use among Puerto Rican males is unexpectedly high.

Discussion

The model tested here is broad, and it presumes that background and lifestyle variables impact the drug use of young people from different racial/ethnic subgroups in much the same way; accordingly, it presumes that subgroup differences in drug use result primarily from subgroup differences in the measured independent variables. To whatever extent this basic presumption is wrong and the variables in the model impact the drug use of young people from different racial/ethnic groups differently, then to that same extent, the additive model we test here would be unable to account fully for the subgroup differences in drug use.

The results of this study indicate that a number of the sizeable racial and ethnic group differences in drug use among high school seniors are largely or at least partially the result of racial/ethnic differences in background and lifestyle factors. Admittedly, the most powerful lifestyle predictors (current frequencies of truancy and of evenings out for fun and recreation), are at least arguably proximal enough to be both causes and consequences of drug use. (They are not, however, nearly as closely related to drug use as the most proximal lifestyle variables such as peer drug use and perceived risk.)

In any case, it should be noted that even after controlling for background and lifestyle differences, some small but significant racial/ethnic differences in levels of drug use remain, particularly between the two largest groups—black and white seniors. Caveats, potential directions toward further explaining racial/ethnic differences in drug use, along with theoretical and policy implications of this research, are presented below.

CAVEATS AND CONCERNS

"Race" as a biological concept has little validity, and objectively measuring race/ethnicity (even as a purely sociological concept) is a difficult and largely subjective task (cf. Smith 1984). Nevertheless, a number of adolescent problem behaviors, including drug use, differ according to the racial/ethnic group with which young people identify themselves.

The research presented here examined drug use differences among six large aggregates of youth. In reality there are numerous refinements and subgroups that could be defined within each racial/ethnic grouping. For example, it has been estimated that "within the broad designation 'Asian/Pacific Islander' are a least 32 different national and ethnic groups" (Austin et al. 1989:1). Similarly, the groups we label "black" and "white" include persons of West Indian, Caribbean, South American, English, Irish,

German, and numerous other descents. Indeed, research that has used more refined race/ethnicity measures than used here has found important within racial/ethnic group differences in alcohol and drug use (e.g., Adlaf et al. 1989; Barnes and Welte 1987). In fact, data presented here, in which youth with Mexican origins are distinguished from those with Puerto Rican and other Latino origins, testify to the potential amount of diversity in drug use behaviors within a particular racial/ethnic group. Unfortunately, geographic clustering and relatively small numbers in the general population make detailed study of numerous groups using our national (versus regional or local) data difficult, if not impossible.

Another obvious caveat is that this study of high school seniors does not include dropouts. We know that drug use among dropouts exceeds that of youth who do not drop out of school (Dryfoos 1990). We also know that dropout rates among black, Hispanic, and Native American youth are higher than average (National Center for Educational Statistics 1989). Although national dropout rates among black and white youth have become more similar in recent years (National Center for Educational Statistics 1989), dropout rates in high poverty, high crime areas of the nation's decaying inner cities may greatly exceed national norms. Because the residents of these areas are often black and Hispanic, the relatively favorable information presented here on drug use among black and Hispanic seniors, relative to white seniors, should not lead to the faulty conclusion that the use and abuse of drugs by black and Hispanic youth is not a problem. The existing research indicates that people of color disproportionately suffer the negative physical and social consequences of drug use. It is estimated that 80 percent of the excess deaths[3] among black and other minority groups each year are at least partially attributable to the use of tobacco, alcohol, and illicit drugs, and that minority group members are disproportionately both victims and perpetrators of drug-related violence (Secretary's Task Force 1986).

In addition to the aforementioned caveats, the reliability and validity of the findings are areas of potential concern. Using the National Longitudinal Survey of Youth, Mensch and Kandel (1988) report that black and Hispanic youth are more likely than white youth to underreport their use of marijuana. It should be noted, however, that this underreporting occurred only at the lowest levels of use, and that no such underreporting was reported for the licit drugs, alcohol and cigarettes, which show the largest subgroup differences in use. Additionally, the National Longitudinal Survey uses face-to-face interviews versus the self-administered, confidential questionnaires used by Monitoring the Future.

Analyses presented elsewhere (Bachman et al. 1991) indicate that the findings of lower drug use among most minority youth relative to white youth replicate over time (from 1976–1989), and thus are reliable. With regard to the validity of these differences, past research has shown that young people who are more heavily involved with drugs perceive less risk in the use of drugs, have more positive attitudes toward drug use, have greater access to drugs, began to use drugs at an early age, and have more friends who use drugs than youth who abstain or use drugs only moderately (Bachman et al. 1989; Bentler and Huba 1987; Harford 1986; Welte and Barnes 1987). Additional analyses of the Monitoring the Future data indicate that relative to white seniors, black seniors perceive greater risk in using drugs, are more likely to disapprove of most forms of drug use, report having greater difficultly obtaining most drugs, began drug use at a later age, and have fewer friends that use drugs (Wallace forthcoming). Based on these and other findings discussed in detail elsewhere (see Bachman et al. 1991), we believe that the self-reports of lower drug use among most minority youth compared to white youth are, on the whole, valid.

THEORETICAL AND POLICY IMPLICATIONS

Despite our oversimplification of racial/ethnic group membership and the omission of dropouts, this study provides important empirical data and potentially valuable theoretical and policy relevant information on subgroup differences in adolescent drug use. The present research documents sizeable racial/ethnic differences in high school seniors' drug use and identifies a number of factors which may help to explain these differences. Understanding the underlying mechanisms by which these differences occur and identifying racial/ethnic differences in these mechanisms should be a priority for future theoretical and empirical research. This is particularly true in instances in which the differences in drug use are particularly pronounced (for example, white-Asian and white-black).

For Asian youth, it appears that their strong commitment to educational advancement and academic success is particularly important in explaining their lower than average use of drugs. Nevertheless, the causal mechanisms that underlie the relationship between their educational success and their low use of drugs are still not clear. Given the strong relationship between truancy and drug use, one might expect that Asian youth do not skip school and thus are not prone to become involved in problem behavior such as drug use. However, examination of the bivariate relationship between truancy and racial/ethnic group (see table 7.B) reveals that the Asian youth are not less likely than average to skip school, and thus differences in truancy rates probably do not contribute to the white-Asian differences in drug use.

Another possible explanation for white-Asian differences in drug use might lie in the fact that Asian youth spend less time in peer-oriented activities than other youth. The reason for this, as well as their concomitant educational success (as measured by grades), may be that they spend a significant portion of their time engaged in educationally-oriented activities (such as doing homework). Hypotheses of this nature are both empirically testable and theoretically interesting.

Like Asian youth, black youth use drugs at considerably lower levels than average. Unlike Asian youth, however, most black youth do not experience greater than average academic success. Black youth are, however, more strongly committed than other youth to religion (Bachman et al. 1987). In light of this fact, one potentially fruitful area of research for explaining black-white differences in drug use would be a careful study of the impact of religion. Past research has shown that religious commitment is a significant deterrent to the use of drugs among adolescents (Bachman et al., 1981; Burkett 1980; Lorch and Hughes 1985). Also, not only are black youth more strongly committed to religion than white youth, they are also more likely than white youth to belong to fundamentalist religious denominations (Bachman et al. 1987). According to Herd (1985), "The Protestant church, especially in its fundamentalist branches is a major force for abstinence in the black population" (163).

The findings presented here reaffirm the importance of two-parent families, educational success, religious commitment, and supervised activities as deterrents to adolescent drug use. At a policy level, comprehensive, cooperative efforts between the school, church, community, and individual families are needed to reduce and prevent drug use and other adolescent problem behaviors. In light of the rather strong negative relationship between academic achievement orientation and drug use as reported by Schulenberg et al. (1990) and others, it appears that tutoring, truancy reduction, and dropout prevention programs are particularly important. Also needed are after-school programs, life-skills training, and programs and policies which can strengthen young people's involvement and commitment to other activities and organizations (e.g., church) shown to deter or reduce involvement in drug use.

The results presented here also indicate that social policies which address the socioeconomic disadvantage that many minority group youth suffer could have important effects on their drug use. For example, the relatively high rates of drug use among Native American youth seem completely explainable in terms of these youths' relatively disadvantaged background. Equally important is the information that if the background status of black and Hispanic youth were more comparable to that of white youth, their levels of drug use might be even lower than reported.

Although we can only speculate, the high rates of drug-related problems which are concentrated among minority group members may result from a relatively small core of heavy drug abusers who not only harm themselves but also prey upon their communities to support their lifestyle. Additionally, the poverty, inadequate educational systems, and joblessness that characterize the inner cities in which many minority youth live, all tend to make the drug trade relatively attractive as a source of income, job training, and employment. While affluent suburban drug users may come to the inner cities to purchase drugs, the violence, prostitution, and other drug-related behaviors and incidents which appear on the evening news and the front page of the newspapers are typically contained within the inner city. Accordingly, the "drug problem" continues to be characterized as a problem of the ghettoes, barrios, and reservations. Among most young people, however, the present findings suggest that the problem is by no means limited to—or even disproportionately concentrated among—the racial/ethnic minority groups.

Appendix A: Variable Names and Descriptions

1. CIGARETTES: How frequently have you smoked cigarettes during the past 30 days? 1 = none, 2 = <1/day, 3 = 1–5/day, 4 = 1/2 pack/day, 5 = 1 pack/day, 6 = 1.5 packs/day, 7 = 2 or more packs/day
2. ALCOHOL: On how many occasions have you had alcoholic beverages to drink during the last 30 days? 1 = 0 occasions, 2 = 1–2, 3 = 3–5, 4 = 6–9, 5 = 10–19, 6 = 20–39, 7 = 40 or more
3. HEAVY ALCOHOL: On how many occasions in the last two weeks have you had 5 or more drinks in a row? 1 = 0 occasions, 2 = 1, 3 = 2, 4 = 3–5, 5 = 6–9, 6 = 10 or more

4. MARIJUANA: On how many occasions (if any) have you used marijuana (grass, pot) or hashsish (hash, hash oil) during the last 12 months? 1 = 0 occasions, 2 = 1–2, 3 = 3–5, 4 = 6–9, 5 = 10–19, 6 = 20–39, 7 = 40 or more

5. COCAINE: On how many occasions have you used cocaine (sometimes called "coke," "crack," or "rock"), during the last 12 months? 1 = 0 occasions, 2 = 1–2, 3 = 3–5, 4 = 6–9, 5 = 10–19, 6 = 20–39, 7 = 40 or more

RACE: respondents racial/ethnic identification.

6. White
7. Black
8. Mexican American
9. Puerto Rican
10. Asian American
11. Native American
12. PARENTAL EDUCATION: mean of parents' education. 1 = completed grade school or less, 2 = some high school, 3 = completed high school, 4 = some college, 5 = completed college, 6 = graduate or professional school after college
13. # PARENTS IN THE HOME: 0 = none, 1 = 1 parent, 2 = 2 both parents
14. URBANICITY: 1 = Farm, 2 = country (not a farm), 3 = Non-SMSA, 4 = Other SMSA, 5 = Large SMSA

REGION

15. Northeast
16. South
17. West
18. North Central
19. CURRICULUM: Which of the following best describes your present high school program? 1 = academic or college prep, 0 = other
20. COLLEGE PLANS: How likely is it that you will graduate from college (four-year) program? 1 = definitely won't, 2 = probably won't, 3 = probably will, 4 = definitely will
21. GRADES: Which of the following best describes your average grade in high school so far? 1 = D, 2 = C-, 3 = C, 4 = C+, 5 = B-, 6 = B, 7 = B+, 8 = A-, 9 = A
22. TRUANCY: mean of number of whole days of school skipped in the last four weeks and number of classes skipped in the last four weeks. Coded from 10–65 where 10 = not at all and 65 = approximately 11+ times truant
23. HOURS WORKED: On average over the school year, how many hours per week do you work in a paid or unpaid job? 1 = none, 2 = 5 or less hours, 3 = 6 to 10 hours, 4 = 11 to 15 hours, 5 = 16 to 20 hours, 6 = 21 to 25 hours, 7 = 26 to 30 hours, 8 = more than 30 hours
24. WEEKLY INCOME: Total weekly income, including job, allowances, etc. 1 = none, 2 = $1–5, 3 = $6–10, 4 = $11–20, 5 = $21–35, 6 = $36–50, 7 = $51–75, 8 = $76–125, 9 = $126+
25. RELIGIOSITY: Mean of how often student attends religious services and how important religion is in the student's life. 1 = very low, 2 = low, 3 = high, 4 = very high
26. POLITICAL VIEWS: How would you describe your political beliefs? 1 = very conservative, 2 = conservative, 3 = moderate, 4 = liberal, 5 = very liberal, 6 = radical

27. EVENINGS OUT: During a typical week, on how many evenings do you go out for fun and recreation? 1 = less than one, 2 = one, 3 = two, 4 = three, 5 = four or five, 6 = six or seven

28. DATING: On average, how often do you go out with a date (or your spouse if you are married)? 1 = never, 2 = once a month or less, 3 = 2 or 3 times a month, 4 = once a week, 5 = 2 or 3 times a week, 6 = over 3 times a week

Notes

This work was supported by Research Grant R 01 DA 01411 from the National institute on Drug Abuse and a Ford Dissertation Fellowship to the first author. The authors thank Lisa Holland, Maria Krysan, Howard Schuman, John Schulenberg, Dan Zahs, and four anonymous reviewers for comments on an earlier version of this chapter. We also thank Sharon Leech for preparation of table 7.B. Correspondence to Wallace, Institute for Social Research, Room 3343, University of Michigan, Ann Arbor, MI 48106-1248.

1. An overall design effect of 4.4 was estimated, thus reducing the total sample from approximately 77,500 to 17,600. The significance tests are based on the reduced N.

2. An analysis of subgroup differences in and variables related to the rate of 30 day use of alcohol produced results that parallel those reported for heavy alcohol use (see correlations in table 7.B).

3. Excess deaths are defined as deaths that would not have occurred if people of color had the same age and sex-specific death rate as the white population (Secretary's Task Force 1986).

References

Adlaf, Edward M., Reginald G. Smart, and S. H. Tan. 1989. "Ethnicity and drug use: A critical look." *International Journal of the Addictions* 24:1–18.

Akers, Ronald L., Marvin D. Krohn, Lonn Lanza-Kaduce, and Marcia Radosevich. 1979. "Social learning and deviant behavior: A specific test of a general theory." *American Sociological Review* 44:636–55.

Austin, Gregory A. 1988. "Substance abuse among minority youth: Native Americans." *Prevention Research Update* 2:1–25.

Austin, Gregory A., and M. Jean Gilbert. 1989. "Substance abuse among Latino youth." *Prevention Research Update* 3:1–26.

Austin, Gregory A., Michael Prendergast, and Harvey Lee. 1989. "Substance abuse among Asian American youth." *Prevention Research Update* 5:1–26.

Bachman, Jerald G., Lloyd D. Johnston, and Patrick M. O'Malley. 1981. "Smoking, drinking, and drug use among American high school students: Correlates and trends, 1975–1979." *American Journal of Public Health* 71:59–69.

Bachman, Jerald G., and Lloyd Johnston. 1978. *The Monitoring the Future Project: Design and Procedures.* (Monitoring the Future Occasional Paper No. 1). Ann Arbor, Mich.: Institute for Social Research.

Bachman, Jerald G., Lloyd D. Johnston, and Patrick M. O'Malley. 1987. *Monitoring the Future: Questionnaire Responses from the Nation's High School Seniors.* Ann Arbor, Mich.: Institute for Social Research.

———. 1990. "Explaining the recent decline in cocaine use among young adults: Further evidence that perceived risks and disapproval lead to reduced drug use." *Journal of Health and Social Behavior* 31:173–184.

Bachman, Jerald G., Lloyd D. Johnston, Patrick M. O'Malley, and Ronald H. Humphrey. 1988. "Explaining the recent decline in marijuana use: Differentiating the effects of perceived risks, disapproval, and general lifestyle factors." *Journal of Health and Social Behavior* 29:92–112.

Bachman, Jerald G., John M. Wallace, Jr., Patrick O'Malley, Lloyd Johnston, and Candace L. Kurth. 1990. Drug use among black, white, Hispanic, Native American, and Asian American high school seniors (1976–1989): Prevalence, trends, and correlates. (Monitoring the Future Occasional Paper No. 30). Ann Arbor, Mich.: Institute for Social Research.

Bachman, Jerald G., John M. Wallace, Jr., Patrick O'Malley, Lloyd Johnston, Candace L. Kurth, and Harold W. Neighbors. 1991. "Racial/ethnic differences in smoking, drinking, and illicit drug use among American high school seniors, 1976–89." *American Journal of Public Health* 81:372–377.

Barnes, Grace M., and John W. Welte. 1986. "Patterns and predictors of alcohol use among 7–12th grade students in New York state." *Journal of Studies on Alcohol* 47:53–62.

Barro, Stephen, and Andrew Kolstad. 1987. "Who drops out of school?: Findings from high school and beyond" cited in National Center for Education Statistics (1989) Dropout Rates in the United States: 1988. Analysis Report September, 1989 U.S. Department of Education Office of Educational Research and Improvement. Washington, D.C.: Government Printing Office.

Burkett, Steven R. 1980. "Religiosity, beliefs, normative standards and adolescent drinking." *Journal of Studies on Alcohol* 41:662–671.

Dryfoos, Joy G. 1990. *Adolescents at Risk.* New York: Oxford University Press.

Furstenberg, Jr., Frank F., S. Philip Morgan, Kristin A. Moore, and James L. Peterson. 1987. "Race differences in the timing of adolescent intercourse." *American Sociological Review* 52:511–518.

Gordon, Nancy P., and Alfred L. McAlister. 1982. "Adolescent drinking: Issues and research." In *Promoting Adolescent Health: A Dialog on Research and Practice,* ed. Thomas Coates, Ann Petersen, and Cheryl Perry, 201–223. New York: Academic Press.

Harford, Thomas C. 1986. "Drinking patterns among black and nonblack adolescents: Results of a national survey." *Annals of the New York Academy of Science* 472:130–141.

Harper, Frederick D. 1988. "Alcohol and black youth: An overview." *Journal of Drug Issues* 18:7–14.

Hayes, Cheryl D., ed. 1987. *Risking the Future: Adolescent Sexuality, Pregnancy, and Childbearing,* Vol. I. Washington, D.C.: National Academy Press.

Herd, Denise. 1985. "Ambiguity in black drinking norms." In *The American Experience with Alcohol: Contrasting Cultural Perspectives,* ed. Linda Bennett and Genevieve Ames, 143–169. New York: Plenum Press.

Hirschi, Travis. 1969. *Causes of Delinquency.* Berkeley, Calif.: University of California Press.

Hofferth, Sandra, and Cheryl D. Hayes, ed. 1987. *Risking the Future: Adolescent Sexuality, Pregnancy, and Childbearing,* Vol. II. Washington, D.C.: National Academy Press.

Jessor, Richard. 1987. "Problem behavior theory, psychosocial, development, and adolescent problem drinking." *British Journal of Addiction* 82:331–342.

Jessor, Richard, and Shirley Jessor. 1977. *Problem Behavior and Psychosocial Development.* New York: Academic Press.

Johnston, Lloyd D., and Patrick M. O'Malley. 1985. "Issues of validity and population coverage in student surveys of drug use." In *Self-Report Methods of Estimating Drug Use,* ed. Beatrice A. Rouse, Nicholas J. Kozel, and Louise G. Richards. National Institute on Drug Abuse Research Monograph No. 57 (ADM) 85-1347. Washington, D.C.: Government Printing Office.

Johnston, Lloyd D., Patrick M. O'Malley, and Jerald G. Bachman. 1989. Drug Use, Drinking, and Smoking: National Survey Results from High School, College, and Young Adult Populations, 1975–1988. National Institute on Drug Abuse. U.S. Department of Health and Human Services Pub. No. (ADM) 89-1638. Washington, D.C.: Government Printing Office.

Kandel, Denise B., Eric Single, and Ronald Kessler. 1976. "The epidemiology of drug use among New York state high school students: Distribution, trends, and change in rates of use." *American Journal of Public Health* 66:43–53.

Kandel, Denise B. 1980. "Drug and drinking behavior among youth." *Annual Review of Sociology* 6:235–285.

Kaplan, Howard, Steven S. Martin, and Cynthia Robbins. 1982. "Application of a general theory of deviant behavior: Self derogation and adolescent drug use." *Journal of Health and Social Behavior* 23:274–294.

Lorch, Barbara R., and Robert H. Hughes. 1985. "Religion and Youth Substance Use." *Journal of Religion and Health* 24:197–208.

Maddahian, Ebrahim, Michael D. Newcomb, and Peter M. Bentler. 1986. "Adolescents' substance use: Impact of ethnicity, income, and availability." *Advances in Alcohol and Substance Abuse* 5:63–78.

Mensch, Barbara S., and Denise B. Kandel. 1988. "Underreporting of substance use in a national longitudinal youth cohort." *Public Opinion Quarterly* 52:100–124.

National Center for Education Statistics. 1989. Dropout Rates in the United States: 1988. Analysis Report September, 1989. U.S. Department of Education Office of Educational Research and Improvement. Washington, D.C.: Government Printing Office.

National Institute on Drug Abuse. 1990. National Household Study on Drug Abuse: Main Findings. U.S. Department of Health and Human Services Publication No. (ADM) 90-1682. Washington, D.C.: Government Printing Office.

Newcomb, Michael D., Ebrahim Maddahian, Rodney Skager, and Peter M. Bentler. 1987. "Substance abuse and psychosocial risk factors among teenagers: Associations with sex, age, ethnicity, and type of school." *American Journal of Drug and Alcohol Abuse* 13:413–433.

Newcomb, Michael D., and Peter M. Bentler. 1988. *Consequences of Adolescent Drug Use.* Newbury Park, Calif.: Sage.

———. 1989 "Substance use among children and teenagers." *American Psychologist* 44:242–248.

Prendergast, Michael L., Gregory A. Austin, Kenneth I. Maton, and Ralph Baker. 1989. "Substance abuse among black youth." *Prevention Research Update* 4:1–27.

Radosevich, Marcia, Lonn Lanza-Kaduce, Ronald L. Akers, and Marvin D. Krohn. 1980. "The sociology of adolescent drug and drinking behavior: A review of the state of the field: Part 2." *Deviant Behavior* 1:145–169.

Rumberger, Russell W. 1983. "Dropping out of high school: The influence of race, sex, and family background." *American Educational Research Journal* 20: 199–220.

Secretary's Task Force on Black and Minority Health. 1985. Vol. I. Summary Volume. U.S. Department of Health and Human Services. Washington, D.C.: Government Printing Office.

Secretary's Task Force on Black and Minority Health. 1986. Vol. VII. Chemical Dependency and Diabetes. U.S. Department of Health and Human Services. Washington, D.C.: Government Printing Office.

Schulenburg, John, Jerald G. Bachman, Patrick M. O'Malley, and Lloyd D. Johnston. 1990. "The impacts of educational commitment and success on drug and alcohol use during the transition from adolescence to young adulthood." Unpublished paper.

Segal, Bernard. 1986. "Age and first experience with psychoactive drugs." *International Journal of the Addictions* 21:1285–1306.

Smith, Tom W. 1984. "The subjectivity of ethnicity." In *Surveying Subjective Phenomena,* 2 vols., ed. Charles P. Turner and Martin Elizabeth, 117–128. New York: Russell Sage Foundation.

Sue, Stanley, and Sumie Okazaki. 1990. "Asian-American educational achievements: A phenomenon in search of an explanation." *American Psychologist* 45:913–920.

Wallace, John M., Jr. Forthcoming. Model Building. Theory Testing, and Explaining Black-White Differences in Adolescent Drug Use. Ph.D. diss., University of Michigan

Welte, John W., and Grace Barnes. 1987. "Alcohol use among adolescent minority groups." *Journal of Studies on Alcohol* 48: 329–336.

CHAPTER 8

Drinking by Black and White Women

RESULTS FROM A NATIONAL SURVEY

Denise Herd

Numerous surveys show that black women are much more likely to abstain from alcoholic beverages than white women or black or white men (Cahalan et al., 1969; Johnson, 1977; Clark and Midanik, 1982; Weschler et al., 1978; Warheit et al., 1976; Caetano, 1984). The reported rates of abstention in national surveys since 1965 range between 49–59 percent for black females and 39–42 percent for white females. At the same time, several of these and other studies indicate that black women display higher rates of heavier drinking and or alcohol related problems than white women. National surveys (Cahalan et al., 1969; Clark and Midanik, 1982) show that rates of heavier drinking are 50–100 percent higher among black women, and community surveys (Bailey et al., 1965; Haberman and Sheinberg, 1967) describe a much lower sex-ratio of alcoholism in black than white respondents (1.2–1.9 for blacks and 4.0–6.2 for whites).

Social theories explaining black women's drinking behavior emphasize both their relative powerlessness in American society and their supposed dominant position in black family life. Taking the first perspective, Knupfer and Room (1964) describe the historical tendency for the more powerful groups in a given society (e.g., whites, males, the middle and upper classes) to have the social and economic privileges that enable them to drink, while less powerful groups (e.g., women, minorities, and the poor) are subject to economic and social restraints (e.g., social criticism and legal policies) that limit their drinking.

On the other hand, some observers explain heavier drinking among black women as the outcome of their greater economic independence and tendency to function as the head of household. For example, Cahalan et al. (1969:48) state that the higher proportion of heavy drinkers among black women may stem from the "frequent filling of the (more 'manlike') role of head of the household among Negro women, which might entail more stress or less of certain kinds of familial constraints against heavy drinking."

Bailey et al. (1965:28) argue that a "permissive drinking culture for [black] women, in addition to combining a major breadwinning role with household responsibilities, might well produce an environment conducive to the development of alcohol problems." Strayer (1961) suggests that the matriarchal position of black women (as economic providers and central caretakers and authority figures) both predisposes them to alcoholism and also spurs them on to be more successful patients in alcoholism treatment. He points out that the black women in his treatment sample are more likely to have careers outside of the home and to be divorced or separated than white women.

Sterne and Pittman (1972) challenge these assumptions by showing that within their sample of black low-income housing project residents, female heavy drinkers are not significantly more likely than other women to be household heads, workers, or relatively more impoverished. They argue instead that factors like urbanization, attitudes towards respectability, tolerance for heavy drinking among men, exposure to heavy drinking, and reasons for drinking differentiated heavy drinking women from other women.

Recent analyses of American women also question the assumption that employment outside of the home or the combination of employment with childrearing and marital roles leads to higher rates of heavier drinking or alcohol-related problems. For example, Wilsnack and Cheloha (1987) argue that the loss of stable marriage and work roles are more associated with adverse drinking behavior and consequences than performing multiple family and work roles.

Although these findings are interesting, applying them to black women is difficult because of the lack of research in this area. For example, the high estimates of heavier drinking rates among black women are based on studies with small numbers of black respondents or on community samples that may not be representative of the population as a whole. There are also several studies that offer conflicting evidence and report lower rates of consumption among black women than whites (Johnson, 1977; Warheit et al., 1976; Knupfer and Lurie, 1961).

This chapter examines the drinking patterns of black and white women, with a special focus on the prevalence of abstention and of heavier drinking. First, I compare the alcohol consumption patterns of black and white women. Then, I describe rates of abstention and heavier drinking in various subgroups according to age, marital status, educational attainment, income, and employment status for the two groups. After a descriptive presentation of the relationship between drinking in various demographic subgroups, I use multivariate analysis to look at the predictors for abstaining and heavier drinking. This analysis enables the reader to address issues raised in the literature about racial differences in the prevalence of drinking and differences in the effects of marital status and employment behavior on alcohol use in black and white women.

Methods

DATA AND SAMPLE

Data for the study were collected through personal interviews with 1,224 black and 1,034 white women in 1984. (Blacks are respondents who classified themselves as "black, not of Hispanic origin," and whites are those who identified themselves as "white, not of Hispanic origin" excluding persons who stated that they were Asians or

Pacific Islanders, American Indians, or Alaskan Natives). A total of 5,221 respondents (including black, white, and Hispanic men and women) were selected using a sample of the adult population of the United States residing in households (excluding Alaska and Hawaii). The survey response rate was 75.9 percent for blacks, 72 percent for Hispanics, and 73.2 percent for the non-Hispanic general population.

The survey was designed to represent the general population of the United States as well as black and Hispanic subgroups. A multistage area probability sample with 110 primary sampling units was designed by the Institute of Survey Research at Temple University. Probability methods were used at each stage of the sampling process (e.g., in the selection of primary sampling units, neighborhoods or census tracts, listing areas, households and eligible respondents) to insure a generalizable sample.

Blacks and Hispanics were oversampled at each stage of the sampling process to obtain adequate and representative minority study populations (see Santos, 1985, on sampling procedure). Weighting was used to counteract the effects of greatly oversampling blacks and Hispanics relative to their proportion in the U.S. population. Weighting was also used to adjust for differences in the probability of being interviewed due to household size and to compensate for non-response rates on the basis of sex, region, and age. The resulting sample, when weighted, thus conforms to the national distribution of the populations (with respect to these characteristics) as reflected in U.S. census data (table available from author).

Trained interviewers surveyed respondents in their homes using a standard interview schedule that took approximately 60 to 75 minutes to complete (interview schedule available from author). The questionnaire included an array of items on the respondent's background, drinking patterns, drinking problems, alcohol treatment experiences, attitudes, and norms regarding alcohol use and information on the social context of drinking behavior. In addition, interviewers asked minority respondents a series of questions on ethnic identification and acculturation.

MEASURES OF DRINKING PATTERNS

As illustrated in table 8.1, alcohol use was measured by a two-dimensional typology on the frequency of consumption (from never to weekly) and the frequency of consuming five or more drinks in the past 12 months (cf. Room, 1985).

A table comparing the overall prevalence of black and white women's drinking patterns using this typology appears in the following section. However, most of the analysis focuses on two subgroups in the typology. These include abstainers, respondents who have never had a drink or have not done so in the past twelve months, and heavier drinkers, respondents who drink weekly and at least occasionally drink five or more drinks ("frequent high maximum" and "frequent heavier drinkers"; see also Herd and Caetano, 1987). "Heavier drinkers" in this analysis does not refer to problem or alcoholic drinkers, but to women who are on the high end of the drinking scale compared to other women. I used this cutoff point because it includes women who might occasionally drink enough to become intoxicated and might therefore be at risk for some, however slight, degree of drinking related problems, and also because it includes

Table 8.1.   Drinking Patterns (Frequency of Drinking by Frequency of Drinking 5 or More Drinks)

	Frequency of Drinking Five or More Drinks		
Frequency of Drinking	Never drinks 5 or more	Drinks 5 or more at least once a year	Drinks 5 or more at least once a week
At least once a week	Frequent Low Maximum (11.2%)	Frequent High Maximum (12.5%)	Frequent Heavy Drinker (12.0%)
1–3 times a month	Less Frequent Low Maximum (12.3%)	Less Frequent High Maximum (6.3%)	
1–11 times a year	Infrequent (15.3%)		
Less than once a year or never	Abstainers (30.2%)		

Note: N = 5221. Weighted data; percentaged on total sample.
Source: 1984 U.S. National Drinking Survey

enough women to do an adequate statistical analysis of subgroup differences. The base for the analysis of heavier drinkers consists of all women including abstainers, allowing use of a consistent population frame throughout the analysis to describe the prevalence of drinking patterns for black and white women as a whole. Future analyses will focus on differences in black and white female drinkers.

Results

AGGREGATE DRINKING PATTERNS

The findings from this survey parallel most other studies, which report a higher proportion of abstainers among black women than white women (Cahalan et al., 1969; Johnson, 1977; Clark and Midanik, 1982; Wilsnack et al., 1984). Table 8.2 shows that nearly half of the black women in the sample (46%) are classified as abstainers compared to about a third of the white women (34%). However, the findings contradict the common assumption that black women drink more heavily than white women (Cahalan et al., 1969; Bailey et al., 1965). About equal proportions of the women fell into the highest drinking category that includes those who drink five or more drinks at a sitting or in a single day at least once a week.

The results of the survey point to different styles in the drinking patterns of black and white women that have been little discussed in prior research. First, on the whole white women drink more frequently than black women. About 26 percent of the whites in the sample drank at least weekly compared to 17 percent of the blacks. Second, white women appear more likely to drink higher quantities of alcohol at a sitting than black women. The rate of consuming five or more drinks at least occasionally

Table 8.2.   Weighted Percent Distribution, Drinking Patterns by Race among Women

	Black	White
Abstainers	46	34
Infrequent Drinkers	16	19
Less Frequent Low Maximum Drinkers	16	14
Less Frequent High Maximum Drinkers	4	7
Frequent Low Maximum Drinkers	9	13
Frequent High Maximum Drinkers	4	8
Frequent Heavier Drinkers	4	5
Total	99%[a]	100%
	(1222)[b]	(1033)

Notes:
a. Does not equal 100% due to rounding error.
b. Numbers in parentheses are unweighted numbers of respondents.

among white women is nearly double the rate for black women; 15 percent of white women compared to 8 percent of black women are described as "high maximum" drinkers either on a "less frequent" or "frequent" basis.

SUBGROUP DIFFERENCES IN ABSTAINING AND HEAVIER DRINKING

Age. In table 8.3 we see that black women in all age categories except those aged 30–39 are considerably more likely to abstain from alcohol use than white women. The two groups of women also differ in patterns of abstaining across different age groups. A sharp increase in rates of abstaining occurs in black women 40 years old and older, but this increase only occurs among white women 60 years old and older.

The prevalence of heavier drinking is significantly lower in black women aged 18–39 than it is for white women of this age group. After age 49, the proportion of heavier drinkers is low and very similar for both groups of women.

These age-related differences parallel findings described by Caetano (1984) in his multiethnic analysis. Black women were more likely to be abstainers than white women, particularly in the younger and older age groups. In addition, in the youngest age group, a noticeably higher percentage of white women reported drinking larger quantities per occasion than did blacks.

Marital Status. The proportion of abstainers is substantially higher for black than white women regardless of marital status. However, table 8.3 shows very striking differences between single women (separated-divorced and never-married) and widowed women. Twice as many black as white women who are never-married or divorced-separated are abstainers, and these rates for widowed women are at least a fourth higher among black women. These racial differences reflect the fact that there is a major split in drinking rates for married versus single women for white but not black women.

Table 8.3.   Sub-Group Differences in Abstaining and Heavier Drinking in Weighted Percents

	Abstainers		Heavier Drinkers[a]		Unweighted	
	Black	White	Black	White	Black	White
Age Group						
18–29	34	22*	12	20*	36	236
30–39	32	30	10	21*	30	217
40–49	56	35*	10	14	13	144
50–59	60	35*	6	5	14	120
60+	69	49*	1	2	25	311
Marital Status						
Married	44	37*	7	12*	32	571
Separated/Divorced	46	23*	7	19*	29	136
Widowed	70	48*	3	3	21	181
Never Married	40	20*	12	19	35	113
Yearly Family Income						
$6,000 or less	53	54	10	8	50	154
$6,001–10,000	45	44	8	8	21	140
$10,001–15,000	50	39	9	11	12	129
$15,001–20,000	28	27	12	17	10	109
$20,001–30,000	29	28	7	13	10	190
$30,001 & over	34	25	5	17*	67	241
Employment Status						
Employed (full-time)	40	23*	8	18*	44	390
Employed (part-time)	31	31	10	15	12	128
Unemployed	43	37	14	16	14	38
Homemaker	57	46*	8	9	25	263
Retired	75	44*	0	4*	16	184

Notes:
a. Combined frequent high maximum and frequent heavier drinkers
*Black-White differences significant at .05 level (Differences in Proportions Test)

Both married and separated-divorced white women are significantly more likely than black women to be classified as heavier drinkers. But black/white differences are particularly strong among separated-divorced women. More than twice as many white as black women in this group are heavier drinkers. A higher rate of heavier drinking also occurs among white never-marrieds, but the difference is not statistically significant.

Previous general population surveys have usually shown that married and widowed women are more likely to be abstainers and light or moderate drinkers, while single and divorced people are often heavier drinkers (Cahalan et al., 1969; Clark and Midanik, 1982; Johnson, 1982; Wilsnack et al., 1984). As observed, these findings are more applicable to white than black women.

Studies of black respondents offer conflicting views on the relationship between marital status and drinking behavior. Sterne and Pittman's (1972) study shows that black separated-divorced women are no more likely to drink at all or to be heavy drinkers than married women. In fact the proportion of abstainers is much higher while the rate of heavier drinking is much lower among separated-divorced than married women. The authors attributed these findings to the possibility that women with broken marriages were no longer living with heavier drinking spouses. However, Caetano and Herd's analysis (1984) of drinking behavior in a large California sample of black women revealed much higher rates of drinking and heavier drinking among single compared to married and widowed women.

Family Income. Income level has a very similar effect on the rates of abstaining among black and white women, as shown in table 8.3. Hence, there were no significant racial differences in the proportion of abstainers according to income level. However, black women with incomes between $10,001 and $15,000 and over $30,001 were considerably more likely to be nondrinkers than white women in these income groups. Among both groups, higher family income is associated with increasing rates of drinking. Two-thirds to three-fourths of the women with incomes of $30,001 or above are classified as drinkers compared to less than half of the women with incomes of $6,000 or less.

Black and white women do show important differences in the relationship between income and heavier drinking. Among white women, increases in income level are generally accompanied by higher rates of heavier drinking. However, among black women, the highest income groups exhibit the lowest rates of heavier drinking. Hence white women with annual family incomes of over $30,001 are more than three times as likely as black women to be heavier drinkers.

Employment Status. Previous studies have shown that employment status has an important effect on women's drinking behavior. Women who work are less likely to be abstainers and more likely to be moderate or heavier drinkers (Johnson, 1977; Wilsnack et al., 1984). To a certain extent these findings were confirmed in table 8.3. Women who work full- or part-time are more likely to be drinkers than women who are unemployed, housewives, or retired. This relationship holds for both black and white women.

The findings from this survey also show that heavier drinking appears strongly related to employment status among white women, but not black women. White women in the work force report noticeably higher rates of heavier drinking than housewives. For example, women with full-time jobs exhibit rates twice as high (18%) as homemakers (9%).

In contrast, rates of heavier drinking are no different for black women with full-time jobs (8%) or for those who identify themselves as homemakers (8%). Among black women, the unemployed exhibit the highest rates of heavier drinking (14%). It was difficult to make a similar comparison among white women because of the comparatively small number who report being unemployed.

Major differences in drinking behavior were observed for black and white employed women. Black employed women include a considerably higher proportion of abstainers (40% versus 23%), but a smaller percentage of heavier drinkers (8% versus 18%) than whites. In addition, there is a significantly higher proportion of abstainers among black homemakers and retired women than among white women in similar roles.

The findings on the comparatively high rates of abstaining and low rates of heavier drinking on the part of black employed women question the assumption that work outside the home is associated with high levels of alcohol consumption among black women. This relationship holds true for white women, but not black women.

MULTIVARIATE ANALYSIS

In previous sections of this chapter, I point to important differences in the drinking patterns of black and white women and the way these differences are related to social characteristics. In general, white women are more likely than blacks to drink at all or to drink large quantities of alcohol at least on an occasional basis. Marital status and employment status appear to affect the drinking patterns of the two groups of women differently. Unlike white women, blacks do not exhibit the split in abstaining or heavier drinking based on whether or not they are married or single, or are employed or homemakers. Although changes in family income level have the same effect on drinking rates in both groups of women, increases are more associated with heavier drinking by white women than blacks.

Log-linear modeling was used to explore whether some of these differences might stem from variation in underlying socio-economic patterns or differences in the way marital or social roles are associated with drinking among the two groups of women. Log-linear modeling is appropriate for analyzing categorical data where the observations are not from populations that are normally distributed with constant variance (Norusis, 1985).

Separate models were developed to examine both abstaining and heavier drinking. Dichotomous variables were created to contrast abstainers versus drinkers, heavier drinkers and all other women, younger (18–39) versus older (40–59) women, married versus single women (never-married and separated-divorced), high (family income of $15,001 a year or more) versus low income (family income of $15,000 or less), and employed women (full- or part-time) versus homemakers.

A hierarchical modeling strategy was followed based on the process described in Knoke and Burke (1980) and Norusis (1985). A number of models were examined and evaluated using the likelihood-ratio chi-square to determine how well the model fit. The models examined ranged from the fully saturated model to progressively simpler models with the smallest number of interaction terms. Models were selected that exhibited a good "fit" with the data (e.g., the likelihood ratio chi-square indicated that there is a high probability that differences between the observed and modeled data are due to sampling error) but also used the fewest possible terms. This avoided complex models with unnecessary variables and interaction terms. This process is analogous to selecting models for regression analysis by examining the effect of variables on R^2.

After selecting suitable models, I generated effect parameters through a logit analysis with the drinking variables (abstainers versus drinkers and heavier drinkers versus all others). The coefficients produced in the analysis provide an indication of the magnitude and direction of the effect of the variables on drinking behavior. The coefficients are lambda parameters that represent the contribution of each independent variable to the logit. When multiplied by two, they indicate the log of the odds of a particular value of the dependent variable. By taking the antilog of the doubled parameter estimate, the odds of being in a particular category of the dependent variable can be observed. For each parameter estimate, standard error, Z values, and confidence intervals are produced. Thus significance levels can be obtained for each coefficient.

The results of the analysis revealed important findings at two different levels. First, the modeling procedure was more successful with white than black women. For white women, it was possible to develop extremely well fitting models with single independent variables. In contrast, for black women, the best models required three- and even four-way interactions. As a result, the selected models for black women achieved only a modest fit with the data. Hence the findings for these women should be interpreted cautiously. Other studies have observed that demographic factors show weaker correlations with drinking behavior in black populations (Caetano and Herd, 1984; Herd, 1985) and have speculated that cultural differences or minority status alters these relationships among blacks.

At another level, the log-linear analysis portrayed similarities but also major differences in the actual predictors of drinking status in the two racial groups. First, the data show that black women are more likely to be abstainers even when controlling for socio-economic status, age level, and marital status. In fact, as table 8.4 illustrates, race is the strongest predictor of being a drinker or abstainer of all the characteristics considered. In addition, the effect of marital status varies significantly by race. The interaction between the two factors reveals that there is a stronger relationship between being a drinker and being white and single than would be expected.

Second, the separate models for white and black women illustrate that employment status significantly predicts drinking in both groups (tables 8.5 and 8.6). As suggested in previous studies (Wilsnack and Cheloha, 1987; Wilsnack et al., 1985), employment outside the home may increase women's drinking by providing more income that can be spent on alcoholic beverages or may put women in work roles where norms encourage or require increased drinking just as they do for men.

In contrast, family income level has a different impact on drinking rates among the two groups. Income independently predicts drinking for white women, but not for blacks. Among blacks only the interaction between income level and employment status is significant. This interaction indicates that the proportion of drinkers is lower for low-income employed women and higher for low-income homemakers than would be expected. These results are in keeping with other studies (Caetano and

Table 8.4.   Model Coefficients: Effects of Age, Marital Status, Income, Employment Status, and Race on Drinking vs. Abstaining in Women

	Coefficient	Coefficient x 2	Antilog
Drinking	.297*	.594	1.811
Drinking by Age (Young)	.145*	.290	1.366
Drinking by Marital Status (Single)	.154*	.308	1.361
Drinking by Income (High)	.130*	.260	1.300
Drinking by Employment Status			
(Employed)	.064	.128	1.136
Drinking by Race (White)	.174*	.348	1.416
Drinking by Race by Marital Status	.103*	.206	1.229
Drinking by Marital Status by			
Employment Status	−.081*	−.162	.850

Notes: Likelihood Ratio Chi-Square = 24.332, df = 22, p = .330
*p < .05

Table 8.5.   Model Coefficients: Effects of Age, Marital Status, Income and Employment Status on Drinking vs. Abstaining in White Women

	Coefficient	Coefficient x 2	Antilog
Drinking	.457*	.914	2.490
Drinking by Marital Status (Single)	.218*	.436	1.546
Drinking by Income (High)	.137*	.274	1.315
Drinking by Employment Status (Employed)	.102*	.204	1.226

Notes: Likelihood Ratio Chi-Square = 7.845, df = 11, p = .727
*p < .05

Herd, 1984; Herd, 1988) that show that the relationship between income level and drinking patterns differs for black and white respondents.

The results also exhibit racial differences in the effects of life-cycle factors on women's drinking. Among white women the odds for being a drinker are significantly affected by whether a woman is married, but not how old she is. This situation is reversed for black women where age, but not marital status, is a predictor for drinking.

In sum, the analysis of predictors for drinking and abstaining revealed that white women are more likely to be drinkers than black women and that within each racial group there are similarities and differences in the predictors of drinking status. White women are significantly more likely to be drinkers if they are single, high income, and employed; and black women have a greater probability of being drinkers if they are young and employed. However, employment is less predictive of being a drinker for low-income black women than one would expect.

The model for predictors of heavier drinking in all women (Table 8.7) shows that race, followed by marital status, and then age are the only variables necessary to predict heavier drinking. Those who are white, single, and under 40 years old are significantly more likely to be heavier drinkers than other women.

When the data were modeled separately for black and white women, major differences appeared in the models and predictors of heavier drinking. Among white women (Table 8.8), age group differences alone are powerful enough to account for heavier drinking in a model that fits the data extremely well (p = .788).

This finding coincides with the patterns observed in a five-way contingency table on age, income, employment, and marital status and heavier drinking that showed that younger white women (18–39 years old) are more likely to be heavier drinkers than

Table 8.6.   Model Coefficients: Effects of Age, Marital Status, Income, Employment Status and Race on Drinking vs. Abstaining in Black Women

	Coefficient	Coefficient x 2	Antilog
Drinking	–.010	–.020	.980
Drinking by Age (Young)	.207*	.414	1.513
Drinking by Income (High)	.002	.004	1.004
Drinking by Employment Status	.188*	.376	1.456
Drinking by Income by Employment	.180*	.360	1.433

Notes: Likelihood Ratio Chi-Square = 13.002, df = 10, p = .224
* p < .05

Table 8.7. Model Coefficients: Effects of Age, Marital Status, Income, Employment Status and Race on Heavier Drinking in Women

	Coefficient	Coefficient x 2	Antilog
Heavier Drinking	−1.022*	−2.044	.130
Heavier Drinking by Age (Young)	.103*	.206	1.229
Heavier Drinking by Marital Status (Single)	.129*	.258	1.294
Heavier Drinking by Race (White)	.220*	.440	1.553

Notes: Likelihood Ratio Chi-Square = 24.620, df = 26, p = .541
* p < .05

middle-aged white women (40–59 years old) in each particular socio-economic or marital group (table available from author).

In contrast, a much more complex model based on the combined interaction of marital status, employment status, and age was necessary to adequately predict heavier drinking in black women (p = .566). The model suggests that the effect of marital status on heavier drinking in these women varies by age group and employment status. Given the complexity of these findings, another model was selected (Table 8.9) that contained only marital status as an independent variable (p = .307). Based on these findings and contingency table analysis (available from the author), it appears that marital status is an important determinant of which black women are likely to be heavier drinkers but that its effect depends on age and employment status. The groups of unmarried black women who seem to be at most risk for heavier drinking are unmarried women who are middle-aged (40–59 years old) and unmarried women who are homemakers.

Interestingly, the above analysis indicates racial differences in the direction of age effects on heavier drinking. Among whites, it is youthful status that predicts higher consumption levels, while among blacks, middle-aged women appear to be at equal or more risk for heavier alcohol use. These findings may reflect differences in cultural patterns related to drinking and aging as well as to different cohort effects experienced by the two groups. For example, recent studies show that the age distribution of heavier drinking differs significantly for black and white men (Caetano, 1984; Herd, 1988).

Given the emphasis placed on the relationship between marital roles and heavier drinking in the Wilsnack et al. study (1984), it is also noteworthy that age emerged as the sole significant predictor of heavier drinking among white women in the present study. While methodological differences prevent an exact comparison of the two studies, the results of the present research underscore the need to control for age when

Table 8.8. Model Coefficients. Effects of Age, Marital Status, Income and Employment Status on Heavier Drinking in White Women

	Coefficient	Coefficient x 2	Antilog
Heavier Drinking	−.895*	−1.790	.167
Heavier Drinking by Age (Young)	.185*	.370	1.448

Notes: Likelihood Ratio Chi-Square = 8.796, df = 13, p = .788
*p < .05

Table 8.9.   Model Coefficients: Effects of Age, Marital Status, Income and Employment Status on Heavier Drinking in Black Women

	Coefficient	Coefficient x 2	Antilog
Heavier Drinking	−1.205*	−2.410	.090
Heavier Drinking by Marital Status (Single)	.166*	.332	1.394

Notes: Likelihood Ratio Chi-Square = 15.00, df = 13, p = .307
*p < .05

looking at the effect of marital status on drinking patterns. Age status influences role behavior such as marriage and childrearing and also determines exposure to social attitudes that may affect drinking patterns.

The emergence of marital status as a major predictor of heavier drinking among black women suggests that some aspects of married life may act as a buffer against heavier drinking in some women. As discussed by Wilsnack et al. (1985), these either could be mechanisms that enhance psychological well-being or that affect the social control of drinking or exposure to alcoholic beverages.

Discussion

The purpose of this analysis was to explore the drinking patterns of black and white women and to examine how they are related to age, marital status, income level, and employment status in women of the two ethnic groups. Based on previous studies, it was especially important to look at the impact of socio-economic status on abstaining and the effects of employment behavior and marriage roles on heavier drinking.

The results confirmed the fact that there are major differences in the drinking patterns of the two groups of women. While the findings echoed previous studies showing higher rates of abstaining in black women, they did not show that these women are more likely to be heavier drinkers. The analysis revealed that although employment predicts drinking in both black and and white women, the two groups differ in other major determinants of drinking. Even more profound differences were observed in the models and variables used to explain heavier drinking in black and white females.

The findings here do not support all of the premises of earlier studies on black women's drinking behavior. First, higher rates of abstaining among black women do not appear to be merely a result of low socio-economic status. Even when income and employment status are taken into account, racial differences in the rates of abstaining persist. It may be that models that include variables on other cultural dimensions (e.g., religious background, regional differences) would better explain black-white differences in rates of drinking. Second, the low rates of heavier drinking in black women question the assumption that distinctive aspects of black women's lifestyles (e.g., high proportion of unmarried women with children) lead to higher levels of alcohol use. Finally, the importance of race as an independent predictor of heavier drinking and the major black-white differences in explanatory models emphasize the need for new conceptual approaches.

These findings imply that a bi-cultural perspective is necessary to understand black women's drinking behavior. While it is clear that some of the same social forces might impact equally on women's drinking behavior in this society (e.g., interacting within the male workplace), it also seems likely that differences in cultural values, social organization, and family life for blacks may affect their drinking patterns. In this light, traditional demographic markers do not adequately describe black women's drinking behavior or explain differences between black and white women's alcohol use. A more fruitful approach might be to try to understand the common experiences that affect all women's drinking patterns as well as the unique social patterns that may occur among women in different subcultural groups.

Note

Preparation of this chapter was supported by grants (AA05595 and AA06050) from the National Institute on Alcohol Abuse and Alcoholism to the Alcohol Research Group, Medical Research Institute of San Francisco. Special thanks to Pam Fox and Judith Remington at the Alcohol Research Group for computer programming on the log-linear model analysis. Correspondence to: Alcohol Research Group, 1816 Scenic Avenue, Berkeley, CA 94609.

References

Bailey, Margaret B., Paul W. Haberman, and Harold Alksne. 1965. "The epidemiology of alcoholism in an urban residential area." *Quarterly Journal of Studies on Alcohol* 26:19–40.

Caetano, Raul. 1984. "Ethnicity and drinking in Northern California: a comparison among whites, blacks and Hispanics." *Alcohol and Alcoholism* 19:31–44.

Caetano, Raul and Denise Herd. 1984. "Black drinking practices in Northern California." *American Journal of Drug Abuse* 10:571–87.

Cahalan, Don, Ira Cisin, and Helen M. Crossley. 1969. *American Drinking Practices. Monograph No. 6.* New Brunswick, NJ: Rutgers Center of Alcohol Studies.

Clark, Walter B. and Lorraine Midanik. 1982. "Alcohol use and alcohol problems among U.S. adults: results of the 1979 national survey." Pp. 3–52 in *Alcohol Consumption and Related Problems, Alcohol and Health Monograph 1.* Department of Health and Human Services No. (ADM) 82–1190. Washington, DC: U.S. Government Printing Office.

Haberman, Paul W. and Jill Sheinberg. 1967. "Implicative drinking reported in a household survey: a corroborative note on subgroup differences." *Quarterly Journal of Studies on Alcohol* 28:538–43.

Herd, Denise. 1985. "The socio-cultural correlates of drinking patterns in black and white Americans: results from a national survey." Ph.D. diss., University of California, San Francisco.

———. 1988. "Sub-group differences in drinking patterns among black and white men: results from a national survey". Unpublished ms. Berkeley, CA: Alcohol Research Group, Medical Research Institute of San Francisco.

Herd, Denise and Raul Caetano. 1987. "Drinking patterns and problems among black, white and Hispanic women in the U.S.: results from a national survey." Paper presented at the Alcohol and Drug Problems Association of North America, National Conference on Women's Issues in Denver, CO, May 3–6.

Hilton, Michael E. 1986. "Abstention in the general population of the U.S.A." *British Journal of Addiction* 81:95–112.

Johnson, Paula B. 1977. "Sex differences and effects of women's roles on drinking practices." RAND Corporation Report WN9913. Unpublished ms.

Johnson, Paula B. 1982. "Sex differences, women's roles, and alcohol use: preliminary national data." *Journal of Social Issues* 38:93–116.

Knoke, David and Peter J. Burke. 1980. *Log-linear Models.* Beverly Hills, CA: Sage Publications.

Knupfer, Genevieve and Elinore E. Lurie. 1961. *Characteristics of Abstainers: A Comparison of Drinkers and Non-drinkers in a Large California City.* Drinking Practices Study Report No. 3. Berkeley, CA: State Department of Public Health.

Knupfer, Genevieve, Raymond Fink, Walter B. Clark, and Angelica S. Goffman. 1963. *Factors Related to Drinking in an Urban Community. Drinking Practices Study Report No. 6.* Berkeley, CA: State Department of Public Health.

Knupfer, Genevieve, and Robin Room. 1964. "Age, sex and social class as factors in amount of drinking in a metropolitan community." *Social Problems* 12:224–40.

Norusis, Marija J. 1984. *SPSSX Advanced Statistics Guide.* New York: McGraw-Hill Book Company.

Room, Robin. 1985. "Measuring alcohol consumption in the U.S.: methods and rationales." Paper presented at the Alcohol Epidemiology Section Meeting, 31st International Institute for the Prevention and Treatment of Alcoholism, Rome, Italy, June.

Santos, Robert. 1985. "One approach to oversampling blacks and Hispanics: the national alcohol survey." Paper presented at the Annual Meeting of the American Statistical Association, Las Vegas, NV.

Sterne, Muriel W. and David J. Pittman. 1972. *Drinking Patterns in the Ghetto.* St. Louis, MO: Social Science Institute, Washington University. Unpublished monograph.

Strayer, Robert. 1961. "A study of the Negro alcoholic." *Quarterly Journal of Studies on Alcohol* 22:111–23.

Warheit, George J., Sandra A. Arey, and Edith Swanson. 1976. "Patterns of drug use: an epidemiological overview." *Journal of Drug Issues* 6:223–37.

Wechsler, Henry, Harold W. Demone, and Nell Gottlieb. 1978. "Drinking patterns of greater Boston adults: subgroup differences on the QFU index." *Journal of Studies on Alcohol* 39:1158–65.

Wilsnack, Richard W. and Randall Cheloha. 1987. "Women's roles and problem drinking across the lifespan." *Social Problems* 34:231–48.

Wilsnack, Sharon C., Albert D. Klassen, and Shelly I. Wright. 1985. "Gender role orientations and drinking among women in a U.S. national survey". Proceedings of the 34th International Congress on Alcoholism and Drug Dependence, August, Calgary, Alberta, Canada. Sponsored by the International Council on Alcohol and Addictions.

Wilsnack, Sharon C., Richard W. Wilsnack, and Albert D. Klassen. 1984. "Women's drinking and drinking problems: patterns from a 1981 national survey." *American Journal of Public Health* 74:1231–38.

CHAPTER 9

Race, Class, and Gender Differences in Substance Abuse

EVIDENCE OF MIDDLE-CLASS/UNDERCLASS POLARIZATION AMONG BLACK MALES

Kellie E. M. Barr, Michael P. Farrell,
Grace M. Barnes, and John W. Welte

Prevalence rates of alcohol and other substance use have been reported for blacks as compared with whites in several recent large population surveys (e.g., Barnes and Welte 1988a; Frank et al. 1988; Hilton 1988; National Institute on Drug Abuse 1985). Overall, blacks have consistently been found to have a higher proportion of abstainers from alcohol than do whites (Barnes and Welte 1988a; Hilton 1988; Knupfer 1989). However, there is less consistency in comparisons of rates of drinking behavior among those who do drink. Rates of daily drinking and being intoxicated were found to be fairly similar in the two races in a national sample (Hilton 1988). In a New York State sample, rates of heavier drinking (consuming an average of over two drinks a day) were similar for black and white females (7 percent), but the rates were higher for black males (31 percent) than for white males (23 percent) (Barnes and Welte 1988a).

Similar inconsistencies characterize epidemiological studies of illicit drug use. National findings show similar rates of lifetime illicit drug use for blacks and whites (approximately 37 percent for both groups) (National Institute on Drug Abuse 1985); but in a New York State sample, Frank and her coauthors (1988) report somewhat higher lifetime use rates for blacks than whites when comparing specific substances, i.e., marijuana (30 percent vs. 28 percent), cocaine (11 percent vs. 8 percent), and heroin (2 percent vs. less than .5 percent).

These inconsistent findings point to the need for research aimed at sorting out the conditions under which blacks and whites differ in substance abuse. One limitation of these descriptive epidemiological reports is that they are not theoretically guided or designed to account for variations in substance abuse by race. It is likely that some of the inconsistencies in findings could be better understood if they were contextualized in a larger theoretical frame. Most notably, recent theorists suggest that socioeconomic status (SES) should be taken into account when comparing blacks and whites, as well as when examining variations within races. Herd (1987) discusses the need to develop and test models of black drinking which adequately address the issues of social change, cultural and class heterogeneity, and disparate determinants of black drinking behavior.

Apart from the epidemiological studies, other research has focused on blacks of lower status (e.g., National Institute on Alcohol Abuse and Alcoholism 1979). These so-called "ghetto studies" have been criticized for assuming blacks are an undifferentiated, impoverished group with a range of pathological behaviors (Dawkins 1980; Harper 1976; Herd 1985). These studies preclude the examination of variations in behavior within the black population, and also do not allow for comparison of blacks with whites, controlling for SES. If the effects of race and SES are not examined together, it is unclear to what degree race is a determining factor in substance abuse, and to what degree SES accounts for the variation.

Wilson's (1978; 1987) recent theorizing about class polarization, race, and gender has potential for explaining a variety of social problems among blacks. He argues that the factors generating an underclass have impinged most dramatically on black males who have been displaced from blue-collar jobs by deindustrialization. In contrast to these lower SES black males who have been left behind, middle-class blacks have benefited from civil rights legislation and affirmative action programs. As middle-class black males have moved into suburban neighborhoods and professional and managerial lifestyles, their behavior and attitudes have become similar to middle-class white males. On the other hand, underclass black males are becoming differentiated from both underclass white males and middle-class black males.

It is well known that deindustrialization has taken its toll on certain groups of black women, most notably single mothers. Nevertheless, the educational attainments of and expansion of employment opportunities for women suggest that the forces creating the class polarization may be affecting black women somewhat less than black men. Between 1960 and 1990, the restructuring of the economic system resulted in a rapid decline in jobs in heavy industry and an increase in service and clerical jobs. Black females have been more than twice as likely to find positions in the expanding sectors of the economy, while black males have remained concentrated in declining areas (Bowman 1991; Wilson 1987). Thus, the class polarization may be more apparent for males than for females.

Wilson's perspective recognizes that blacks should not be regarded as a homogeneous group, but examined as a diversified group which comprises different occupational, educational, and economic levels. If his theory is taken into consideration in examining rates of alcohol consumption and substance abuse among blacks, and if these rates are treated as indicators of behavior problems, then differences should be seen between rates of drinking and other drug use in the black middle class and underclass. If the black middle class is moving rapidly ahead while the underclass is falling further behind, this polarization would be reflected in alcohol and other substance abuse problems. If, relatively speaking, more opportunities are available for black women, we would expect to find that they are less affected by the polarization than men.

Hypothesis 1. If blacks are becoming polarized into a relatively affluent middle class and a disadvantaged underclass, then SES will be more strongly related to alcohol consumption, alcohol-related problems, and illicit drug use for blacks than for whites.

Hypothesis 2. If polarization affects black males most severely, then black males in the lowest SES group will have disproportionately high levels of alcohol consumption, alcohol-related problems, and illicit drug use when compared to other race and gender groups.

Methods

SAMPLING AND INTERVIEWING PROCEDURES

To fully test Wilson's theory would require a longitudinal design using time trend analysis to examine changes in drug and alcohol use before and after the eras of civil rights legislation and deindustrialization. Although such a design is beyond the scope of this study, a cross-sectional design can provide evidence bearing on the theory. Findings from a cross-sectional analysis which support the theory will be reason to follow up with longitudinal studies.

The data for this analysis are based on an extensive study of alcohol and substance use among a representative sample of 6,364 adults, age 18 and older living in New York State. The sampling, interviewing procedures, and descriptive findings are reported in a detailed monograph (Barnes and Welte 1988a). Briefly, the overall sample had four components—a telephone household sample of adults (n = 5,070); a supplemental sample designed to reach college students living in dormitories who would not be accessible through the household sample (n = 483); a sample of persons living in shelters for the homeless (n = 412); and a New York City nontelephone sample (n = 399) to compensate for those areas where telephone penetration rates were below 90 percent. Blacks were oversampled to allow for more detailed statistical analysis. The actual number of blacks interviewed was 888, and the actual number of whites interviewed was 4,099. The weighted sample corrects for the oversample (whites = 4,793; blacks = 777). For the present study, white respondents constitute 75 percent of the weighted sample, and black respondents constitute 12 percent of the weighted sample, which is comparable to their proportions of New York State's population at the time of the survey. Other racial/ethnic groups, primarily Hispanics and Asians, constitute approximately 13 percent of the sample, but are eliminated from the present analysis.

Household and college interview subsamples were conducted on the telephone by trained interviewers under a contract with Louis Harris and Associates, using computer-assisted telephone interviewing (CATI). Interviews of the sample of homeless living in shelters also used the telephone method; a field worker obtained their cooperation and dialed the number to make contact with the survey research contractor. The nontelephone household sample was interviewed personally.

The descriptive analyses presented here are weighted to represent the general population of New York State. In the regression analysis, we use the unweighted sample, thereby taking advantage of the actual number of black respondents in the sample. Making use of the larger number of blacks does not affect the relationships between variables, yet allows for more detailed analysis of subgroups within each race without concern that the number of cases is too small to allow confidence in the generalizability of findings.

DEPENDENT VARIABLES

Alcohol consumption. Alcohol consumption was measured by self-reports of the frequency and quantity of drinking beer, wine, and liquor during the past 12 months. For example, respondents were asked, "How often do you usually drink wine?" Response categories ranged from three or more times a day to never. Next, respondents were asked, "When you drink wine, how many four-ounce wine glasses do you usually have at one time, on the average?" Comparable frequency and quantity questions were asked for beer and for liquor. For this analysis, alcohol consumption was a continuous variable representing the average number of ounces of absolute alcohol consumed per day. For example, an absolute alcohol score of .5 is roughly equivalent to drinking an average of one can of beer, or one four-ounce glass of wine, or a mixed drink containing from one to one and one-half ounces of liquor per day.

Alcohol-related problems. Alcohol problems were indicated by self-reports of the number of alcohol-related problems occurring in the past 12 months. The social behavior items included: having trouble with one's boss or fellow workers, friends, family members, or police as a result of drinking; driving after having a good bit to drink; or having an accident in a car or home because of drinking. Behaviors indicating possible signs of alcohol dependence were also included in the alcohol problems scale; for example, forgetting things done while drinking, quickly tossing down several drinks to get a faster effect, drinking when getting up in the morning, not stopping drinking before becoming intoxicated, and unsuccessfully trying to cut down or quit drinking.

ILLICIT DRUG USE

Illicit drug use was measured by self-reports of the total number of times in the past 30 days the respondent used any of 12 types of illicit drugs. These drugs included marijuana, cocaine, hallucinogens, inhalants, and heroin.

INDEPENDENT VARIABLES

The independent variables were gender, race (black and white), and two measures of socioeconomic status—years of education and family income in the preceding year.

Results

DISTRIBUTION OF SOCIOECONOMIC FACTORS

Table 9.1 gives the race and sex-specific distributions for the two SES indicators. Not surprisingly, we find a relationship between race and education. A larger proportion of blacks (31 percent) than whites (14 percent) have less than a high school education; similarly, blacks have a lower proportion of four-year college graduates (13 percent) in comparison to whites (27 percent). Little difference was seen in the comparison of blacks and whites in the middle educational group (56 percent and 59 percent, respectively).

Table 9.1. Distribution of SES Factors According to Race and Sex (Weighted Analysis)

	Black						White					
	Male		Female		Total		Male		Female		Total	
	%	N	%	N	%	N	%	N	%	N	%	N
Education												
Less than High School	30		32		31		15		13		14	
High School Graduate/Some College	57		56		56		53		64		59	
4-Year College Graduate	13		12		13		32		23		27	
	100	(333)	100	(440)	100	(773)	100	(2224)	100	(2550)	100	(4774)
Income												
< $7,000	20		22		21		3		8		6	
$7,000–14,999	16		18		17		11		12		11	
$15,000–24,999	30		34		32		23		30		27	
$25,000+	34		26		30		63		50		56	
	100	(337)	100	(440)	100	(777)	100	(2238)	100	(2555)	100	(4793)

Twenty-one percent of all black respondents reported yearly household incomes under $7,000, while only 6 percent of the white population reported this level of income. While over half of all white respondents (56 percent) reported yearly household incomes of $25,000 or more, less than a third (30 percent) of all black respondents were in this income bracket. These findings underline the importance of taking SES into account when comparing racial groups.

DISTRIBUTION OF ALCOHOL CONSUMPTION, ALCOHOL-RELATED PROBLEMS, AND ILLICIT DRUG USE

Table 9.2 shows the prevalence of alcohol consumption, alcohol-related problems, and illicit drug use in the last 30 days broken down for race and gender groups. For alcohol consumption, black males and females had higher abstention rates than their white counterparts. Black and white females had similar rates of heavier drinking (defined as consuming more than an average of two drinks per day); however, black males had a higher rate of heavier drinking (31 percent) than did white males (23 percent), and black males had a higher mean rate of alcohol consumption per day than white males.

Black and white females showed very similar patterns of alcohol-related problems, whereas a higher proportion of black males had three or more problems. Black males also had a higher mean level of problems than white males or females as a whole. This same pattern holds for illicit drug use, with black males showing the highest use rates. These descriptive findings are similar to those reported elsewhere (e.g., Herd 1990).

EFFECTS OF RACE, GENDER, AND SES ON THREE MEASURES OF SUBSTANCE ABUSE

To test our hypotheses about the interaction of race, gender, and SES, we carried out separate regression analyses for each dependent variable (alcohol consumption, alcohol-related problems, and drug use). Dummy variables were used for gender (0 = female, 1 = male) and race (0 = white, 1 = black). To avoid problems with multicollinearity due to the high correlation between income and education, we computed separate equations for each of these indicators of SES. To test the hypotheses that SES has stronger effects on black males than on other groups, it was necessary to examine the interaction of gender, race, and SES. As Aiken and West (1991) suggest, when examining interaction effects it is necessary to center the independent variables of education and income by setting their means to zero. This procedure reduces the intercorrelations between main effects and interaction effects.

Looking first at the main effects (tables 9.3 and 9.4), gender had a significant effect on all three dependent variables. Not surprisingly, males drank more than females, had more problems as a consequence of drinking, and were more likely to use drugs. We also find that race has a significant main effect; black respondents drank more, had more alcohol-related problems, and used more drugs. Finally, with more years of education, less substance use and fewer problems occurred. However, because the two- and

Table 9.2. Distribution of Alcohol Consumption, Alcohol-Related Problems, and Illicit Drug Use (Weighted Analysis)

	Black			White		
	Male (N = 337)	Female (N = 440)	Total (N = 777)	Male (N = 2238)	Female (N = 2555)	Total (N = 4793)
Alcohol Consumption (Average ounces of absolute alcohol per day)						
0 (Abstainer)	29%	42%	37%	17%	26%	22%
Greater than 0 and less than or equal to 1	40%	51%	46%	60%	67%	64%
Greater than 1 (i.e., over 2 drinks/day)	31%	7%	17%	23%	7%	14%
	100%	100%	100%	100%	100%	100%
Mean Absolute Alcohol/Day	1.37	.33	.78	.94	.30	.60
Alcohol-Related Problems (12 months)						
None	69%	89%	81%	74%	88%	81%
1 or 2	11%	5%	7%	12%	6%	9%
3 or more	20%	6%	12%	14%	6%	10%
	100%	100%	100%	100%	100%	100%
Mean Alcohol-Related Problems	5.5	1.6	3.3	2.8	.9	1.8
Illicit Drug Use (30 days)						
No drug use	84%	93%	89%	92%	94%	93%
Used 1 or 2 times	4%	2%	3%	3%	3%	3%
Used 3 or more times	12%	5%	8%	5%	3%	4%
	100%	100%	100%	100%	100%	100%
Mean Drug Use	2.0	1.0	1.4	.9	.4	.6

Table 9.3 Regression Equations: Main and Interaction Effects of Gender, Race, and Income on Alcohol Consumption, Problem Behavior, and Drug Abuse (Beta coefficients in parentheses)

	Dependent Variables					
	Average Ounces of Alcohol/Day		Alcohol Problems 12 Months		Drug Use 30 Days	
	Without Interaction Effects	With Interaction Effects	Without Interaction Effects	With Interaction Effects	Without Interaction Effects	With Interaction Effects
Independent Variables						
Gender (0 = female, 1 = male)	1.02***	.80***	4.78***	3.05***	1.07***	.55**
	(.17)	(.14)	(.10)	(.06)	(.09)	(.04)
Race (0 = white, 1 = black)	.77***	.09	5.33***	.41	2.23***	.68*
	(.10)	(.01)	(.09)	(.01)	(.14)	(.04)
Income	-.003	.01*	-.02	.03	-.01*	-.004
	(-.02)	(.04)	(-.02)	(.03)	(-.03)	(.02)
Constant	0.0		.93		.41	
Multiple R	.23		.14		.17	
R²	.04		.02		.03	
Interaction Effects						
Race × Gender		.67**		4.77**		1.49**
		(.06)		(.06)		(.07)
Income × Gender		-.01**		-.04		-.002
		(-.04)		(-.03)		(.005)
Income × Race		-.02**		-.09		-.04**
		(-.05)		(-.03)		(-.06)
Income × Gender × Race		-.04***		-.40***		-.10***
		(-.09)		(-.10)		(-.10)
Constant		.34		1.60		.60
Multiple R		.25		.19		.23
R²		.06		.04		.05

Notes:
* p < .05   ** p < .01   *** p < .001

Table 9.4 Regression Equations: Main and Interaction Effects of Gender, Race, and Education on Alcohol Consumption, Problem Behavior, and Drug Abuse (Beta coefficients in parentheses)

	Dependent Variables					
	Average Ounces of Alcohol/Day		Alcohol Problems 12 Months		Drug Use 30 Days	
	Without Interaction Effects	With Interaction Effects	Without Interaction Effects	With Interaction Effects	Without Interaction Effects	With Interaction Effects
Independent Variables						
Gender (0 = female, 1 = male)	1.02***	.83***	4.75***	2.97***	1.06***	.54**
	(.17)	(.14)	(.10)	(.06)	(.09)	(.04)
Race (0 = white, 1 = black)	.73***	.14	5.30***	.75	2.24***	.90**
	(.10)	(.02)	(.09)	(.01)	(.14)	(.06)
Education (in years)	-.05***	.02	-.24*	.07	-.07**	-.02
	(-.05)	(.02)	(-.03)	(.01)	(-.03)	(-.01)
Constant	0.0		.97		.42	
Multiple R	.21		.14		.17	
R^2	.04		.02		.03	
Interaction Effects						
Race × Gender		.98***		7.46***		2.31***
		(.09)		(.09)		(.10)
Education × Gender		-.08**		-1.5		.02
		(-.05)		(-.01)		(.01)
Education × Race		.10*		-.30		-.14
		(-.04)		(-.02)		(-.03)
Education × Gender × Race		-.18**		-2.39***		-.47**
		(-.05)		(-.08)		(-.06)
Constant		.35		1.67		.63
Multiple R		.24		.18		.21
R^2		.06		.03		.04

Notes:
* $p < .05$ ** $p < .01$ *** $p < .001$

three-way interaction effects are significant, these coefficients should not be interpreted without taking into account the coefficients for the interaction terms (Aiken and West 1991; Stolzenberg 1980). In other words, the significant interaction effects tell us that the effects of one variable depend upon the level of another variable.

In hypothesis 1 we proposed that for blacks, SES would be more strongly related to all three dependent variables than for whites. If this is true, then we should find significant interactions between race and education, as well as between race and income. The interaction effects show support for the hypothesis when the independent variable was income and the dependent variables were alcohol use and drug use (table 9.3). For both of these dependent variables, there was a significant interaction between income and race. Likewise, the hypothesis was supported when the independent variable was education and the dependent variable was alcohol use (table 9.4). However, the hypothesis was not supported when the dependent variable was alcohol problems. To understand the last finding, it is necessary to examine the three-way interactions as we discuss hypothesis 2 below. But before doing so, we first examine the two-way interactions more closely.

To aid in interpreting the interaction effects, the mean scores for each dependent variable for black and white males and females at four income levels are displayed in figures 9.1 through 9.3. Means for each group at three levels of education are displayed in figures 9.4 through 9.6. The interaction effects are strongest for INCOME X RACE on alcohol consumption (figure 9.1) and drug use (figure 9.3). For both, apart from gender differences, there was no difference between blacks and whites in the highest income group ($25,000 or more). In other words, at the higher income levels, blacks and whites look very much alike in their rates of alcohol and drug use. Figure 9.3 indicates that for black men and women, as income decreased, drug use increased. The trend is less clear for whites. Likewise, for blacks especially, as income decreased, the average amount of

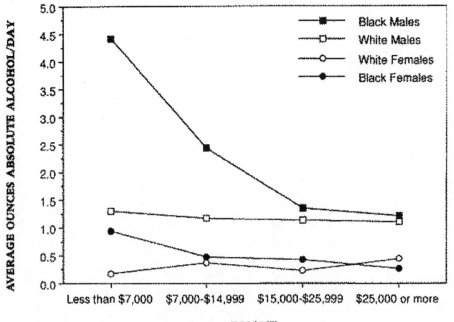

Figure 9.1.   Mean Ounces Absolute Alcohol by Income, Race and Gender

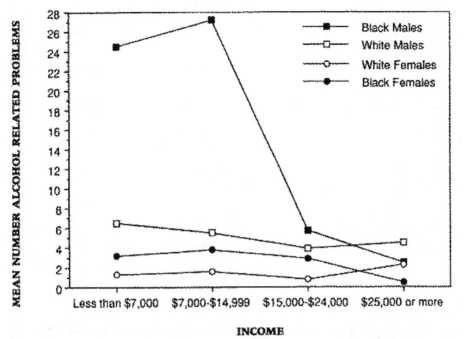

Figure 9.2.   Mean Number Alcohol-Related Problems by Income, Race and Gender

alcohol consumed increased (figure 9.1). A similar pattern occurs when we examine the effects of education level on alcohol use for each race (figure 9.4). At the highest education level, there were virtually no differences between black females and white females, and little difference between black and white males. But as education declined, the rate of alcohol use increased most clearly for black men and women.

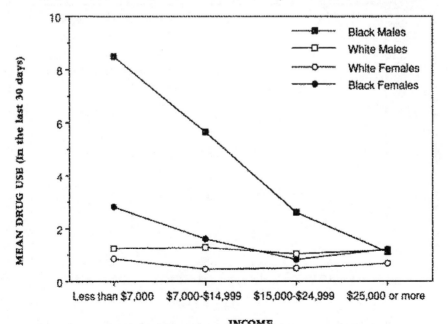

Figure 9.3.   Mean Drug Use in the Last 30 Days by Income, Race and Gender

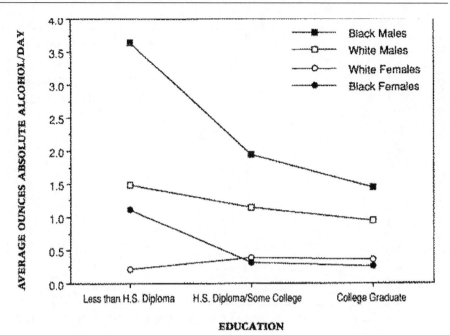

Figure 9.4.   Mean Ounces Absolute Alcohol by Education, Race, and Gender

In Hypothesis 2, we proposed that the effects of low SES would be most dramatic for black males. If this is true, there should be a significant three-way interaction for GENDER X RACE X INCOME and for GENDER X RACE X EDUCATION. The results in tables 9.2 and 9.3 support the hypothesis. Regardless of the indicator of SES, and regardless of the dependent variable, three-way interactions are significant. Figures

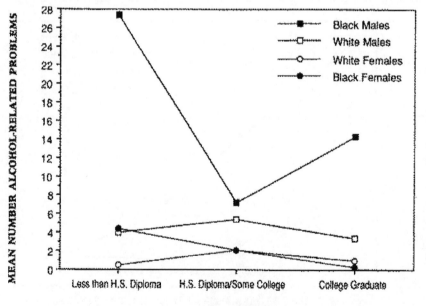

Figure 9.5.   Mean Number Alcohol-Related Problems by Education, Race, and Gender

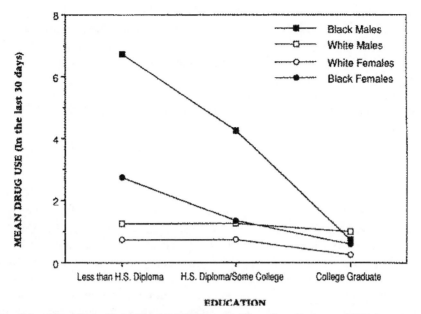

Figure 9.6.   Mean Drug Use in the Last 30 Days by Education, Race, and Gender

9.1 through 9.6 show that in all cases, the indicators of substance abuse were more strongly affected by SES for black males than for any other group. While middle-class black males were not very different from middle-class white males, black males with little education or income were sharply differentiated from white males. Furthermore, as the theory predicts, black males at the lowest SES level were also sharply differentiated from black females. They stand out dramatically with the highest rates of alcohol and drug consumption and the highest rates of alcohol-related problems.

Recent findings about the differences in drinking histories over the life course of black and white males raise questions about how age might affect these findings (Barnes and Welte 1988b). Since age is correlated with both education and income, it might alter the findings significantly if it was included in the analysis. However, the findings remained the same when the data were reanalyzed with age included as a main effect in the regression.

The differences are conveyed most clearly if we compare the means for blacks and whites in the lowest income group, those earning less than $7,000 (figures 9.1–9.3). The gender effect is apparent for this income group—for each race males score higher than females across all three dependent variables. Although there were some interesting fluctuations, means for white males in the lowest income group were relatively close to those for black and white females. The strong interaction effects were most apparent when we compared the means of black and white males in this income group. While white males in the lowest income group consumed, on average, 1.31 ounces of alcohol per day, black males consumed an average of 4.41 ounces (figure 9.1). While low-income white males experienced an average of 6.5 alcohol-related problems per year, black males reported an average of 24.5 problems (figure 9.2). Finally, while white males in the low-income group reported using drugs an average of 1.3 times in the past 30 days, black males reported using drugs an average of 8.5 times (figure 9.3). These findings are consistent with the hypothesis that black males in the lowest SES group are most likely to fall out of the system and to engage in substance abuse.

The only exception to the general trend for black males to show fewer problems as SES increased occurred when we examined the effects of education on alcohol-related problems. Figure 9.5 shows that the relationship between education and alcohol-related problems is curvi-linear. The more education black men received, the fewer alcohol problems they experienced, until they reached the highest levels of education, where problems increased again. Black males with college degrees or above experienced, on average, 13.7 alcohol-related problems per year, while white males experienced, on average, 3.4 problems.

Discussion

Wilson (1987) asks why the social conditions of the black underclass have deteriorated in recent years. He points out that the increasing problems of crime, out-of-wedlock births, female-headed families, and welfare dependency cannot be explained by simplistic theories of racial discrimination, nor by equally simplistic theories of a culture of poverty. Instead, he suggests that these problems are a result of several factors, including deindustrialization and the geographical relocation of stores and factories outside of urban areas. The collapse of blue-collar industries and loss of manufacturing jobs from the 1970s through the 1990s has hit young black males hardest. Declining opportunities have led to higher rates of unemployment, imprisonment, and mortality. However, expanding educational and employment opportunities for women, coupled with support from the welfare system and informal familial networks, may have reduced the impact of deindustrialization on black women. Thus, black males and females experience the effects of deindustrialization differently. Wilson further argues that changes in the black class structure may also be contributing factors. Most notably, reduced discrimination and new opportunities may have resulted in middle-class blacks moving ahead economically and becoming less connected to lower-class blacks in impoverished areas. With less segregation, middle-class blacks are not as constrained to live with and address the needs of the underclass. Ironically, the relative success of middle-class blacks has contributed to isolation, and to the intensification of some inner city problems.

We proposed that Wilson's theory had implications for expected differences in the relationship between substance abuse and SES for blacks and whites, and males and females. The theory implies that middle-class blacks will resemble middle-class whites in their rates of drinking and substance abuse, but that blacks' rates will increase more rapidly as income and education decline. Furthermore, the negative effects of poverty and lack of education will be more dramatic for black men than for black women. By and large the findings support these hypotheses (for similar findings on black men, see Herd 1990).

An examination of the effects of education on alcohol and drug consumption showed that black and white male college graduates differed little in alcohol and drug use. However, as education declines, use increases to the point that black males with less than a high school education drink and use drugs more than three times as much as white males. The only exception to the pattern occurs for the relationship between education and alcohol-related problems. The more education men have, the less they drink, whether they are black or white. Yet, when highly educated black men do drink, they are more likely to have problems (figure 9.5). This finding is not explained by Wilson's theory. Kanter (1977) argues that minorities in higher status positions are more closely scrutinized and their nonconforming behavior is more readily detected. Perhaps the high visibility of black men in the middle class makes them more susceptible to stigmatization over problems related to alcohol use (Park 1983). This question should be examined in future research (for recent research addressing these issues, see Hilton 1987).

The effects of SES on substance abuse are most dramatic when we use income as the indicator of SES. On the average, impoverished black men use drugs at more than five times the rate of impoverished white men; impoverished black men drink at more than three times the rate of other groups. When they drink, they are three to four times more likely to experience drinking-related problems than comparable white men. These findings on the relationship between poverty and deviant behavior among black men are consistent with other recent findings (see, for example, Gibbs 1988; Sterne and Pittman 1976). They are also consistent with Wilson's thesis that lower SES black men are particularly hard hit by the polarization of blacks in the wake of deindustrialization.

Alcohol and drug consumption should be included in attempts to understand how black males are affected by the emerging class structure in the postindustrial society. Although our findings can be interpreted within the context of Wilson's theory, they leave many unanswered questions that should be explored in future research. Wilson's sociohistorical analysis implies that the polarization of black males intensified during the 1970s and 1980s. Our cross-sectional data do not allow us to examine whether the polarization of drug and alcohol use occurred in concert with other indicators of change. This question should be explored with longitudinal or panel data.

It is not clear how drug and alcohol consumption fit into the larger frame of the life course of black males in the underclass. To what extent are the higher rates of consumption a cause or a consequence of the marginal, anomic roles of impoverished black males outside economic and familial systems? Are drugs and alcohol used as a means to cope by some men who are cut off from economic opportunities as well as emotional support? Or is substance abuse part of an adolescent lifestyle that culminates with disengagement?

Answers to these questions might emerge from closer analysis of some of the intriguing findings about the relationships among age, race, and patterns of alcohol consumption. Heavy drinking by black males increases as they move through young adulthood and into middle age (Barnes and Welte 1988b; Herd 1990). The reverse is true for white males, whose rates of alcohol consumption exceed blacks when they are young, but decline as they mature and age. It may be that the white pattern reflects the stresses of the young adult transition, which declines with age, while the black pattern reflects the cumulative impact with age of the frustrations of marginalization from economic and familial systems. The findings in this study held up even when we introduced age into the regression as a control variable. However, future research should look more closely at the ways in which age fits into the emerging pattern of race, class, and gender dynamics.

Like previous researchers, we find that both abstention and heavy drinking are high among blacks. How do we account for the "two worlds" of orientation toward alcohol among blacks? What is the relationship between the abstaining pattern and race, class, gender, and age? How does this pattern fit into the larger frame of the transformation of the structure of black life that has paralleled deindustrialization? Are the abstainers part of a life structure that is growing or eroding in face of change? These questions are not addressed in this chapter, but they are important to ask if we are to understand the effects of deindustrialization and to develop policies that might reduce drug and alcohol consumption.

Although this chapter's purpose has not been to address policy issues, it is appropriate to close by pointing out one obvious policy implication. Drug and alcohol use are both a symptom and a cause of a number of social problems. Our findings show that they are a significant factor in the lives of disadvantaged black males. If, as Wilson has suggested, many problems of blacks in the underclass hinge on the marginalization of black males, and if alcohol and drugs play a part in that marginalization, then special emphasis should be placed on meeting black men's needs through increasing economic opportunities and education and rehabilitation programs aimed at reducing drug and alcohol consumption.

Note

The authors would like to thank Dr. Blanche Frank and staff of the New York State Division of Substance Abuse Services for their efforts in carrying out this study, Barbara Dintcheff for assistance in data analysis, and Audrey Topinko for preparing the manuscript for publication. Correspondence to: Barnes, Research Institute on Addictions, 1021 Main Street, Buffalo, NY 14203.

References

Aiken, Leona S., and Stephen G. West. 1991. *Multiple Regression: Testing and Interpreting Interactions.* Newbury Park, Calif.: Sage Publications.

Barnes, Grace M., and John W. Welte. 1988a. *Alcohol Use and Abuse Among Adults in New York State* (Monograph). Buffalo, N.Y.: Research Institute on Alcoholism.

———. 1988b. "Drinking among black, Hispanic and white adults in New York State." Poster presented at the annual meeting of the Research Society on Alcoholism, Wild Dunes, S.C.

Bowman, Phillip J. 1991. "Work life." In *Life in Black America,* ed. James S. Jackson, 124–155. Newbury Park, Calif.: Sage Publications.

Dawkins, Marvin P. 1980. "Alcohol information on black Americans: Current status and future needs." *Journal of Alcohol and Drug Education* 25:28–40.

Frank, Blanche, Rozanne Marel, James Schmeidler, and Michael Maranda. 1988. *State Household Survey of Substance Abuse, 1986.* New York: New York State Division of Substance Abuse Services.

Gibbs, Jewelle Taylor. 1988. *Young, Black and Male in America.* New York: Auburn House.

Harper, Frederick D. 1976. "Overview: Alcohol and blacks." In *Alcohol Abuse and Black America,* ed. Frederick D. Harper, 1–12. Alexandria, Va.: Douglass Publishers.

Herd, Denise. 1985. *Social Contexts of Drinking Among Black and White Americans.* Berkeley, Calif.: Alcohol Research Group.

———. 1987. "Rethinking black drinking." *British Journal of Addiction* 82:219–223.

———. 1990. "Subgroup differences in drinking patterns among black and white men: Results from a national survey." *Journal of Studies on Alcohol* 51:221–232.

Hilton, Michael E. 1987. "Demographic characteristics and the frequency of heavy drinking as predictors of self reported drinking problems." *British Journal of Addiction* 82:913–925.

———. 1988. "The demographic distribution of drinking patterns in 1984." *Drug and Alcohol Dependence* 22:37–47.

Kanter, Rosabeth Moss. 1977. *Men and Women of the Corporation.* New York: Basic Books.

Knupfer, Genevieve. 1989. "The prevalence in various social groups of eight different drinking patterns, from abstaining to frequent drunkenness: Analysis of 10 U.S. surveys combined." *British Journal of Addiction* 84:1305–1318.

National Institute on Alcohol Abuse and Alcoholism. 1979. *Alcohol Topics in Brief: Alcohol and Blacks.* Rockville, Md.: National Clearinghouse for Alcohol Information.

National Institute on Drug Abuse. 1985. *National Household Survey on Drug Abuse.* Rockville, Md.: National Institute on Drug Abuse.

Park, Peter. 1983. "Social-class factors in alcoholism." In *The Biology of Alcoholism, Vol. 6, The Pathogenesis of Alcoholism: Psychosocial Factors,* ed. Benjamin Kissin and Henri Begleiter, 365–404. New York: Plenum.

Sterne, Muriel W., and David J. Pittman. 1976. "Alcohol abuse and the black family." In *Alcohol Abuse and Black America,* ed. Frederick D. Harper, 177–185. Alexandria, Va.: Douglass Publishers.

Stolzenberg, Ross M. 1980. "The measurement and decomposition of causal effects in nonlinear and nonadditive models." In *Sociological Methodology,* ed. Karl L. Schuessler, 459–488. San Francisco: Jossey-Bass.

Wilson, William J. 1978. *The Declining Significance of Race.* Chicago: University of Chicago Press.

———. 1987. *The Truly Disadvantaged.* Chicago: University of Chicago Press.

Part IV

SOCIAL WORLDS: QUALITATIVE RESEARCH

Qualitative research is designed to provide authentic and detailed accounts of the lives, troubles, and routine activities of people in their natural settings. Using qualitative techniques like field observation and in-depth interviews, ethnographic researchers have contributed richly textured portraits of the social worlds of drinkers and drug users to the literature on social problems. Watching and listening to people in the settings where they live, work, and play allows the sociological observer to see and feel "reality" first-hand from the insider's perspective. Thus, qualitative research aims at fuller understanding of the social contexts, shared meanings, and personal decisions that affect the initiation and development of drug-using careers.

A classic example of how qualitative research can provide valuable insight into the social bases of drug use and drug experiences is Howard Becker's study, "Becoming a Marihuana User" (1953; 1963). During the late 1940s Becker worked professionally as a jazz musician, one of the few occupational groups in which marijuana smoking was relatively common at that time. This gave him a unique opportunity to observe marijuana use in natural settings, such as jazz clubs, and to make contacts with musicians and other drug users in this deviant social world. Based on his field observations and interviews with numerous marijuana users, Becker concluded that an individual's ability to get high on marijuana as well as the necessary motivation for continued use of the drug were acquired through a process of social interaction with other users. Becker's convincing, qualitative account of marijuana use as a socially learned activity contrasts markedly with individualistic explanations of drug use that were prevalent during the 1940s and continue to be popular today.

Similar to Becker's study, the first chapter in this part by Don Zimmerman and Lawrence Wieder uses qualitative methods to shed light on the socially organized character of marijuana use. In initial fieldwork in a drug-using community in Southern California in the early 1970s, Zimmerman and Wieder heard one of their informants say that "you can't help but get stoned" on marijuana whenever members of this community got together socially. In contrast, other members of this community described marijuana smoking as a spontaneous, unplanned act of individuals that in no way involved group coercion or "peer pressure." Zimmerman and Wieder went on to examine how these seemingly different ways of talking about marijuana use—as inevitable

185

or as spontaneous—both made sense in the context of the ritual organization of marijuana smoking situations in this community. For instance, they noted that in any social gathering it was virtually certain that someone would have marijuana and that
someone would "spontaneously" want to smoke. Once use began, the drug was ritu-
ally circulated to all those present so that any participant "couldn't help but get
stoned." In addition to their useful ethnographic account of marijuana smoking rituals during the heyday of the "counterculture," Zimmerman and Wieder show that the
meanings and motives that people attach to their drug-using activity are intimately tied
to the social organization of the settings in which use occurs.

In the second chapter, Patricia and Peter Adler present an insider's perspective on a
deviant occupational world in their analysis of career entry, shifts, and retirements of
drug dealers and smugglers in the marijuana and cocaine trade. Based on six years of
participant observation and interviews with 65 dealers and smugglers, the Adlers focus
on how drug traffickers enter the business, how they rise to the top, how they become
disenchanted and leave the business, and why most return. Dealers usually start as drug
users and movement to the higher echelons of dealing is very competitive and difficult.
Nearly all quit the drug business at one time or another because of the risks of the work,
disillusionment, and burnout. Many who leave or who are forced out re-enter the business; relatively few remain permanently retired. This study is one of the few that provides a detailed exploration of the occupational world of upper-level drug dealers. As
you read this insightful ethnography, consider how the career paths of individuals in the
drug business parallel or differ from those of people involved in legal enterprises.

References

Becker, Howard S. 1953. "Becoming a marihuana user." *American Journal of Sociology*
    59:235–243.
———. 1963. *Outsiders: Studies in the Sociology of Deviance.* New York: Free Press.

CHAPTER 10

You Can't Help but Get Stoned

NOTES ON THE SOCIAL ORGANIZATION OF MARIJUANA SMOKING

Don H. Zimmerman and D. Lawrence Wieder

In the course of a year-long ethnographic study of one local manifestation of the counter-culture,[1] one of our informants volunteered the following remark, "You can't help but get stoned. It's really hard to turn the thing down."

Given our interest in the pattern of drug use, particularly marijuana, this comment immediately caught our attention. What the informant seemed to be saying was that there existed an environment of continuous opportunity for smoking marijuana ("everywhere you go . . .").[2] Moreover, beyond its sheer availability, the remark implies that the settings through which this informant moved were focal points for external pressures which made it difficult to avoid smoking ("hard to turn . . . down"). It was as if members of the community were fated to come under the influence, no matter who they were with or where they were ("you can't help but get stoned").

Upon first reflection, the remark suggested to us that the social group we were studying explicitly provided for—if it did not mandate—many and diverse occasions for the express purpose of smoking marijuana. Yet, as we pursued this idea in contacts with other informants, we discovered that they did not view their day-to-day social encounters as primarily occasions for smoking. A few situations, e.g., parties, going to certain movies or rock concerts, or introducing someone to marijuana for the first time (cf. Becker, 1963:41–58), were designated as all but ritual times for getting stoned for which some explicit forethought and anticipation might be expected. But by and large, our informants insisted that marijuana smoking "just happened," and that no one in particular planned it. The activity of getting stoned, which occurred with predictable regularity, was characterized as an essentially "spontaneous" or "impulsive" event (Cf. Cavan, 1972:82 and *passim;* Turner, 1976:997–1000).

We thus faced the issue of how to regard these two accounts. On the one hand, we have "getting stoned" portrayed as an all but coerced behavior, an unavoidable concomitant of participation in the daily life of the community—something like *a social fact* in Durkheim's sense (1966: 1–13). On the other, we are told that marijuana smoking occurs at the whim of the individual and is not to be viewed as a socially regimented activity.

Neither account fit exactly with information we had already gathered. That is, we were reasonably sure that members of the community did not, to the last individual, get stoned at each and every opportunity, and it was also apparent that individuals often did make careful provision to ensure that smoking would occur on specific occasions other than the ones designated above. Perhaps the account "You can't help but get stoned" was merely an exaggeration of the facts. The claim that smoking was "spontaneous" could be an essentially ideological response to our queries. Our informants, after all, were participants in a subculture which valued "freedom" and "orientation to the present moment" (Wieder and Zimmerman, 1974:141–142; 1976:312–330) so it is understandable that they described their behavior in terms compatible with such ideals. It is also possible to view the alleged inability to avoid marijuana intoxication as simply a consequence of the fact that *most* members of community (a "drug culture") were "spontaneously" moved to smoke *most* of the time.

It is likely that each of the interpretations captures an aspect of the truth. Yet these interpretations required that we view our informants' accounts as merely candidate ethnographic descriptions to be tested in further investigation. We suggest that treating informants' statements as quasi-social-scientific observations diverts attention from a research task prior to the determination of the truth of a given account, namely, the specification of how to *hear* remarks like, "You can't help but get stoned," or "smoking is spontaneous," that is to locate their sense within the context of the social arrangements of which they are a part and which they describe. Such statements are not so much propositions advancing truth-claims as they are *instructions* informing the initiate or the outsider how to "see" or "understand" events from the point of the native (Cf. Cavan, 1972:199–207; Wieder, 1974:184–218).

The problem for the outsider, of course, is how correctly to interpret the instructions when they themselves are conveyed by natural language expressions whose context is the same set of affairs the instructions seek to explain. While members of the same society usually share a common language, this general observation does not guarantee that natural language expressions can be analyzed for their meaning without reference to their context. Mills (1940) understood this when he proposed studying the situated character of motive accounts. Others have called attention to the numerous aspects of the importance of context through the concepts of "domain of discourse" (Conklin, 1962; Frake, 1962), "indexicality of expressions" (Garfinkel, 1967:1–34; Garfinkel and Sacks, 1970; Cicourel, 1974:56, 87–88, 113–114 ff.; Bar-Hillel, 1954), "setting" (Hymes, 1962), and "embedded instructions" (Garfinkel, 1966: Wieder, 1974:183–214). These concepts point to the wide variation in situated accounts and to their being largely understandable as aspects of features of the scenes they illuminate.

Informants' remarks are seldom disinterested, detached, or idle, as if motivated by mere theoretical interest; they are descriptions done from *within,* reflecting the practical concerns of the speaker. They are addressed to an outsider, one who is, moreover, given to incessant and, from the insider's point of view, frequently naive questioning. Often, no amount of interrogation is sufficient to bridge the gap between the ethnographer and the native; the latter must lead the former by the hand to the round of social life where the dialogue becomes enriched by the particulars of interaction. Indeed, it is the specific aim of the strategy of participant observation to develop the ability to see and to hear in *native* terms through involvement in the research setting-up to the limit imposed by the constraints of disciplined inquiry (Cf. Malinowski, 1922:25; Kluckhohn, 1949:299–300; Bruyn, 1966:15, 21; Williams, 1967:61; Lofland, 1971:4, 7; and Bogdan and Taylor, 1975:8–11).

In this chapter, we offer a description of what may be termed the "social organization of marijuana smoking," that is, a characterization of the social context for the two descriptions of the practice of smoking marijuana that we have discussed. Our concern is less with the substantive details of this activity than with the discovery of those features of its organization which would *warrant* its characterization by participants in particular ways, e.g., as "spontaneous" and "unavoidable." We pay particular attention to how this organization methodically provides for the routine occurrence of marijuana use, particularly in relation to the structure of social gatherings, and how marijuana smoking is initiated or resumed in those gatherings. Our objective is not to determine whether the occurrence of marijuana smoking is really spontaneous in some ultimate sense, or whether it is in fact unavoidable. Instead, we want to consider how daily activities are organized so that the "here-now-this-that" of interaction, its particulars, are produced and exhibited to participants such that the expressions "You can't help but get stoned," and "It just happens," could both be generated from the everyday possibilities made available by that social organization (Cf. Sacks, 1975). To approach this task is to approach an understanding, albeit limited, of the relationship between talk and action in a social setting (Cf. Wieder, 1974).

The Social Organization of Marijuana Smoking

The pursuit of our problem involves the examination of a number of related topics in the social organization of marijuana use—the availability of marijuana for consumption, how marijuana is defined as a social object, the ritual and etiquette of marijuana smoking, the nature of social gatherings, and the structure of smoking occasions. These topics illuminate the warrant for talk about the inevitability of "getting stoned" and the "spontaneous" character of marijuana smoking.

SUPPLY

Since space does not permit a detailed discussion of the community network through which marijuana was obtained, we simply note that, at any given time, any individual was likely to have some friend who was dealing, usually on a casual, part-time basis, or who knows someone who was dealing. Involvement in normal friendship patterns in the community all but guaranteed regular and ready access to a supply when marijuana is available in the area. For residents of the community, marijuana was relatively safe to sell and relatively easy to buy. Hence, it was ordinarily readily available (Cf. Cavan, 1972:118–128).

SMOKING ETIQUETTE

Smoking marijuana in the company of others is a practice guided by a set of rituals and expectations, familiar to those with even a casual knowledge of counter-culture settings.

1. Persons possessing marijuana are expected to share it. If people are gathered in someone's house or apartment, the host—if she/he has a supply—typically offers it to visitors, much in the same way coffee or an alcoholic beverage is offered to guests in other social settings. Alternatively, a visitor may provide a joint if, for example, the host's supply is exhausted, or if the host has the reputation for not keeping a personal "stash." Often visitors will bring a joint or two to share with friends, particularly if they have marijuana they consider exceptionally potent. In summary, marijuana is socially defined as a communal commodity, to be freely offered and freely requested.

2. Given that marijuana is to be smoked on some occasion, the joint or pipe is passed around to everybody present. The ritual of passing a joint or a pipe around is a highly routinized practice in the community studied, as elsewhere. Regardless of who provides the marijuana or how the occasion is initiated, it is to be shared in this fashion by anyone present who wishes to participate. It would be an egregious breach of etiquette for someone to produce a joint, light and smoke it without passing it. For example, when presented with a hypothetical situation in which someone did not pass a joint, one informant exploded: "[It] just doesn't happen. Nobody would let it happen; they'd just take it away from him" (Cf. Cavan, 1972: 138, n.30).

Obviously, when individuals smoke alone, the ritual does not supply. The striking fact is that when one is engaged in smoking, in the company of others, the joint is almost always passed. This pattern also appears when several joints are lit. Even when the parties involved do not know each other (as in the case of a rock concert or other public gathering at which it is cool to smoke), it is extremely rare for individuals who are sitting near or next to each other to smoke separate joints when they are co-participants in a gathering.

Although the ritual of passing the joint may seem trivial, subsequent analysis will show that this practice is a critical feature of the social arrangements examined here.

3. Smoking marijuana with others entails a commitment to an on-going social occasion. Sharing a joint with friends establishes the expectation that an exchange of sociable talk or activity will also be shared; for a smoking occasion entails social obligations beyond taking a "hit" or two as the joint makes its round. It would be easy to overemphasize the obligation not to "smoke and run." Smoking occasions are frequently characterized by shifting personnel, and particularly for members of the counter-culture, the emphasis on "doing your own thing" softens the constraint implied by this expectation.

However, a smoking occasion is first and foremost a sociable gathering. When friends come together, they talk, play music, eat, and go out to movies and other public events. As noted, informants uniformly balk at identifying most social occasions, or phases of social occasions, as necessarily calling for the use of marijuana or any other drug. Instead, they prefer to view smoking as something that "just happens" along with other events that ordinarily occur when people get together. It is worth noting that this contrasts markedly with the typical circumstances under which more potent drugs such as LSD are ingested (Cf. Zimmerman and Wieder, 1971: Chapter 4; Stoddart, 1974).

4. Within the limits of the marijuana available, persons may smoke as much as they desire: persons are free to get as stoned as they wish. Much of the etiquette governing this form of "hospitality" and "sociability" is similar to other forms, for example, the hospitality governing the serving of food and beverages. In contrast to most occasions of alcohol use, there appear to be no social sanctions controlling the amount of marijuana an individual may properly consume.

A common consequence of a high intake of marijuana appears to be a turn inward, a lapse into silence, an individual and private "tripping," for example, absorption into the music playing on the stereo or fascination with a candle flame. One way of characterizing this effect of smoking is a lapse of *social presence*. The individual need not necessarily be available for conversation or other group activities. Such a lapse is not defined as inappropriate, as it might be at a cocktail party where such a failure of social presence might be taken as a sign of drunkenness or unsociability. Being very stoned and withdrawing is an accepted form of participation in a smoking occasion, another way of "doing one's own thing" (as, for example, would be the opposite, extreme gregariousness).

One obvious consequence of the lack of social constraint on the amount of marijuana consumed is that persons may continue to smoke over some period of time or, if smoking has been terminated, resume smoking at a later time. This suggests that, structurally, a smoking occasion has no definite boundaries in time.

This loose temporal structure is related to the treatment of newcomers to a gathering. A characteristic of social life in the community is that people drop in on each other, day or night, often unannounced, and do so frequently. If someone drops in on a gathering where smoking is in progress, the newcomers will be included as a matter of course. Or, the newcomers may reinitiate smoking by reason of the etiquette governing hospitality.

GATHERINGS

Regular marijuana smokers often smoke alone. Of concern here is the marijuana smoking that occurs in social situations. Gatherings happen when friends visit each other or when they decide to go somewhere together (for example to a movie or some other public event, to the mountains, etc.) or when they decide to have a party. We will focus on gatherings of friends at someone's house or apartment. Our diary materials suggest that this is the most typical type of socializing. In contrast to gatherings for the purpose of going out, gatherings at someone's house are more frequently spontaneous and uncoordinated, involving no invitations or advance notice from host or guests. There are no real hosts. It is precisely the casualness of such gatherings that contributes most directly to the environment of continuous opportunity and the spontaneity of smoking.

A relatively obvious factor influencing the frequency of social gatherings is time. In simple terms, a gathering consumes time—the time spent in sociable interaction and the time spent in transit for those not residing in the gathering place.

Individuals deeply involved in this sub-culture tend to emphasize the here-and-now and to reject the transitional middle-class emphasis on work, career, and the rational use of time (Wieder and Zimmerman, 1974: 141–144; 1976: 327–330). For such a person, much of the day may be consumed in social gatherings. One pattern of interaction prominent in the community is what one informant termed "the circuit." The circuit consists of a number of apartments or houses occupied by particular friends who may be visited at virtually any time and where it is normal to find others gathered. Often such places may be visited serially for a congenial gathering or gatherings.

The availability of persons and places to being "visited" is a feature attended to by members of the community. The permissibility of participating in and thus sustaining such a pattern is something to which persons "within the scene" are socialized.

The casualness that characterizes the pattern of visiting directly supports the value of spontaneity, of "hanging loose." Community members expect each other to be prepared for and, more important, to be open to unannounced visits possibly developing into extended interaction.

Given the institution of the circuit and the emphasis on unplanned social contacts, a routine day for many young people in the community consists of a series of impromptu gatherings across constantly changing collections of persons and shifting locations. These social contacts, as they coalesce into gatherings, represent points at which a smoking occasion may be initiated or resumed.

This generalization, however, holds as stated for gatherings of mutual friends. If some persons in a gathering are known to only some of those present, those unacquainted with them are typically reluctant to initiate smoking. The usual procedure would be to allow those who know the individuals in question to decide the issue of smoking since they presumably are in a position to know if it would be "cool" (meaning in this instance *safe,* or at least socially acceptable) to smoke in their presence.

Discussion

We have briefly examined a set of features intimately involved with marijuana use: the organization of marijuana distribution at the "street level," the etiquette or social expectations regulating the use of marijuana on social occasions, and the pattern of "getting together" characterizing the usual mode of sociable interaction among the young people in question. Now let us reconsider the notion of "spontaneity."

SPONTANEITY

As suggested earlier, the notion of spontaneity implies that an event is unplanned, unannounced, unscheduled, and that no particular account of it is needed. Most particularly, no appeal need be made to any social circumstance or convention which, from without, dictates, calls for, condones, excuses, or can be assigned responsibility for the event. For example, an informant was asked why she smoked a joint with a friend on a particular occasion, and she answered, "I suppose I just felt like it. It was a nice sunny day."

Similar questioning often prompted other informants to respond with variants of the above: "just felt like it," "there was nothing specific to do," or "to pass the afternoon." The explicitly stated "motives" appear to stress the orientation of the individual *outward* to the environment rather than the press of external events or social custom *inward* on the person.

The question "Why did you smoke *then?*" is far from a neutral probe for it implies that the behavior under scrutiny, namely, marijuana smoking, calls for some explanation. Blum and McHugh (1971:103–104) suggest that motive functions as an observer's rule for linking biographies with events and for detecting the methodical character of an action. In these terms, the request for a specific motive for smoking—given the assumption that persons are at least tacitly oriented to the nature of motives in the sense that Blum and McHugh (1971) propose—suggests inferences concerning what *kind* of person it is that is smoking and *what* the smoking is meant to accomplish. To counter with the claim that motives are various is to argue that no single rule is available which will link biography to event and that the event itself is non-methodical, that is, is not a means to accomplish some display. Paradoxically, the variability of "motive" and the noninstrumental character of smoking is taken to be *expressive* of spontaneity. This paradox is resolved, however, if we recognize that the rules which provide for linkage are features of social organization, and as such, can operate to sever linkages to individual biography. Routine action is action which is "motivationally transparent" (Cf. Zimmerman, 1970: 326–327) and which ordinarily requires no special account. What our informants were telling us was that our question was inappropriate and "unaskable." (That is, if the question was understood to mean, how do you arrange your environment so as to have handy excuses to smoke—in the same sense that heavy drinkers might find many occasions to celebrate).

These responses elaborate our earlier point concerning the possible ideological character of the insistence on the spontaneity of marijuana smoking: the community celebrates doing what one feels like, whenever one likes, for whatever reason, free of middle-class "hangups" (Cf. Spates, 1976:870–871; Turner, 1976:492–945; 997–1000).

We may now address the issue of how to hear remarks concerning spontaneity by virtue of having in hand a description of how marijuana smoking is organized. We suggest that what is at work is an elegant mechanism which, if it does not hide its operation from those who employ it, relieves them of the necessity of explicitly acknowledging it. It is, in short, a form of organization adequate to provide for the regular occurrence of marijuana smoking, while rendering the methodical social practices which insure its initiation as merely individual choices or the selection of one among many options available. The question that emerges quite naturally at this point is, "How is the spontaneous smoking of marijuana routinized?"

ENSURING THAT MARIJUANA SMOKING "JUST HAPPENS" ON AN EVERYDAY BASIS

On the basis of the description of the social organization of marijuana smoking already accomplished, the following formulation may be suggested: whenever people in the community get together, *any one of them may properly initiate a smoking occasion.*

Marijuana may be offered or requested by any participant in a gathering, and if it is available, it is to be shared.

These seemingly trivial points of etiquette become quite consequential when considered in conjunction with other expectations operating in the scene. The socially appropriate use of marijuana is not constrained to designated times of day, nor is it restricted to ceremonial or other regularized social occasions such as lunchtime or dinnertime or a nightcap. Thus, the motivations of individual persons to smoke are not pointedly coordinated in the same sense that the motivations of individuals to drink are integrated via ritualized times and occasions.

The mechanism for involving a set of individuals (who may or may not have had a specific intention to smoke at the time and place in question) is rather simple. Whenever a joint is lit, it is inevitably passed around to all present. Since anyone can properly initiate a smoking occasion, only one person need decide to smoke. Once smoking is initiated, it is *structurally* a group practice. No specific agreement among parties present—in the sense of an explicit alignment of individual intentions—is required to generate a smoking occasion. The group valued ideal of spontaneity, the claim that it "just happens" without plan or forethought, is upheld by virtue of the fact that the practice is organized and resources made available in such a way that the responsibility for initiation of smoking is diffused among group members. Even if it happens that everyone present wishes to smoke, anticipated smoking, brought their own supply just in case, the mode of occurrence requires no explicit collective decision. The fact that someone will usually want to smoke, and that someone will usually have a supply is sufficient guarantee that the practice will occur not only regularly, but predictably.

This analysis does not propose that members of the group do not, as individuals, plan or scheme to ensure the occurrence of smoking, or that they are overwhelmed by its spontaneity. What the analysis does suggest is that in this community, the sub-culture has generated a social context relatively free of the conventions and schedules that regulate the use of the recreational drug of choice in the larger society. The loose temporal structure of gatherings, the etiquette of marijuana use, and the lack of social necessity for justifying involvement in smoking at any given time or place instead specify the located sense of the notion of "spontaneity." That smoking "just happens" does not mean that it is not socially organized, and thus is random or haphazard in nature, but rather that it is an event of a particular kind of social organization, so constructed that its methodical generation is routinely obscured in its very mode of occurrence. Thus groups organize themselves to uphold the values they espouse.

That the systematic bases for marijuana smoking apparently are not explicitly acknowledged by members of the group does not mean that the consequences of such organization are not experienced and commented upon.

"YOU CAN'T HELP BUT GET STONED"

The analysis provided here of the social mechanism sustaining the group member's sense that marijuana smoking is a spontaneous event also depicts the circumstances which warrant the proposal that: "You can't help but get stoned. Just everywhere you go everyone has it. It's hard to turn the thing down."

Since the joint, once lit, is passed to all present, participants in a gathering that has become a smoking occasion are repeatedly presented with the choice of declining to smoke and to "pass" as the joint makes its rounds. Thus, the situation is structured to promote smoking and by its very organization focuses attention on the non-smoker who must continue to refuse the joint as it is passed. When an individual declines to smoke, she/he often offers an account likely to be acceptable to the group, for example being "into meditation," which is heard as *"I would* smoke but I'm doing something now that requires that I abstain." A newcomer to the group, or someone unknown to some of those present, may create uneasiness if not paranoia by declining since it is by participation that the smoking occasion is validated and situationally appropriate identities established. Not smoking is thus a problematic matter once smoking has been initiated. But given that marijuana is available, that individuals frequently carry their own supply, and that the patterns of visiting and the constantly shifting composition of gatherings of friends enhance the chance that smoking will be re-initiated over the course of the day, the informant has provided a very succinct account of this aspect of life in the community.

It is not clear, however, that we should regard the above characterization as simply a useful generalization provided by an unusually perceptive informant. It is not simply that she noted to herself the availability of marijuana or its distribution, or that it is usually offered to all present. Nor is it the case that contrary instances—unavailability, gaps in distribution, stingy hosts, persons who declined to smoke—would constitute a serious challenge to the picture she provided. We suggested instead that the informant's remarks are warranted by the social organization we have described, that is, on an appreciation of how effective such social arrangements were in facilitating marijuana use. Thus, "everywhere" and "everyone" are those typical places and persons that come under the jurisdiction of those arrangements while the inability to refuse is not so much an admission of weak will or uncontrollable craving as a depiction of the typical structuring of choice—one must choose *not* to smoke. Once a member of the community and a participant in and contributor to its ways of organizing life, one may not be able to "avoid" marijuana intoxication by virtue of the fact that one is party to the very activities which sustain this mode of managing marijuana use.

Conclusion

In this chapter we have explored a particular type of social organization in relation to informants' characterizations of the state of affairs it methodically provides for. Our guiding notion was that indigenous descriptions produced by parties to a social setting may be viewed as instructions for grasping the nature of events from a native's perspective. We proposed that such instructions must be referred to the organization of such settings for their sense. This decision permitted us to entertain the possibility that the claim that practices such as marijuana smoking were spontaneous—which at first glance appeared ideological—nonetheless possessed some definite organizational sense and warrant. The question was: what was the nature of this organization? We were able to view the assertion that marijuana smoking "just happened" from the same stance.

It should be clear by now that we proceeded by employing our informant's remarks—in the context of what we already understood about the community we were studying—as guides to further inquiry, instructions, as it were, for assembling disparate observations into a coherent pattern of activity. In turn, the emergence of pattern further deepened our grasp of *how* our informants' commentaries articulated with social arrangements in the setting. Thus what we heard from the people we studied was both resource and topic and yielded a picture of social organization sustained by our independent investigation but consonant with out subjects' accounts of its consequences. Our informants were not simply surrogate ethnographers furnishing disinterested descriptions of their activities, but neither were they dupes fooled by collective prejudices into thinking their activities were of one sort when they "really" were of quite another. The problem was to discover in what way to regard what was said.

In the final analysis, the talk that goes on in and about social settings cannot be regarded as distinct from the setting, as something that can be detached and examined at leisure apart from the lively context of its occurrence. The contours of socially organized settings (and the internal structure of the organization itself) often require an instructed gaze provided by indigenous accounts; but it is the working of that social organization which invests the accounts with specific sense. If in some setting group members complain of the inevitability of conflict as an existential condition, we should be alert to the challenge thereby posed, namely, to discover the relationship between the account offered and management of daily life in the setting. To the extent that there is a demonstrable relationship, there is then some reason to believe that we are in the presence of consequential talk embedded in the workings of an actual social organization.

Notes

This chapter is based on ethnographic research funded by Grant 70-039, Law Enforcement Assistance Administration, United States Department of Justice. The findings and interpretations drawn in this article do not necessarily reflect the policies or official positions of the funding agency. We wish to acknowledge the assistance of Dorothy Miller and of Suzanne Wedow, Ron Kaiman, Peter Suczek, Tom Wallace, and Steve Plevin, by whose efforts much of the data were collected. Gail Jefferson, Harvey Molotch, Melvin Pollner, and Thomas Wilson provided helpful comments.

1. We employed five research assistants and two secretary-typists who lived in and to varying degrees identified with the community under study. On the basis of lengthy tape-recorded interviews with them, we forged an initial description of the value-themes of the community. Through contacts provided by our research assistants we obtained twenty additional biographic interviews with community members. More extensive material which overlapped with this body of data was obtained by a method we have referred to elsewhere (Zimmerman & Wieder, 1977) as the "Diary-Diary-Interview Method." Sixty community members kept diaries for us for seven consecutive days. These diaries were subjected to a preliminary analysis which served as the basis for interviews tailored to the commentaries provided by each diarist. Biographic and diary data were comple-

mented by our own field notes and those of our assistants. For a more detailed description of our methods, see Wieder and Zimmerman (1974) and Zimmerman and Wieder (1977).

2. A survey of households in the community conducted by independent researchers one year after the conclusion of our field study revealed that sixty-seven percent of those sampled currently smoked marijuana. A secondary analysis of the data found that of those whose responses to selected questions most closely approximated the value themes of the counterculture displayed in our ethnographic materials, ninety percent currently smoked (Cf. Wieder and Zimmerman, 1974:146–147).

References

Bar-Hillel, Y. 1954. "Indexical expressions," *Mind* 63:359–79.

Becker, Howard S. 1963. *Outsiders: Studies in the Sociology of Deviance.* New York: The Free Press.

Bogdan, Robert and Steven J. Taylor. 1975. *Introduction to Qualitative Research Methods.* New York: Wiley-Interscience.

Bruyn, Sevryn T. 1966. *The Human Perspective in Sociology.* Englewood Cliffs, N.J.: Prentice-Hall.

Cavan, Sherri. 1972. *Hippies of the Haight.* St. Louis: New Critics Press.

Cicourel, Aaron V. 1974. *Cognitive Sociology.* New York: The Free Press.

Conklin, Harold C. 1962. "Comment on Frake," *Anthropology and Human Behavior,* The Anthropological Society of Washington, Washington, D.C., pp. 86–93.

Durkheim, Emile. 1966. *The Rules of the Sociological Method.* New York: The Free Press.

Frake, Charles. 1962. "The ethnographic study of cognitive systems," *Anthropology and Human Behavior,* The Anthropological Society of Washington, Washington, D.C., pp. 72–85.

Garfinkel, Harold. 1966. "The Berkeley talk," Photocopied Manuscript.

———. 1967. *Studies in Ethnomethodology.* Englewood Cliffs, N.J.: Prentice-Hall.

———, and Harvey Sacks. 1970. "On formal structures of Practical actions." In *Theoretical Sociology,* John McKinney and Edward Tiryakian (eds.). New York: Appleton-Century-Crofts, pp. 338–366.

Hymes, Dell H. 1962. "The ethnography of speaking." In *Anthropology and Human Behavior,* The Anthropological Society of Washington, Washington, D.C., pp. 13–53.

Kluckhohn, Clyde. 1949. *Mirror for Man.* New York: McGraw-Hill.

Lofland, John. 1971. *Analyzing Social Settings.* Belmont, Calif.: Wadsworth.

Malinowski, Bronislaw (19–2). 1961. *Argonauts of the Western Pacific.* London: Routledge. (Dutton, New York).

Mills, C. Wright. 1940. "Situated actions and vocabularies of motive." *American Sociological Review* 5:904–913.

Stacks, Harvey. 1975. "Everyone has to lie." In *Ritual, Reality and Innovation in Language Use,* Blount and Sanchez (eds.). New York: Seminar Press.

Stoddart, Kenneth. 1974. "The facts of life about dope: Observations of a local pharmacology." *Urban Life and Culture* 3:179–203.

Spates, James L. 1976. "Counterculture and dominant culture values: A cross-national analysis of the underground press and dominant culture magazines." *American Sociological Review,* 41:868–883.

Turner, Ralph. 1976. "The Real Self: From Institution to Impulse." *American Journal of Sociology* 81:989–1016.

Wieder, D. Lawrence. 1974. *Language and Social Reality.* The Hague: Mouton.

Wieder, D. Lawrence and Don H. Zimmerman. 1974. "Generational experience and the development of freak culture." *Journal of Social Issues* 30:137–161.

Williams, Thomas Rhys. 1974. *Field Methods in the Study of Culture.* New York: Holt, Rinehart, and Winston.

Zimmerman, Don H. and D. Lawrence Wieder. 1971. *The Social Bases of Illegal Behavior in the Student Community,* Department of Commerce, PB-211 657.

Zimmerman, Don H. and D. Lawrence Wieder. 1977. "The diary-diary-interview method." *Urban Life: A Journal of Ethnographic Research,* 5:479–498.

Zimmerman, Don H. 1970. "Record-keeping and the intake process in a public welfare agency." In Stanton Wheeler (ed.) *On Record: Files and Dossiers in American Life.* New York: Basic Books.

CHAPTER 11

Shifts and Oscillations in Deviant Careers

THE CASE OF UPPER-LEVEL DRUG DEALERS AND SMUGGLERS

Patricia A. Adler and Peter Adler

The upper echelons of the marijuana and cocaine trade constitute a world which has never before been researched and analyzed by sociologists. Importing and distributing tons of marijuana and kilos of cocaine at a time, successful operators can earn upwards of a half million dollars per year. Their traffic in these so-called "soft"[1] drugs constitutes a potentially lucrative occupation, yet few participants manage to accumulate any substantial sums of money, and most people envision their involvement in drug trafficking as only temporary. In this study we focus on the career paths followed by members of one upper-level drug dealing and smuggling community. We discuss the various modes of entry into trafficking at these upper levels, contrasting these with entry into middle- and low-level trafficking. We then describe the pattern of shifts and oscillations these dealers and smugglers experience. Once they reach the top rungs of their occupation, they begin periodically quitting and re-entering the field, often changing their degree and type of involvement upon their return. Their careers, therefore, offer insights into the problems involved in leaving deviance.

Previous research on soft drug trafficking has only addressed the low and middle levels of this occupation, portraying people who purchase no more than 100 kilos of marijuana or single ounces of cocaine at a time (Anonymous, 1969; Atkyns and Hanneman, 1974; Blum *et al.*, 1972; Carey, 1968; Goode, 1970; Langer, 1977; Lieb and Olson, 1976; Mouledoux, 1972; Waldorf *et al.*, 1977). Of these, only Lieb and Olson (1976) have examined dealing and/or smuggling as an occupation, investigating participants' career developments. But their work, like several of the others, focuses on a population of student dealers who may have been too young to strive for and attain the upper levels of drug trafficking. Our study fills this gap at the top by describing and analyzing an elite community of upper-level dealers and smugglers and their careers.

We begin by describing where our research took place, the people and activities we studied, and the methods we used. Second, we outline the process of becoming a drug trafficker, from initial recruitment through learning the trade. Third, we look at the different types of upward mobility displayed by dealers and smugglers. Fourth, we examine the career shifts and oscillations which veteran dealers and smugglers display, outlining the multiple, conflicting forces which lure them both into and out of drug trafficking.

We conclude by suggesting a variety of paths which dealers and smugglers pursue out of drug trafficking and discuss the problems inherent in leaving this deviant world.

Setting and Method

We based our study in "Southwest County," one section of a large metropolitan area in southwestern California near the Mexican border. Southwest County consisted of a handful of beach towns dotting the Pacific Ocean, a location offering a strategic advantage for wholesale drug trafficking.

Southwest County smugglers obtained their marijuana in Mexico by the ton and their cocaine in Colombia, Bolivia, and Peru, purchasing between 10 and 40 kilos at a time. These drugs were imported into the United States along a variety of land, sea, and air routes by organized smuggling crews. Southwest County dealers then purchased these products and either "middled" them directly to another buyer for a small but immediate profit of approximately $2 to $5 per kilo of marijuana and $5,000 per kilo of cocaine, or engaged in "straight dealing." As opposed to middling, straight dealing usually entailed adulterating the cocaine with such "cuts" as manitol, procaine, or inositol, and then dividing the marijuana and cocaine into smaller quantities to sell them to the next-lower level of dealers. Although dealers frequently varied the amounts they bought and sold, a hierarchy of transacting levels could be roughly discerned. "Wholesale" marijuana dealers bought directly from the smugglers, purchasing anywhere from 300 to 1,000 "bricks" (averaging a kilo in weight) at a time and selling in lots of 100 to 300 bricks. "Multi-kilo" dealers, while not the smugglers' first connections, also engaged in upper-level trafficking, buying between 100 to 300 bricks and selling them in 25 to 100 brick quantities. These were then purchased by middle-level dealers who filtered the marijuana through low-level and "ounce" dealers before it reached the ultimate consumer. Each time the marijuana changed hands its price increase was dependent on a number of factors: purchase cost; the distance it was transported (including such transportation costs as packaging, transportation equipment, and payments to employees); the amount of risk assumed; the quality of the marijuana; and the prevailing prices in each local drug market. Prices in the cocaine trade were much more predictable. After purchasing kilos of cocaine in South America for $10,000 each, smugglers sold them to Southwest County "pound" dealers in quantities of one to 10 kilos for $60,000 per kilo. These pound dealers usually cut the cocaine and sold pounds ($30,000) and half-pounds ($15,000) to "ounce" dealers, who in turn cut it again and sold ounces for $2,000 each to middle-level cocaine dealers known as "cut-ounce" dealers. In this fashion the drug was middled, dealt, divided, and cut—sometimes as many as five or six times—until it was finally purchased by consumers as grams or half-grams.

Unlike low-level operators, the upper-level dealers and smugglers we studied pursued drug trafficking as a full-time occupation. If they were involved in other businesses, these were usually maintained to provide them with a legitimate front for security purposes. The profits to be made at the upper levels depended on an individual's style of operation, reliability, security, and the amount of product he or she consumed.

About half of the 65 smugglers and dealers we observed were successful, some earning up to three-quarters of a million dollars per year.[2] The other half continually struggled in the business, either breaking even or losing money.

Although dealers' and smugglers' business activities varied, they clustered together for business and social relations, forming a moderately well-integrated community whose members pursued a "fast" lifestyle, which emphasized intensive partying, casual sex, extensive travel, abundant drug consumption, and lavish spending on consumer goods. The exact size of Southwest County's upper-level dealing and smuggling community was impossible to estimate due to the secrecy of its members. At these levels, the drug world was quite homogeneous. Participants were predominantly white, came from middle-class backgrounds, and had little previous criminal involvement. While the dealers' and smugglers' social world contained both men and women, most of the serious business was conducted by the men, ranging in age from 25 to 40 years old.

We gained entry to Southwest County's upper-level drug community largely by accident. We had become friendly with a group of our neighbors who turned out to be heavily involved in smuggling marijuana. Opportunistically (Riemer, 1977), we seized the chance to gather data on this unexplored activity. Using key informants who helped us gain the trust of other members of the community, we drew upon snowball sampling techniques (Biernacki and Waldorf, 1981) and a combination of overt and covert roles to widen our network of contacts. We supplemented intensive participant-observation, between 1974 and 1980,[3] with unstructured, taped interviews. Throughout, we employed extensive measures to cross-check the reliability of our data, whenever possible (Douglas, 1976). In all, we were able to closely observe 65 dealers and smugglers as well as numerous other drug world members, including dealers' "old ladies" (girlfriends or wives), friends, and family members.

Becoming a Drug Trafficker

There are three routes into the upper levels of drug dealing and smuggling. First, some drug users become low-level dealers, gradually working their way up to middle-level dealing. It is rare, however, for upper-level dealers to have such meager origins. Second, there are people who enter directly into drug dealing at the middle level, usually from another occupation. Many of these do extremely well right away. Third, a number of individuals are invited into smuggling because of a special skill or character, sometimes from middle-level drug trafficking careers and other times from outside the drug world entirely. We discuss each of these in turn.

LOW-LEVEL ENTRY

People who began dealing at the bottom followed the classic path into dealing portrayed in the literature (Anonymous, 1969; Blum *et al.,* 1972; Carey, 1968; Goode,

1970; Johnson, 1973). They came from among the ranks of regular drug users, since, in practice, using drugs heavily and dealing for "stash" (one's personal supply) are nearly inseparable. Out of this multitude of low-level dealers, however, most abandoned the practice after they encountered their first legal or financial bust, lasting in the business for only a fairly short period (Anonymous, 1969; Carey, 1968; Lieb and Olson, 1976; Mandel, 1967). Those who sought bigger profits gradually drifted into a fulltime career in drug trafficking, usually between the ages of 15 and 22. Because of this early recruitment into dealing as an occupation, low-level entrants generally developed few, if any, occupational skills other than dealing. One dealer described his early phase of involvement:

> I had dealt a limited amount of lids [ounces of marijuana] and psychedelics in my early college days without hardly taking it seriously. But after awhile something changed in me and I decided to try to work myself up. I probably was a classic case-started out buying a kilo for $150 and selling pounds for $100 each. I did that twice, then I took the money and bought two bricks, then three, then five, then seven.

This type of gradual rise through the ranks was characteristic of low-level dealers; however, few reached the upper levels of dealing from these humble beginnings. Only 20 percent of the dealers we observed in Southwest County got their start in this fashion. Two factors combined to make it less likely for low-level entrants to rise to the top. The first was psychological. People who started small, thought small; most had neither the motivation nor vision to move large quantities of drugs. The second, and more critical factor, was social. People who started at the bottom and tried to work their way up the ladder often had a hard time finding connections at the upper levels.[4] Dealers were suspicious of new customers, preferring, for security reasons, to deal with established outlets or trusted friends. The few people who did rise through the ranks generally began dealing in another part of the country, moving to Southwest County only after they had progressed to the middle levels. These people were lured to southwestern California by its reputation within drug circles as an importation and wholesale dealing market.

MIDDLE-LEVEL ENTRY

About 75 percent of the smugglers and dealers in Southwest County entered at the middle level. Future big dealers usually jumped into transacting in substantial quantities from the outset, buying 50 kilos of "commercial" (low-grade) marijuana or one to two ounces of cocaine. One dealer explained this phenomenon:

> Someone who thinks of himself as an executive or an entrepreneur is not going to get into the dope business on a small level. The average executive just jumps right into the middle. Or else he's not going to jump.

This was the route taken by Southwest County residents with little or no previous involvement in drug trafficking. For them, entry into dealing followed the establishment of social relationships with local dealers and smugglers. (Naturally, this implies a self-selecting sample of outsiders who become accepted and trusted by these upper-level traffickers, based on their mutual interests, orientation, and values.) Through their friendships with dealers, these individuals were introduced to other members of the dealing scene and to their "fast" lifestyle. Individuals who found this lifestyle attractive became increasingly drawn to the subculture, building networks of social associations within it. Eventually, some of these people decided to participate more actively. This step was usually motivated both by money and lifestyle. One dealer recounted how he fell in with the drug world set:

> I used to be into real estate making good money. I was the only person at my firm renting to longhairs and dealing with their money. I slowly started getting friendly with them, although I didn't realize how heavy they were. I knew ways of buying real estate and putting it under fictitious names, laundering money so that it went in as hot cash and came out as spendable income. I slowly got more and more involved with this one guy until I was neglecting my real estate business and just partying with him all the time. My spending went up but my income went down, and suddenly I had to look around for another way to make money fast. I took the money I was laundering for him, bought some bricks from another dealer friend of his, and sold them out of state before I gave him back the cash. Within six months I was turning [selling] 100 bricks at a time.

People who entered drug dealing at these middle levels were usually between the ages of 25 and 35 and had been engaged in some other occupation prior to dealing seriously. They came from a wide range of occupational backgrounds. Many drifted into the lifestyle from jobs already concentrated in the night hours, such as bartender, waiter, and nightclub bouncer. Still others came from fields where the working hours were irregular and adaptable to their special schedules, such as acting, real estate, inventing, graduate school, construction, and creative "entrepreneurship" (more aptly called hand-to-mouth survival, for many). The smallest group was tempted into the drug world from structured occupations and the professions.

Middle-level entrants had to learn the trade of drug trafficking. They received "on-the-job training" (Miller and Ritzer, 1977:89) in such skills as how to establish business connections, organize profitable transactions, avoid arrest, transport illegal goods, and coordinate participants and equipment. Dealers trained on-the-job refined their knowledge and skills by learning from their mistakes. One dealer recalled how he got "burned" with inferior quality marijuana on his first major "cop" [purchase] because of his inexperience:

> I had borrowed around $7,000 from this friend to do a dope deal. I had never bought in that kind of quantity before but I knew three or four guys who I got it from. I was nervous so I got really stoned before I shopped around and I ended up being hardly able to tell about the quality. Turned out you just couldn't get high off the stuff. I ended up having to sell it below cost.

Once they had gotten in and taught themselves the trade, most middle-level entrants strove for upward mobility. About 80 percent of these Southwest County dealers jumped to the upper levels of trafficking. One dealer described her mode of escalation:

> When I started to deal I was mostly looking for a quick buck here or there, something to pay some pressing bill. I was middling 50 or 100 bricks at a time. But then I was introduced to a guy who said he would front me half a pound of coke, and if I turned it fast I could have more, and on a regular basis. Pretty soon I was turning six, seven, eight, nine, 10 pounds a week— they were passing through real fast. I was clearing at least 10 grand a month. It was too much money too fast. I didn't know what to do with it. It got ridiculous, I wasn't relating to anyone anymore, I was never home, always gone. The biggest ego trip for me came when all of a sudden I turned around and was selling to the people I had been buying from. I skipped their level of doing business entirely and stage-jumped right past them.

Southwest County's social milieu, with its concentration of upper-level dealers and smugglers, thus facilitated forming connections and doing business at the upper levels of the drug world.

SMUGGLING

Only 10 percent of Southwest County drug smugglers were formerly upper-level dealers who made the leap to smuggling on their own; the rest were invited to become smugglers by established operators. About half of those recruited came directly from the drug world's social scene, with no prior involvement in drug dealing. This implies, like middle-level entry into dealing, both an attraction to the drug crowd and its lifestyle, and prior acquaintance with dealers and smugglers. The other half of the recruits were solicited from among the ranks of middle-level Southwest County dealers.

The complex task of importing illegal drugs required more knowledge, experience, equipment, and connections than most non-smugglers possessed. Recruits had some skill or asset which the experienced smuggler needed to put his operation together. This included piloting or navigating ability, equipment, money, or the willingness to handle drugs while they were being transported. One smuggler described some of the criteria he used to screen potential recruits for suitability as employees in smuggling crews:

> Pilots are really at a premium. They burn out so fast that I have to replace them every six months to a year. But I'm also looking for people who are cool: people who will carry out their jobs according to the plan, who won't panic if the load arrives late or something goes wrong, 'cause this happens a lot. . . . And I try not to get people who've been to prison before, because they'll be more likely to take foolish risks, the kind that I don't want to have to.

Most novice smugglers were recruited and trained by a sponsor with whom they forged an apprentice-mentor relationship. Those who had been dealers previously knew the rudiments of drug trafficking. What they learned from the smuggler was how to fill a particular role in his or her highly specialized operation.

One smuggler we interviewed had a slightly larger than average crew. Ben's commercial marijuana smuggling organization was composed of seven members, not including himself. Two were drivers who transported the marijuana from the landing strip to its point of destination. One was a pilot. The dual roles of driver and co-pilot were filled by a fourth man. Another pilot, who operated both as a smuggler with his own makeshift crew and as a wholesale marijuana dealer who was supplied by Ben, flew runs for Ben when he wasn't otherwise occupied. The sixth member was Ben's enforcer and "stash house" man; he lived in the place where the marijuana was stored, distributed it to customers, and forcibly extracted payments when Ben deemed it necessary. The seventh member handled the financial and legal aspects of the business. He arranged for lawyers and bail bondsmen when needed, laundered Ben's money, and provided him with a legitimate-looking business front. Most of these family members also dealt drugs on the side, having the choice of taking their payment in cash ($10,000 for pilots; $4,000 for drivers) or in kind. Ben arranged the buying and selling connections, financed the operation, provided the heavy equipment (planes, vans, radios) and recruited, supervised, and replaced his crew.

Relationships between smugglers and their recruits were generally characterized by a benign paternalism, leading apprentices to form an enduring loyalty to their sponsor. Once established in a smuggling crew, recruits gained familiarity with the many other roles, the scope of the whole operation, and began to meet suppliers and customers. Eventually they branched out on their own. To do so, employees of a smuggling crew had to develop the expertise and connections necessary to begin running their own operations. Several things were required to make this move. Acquiring the technical knowledge of equipment, air routes, stopovers, and how to coordinate personnel was relatively easy; this could be picked up after working in a smuggling crew for six months to a year. Putting together one's own crew was more difficult because skilled employees, especially pilots, were hard to find. Most new smugglers borrowed people from other crews until they became sufficiently established to recruit and train their own personnel. Finally, connections to buy from and sell to were needed. Buyers were plentiful, but securing a foreign supplier required special breaks or networks.

Another way for employees to become heads of their own smuggling operations was to take over when their boss retired. This had the advantage of keeping the crew and style of operation intact. Various financial arrangements could be worked out for such a transfer of authority, from straight cash purchases to deals involving residual payments. One marijuana smuggler described how he acquired his operation:

> I had been Jake's main pilot for a year and, after him, I knew the most about his operation. We were really tight, and he had taken me all up and down the coast with him, meeting his connections. Naturally I knew the Mexican end of the operation and his supplier since I used to make the runs, flying down the money and picking up the dope. So when he told me he wanted to get out of the business, we made a deal. I took over the set-up and gave him a residual for every run I made. I kept all the drivers, all the connections—everything the guy had—but I found myself a new pilot.

In sum, most dealers and smugglers reached the upper levels not so much as a result of their individual entrepreneurial initiative, but through the social networks they formed in the drug subculture. Their ability to remain in these strata was largely tied to the way they treated these drug world relationships.[5]

Shifts and Oscillations

We have discussed dealers and smugglers separately up to this point because they display distinct career patterns. But once individuals entered the drug trafficking field and rose to its upper levels, they became part of a social world, the Southwest County drug scene, and faced common problems and experiences. Therefore, we discuss them together from here on.

Despite the gratifications which dealers and smugglers originally derived from the easy money, material comfort, freedom, prestige, and power associated with their careers, 90 percent of those we observed decided, at some point, to quit the business. This stemmed, in part, from their initial perceptions of the career as temporary ("Hell, nobody wants to be a drug dealer all their life"). Adding to these early intentions was a process of rapid aging in the career: dealers and smugglers became increasingly aware of the restrictions and sacrifices their occupations required and tired of living the fugitive life. They thought about, talked about, and in many cases took steps toward getting out of the drug business. But as with entering, disengaging from drug trafficking was rarely an abrupt act (Lieb and Olson, 1976:364). Instead, it more often resembled a series of transitions, or oscillations,[6] out of and back *into* the business. For once out of the drug world, dealers and smugglers were rarely successful in making it in the legitimate world because they failed to cut down on their extravagant lifestyle and drug consumption. Many abandoned their efforts to reform and returned to deviance, sometimes picking up where they left off and other times shifting to a new mode of operating. For example, some shifted from dealing cocaine to dealing marijuana, some dropped to a lower level of dealing, and others shifted their role within the same group of traffickers. This series of phase-outs and re-entries, combined with career shifts, endured for years, dominating the pattern of their remaining involvement with the business. But it also represented the method by which many eventually broke away from drug trafficking, for each phase-out had the potential to be an individual's final departure.

AGING IN THE CAREER

Once recruited and established in the drug world, dealers and smugglers entered into a middle phase of aging in the career. This phase was characterized by a progressive loss of enchantment with their occupation. While novice dealers and smugglers found that participation in the drug world brought them thrills and status, the novelty gradually faded. Initial feelings of exhilaration and awe began to dull as individuals became increasingly jaded. This was the result of both an extended exposure to the mundane, everyday business aspects of drug trafficking and to an exorbitant consumption of drugs (especially cocaine). One smuggler described how he eventually came to feel:

> It was fun, those three or four years. I never worried about money or anything. But after awhile it got real boring. There was no feeling or emotion or anything about it. I wasn't even hardly relating to my old lady anymore. Everything was just one big rush.

This frenzy of overstimulation and resulting exhaustion hastened the process of "burnout" which nearly all individuals experienced. As dealers and smugglers aged in the career they became more sensitized to the extreme risks they faced. Cases of friends and associates who were arrested, imprisoned, or killed began to mount. Many individuals became convinced that continued drug trafficking would inevitably lead to arrest ("It's only a matter of time before you get caught"). While dealers and smugglers generally repressed their awareness of danger, treating it as a taken-for-granted part of their daily existence, periodic crises shattered their casual attitudes, evoking strong feelings of fear. They temporarily intensified security precautions and retreated into near isolation until they felt the "heat" was off.

As a result of these accumulating "scares," dealers and smugglers increasingly integrated feelings of "paranoia"[7] into their everyday lives. One dealer talked about his feelings of paranoia:

> You're always on the line. You don't lead a normal life. You're always looking over your shoulder, wondering who's at the door, having to hide everything. You learn to look behind you so well you could probably bend over and look up your ass. That's paranoia. It's a really scary, hard feeling. That's what makes you get out.

Drug world members also grew progressively weary of their exclusion from the legitimate world and the deceptions they had to manage to sustain that separation. Initially, this separation was surrounded by an alluring mystique. But as they aged in the career, this mystique became replaced by the reality of everyday boundary maintenance and the feeling of being an "expatriated citizen within one's own country." One smuggler who was contemplating quitting described the effects of this separation:

> I'm so sick of looking over my shoulder, having to sit in my house and worry about one of my non-drug world friends stopping in when I'm doing business. Do you know how awful that is? It's like leading a double life. It's ridiculous. That's what makes it not worth it. It'll be a lot less money [to quit], but a lot less pressure.

Thus, while the drug world was somewhat restricted, it was not an encapsulated community, and dealers' and smugglers' continuous involvement with the straight world made the temptation to adhere to normative standards and "go straight" omnipresent. With the occupation's novelty worn off and the "fast life" taken-for-granted, most dealers and smugglers felt that the occupation no longer resembled their early impressions of it. Once they reached the upper levels of the occupation, their experience began to change. Eventually, the rewards of trafficking no longer seemed to justify the strain and risk involved. It was at this point that the straight world's formerly dull ambiance became transformed (at least in theory) into a potential haven.

PHASING-OUT

Three factors inhibited dealers and smugglers from leaving the drug world. Primary among these factors were the hedonistic and materialistic satisfactions the drug world provided. Once accustomed to earning vast quantities of money quickly and easily, individuals found it exceedingly difficult to return to the income scale of the straight world. They also were reluctant to abandon the pleasures of the "fast life" and its accompanying drugs, casual sex, and power. Second, dealers and smugglers identified with, and developed a commitment to, the occupation of drug trafficking (Adler and Adler, 1982). Their self-images were tied to that role and could not be easily disengaged. The years invested in their careers (learning the trade, forming connections, building reputations) strengthened their involvement with both the occupation and the drug community. And since their relationships were social as well as business, friendship ties bound individuals to dealing. As one dealer in the midst of struggling to phase-out explained:

> The biggest threat to me is to get caught up sitting around the house with friends that are into dealing. I'm trying to stay away from them, change my habits.

Third, dealers and smugglers hesitated to voluntarily quit the field because of the difficulty involved in finding another way to earn a living. Their years spent in illicit activity made it unlikely for any legitimate organizations to hire them. This narrowed their occupational choices considerably, leaving self-employment as one of the few remaining avenues open. Dealers and smugglers who tried to leave the drug world generally fell into one of four patterns.[8] The first and most frequent pattern was to postpone quitting until after they could execute one last "big deal." While the intention was sincere, individuals who chose this route rarely succeeded; the "big deal" too often remained elusive. One marijuana smuggler offered a variation of this theme:

> My plan is to make a quarter of a million dollars in four months during the prime smuggling season and get the hell out of the business.

A second pattern we observed was individuals who planned to change immediately, but never did. They announced they were quitting, yet their outward actions never varied. One dealer described his involvement with this syndrome:

> When I wake up I'll say, "Hey, I'm going to quit this cycle and just run my other business." But when you're dealing you constantly have people dropping by ounces and asking, "Can you move this?" What's your first response? Always, "Sure, for a toot."

In the third pattern of phasing-out, individuals actually suspended their dealing and smuggling activities, but did not replace them with an alternative source of income. Such withdrawals were usually spontaneous and prompted by exhaustion, the influence of a person from outside the drug world, or problems with the police or other associates. These kinds of phase-outs usually lasted only until the individual's money ran out, as one dealer explained:

> I got into legal trouble with the FBI a while back and I was forced to quit dealing. Everybody just cut me off completely, and I saw the danger in continuing, myself. But my high-class tastes never dwindled. Before I knew it I was in hock over $30,000. Even though I was hot, I was forced to get back into dealing to relieve some of my debts.

In the fourth pattern of phasing-out, dealers and smugglers tried to move into another line of work. Alternative occupations included: (1) those they had previously pursued; (2) front businesses maintained on the side while dealing or smuggling; and (3) new occupations altogether. While some people accomplished this transition successfully, there were problems inherent in all three alternatives.

(1) Most people who tried resuming their former occupations found that these had changed too much while they were away. In addition, they themselves had changed: they enjoyed the self-directed freedom and spontaneity associated with dealing and smuggling, and were unwilling to relinquish it.

(2) Those who turned to their legitimate front business often found that these businesses were unable to support them. Designed to launder rather than earn money, most of these ventures were retail outlets with a heavy cash flow (restaurants, movie theaters, automobile dealerships, small stores) that had become accustomed to operating under a continuous subsidy from illegal funds. Once their drug funding was cut off they could not survive for long.

(3) Many dealers and smugglers utilized the skills and connections they had developed in the drug business to create a new occupation. They exchanged their illegal commodity for a legal one and went into import/export, manufacturing, wholesaling, or retailing other merchandise. For some, the decision to prepare a legitimate career for their future retirement from the drug world followed an unsuccessful attempt to phase-out into a "front" business. One husband-and-wife dealing team explained how these legitimate side businesses differed from front businesses:

> We always had a little legitimate "scam" [scheme] going, like mail-order shirts, wallets, jewelry, and the kids were always involved in that. We made a little bit of money on them. Their main purpose was for a cover. But [this business] was different; right from the start this was going to be a legal thing to push us out of the drug business.

About 10 percent of the dealers and smugglers we observed began tapering off their drug world involvement gradually, transferring their time and money into a selected legitimate endeavor. They did not try to quit drug trafficking altogether until they felt confident that their legitimate business could support them. Like spontaneous phase-outs, many of these planned withdrawals into legitimate endeavors failed to generate enough money to keep individuals from being lured into the drug world.

In addition to voluntary phase-outs caused by burnout, about 40 percent of the Southwest County dealers and smugglers we observed experienced a "bustout" at some point in their careers.[9] Forced withdrawals from dealing or smuggling were usually sudden and motivated by external factors, either financial, legal, or reputational. Financial bustouts generally occurred when dealers or smugglers were either "burned" or "ripped-off" by others, leaving them in too much debt to rebuild their base of operation. Legal bustouts followed arrest and possibly incarceration: arrested individuals were so "hot" that few of their former associates would deal with them. Reputational bustouts occurred when individuals "burned" or "ripped-off" others (regardless of whether they intended to do so) and were banned from business by their former circle of associates. One smuggler gave his opinion on the pervasive nature of forced phase-outs:

> Some people are smart enough to get out of it because they realize, physically, they have to. Others realize, monetarily, that they want to get out of this world before this world gets them. Those are the lucky ones. Then there are the ones who have to get out because they're hot or someone else close to them is so hot that they'd better get out. But in the end when you get out of it, nobody gets out of it out of free choice; you do it because you have to.

Death, of course, was the ultimate bustout. Some pilots met this fate because of the dangerous routes they navigated (hugging mountains, treetops, other aircrafts) and the sometimes ill-maintained and overloaded planes they flew. However, despite much talk of violence, few Southwest County drug traffickers died at the hands of fellow dealers.

RE-ENTRY

Phasing-out of the drug world was more often than not temporary. For many dealers and smugglers, it represented but another stage of their drug careers (although this may not have been their original intention), to be followed by a period of reinvolvement. Depending on the individual's perspective, re-entry into the drug world could be viewed as either a comeback (from a forced withdrawal) or a relapse (from a voluntary withdrawal).

Most people forced out of drug trafficking were anxious to return. The decision to phase-out was never theirs, and the desire to get back into dealing or smuggling was based on many of the same reasons which drew them into the field originally. Coming back from financial, legal, and reputational bustouts was possible but difficult and was not always successfully accomplished. They had to re-establish contacts, rebuild their organization and fronting arrangements, and raise the operating capital to resume dealing. More difficult was the problem of overcoming the circumstances surrounding their departure. Once smugglers and dealers resumed operating, they often found their former colleagues suspicious of them. One frustrated dealer described the effects of his prison experience:

> When I first got out of the joint [jail], none of my old friends would have anything to do with me. Finally, one guy who had been my partner told me it was because everyone was suspicious of my getting out early and thought I made a deal [with police to inform on his colleagues].

Dealers and smugglers who returned from bustouts were thus informally subjected to a trial period in which they had to re-establish their trustworthiness and reliability before they could once again move in the drug world with ease.

Re-entry from voluntary withdrawal involved a more difficult decision-making process, but was easier to implement. The factors enticing individuals to re-enter the drug world were not the same as those which motivated their original entry. As we noted above, experienced dealers and smugglers often privately weighed their reasons for wanting to quit and wanting to stay in. Once they left, their images of and hopes for the straight world failed to materialize. They could not make the shift to the norms, values, and lifestyle of the straight society and could not earn a living within it. Thus, dealers and smugglers decided to re-enter the drug business for basic reasons: the material perquisites, the hedonistic gratifications, the social ties, and the fact that they had nowhere else to go.

Once this decision was made, the actual process of re-entry was relatively easy. One dealer described how the door back into dealing remained open for those who left voluntarily:

> I still see my dealer friends, I can still buy grams from them when I want to. It's the respect they have for me because I stepped out of it without being busted or burning someone. I'm coming out with a good reputation, and even though the scene is a whirlwind—people moving up, moving down, in, out—if I didn't see anybody for a year I could call them up and get right back in that day.

People who relapsed thus had little problem obtaining fronts, re-establishing their reputations, or readjusting to the scene.

CAREER SHIFTS

Dealers and smugglers who re-entered the drug world, whether from a voluntary or forced phase-out, did not always return to the same level of transacting or commodity which characterized their previous style of operation. Many individuals underwent a "career shift" (Luckenbill and Best, 1981) and became involved in some new segment of the drug world. These shifts were sometimes lateral, as when a member of a smuggling crew took on a new specialization, switching from piloting to operating a stash house, for example. One dealer described how he utilized friendship networks upon his re-entry to shift from cocaine to marijuana trafficking:

> Before, when I was dealing cocaine, I was too caught up in using the drug and people around me were starting to go under from getting into "base" [another form of cocaine]. That's why I got out. But now I think I've got

> myself together and even though I'm dealing again I'm staying away from
> coke. I've switched over to dealing grass. It's a whole different circle of peo-
> ple. I got into it through a close friend I used to know before, but I never
> did business with him because he did grass and I did coke.

Vertical shifts moved operators to different levels. For example, one former smuggler returned and began dealing; another top-level marijuana dealer came back to find
that the smugglers he knew had disappeared and he was forced to buy in smaller quantities from other dealers. Another type of shift relocated drug traffickers in different
styles of operation. One dealer described how, after being arrested, he tightened his security measures:

> I just had to cut back after I went through those changes. Hell, I'm not get-
> ting any younger and the idea of going to prison bothers me a lot more than
> it did 10 years ago. The risks are no longer worth it when I can have a com-
> fortable income with less risk. So I only sell to four people now. I don't care
> if they buy a pound or a gram.

A former smuggler who sold his operation and lost all his money during phase-out returned as a consultant to the industry, selling his expertise to those with new money
and fresh manpower:

> What I've been doing lately is setting up deals for people. I've got foolproof
> plans for smuggling cocaine up here from Colombia; I tell them how to
> modify their airplanes to add on extra fuel tanks and to fit in more weed,
> coke, or whatever they bring up. Then I set them up with refueling points
> all up and down Central America, tell them how to bring it up here, what
> points to come in at, and what kind of receiving unit to use. Then they do
> it all and I get 10 percent of what they make.

Re-entry did not always involve a shift to a new niche, however. Some dealers and
smugglers returned to the same circle of associates, trafficking activity, and commodity they worked with prior to their departure. Thus, drug dealers' careers often peaked
early and then displayed a variety of shifts, from lateral mobility, to decline, to hold-
ing fairly steady.

A final alternative involved neither completely leaving nor remaining within the
deviant world. Many individuals straddled the deviant and respectable worlds forever by continuing to dabble in drug trafficking. As a result of their experiences in
the drug world they developed a deviant self-identity and a deviant *modus operandi*.
They might not have wanted to bear the social and legal burden of full-time deviant
work but neither were they willing to assume the perceived confines and limitations
of the straight world. They therefore moved into the entrepreneurial realm, where
their daily activities involved some kind of hustling or "wheeling and dealing" in an
assortment of legitimate, quasi-legitimate, and deviant ventures, and where they
could be their own boss. This enabled them to retain certain elements of the deviant
lifestyle, and to socialize on the fringes of the drug community. For these individu-

als, drug dealing shifted from a primary occupation to a sideline, though they never abandoned it altogether.

Leaving Drug Trafficking

This career pattern of oscillation into and out of active drug trafficking makes it difficult to speak of leaving drug trafficking in the sense of a final retirement. Clearly, some people succeeded in voluntarily retiring. Of these, a few managed to prepare a post-deviant career for themselves by transferring their drug money into a legitimate enterprise. A larger group was forced out of dealing and either didn't or couldn't return; their bustouts were sufficiently damaging that they never attempted re-entry, or they abandoned efforts after a series of unsuccessful attempts. But there was no way of structurally determining in advance whether an exit from the business would be temporary or permanent. The vacillations in dealers' intentions were compounded by the complexity of operating successfully in the drug world. For many, then, no phase-out could ever be definitely assessed as permanent. As long as individuals had the skills, knowledge, and connections to deal they retained the potential to re-enter the occupation at any time. Leaving drug trafficking may thus be a relative phenomenon, characterized by a trailing-off process where spurts of involvement appear with decreasing frequency and intensity.

Summary

Drug dealing and smuggling careers are temporary and fraught with multiple attempts at retirement. Veteran drug traffickers quit their occupation because of the ambivalent feelings they develop toward their deviant life. As they age in the career their experience changes, shifting from a work life that is exhilarating and free to one that becomes increasingly dangerous and confining. But just as their deviant careers are temporary, so too are their retirements. Potential recruits are lured into the drug business by materialism, hedonism, glamor, and excitement. Established dealers are lured away from the deviant life and back into the mainstream by the attractions of security and social ease. Retired dealers and smugglers are lured back in by their expertise, and by their ability to make money quickly and easily. People who have been exposed to the upper levels of drug trafficking therefore find it extremely difficult to quit their deviant occupation permanently. This stems, in part, from their difficulty in moving from the illegitimate to the legitimate business sector. Even more significant is the affinity they form for their deviant values and lifestyle. Thus few, if any, of our subjects were successful in leaving deviance entirely. What dealers and smugglers intend, at the time, to be a permanent withdrawal from drug trafficking can be seen in retrospect as a pervasive occupational pattern of mid-career shifts and oscillations. More research is needed into the complex process of how people get out of deviance and enter the world of legitimate work.

Notes

An earlier version of this chapter was presented at the annual meetings of the American Society of Criminology, Denver, Colorado, November, 1983. Correspondence to: Department of Sociology, University of Tulsa, Tulsa, Oklahoma 74104.

1. The term "soft" drugs generally refers to marijuana, cocaine and such psychedelics as LSD and mescaline (Carey, 1968). In this chapter we do not address trafficking in psychedelics because, since they are manufactured in the United States, they are neither imported nor distributed by the group we studied.

2. This is an idealized figure representing the profit a dealer or smuggler could potentially earn and does not include deductions for such miscellaneous and hard-to-calculate costs as: time or money spent in arranging deals (some of which never materialize); lost, stolen, or unrepaid money or drugs; and the personal drug consumption of a drug trafficker and his or her entourage. Of these, the single largest expense is the last one, accounting for the bulk of most Southwest County dealers' and smugglers' earnings.

3. We continued to conduct follow-up interviews with key informants through 1983.

4. The exception to this was where low-level dealers rose on the "coattails" of their suppliers: as one dealer increased the volume of his or her purchases or sales, some of his or her customers followed suit.

5. For a more thorough discussion of the social networks and relationships in Southwest County's drug world see Adler and Adler (1983).

6. While other studies of drug dealing have also noted that participants did not maintain an uninterrupted stream of career involvement (Slum *et al.*, 1972; Carey, 1968; Lieb and Olson, 1976; Waldorf *et al.*, 1977), none have isolated or described the oscillating nature of this pattern.

7. In the dealers' vernacular, this term is not used in the clinical sense of an individual psychopathology rooted in early childhood traumas. Instead, it resembles Lemert's (1962) more sociological definition which focuses on such behavioral dynamics as suspicion, hostility, aggressiveness, and even delusion. Not only Lemert, but also Waldorf *et al.* (1977) and Wedow (1979) assert that feelings of paranoia can have a sound basis in reality, and are therefore readily comprehended and even empathized with others.

8. At this point, a limitation to our data must be noted. Many of the dealers and smugglers we observed simply "disappeared" from the scene and were never heard from again. We therefore have no way of knowing if they phased-out (voluntarily or involuntarily), shifted to another scene, or were killed in some remote place. We cannot, therefore, estimate the numbers of people who left the Southwest County drug scene via each of the routes discussed here.

9. It is impossible to determine the exact percentage of people falling into the different phase-out categories: due to oscillation, people could experience several types and thus appear in multiple categories.

References

Adler, Patricia A., and Peter Adler. 1982. "Criminal commitment among drug dealers." *Deviant Behavior* 3:117–135.

———. 1983. "Relations between dealers: The social organization of illicit drug transactions." *Sociology and Social Research* 67(3):260–278.

Anonymous. 1969. "On selling marijuana." Pp. 92–102 in Erich Goode (ed.), *Marijuana*. New York: Atherton.

Atkyns, Robert L., and Gerhard J. Hanneman. 1974. "Illicit drug distribution and dealer communication behavior." *Journal of Health and Social Behavior* 15(March):36–43.

Biernacki, Patrick, and Dan Waldorf. 1981. "Snowball sampling." *Sociological Methods and Research* 10(2):141–163.

Blum, Richard H., and Associates. 1972. *The Dream Sellers*. San Francisco: Jossey-Bass.

Carey, James T. 1968. *The College Drug Scene*. Englewood Cliffs, NJ: Prentice-Hall.

Douglas, Jack D. 1976. *Investigative Social Research*. Beverly Hills, CA: Sage.

Goode, Erich. 1970. *The Marijuana Smokers*. New York: Basic.

Johnson, Bruce D. 1973. *Marijuana Users and Drug Subcultures*. New York: Wiley.

Langer, John. 1977. "Drug entrepreneurs and dealing culture." *Social Problems* 24(3):377–385.

Lemert, Edwin. 1962. "Paranoia and the dynamics of exclusion." *Sociometry* 25(March):2–20.

Lieb, John, and Sheldon Olson. 1976. "Prestige, paranoia, and profit: On becoming a dealer of illicit drugs in a university community." *Journal of Drug Issues* 6(Fall):356–369.

Luckenbill, David F., and Joel Best. 1981. "Careers in deviance and respectability: The analogy's limitations." *Social Problems* 29(2):197–206.

Mandel, Jerry. 1967. "Myths and realities of marijuana pushing." Pp. 58–110 in Jerry L. Simmons (ed.), *Marijuana: Myths and Realities*. North Hollywood, CA: Brandon.

Miller, Gale, and George Ritzer. 1977. "Informal socialization: Deviant occupations," Pp. 83–94 in George Ritzer, *Working: Conflict and Change*. 2nd edition. Englewood Cliffs, NJ: Prentice-Hall.

Mouledoux, James. 1972. "Ideological aspects of drug dealership." Pp. 110–122 in Ken Westhues (ed.), *Society's Shadow: Studies in the Sociology of Countercultures*. Toronto: McGraw-Hill, Ryerson.

Redlinger, Lawrence J. 1975. "Marketing and distributing heroin." *Journal of Psychedelic Drugs* 7(4):331–353.

Riemer, Jeffrey W. 1977. "Varieties of opportunistic research." *Urban Life* 5(4):467–477.

Waldorf, Dan, Sheigla Murphy, Craig Reinarman, and Bridget Joyce. 1977. *Doing Coke: An Ethnography of Cocaine Users and Sellers*. Washington, DC: Drug Abuse Council.

Wedow, Suzanne. 1979. "Feeling paranoid: The organization of an ideology." *Urban Life* 8(1):72–93.

Part V

LINKS TO OTHER SOCIAL PROBLEMS

Over the past century, claims-making groups have blamed a multitude of social problems on the use and effects of alcohol and drugs. Moral crusades such as the Prohibition Movement or the War on Drugs linked drinking and drug use to crises in virtually every social institution—the collapse of families, violence in schools and communities, lost productivity in the workplace. Claims such as these are fueled in part by the desire to find simple (and inexpensive) answers to troubling social issues and to "crack down" on these problems by passing strict laws against the sale or use of drugs. However, as the three studies in this final part illustrate, the empirical relationships between drinking or drug use and other social problems are quite complex and defy easy explanation. Historical experience also shows that "tough" policies against alcohol and drugs can sometimes backfire and make other social problems worse. Consequently, a growing number of researchers are systematically exploring these links and working toward more informed perspectives on the impact of drinking and drug use on crime, disease, and other problematic conditions.

In the first chapter, Glenda Kaufman Kantor and Murray Straus use data from a large, nationally representative survey of U.S. households to examine a widely held belief about the link between alcohol use and domestic violence—the "drunken bum" theory of wife beating. As shown in their figure 1, they do indeed find a strong statistical association between patterns of heavy or binge drinking by husbands and the rate (percent) of abusive violence against wives. However, Kantor and Straus also report other results that raise some significant doubts about the direct, causal impact of drinking on spouse abuse. For instance, they find that in the vast majority of cases neither husbands nor wives were using alcohol prior to recent incidents of husband-to-wife violence. Furthermore, as figure 2 in their article suggests, the strength of the relationship between husbands' drinking patterns and rates of wife abuse depends in part on social class and cultural norms that support violence. These and other results lead to the conclusion that programs focused mainly on reducing drinking are not the answer to the complex problem of wife abuse. As Kantor and Straus indicate, this problem is more deeply rooted in economic inequality and a cultural tradition that glorifies violence as an instrument of male dominance.

217

Charles Faupel and Carl Klockars tackle another important causal puzzle in their analysis of alternative explanations of the association between heroin use and crime. Does the high cost of drug addiction motivate criminal activity? Or does involvement in delinquency or crime lead to the use of heroin and other illegal drugs? To shed light on these competing views of the "drugs-crime connection," Faupel and Klockers use evidence from intensive interviews with thirty-two heroin addicts with a long history of criminal activity. Their findings indicate that each explanation works better at some stages of addicts' criminal careers than at others, depending on (1) the availability of heroin and (2) the degree of structure in their daily lives. In particular, the conventional stereotype of the "street addict" who must support a habit through extensive criminal activity mainly characterizes late-stage addicts who have relatively limited access to heroin and a low degree of life structure. At other stages, criminal activity appears either to facilitate heroin use by increasing availability of the drug or, paradoxically, to reduce drug use by adding structure to addicts' lives. In general, Faupel and Klockers argue that simple causal models cannot adequately capture the dynamic, shifting connections between crime and drug use among heroin addicts. Similarly, they conclude that the vision and effectiveness of drug-control policy in the United States have been seriously limited by a narrow, criminal conception of addicts and their behavior.

Finally, Philippe Bourgois, Mark Lettiere, and James Quesada present a powerful ethnographic account of how needle sharing and other unsafe practices expose heroin users to the risk of HIV/AIDS infection. Whereas most public health researchers rely on quantitative analyses of survey data to study the behaviors that link injecting drug use (IDU) to HIV/AIDS transmission, Bourgois and his associates base their work on several years of participant observation in which they were in almost daily contact with a network of street addicts in San Francisco. They observed numerous instances in which potentially contaminated blood was passed from one person to another in the process of heroin injection. Addicts were well aware that they were engaging in risky behavior, although they frequently lied about these practices when asked by epidemiological researchers and outreach workers. In an insightful theoretical interpretation of their ethnographic observations, Bourgois et al. show how broader relations of power and inequality figure into these patterns of risky IDU behavior and contribute to misleading results in public health research on HIV/AIDS. In particular, they argue that repressive strategies for dealing with drug problems in the United States have created oppressive conditions under which the AIDS epidemic thrives among injecting drug users. Here, as in other cases, links between drug use and other social problems have been forged as indirect consequences of antidrug crusades and "tough" policies of social control.

CHAPTER 12

The "Drunken Bum" Theory of Wife Beating

Glenda Kaufman Kantor and Murray A. Straus

The belief that male drunkenness is a major cause of wife beating has been part of American consciousness at least since the Temperance movement (Bordin, 1981; Pleck, 1987). American cultural images of the association between alcohol and violence are also evident in films depicting wild-west barroom brawls and in Tennessee Williams' notable characterization of the drunken, boorish Stanley Kowalski striking his pregnant wife, Stella. These images link alcohol and aggression, and suggest, first, that excess drinking is the principal cause of violence; and second, that drunkenness and wife beating are culturally scripted masculine behaviors. A third part of this cultural script portrays wife beating as a phenomenon of the underclass. Together, these images identify the "drunken bum" as the prototypical wife beater.

In this analysis we consider both aspects of this folk theory of the causes of intra-family violence. First we examine alcohol and class explanations of intra-family violence, and their convergence in the "drunken bum" theory of violence. Then we use data from a nationally representative sample of American families to test these ideas empirically. The three major questions we address are: (1) Do men who drink heavily have a higher rate of wife beating than others? (2) To what extent does drinking occur at the time of the violent incident? (3) Are such linkages between drinking and wife beating found primarily among working class men?

Explanations of the Drinking-Violence Relationship

DISINHIBITION THEORY

Central to suppositions of a direct alcohol-violence linkage are centuries-old and widely held beliefs that alcohol releases inhibitions and alters judgment. This belief has persisted for the greater part of this century as well. It has been bolstered by the medical, biological, and psychoanalytic opinion that alcohol's effects on the central nervous system release inhibitions by depressing brain function or suppressing super-ego function thereby allowing the expression of rage. However, disinhibition theory has recently fallen into disrepute as researchers develop a growing awareness of the complexity of the alcohol-violence syndrome. Mayfield (1983:142) points out that the location of the inhibition center of the brain is unknown and "disinhibition is no more than a tautological expression for drunkenness." Contemporary alcohol researchers now regard disinhibition as a complex process resulting from alcohol's pharmacologically-induced "cognitive disruption" (Leonard, 1984:79) and mood-altering effects (Blum, 1981) interacting with varying individual expectancies about alcohol's powers (Marlatt and Rohsenow, 1980; Sher, 1985).

SOCIAL LEARNING AND DEVIANCE DISAVOWAL THEORY

MacAndrew and Edgerton's (1969) classic cross-cultural analysis provides an alternative explanation of the alcohol-violence linkage. These authors argue that drunken comportment is learned and may take the form of "time-out behavior" (1969:90). When individuals take time out by drinking, they are exempted from the usual behavioral constraints associated with sobriety. Similar doubts about disinhibition theory are expressed by other researchers (Coleman and Straus, 1983; Gelles, 1974; Gottheil et al., 1983; Pernanen, 1976; Taylor and Leonard, 1983). Coleman and Straus's (1983) analysis of data for 2,143 families suggests that social learning and deviance disavowal theories provide a better accounting of the alcohol-violence relationship within families. They argue that people learn a "script" for violence by observing that individuals are excused and forgiven for violent behavior which occurs while drinking ("It was the booze made me do it"). Gelles's study (1974) of 80 families led him to conclude that "individuals who wish to carry out a violent act become intoxicated in order to carry out the violent act" (1974:117). Moreover, McClelland and his associates (1972) found that men drink to heighten their sense of power—a finding consistent with the attributions of intentionality implicit in deviance disavowal views. Furthermore, Room (1980:8) argues that alcohol is "an instrument of intimate domination" used to excuse the exercise of illegitimate force against subordinates.

INTEGRATED THEORETICAL MODELS

Pernanen's comprehensive theoretical reviews (1976, 1981) demonstrate the complexity of the association between alcohol and violence. Pernanen notes, as do other researchers (Blum, 1981; Boyatzis, 1983; Brown et al., 1980; Levinson, 1983; Powers and Kutash, 1982) that many factors may intervene to determine alcohol-violence outcomes. These include, but are not limited to, the symbolic meaning attached to alcohol use and expectancies about alcohol's effects; contextual factors present in the setting or the interaction of individuals; and perceptual and cognitive changes produced by alcohol. Disentangling these relationships can constitute a major difficulty for researchers.

Theoretical understanding is also hampered by narrow empirical tests of single cause-effect relationships and by implying that association equals causality. Instead of reflecting a causal relationship, the link between alcohol abuse and family violence may be "spurious" in the sense that both the drinking and the violence may reflect an underlying third factor or factors. The underlying factors may be at the individual, structural, or cultural level. At the structural level, the high degree of conflict inherent in American family structure may lead to marital discord and violence (Hotaling and Straus, 1980) as well as to alcohol abuse as a response to this stress (Linsky et al., 1985). This would produce a correlation between alcohol abuse and violence even though there is no causal relationship. At the cultural level, norms that legitimate violence as a masculine form of power assertion may co-exist with norms regarding the husband as the "head" of the household and excess drinking as acceptable masculine behavior.

Finally, these and other factors may interact with family socioeconomic status. First, while there has been considerable debate over the existence of a subculture of violence (Baron and Straus, 1987; Loftin and Hill, 1974), there do seem to be regional and social class differences in actual violence (Straus et al., 1980). Second, there is some consensus that alcohol abuse problems are most prevalent among lower-class men (Cahalan, 1970; Cahalan et al., 1969). Third, Brown and her associates (1980) found that heavy drinkers are more likely than others to believe that drinking increases sexual and aggressive behavior. In addition, some researchers (Cahalan, 1970, Cahalan and Room, 1974) have found that lower-class men more often express aggressive feelings while drinking. Fourth, lower blue-collar families have been described as the last bastion of patriarchy (Komarovsky, 1967) where wife beating, although infrequent, occurs more often than within higher socioeconomic status families (Allen and Straus, 1980; Straus et al., 1980). These presumed characteristics of low socioeconomic status individuals and families seem to provide the basis for the drunken bum theory.

Empirical Research on Alcohol Abuse and Intra-Family Violence

A substantial body of literature exists on alcohol and violent interpersonal crimes.[1] However, there are many methodological problems with this research (see Greenberg, 1981; Pernanen, 1976, 1981). The major criticisms include sample biases, nonuniform measures of alcohol use and crime, and failure to specify antecedent conditions under which alcohol use and crimes occur. There are a number of general reviews of the relationship between alcohol abuse and family violence (Critchlow, 1983; Klein, 1981; Morgan, 1982, 1983; Room and Collins, 1983). Therefore, we limit our review of the literature to the link between alcohol and spouse abuse which is our empirical focus.

ASSOCIATION OF ALCOHOL WITH INTRA-FAMILY VIOLENCE

To a great extent, there is little consensus in the literature even on the elementary question of whether there is a *correlation* between drinking and intra-family violence. Take for example two of the most frequently cited works. Bard and Zacker's study (1974) of domestic assaults reported to police found little association between alcohol and family violence; whereas Wolfgang (1958) found that victims of family violence were frequently drinking. One difference between these studies is that Wolfgang studied the most extreme end of the family violence continuum—spousal homicide—while Bard and Zacker focused on assault.

Our systematic examination of 15 empirical studies produced a wide range of estimates of alcohol involvement in spousal violence–from 6 to 85 percent.[2] However, this is not surprising given the limitations of these studies. Most used descriptive or bivariate statistics and therefore lack controls for confounding variables. Some are based on clinical samples and others on more-or-less representative community samples. Some use self-reports, whereas others use the report of the spouse, and still others use the report of a police officer. Finally, the 15 studies employed a variety of measures of both alcohol use and wife abuse.

Six of the 15 studies (Byles, 1978; Caesar, 1985; Coleman and Straus, 1983; Gelles, 1974; Rosenbaum and O'Leary, 1981; Van Hasselt et al., 1985) used a violent vs. non-violent research design; and two (Coleman and Straus, 1983; Eberle, 1980) compared drinking with non-drinking couples. All seven of these comparative design studies found an association between drinking and marital violence. This is consistent with Hotaling and Sugarman's (1986) comprehensive analysis of case-controlled studies of husband-to-wife violence. They found that alcohol abuse was one of the risk factors which met their criteria for consistency across two-thirds or more of the studies, they reviewed. Thus, alcohol seems to be an important correlate of wife abuse.

Even if one grants that the evidence supports a *correlation* between alcohol use and wife abuse, there are many inconsistencies and shortcomings in existing studies. For example, only one study (Van Hasselt et al., 1985) used a Quantity-Frequency Index to measure alcohol consumption, but the study was limited to a clinical population. Moreover, because the previous research is almost entirely descriptive or bivariate, it does not provide information appropriate to testing the complex interrelation of factors specified by the theories we reviewed earlier. In our analysis below, we use a modified Quantity-Frequency Index measure of alcohol use for a large, representative sample of American families. We also use multivariate techniques that allow us to take into account the complex factors which figure prominently in existing theories—alcohol, occupational status, and norms concerning violence.

Methods

SAMPLE

The data for this study come from a national probability sample of 6,002 households, obtained by telephone interviews in 1985.[3] Eligible households had to include an adult 18 years of age or older who was: (1) presently married, or (2) presently living as a male-female couple; or (3) divorced or separated within the last two years; or (4) single parent with a child under 18 and living in the household. When more than one eligible adult was in the household, a random procedure was used to select one respondent according to gender and marital status. Thus, one member of each household; either the husband or the wife, was interviewed.[4] The interviews lasted an average of 35 minutes. The response rate, calculated as "completed portion of eligibles," was 84 percent. The spouse abuse data are based on the 5,159 households containing a currently married or cohabiting couple. For more information on the sample, see Straus and Gelles (1986).

ALCOHOL ABUSE MEASURES

Drinking Index. The first of our two measures of alcohol abuse is the Drinking Index. It combines data from two survey questions:

(1) In general, how often do you consume alcoholic beverages–that is, beer, wine or liquor? never, less than 1 day a month, 1–3 days a month, 1–2 days a week, 3–4 days a week, 5–6 days a week, daily? (The median frequency of drinking was 1–3 times a month.)
(2) On a day when you do drink alcoholic beverages, on the average, how many drinks do you have? By a "drink" we mean a drink with a shot of 1½ ounces of hard liquor, 12 ounces of beer, or 5 ounces of wine. (The median number of drinks per day was two.)

We used the frequency and amount data from these questions to develop six categories of drinking:

0 = Abstinent: Never drinks (30.6 percent).
1 = Low: Drinks on infrequent occasions, ranging from less than once a month up to 1–2 times a week; never more than 1 drink at a time. Drinks less than once a month and no more than 2 drinks at a time (26.8 percent).
2 = Low Moderate: Drinks from 1 to 3 times a month up to daily; never more than 2 drinks (22.1 percent).
3 = High Moderate: Drinks less than once a month up to 1 to 2 times a week; 3–4 drinks a day (10.5 percent).
4 = High: Drinks 3–4 times a week up to daily; 3 or more drinks a day (4.9 percent).
5 = Binge: Drinks on infrequent occasions—once a month up to 1 to 2 times a week; 5 or more drinks a day (4.6 percent).

The distribution for the Drinking Index reveals that over half the sample were abstinent or low drinkers, and for the individuals who did drink, moderate patterns predominated. Significant sex differences in drinking patterns were also present. Two-thirds of women were abstinent or infrequent drinkers, and less than 5 percent of women were high or binge drinkers. These findings are comparable to previous national surveys that investigate drinking patterns (ADAMHA, 1980; Cahalan, 1970; Gallup 1978).

Although the distribution of drinking types is roughly consistent with previous drinking survey data, there are some possible limitations of this measure. First, it measures the average drinking pattern of each respondent and does not provide information on days when an individual departs from his/her typical drinking pattern. Thus the index may miss those who are normally moderate drinkers but binge on occasion. Second, the Drinking Index differs from the traditional Quantity-Frequency measure developed by Cahalan and associates (1969) because it does not estimate absolute alcohol content. However, this measure is comparable to those used by other researchers (e.g., Neff and Husaini, 1985) and does differentiate patterns and levels of drinking. The Drinking Index is also sensitive to binge patterns of drinking, a pattern important for our analysis, but not identified by typical quantity-frequency indexes.

Drinking at Time of Violence Measure (DTV). For purposes of this study, the most serious limitation of the Drinking Index is that it does not provide information about whether drinking was one of the immediate antecedents of violence. Therefore, we included a third question in the survey to provide a "Drinking at the Time of Violence" (DTV) measure. We asked this question of all respondents who reported incidents of physical violence. The most recent and most severe act of violence (see below) was used as the reference, and the respondents were asked (in reference to the most recent and most violent act): "Were either or both of you drinking right before the conflict started?" However, this measure does not indicate the amount of alcohol consumed at that time. Although this measure may be further limited by its reliance on self and spousal reports of drinking at the time of violence, a substantial literature exists validating both self and spousal reports of drunkenness (e.g., Hesselbrock et al., 1983; Maisto et al., 1979; Polich, 1982; Sobell and Sobell, 1978; Van Hasselt et al., 1985; Vernis, 1983).

APPROVAL OF VIOLENCE

To measure norms tolerating wife abuse, we replicated the measure first employed in a 1968 survey conducted for the President's Commission on the Causes and Prevention of Violence: "Are there situations that you can imagine in which you would approve of a husband slapping his wife?" (Owens and Straus, 1975; Stark and McEvoy, 1970).

VIOLENCE MEASURE

The definition of violence used here is "an act carried out with the intention or perceived intention of causing physical pain or injury to another person."[5] We used the "Conflict Tactics Scale" (CTS) to measure the incidence of violence (Straus, 1979). The CTS has been used and refined in a number of studies of intra-family violence (Allen and Straus, 1980; Giles-Sims, 1983; Hornung et al., 1981; Jorgensen, 1977; Straus, 1979; Straus and Gelles, 1986; Steinmetz, 1977). We use the 1985 revision of the CTS (Straus and Gelles, 1986) in this analysis, and specifically the following acts of physical violence: threw an object at the spouse; pushed, grabbed, or shoved spouse; slapped spouse; kicked; punched; hit with object; beat-up; choked; threatened with knife or gun; used knife or gun.

While we consider both husband-to-wife and wife-to-husband violence to be important, we believe that they cannot be equated. Assaults on women are a far more serious problem given men's greater size and strength. Men, in fact, may laugh at their wife's attempts to slap or punch them, and much of the violence by wives is in self-defense (Saunders, 1986; Straus, 1980). Consistent with this, our data on the effects of violence show that women are three times more likely to require medical care for injuries sustained in family assaults. Therefore, we chose to focus this chapter on husband-to-wife acts of physical violence. For brevity and convenience, this will be referred to as "wife abuse" for the balance of the chapter. Wife abuse existed if the husband engaged in one or more of the violent acts listed above during the one-year referent period of the survey.

OCCUPATIONAL STATUS MEASURE

Each respondent was asked: What kind of work do you do? What kind of work does your spouse/partner do? This information was coded using the Bureau of Labor Statistics revised Occupational Classification System. Then, each Bureau of Labor Statistics occupation code was classified as either "blue-collar" or "white-collar" using the list of occupations falling into these categories by Rice (see Robinson et al., 1969).

Drinking Patterns and Wife Abuse

As a first approach to the question of the link between drinking and family violence, we computed the wife abuse rates for each of the six types of drinkers identified by the Drinking Index. The results in figure 12.1 provide strong evidence of a linear as-

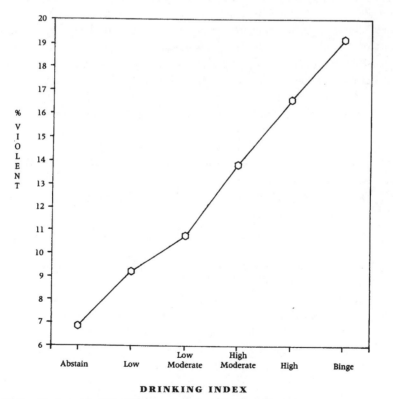

DRINKING INDEX

Figure 12.1. Husband-to-Wife Violence Rate by Drinking Index

sociation between drinking and wife abuse. The percentage of violent husbands rises monotonically from 6.8 percent for abstainers to a three times higher rate of violence (19.2 percent) for the binge drinkers. It appears that the more potentially problematic the drinking level, the higher the rate of violence between spouses. However, it is extremely important not to overlook the substantial amount of wife abuse by abstainers and moderate drinkers.

Drinking at the Time of the Violent Incident

As indicated earlier, an important limitation of the Drinking Index is that it refers to the respondents' *usual* pattern of drinking, and does not provide information on whether there was drinking at the time of the violence. However, the DTV (Drinking at Time of Violence) measure provides this information and permits us to test the hypothesis that drinking is one of the immediate antecedents of family violence. Our data clearly demonstrate that alcohol was *not* used immediately prior to the conflict in the majority (76 percent) of cases. On the other hand, it is also important that in a substantial number of couples (24 percent) one or both partners *were* drinking at the time of the violent incident. In 14 percent of these couples only the male was drinking, in 2 percent only the female was drinking, while in 8 percent both were drinking.

We also investigated whether there is a link between the respondent's usual pattern of drinking and the drinking that occurred at the time of the violence by cross tabulating the DTV measure by the Drinking Index. One might expect that the more one usually drinks, the greater the likelihood that drinking will be involved in a specific incident of wife abuse. This expectation finds strong support in these data (chi-square = 77.65, p < .001). The percent drinking at the time of violence increased from 19.4 percent for the low drinking categories, to 20.8 percent for the high moderates, 47.5 percent for the highs, and 48.4 percent for the binge drinkers. Thus, there is little or no difference between the abstainers, low drinkers, low moderate drinkers, and high moderate drinkers with respect to the percentage of couples in which one or both of the spouses was drinking at the time of the violence. However, for high drinkers and bingers, the percent with alcohol involvement at the time of the violence more than doubles, to about half of all such couples.

Socioeconomic Status and Violence Norms

The thesis that there is a lower-class "culture of violence" (Wolfgang and Ferracuti, 1967) is widely disputed by both criminologists and sociologists who study social stratification. Steinmetz and Straus (1974) and Ball-Rokeach (1973) are among many who question this theory. Instead they argue that class differences in violence are a product of lower resources and higher economic and occupational frustration, and they note there are large differences in approval of violence *within* classes. Nevertheless, as we pointed out earlier, the belief persists that wife beating is perpetrated largely by drunken, lower-class men. To test this theory, we simultaneously considered three of its key elements—occupational status, norms concerning violence, and alcohol abuse. However, before examining the joint effects, table 12.1 permits us to look at all three elements of the "drunken bum theory" one-by-one.

OCCUPATIONAL STATUS DIFFERENCES IN DRINKING, APPROVAL OF VIOLENCE, AND WIFE ABUSE

The results in table 12.1 are consistent with those of other national surveys that show greater levels of both abstinence and high consumption patterns for working-class males (Cahalan, 1970). Binge and weekend drinking among the lower classes and conflict with spouses when drinking have been more frequently identified in lower socioeconomic groups (Cahalan, 1970; Cahalan and Room, 1974).

Table 12.1 also shows that tolerance of wife abuse is more prevalent among blue-collar males (18.5 percent) than among white-collar males (14.4 percent). However, the great majority of men express disapproval of wife slapping regardless of their occupational status. Finally, the last row of table 12.1 shows that blue-collar men are more likely to abuse their wives than are white-collar men.

The results of the bivariate analyses presented in table 12.1 are consistent with previous research on status differences in alcohol abuse and wife abuse, and they provide some support for the "drunken bum theory." However, while all the predicted differences are statistically significant, none are very large.

Table 12.1   Occupational Class Differences in Drinking Patterns, Approval of Violence, and Wife Abuse[a]

Variable		Blue Collar	White Collar
Husband's Drinking Pattern			
Abstinent		29.4%	20.4%
Rare		19.8	24.1
Low Moderate		16.9	31.8
High Moderate		14.1	10.6
High		10.5	7.7
Binge		9.2	5.4
	N =	1089	1266
		Chi-square = 98.85, p <.001	
Husband's Approval of			
Slapping a wife		18.5%	14.4%
	N =	1079	1253
		Chi-square = 6.74, p <.01	
Violent Husbands		13.4%	10.4%
	N =	2462	2568
		Chi-square = 11.17, p <.004	

Note:
a. The N's for Husband's Drinking Pattern and Husband's Approval of Slapping are the number of husbands in the sample, whereas the N for the Wife Abuse Rate is the number of couples.

THE DRUNKEN BUM THEORY

We used a hierarchical log-linear analysis to examine the adequacy of the drunken bum model and to determine the relative importance of drinking, occupational status, and norms. This is a more appropriate test of the "drunken bum theory" because, unlike the tests in table 12.1, the log-linear analysis enables us to look at the interaction of the three key elements of the theory: drinking patterns, violence norms, and occupational status.

    We used a backward elimination procedure (Benedetti and Brown, 1978) to select the best-fitting theoretical model. This method systematically removes effects that produce the least significant changes in the likelihood-ratio chi-squares. The first model tested, a saturated model, examines all main and interaction effects between husband-to-wife violence, the drinking index, norms, and occupational status. The final, best-fitting model includes the three-way interaction between drinking levels, occupational status, and norms, and the two-way interactions between occupational status and violence, and norms and violence (Likelihood-ratio chi-square = 13.022, df = 17; p = .735). Figure 12.2 presents the percentages in each cell.[6]

    Reading across figure 12.2 shows that within all four of the sub-groups, the husbands' drinking pattern is related to the probability of wife abuse. Even for the group whose violence seems to be least affected by alcohol—white-collar men who do not ap-

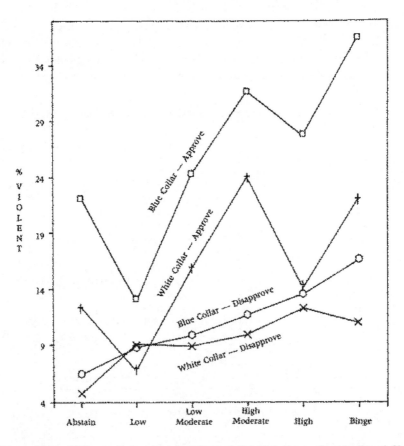

Figure 12.2. Violence Rate as a Function of Drinking Type, Occupational Status and Violence Norms

Table 12.2   Tests of Partial Associations for Wife Abuse, Drinking Types, Norms, and Occupational Status

Effects	L.R. X²	Partial df p Value	
D.T.ª by Occ. by Norms	13.46	5	.019
Wife Abuse by D.T.	18.11	5	.003
Wife Abuse by Occ.	3.95	1	.047
D.T. by Occ.	95.02	5	.000
Wife Abuse by Norms	26.21	1	.000
D.T. by Norms	42.45	5	.000
Occ. by Norms	2.97	1	.080
D.T.	482.20	5	.000
Occ.	15.44	1	.000
Norms	1103.61	1	.000

ªD.T. = Drinking Type

prove of violence—the percent violent among binge drinkers is more than double the percent for abstainers.[7]

Figure 12.2 also shows that men who believe that there are circumstances under which they "would approve of a husband slapping his wife" have higher percentages of violence than men who disagreed with this statement. The differences between the two groups are large and consistent: 11 of the 12 comparisons possible in figure 12.2 show that those who agreed with this traditional view had a higher rate of wife abuse than did those who disagreed.

The top two lines of figure 12.2 show that among men who approve of wife slapping, blue-collar men have a substantially higher rate of wife abuse. The lower two lines of figure 12.2 show that the blue-collar rate of wife abuse is also higher than the white-collar rate among men who disapprove of wife slapping, but the differences are small. In general, figure 12.2 demonstrates that blue-collar men have a higher rate of wife abuse, even after controlling for norms approving violence and drinking. However, normative effects appear to outweigh those of occupational status.

As a further test of the theoretical model, we computed the partial chi-square values to determine which variables exert the strongest net effects. Table 12.2 shows that there is a significant three-way interaction between drinking type, approval of violence, and occupational status. All of the two-way interactions are also significant. Most marked of all the effects are the main effects for drinking types and norms. However, it is clear from the very large Likelihood-ratio chi-square that the most pronounced relationship is between norms regarding violence and wife abuse.[8]

Summary and Conclusions

In this study, we used survey data based on a nationally representative sample of 5,159 couples to examine three questions: (1) Do men who drink heavily have a higher probability of wife beating than others? (2) To what extent does drinking occur at the time of the violent incident? (3) Are such linkages between drinking and wife beating found primarily among working-class men?

Our findings revealed a strong link between alcohol use and physical abuse of wives. We found that the usual pattern of drinking of the respondent (as measured by a Drinking Index with six categories ranging from abstainers to binge drinkers) was directly related to the percent of wife abuse. Moreover, our analyses of drinking as an immediate antecedent of the violence revealed that alcohol was involved in about one out of four instances of wife abuse. When alcohol was an immediate antecedent, it was drinking by the husband alone, or by both the husband and the wife, and only rarely drinking by the wife alone that preceded the violent incident.

On the other hand, it is important not to overstate the extent of the link between alcohol use and wife abuse. For example, although figure 12.1 shows that men who were classified as high or binge drinkers had a two-to-three times greater rate of assaulting their wives than did husbands who abstained, we should stress that about 80 percent of the men in both the high and binge drinking groups did *not* hit their wives at all during the year of this survey. Similarly, while we found that alcohol was often an immediate antecedent of wife abuse, most instances of such abuse took place when neither the husband nor the wife had been drinking. Thus, it is evident that alcohol use at the time of violence is far from a necessary or sufficient cause for wife abuse despite the stereotype that all drunks hit their wives or all wife hitting involves drunks.

Although blue-collar husbands tended to have a higher rate of wife abuse than white-collar husbands, figure 12.2 shows that the *combination* of blue-collar occupational status, drinking, and approval of violence is associated with the highest likelihood of wife abuse. Men with these characteristics have a rate of wife abuse which is 7.8 times greater than the wife-abuse rate of white-collar men who do little drinking and do not approve of slapping a wife under any circumstances. These findings clearly fit the "drunken bum" theory. However, because these are cross-sectional data, the causal order of violence approval is unknown. For some men, normative approval of violence may be an antecedent condition, while for others it may be a rationalization of past wife beating.

Finally, even though we found that the rate of wife abuse is seven times greater among binge-drinking blue-collar men who approve of violence, two-thirds of men with these characteristics did *not* assault their wives during the year of the study. Thus, although the results of this study show that there is more than a "kernel of truth" in the drunken bum theory of wife beating, the findings also provide the basis for demythologizing this stereotype.

Toward an Integrated Theory of the Alcohol-Violence Link

Because some of the results of this study replicate those of a previous study using a large, representative sample (Coleman and Straus, 1983), there are grounds to believe that alcohol use is associated with an increased probability of wife abuse. However, the processes which produce this linkage have yet to be examined empirically, despite a large literature on the subject. For example, Kaufman (1985:79) holds, as do others (Flanzer, 1982; Gelles, 1974), that:

Many arguments are triggered by drinking and drunkenness. Fights start over how much alcohol has been consumed and whether the spouse is drunk or not, and may escalate over related sensitive matters. The ensuing verbal fights are intense and use ammunition from a wide range of issues in the relationship.

Although this is a plausible scenario, experimental studies of marital conflict during drinking (Billings et al., 1979; Frankenstein et al., 1985; Gorad, 1971; Leonard, 1984; Steinglass et al., 1977) have yielded conflicting results on the effect of intoxication on verbal aggression, and also varying theoretical interpretations. Similar ambiguities exist in survey research findings. For example, Coleman and Straus (1983) argue that their findings demonstrate a link between drinking and marital violence, and reflect processes of social learning and deviance disavowal, but they present no empirical evidence to back up this interpretation.

The evidence is somewhat stronger, but hardly definitive, for certain other causal processes and etiological factors. For example, the motivation or purpose of drinking may account for part of the drinking-marital violence relationship. Several researchers have found an association between power motivation and drinking (Brown et al., 1980; Cahalan, 1970; McClelland et al., 1972; Room, 1980). Thus, heavy drinking may be a means of asserting power and control in the marital relationship. Men who are concerned about demonstrating their masculinity may try to accomplish this symbolically by drunkenness, by dominance over women, and by the exertion of physical force on others.

The results reported here suggest that, whatever other factors may be operating, norms concerning violence in combination with low socioeconomic status are important. This is most clearly indicated by the finding that when neither of these factors are present—i.e., among white-collar men who reject the legitimacy of hitting a wife—there is a limited relationship between alcohol abuse and wife abuse. Among other men, alcohol abuse may be only the most visible correlate of family violence, or it may be an important facilitating factor.

The facilitating process can be illustrated by considering men who reject the traditional norm permitting a man to slap his wife. For these men, we found that alcohol *is* associated with wife abuse. The process underlying this association may well involve a combination of the factors we discussed above. At the individual level, it probably includes acting on a belief in the disinhibiting power of alcohol—i.e., that drinking enables one to engage in activities that one would otherwise hesitate to engage in, such as extramarital sex, telling off the boss, or slapping the spouse. At the societal level, the underlying process probably includes norms which excuse "drunken comportment," especially in the form of binge drinking (see MacAndrew and Edgerton, 1969). This socially accepted "time out" from normal rules permits men who reject the legitimacy of hitting their wives to disavow responsibility for their otherwise reprehensible behavior.

These speculations suggest some of the interrelationships among the various theories purporting to explain the alcohol-violence link. These different theories are not necessarily at odds, but may be complementary. Much work needs to be accomplished before a logically integrated and empirically verified theory can be produced.

However, the results of our study call into question the use of alcohol treatment programs as a means of combating wife abuse. As desirable as alcohol treatment programs may be on other grounds, most intra-family violence occurs in the absence of alcohol. Moreover, reducing alcohol abuse does not deal with what are probably the basic factors underlying the high rate of wife abuse in the United States. To the extent that this is the case, steps to reduce wife abuse should focus on these underlying factors—especially the high rate of poverty and economic inequality, and the cultural tradition which glorifies violence, assumes male dominance, and tolerates violence by men against women.

Notes

This is a revised version of a paper presented at the National Alcoholism Forum conference on "Alcohol and The Family," San Francisco, CA, April 18, 1986. This research was made possible by funds provided by the National Institute on Alcohol Abuse and Alcoholism and the National Institute of Mental Health (Grants R01 MH40027 and MH 15161). We would like to acknowledge the helpful comments of Lawrence Hamilton, Robin Room, and three anonymous reviewers, and to express our appreciation to the members of the Family Violence Research Program Seminar for their comments and criticisms. This research is part of the Family Violence Research Program at the University of New Hampshire. A program description and list of publications is available upon request. Correspondence to: Kaufman Kantor, Family Research Laboratory, University of New Hampshire, Durham, NH 03824.

1. For example see Amir (1971), Collins (1981), Greenberg (1981), Rada (1978), Roizen (1981), Roizen and Schneberk (1977), Shupe (1954), and Wolfgang (1958).

2. These 15 studies are: Bard and Zacker (1974); Byles (1978); Caesar (1985); Coleman and Straus (1983); Dobash and Dobash (1979); Eberle (1980); Gelles (1974); Labell (1977); Nisonoff and Bitman (1979); Okun (1986); Rosenbaum and O'Leary (1981); Roy (1977); Van Hasselt, Morrison and Bellock (1985); and Walker (1979, 1984).

3. Experience with studies of family problems, including spouse abuse, rape, and parental kidnapping (Gelles, 1983) shows that telephone interviewing produces higher response rates than face-to-face interviews on sensitive family topics. Not only do the flexibility and anonymity of the telephone lead to a higher response rate, but there is reason to believe that these attributes also yield data which are equivalent in reliability and validity to those gathered by face-to-face interviews. For example, Bradburn et al. (1979) found statistically indistinguishable differences in admitting to a conviction for drunken driving among persons who had in fact been convicted of that offense between face-to-face and phone surveys.

4. For convenience and economy, we use terms such as "marital," and "spouse," and "wife," and "husband" to refer to the respondents, regardless of whether they were married or a non-married cohabiting couple. For an analysis of differences and similarities between married and cohabiting couples with respect to violence and other characteristics, see Yllo (1978), and Yllo and Straus (1981).

5. See Gelles and Straus (1979) for an explication of this definition and an analysis of alternative definitions.

6. We used the SPSSX program, HILOGLINEAR for these analyses. The cell frequencies used to compute the percentages in figure 12.2 are from the observed cell frequencies included in the log-linear analysis output.

7. Figure 12.2 also shows that there is considerable fluctuation around each of the four trend lines. This can be interpreted as indicating that the relationship between drinking and wife abuse is not simply "the more drinking, the higher the rate of wife abuse." For example, among white-collar men who express approval of slapping a wife, the proportion violent is greatest at the "High Moderate" level of drinking, declines for the "High" category, and rises again for "Binge" drinkers, though not to the same level as among the "High Moderate" drinkers. This is consistent with Coleman and Straus (1983) who also found a similar drop in violence for those with the most serious alcohol abuse. However, as is almost always the case for a multi-dimensional cross-tabulation, there are a number of cells with relatively few cases. In such instances, a shift of one or two cases from the non-violent to the violent category can produce a large change in the percent violent. Consequently, it is best to concentrate on the two main findings shown in figure 12.2: the general upward trend in violence as drinking increases, and the higher actual rate of wife abuse among men who believe that there are "situations that you can imagine in which you would approve of a husband slapping his wife." Because the findings are subject to varying interpretations, and especially because others may want to re-analyze the data, it is desirable to document the actual Ns which are the basis for the percentages in figure 12.1. Reading from left to right for each plot line these Ns are: Blue collar-Approve = 36, 23, 37, 22, 36, 30. White collar—Approve = 32, 30, 50, 29, 21, 9. Blue collar—Disapprove = 264, 181, 131, 118, 65, 65. White collar—Disapprove = 213, 261, 329, 99, 64, 54.

8. Given the relatively high rates of husband-to-wife violence that Straus et al. (1980:129) found for unemployed and part-time workers, and the relevance for the drunken bum stereotype, we examined the relationship between unemployment and wife abuse. Consistent with the previous study, we found that a larger percentage of unemployed men assaulted their wives during the year of the survey. When unemployment was added to the log-linear model, it continued to be significant, but the overall model did not meet the goodness-of-fit criterion as well as the model presented in this section. To the extent that the drunken bum stereotype includes unemployment, we think it refers to the *chronically* unemployed, whereas most of the unemployed husbands in this sample are probably not chronically unemployed. We infer this from the fact that most unemployment is transitory. Therefore, if our sample is representative of adult males, most of the unemployed in the sample are also temporarily unemployed.

References

A.D.A.M.H.A. 1980. National Data Book. Alcohol, Drug Abuse and Mental Health Administration DHEW No. (ADM) 80-938. Rockville, MD.

Allen, Craig M., and Murray A. Straus. 1980. "Resources, power, and husband-wife violence." Pp. 188–208 in Murray A. Straus and Gerald T. Hotaling (eds.), *The Social Causes of Husband-Wife Violence.* Minneapolis: University of Minnesota Press.

Amir, Menachem. 1971. Patterns in Forcible Rape. Chicago: University of Chicago Press.

Ball-Rokeach, Sandra J. 1973. "Values and violence: a test of the subculture of violence thesis." *American Sociological Review* 38:736–49.

Bard, Morton, and J. Zacker. 1974. "Assaultiveness and alcohol use in family disputes: police perceptions." *Criminology* 12:281–92.

Baron, Larry, and Murray A. Straus. 1987. "Legitimate violence, violent attitudes, and rape: a test of the cultural spillover theory." Annals of the New York Academy of Sciences: Forthcoming.

Benedetti, Jacqueline K., and Morton B. Brown.1978. "Strategies for the selection of log-linear models." *Biometrics* 34:680–86.

Billings, Andrew G., Marc Kessler, Christopher A. Gomberg and Sheldon Weiner. 1979. "Marital conflict resolution of alcoholic and nonalcoholic couples during drinking and nondrinking sessions." *Journal of Studies on Alcohol* 40:183–95.

Blum, Richard H. 1981. "Violence, alcohol, and setting: an unexplored nexus." Pp. 110–42 in James J. Collins, Jr. (ed.), *Drinking and Crime: Perspectives on the Relationships between Alcohol Consumption and Criminal Behavior.* New York: Guilford Press.

Bordin, Ruth. 1981. *Woman and Temperance: A Quest for Power and Liberty, 1873–1900.* Philadelphia: Temple University Press.

Boyatzis, Richard E. 1983. "Who should drink what, when, and where if looking for a fight." Pp. 314–29 in Edward Gottheil, Keith A. Druley, Thomas E. Skoloda, and Howard M. Waxman (eds.), *Drug Abuse and Aggression.* Springfield, IL: Charles C. Thomas.

Bradbum, Norman M., Seymour Sudman and Associates. 1979. *Improving Interview Method and Questionnaire Design.* San Francisco: Jossey-Bass.

Brown, Sandra A., Mark S. Goldman, Andres Inn, and Lynn R. Anderson. 1980. "Expectations of reinforcement from alcohol: their domain and relation to drinking patterns." *Journal of Consulting and Clinical Psychology* 48:419–26.

Byles, John A. 1978. "Violence, alcohol problems and other problems in disintegrating families." *Journal of Studies on Alcohol* 39:551–53.

Caesar, Patti Lynn. 1985. "The wife beater: personality and psychosocial characteristics." Paper presented at the annual meeting of the American Psychological Association, Los Angeles.

Cahalan, Don. 1970. *Problem Drinkers: A National Survey.* San Francisco: Jossey-Bass.

Cahalan, Don, Ira H. Cisin, and Helen M. Crossley. 1969. *American Drinking Practices: A National Study of Drinking Behavior and Attitudes.* New Brunswick, NJ: Rutgers Center for Alcohol Studies.

Cahalan, Don, and Robin Room. 1974. *Problem Drinking Among American Men.* New Brunswick, NJ: Rutgers Center for Alcohol Studies.

Coleman, Diane H., and Murray A. Straus. 1983. "Alcohol abuse and family violence." Pp. 104–24 in Edward Gottheil, Keith A. Druley, Thomas E. Skoloda, and Howard M. Waxman (eds.), *Alcohol, Drug Abuse and Aggression.* Springfield, IL: Charles C. Thomas.

Collins, James J., Jr. 1981. "Alcohol use and criminal behavior: an empirical, theoretical and methodological overview." Pp. 288–316 in James J. Collins, Jr. (ed.), *Drinking and Crime: Perspectives on the Relationships Between Alcohol Consumption and Criminal Behavior.* New York: Guilford Press.

Critchlow, Barbara. 1983. "Blaming the booze: the attribution of responsibility for drunken behavior." *Personality and Social Psychology Bulletin* 9:451–73.

Dobash, R. Emerson, and Russell Dobash. 1979. *Violence Against Wives: A Case Against Patriarchy.* New York: Free Press.

Eberle, Patricia A. 1980. "Alcohol abusers and non-users: a discriminant analysis of differences between two subgroups of batterers." Paper presented at the annual meeting of the Society for the Study of Social Problems, Toronto.

Flanzer, Jerry. 1982. "Alcohol and family violence: double trouble." Pp. 136–42 in Maria Roy (ed.), *The Abusive Partner.* New York: Van Nostrand Reinhold.

Frankenstein, William, William M. Hay, and Peter E. Nathan. 1985. "Effects of intoxication on alcoholics' marital communication and problem solving." *Journal of Studies on Alcohol* 46:1–6.

Gallup, George. 1978. "More Americans drink and they're drinking more." *Boston Globe*, July 2:C1-C3.

Gelles, Richard J. 1974. *The Violent Home*. Beverly Hills, CA: Sage.

———. 1983. "Parental child snatching: the use of telephone survey techniques to study a hidden family problem." Paper presented at the National Council on Family Relations, Theory Construction and Research Methods Workshop, Minneapolis.

Gelles, Richard J., and Murray A. Straus. 1979. "Determinants of violence in the family: toward a theoretical integration." Pp. 549–81 in Wesley R. Burr, Rueben Hill, F. Ivan Nye, and Ira L. Reiss (eds.), *Contemporary Theories about the Family*. New York: Free Press.

Giles-Sims, Jean. 1983. *Wife Battering: A Systems Theory Approach*. New York: Guilford Press.

Gorad, Stephen L. 1971. "Communicational styles and interaction of alcoholics and their wives." *Family Process* 10:475–89.

Gottheil, Edward, Keith A. Druley, Thomas E. Skoloda, and Howard W. Waxman. 1983. "Aggression and addiction: summary and overview." Pp. 333–56 in Edward Gottheil, Keith A. Druley, Thomas E. Skoloda, and Howard M. Waxman (eds.), *Drug Abuse and Aggression*. Springfield, IL: Charles C. Thomas.

Greenberg, Stephanie W. 1981. "Alcohol and crime: a methodological critique of the literature." Pp. 70–106 in James J. Collins, Jr. (ed.), *Drinking and Crime: Perspectives on the Relationships Between Alcohol Consumption and Criminal Behavior*. New York: Guilford Press.

Hesselbrock, Michie, Thomas F. Babor, Victor Hesselbrock, Roger E. Meyer, and Cathy Workman. 1983. "Never believe an alcoholic? On the validity of self-report measures of alcohol dependence and related constructs." *International Journal of the Addictions* 18:593–609.

Hornung, Carlton A., B. Claire McCullough, and Taichi Sugimoto. 1981. "Status relationships in marriage: risk factors in spouse abuse." *Journal of Marriage and the Family* 43:675–92.

Hotaling, Gerald T., and Murray A. Straus. 1980. "Culture, social organization, and irony in the study of family violence." Pp. 3–22 in Murray A. Straus and Gerald T. Hotaling (eds.), *The Social Causes of Husband-Wife Violence*. Minneapolis: University of Minnesota Press.

Hotaling, Gerald T. and David B. Sugarman. 1986. "An analysis of risk markers in husband to wife violence: the current state of knowledge." *Violence and Victims* 1:101–24.

Jorgensen, Stephen R. 1977. "Societal class heterogamy, status striving, and perception of marital conflict: a partial replication and revision of Pearlin's Contingency Hypothesis." *Journal of Marriage and the Family* 39:653–89.

Kaufman, Edward. 1985. *Substance Abuse and Family Therapy*. New York: Grune and Stratton.

Klein, Dorie. 1981. "Drinking and battering: some preliminary considerations on alcohol, gender domination, and marital violence." Paper presented at the annual meeting of the Society for the Study of Social Problems, Toronto.

Komarovsky, Mirra. 1967. *Blue-Collar Marriage*. New York: Random House.

Labell, Linda S. 1977. "Wife abuse: a sociological study of battered women and their mates." *Victimology* 4:258–67.

Leonard, Kenneth E. 1984. "Alcohol consumption and escalatory aggression in intoxicated and sober dyads." *Journal of Studies of Alcohol* 45:75–80.

Levinson, David. 1983. "Social setting, cultural factors and alcohol-related aggression." Pp. 41–58 in Edward Gottheil, Keith A. Druley, Thomas E. Skoloda, and Howard M. Waxman (eds.), *Drug Abuse and Aggression*. Springfield, IL: Charles C. Thomas.

Linsky, Arnold S., Murray A. Straus, and John P. Colby, Jr. 1985. "Stressful events, stressful conditions and alcohol problems in the United States: a partial test of Bales' theory of alcoholism." *Journal of Studies on Alcohol* 46:72–80.

Loftin, Colin, and Robert H. Hill. 1974. "Regional subculture and homicide: an examination of the Gastil-Hackney thesis." *American Sociological Review* 39:714–24.

MacAndrew, Craig, and Robert B. Edgerton. 1969. *Drunken Comportment*. Chicago: Aldine.

Maisto, Stephen A., Linda C. Sobell, and Mark B. Sobell. 1979. "Comparison of alcoholics' self-reports of drinking behavior with reports of collateral informants." *Journal of Consulting and Clinical Psychology* 47:106–12.

Marlatt, G. Allan, and Damaris J. Rohsenow. 1980. "Cognitive processes in alcohol use: expectancy and the balanced placebo design." Pp. 159–99 in Nancy K. Mello (ed.), *Advances in Substance Abuse: Behavioral and Biological Research*. A Research Annual, Volume 1. Greenwich, CT: JAI Press.

Mayfield, Demmie. 1983. "Substance abuse and aggression: a psychopharmacological perspective." Pp. 139–49 in Edward Gottheil, Keith A. Druley, Thomas E. Skoloda, and Howard M. Waxman (eds.), *Drug Abuse and Aggression*. Springfield, IL: Charles C. Thomas.

McClelland, David C., William N. Davis, Rudolph Kalin, and Eric Wanner. 1972. *The Drinking Man*. New York: Free Press.

Morgan, Patricia. 1982. "Alcohol and family violence: a review of the literature." Pp. 223–59 in *Alcohol Consumption and Related Problems, Alcohol and Health Monograph 1,* DHHS Publication (ADM) 82-1190. Washington, DC: U.S. Government Printing Office.

———. 1983. "Alcohol, disinhibition, and domination: a conceptual analysis." Pp. 405–20 in Robin Room and Gary Collins (eds.), *Alcohol and Disinhibition: Nature and Meaning of the Link*. Washington, DC: U.S. Government Printing Office.

Neff, James A., and Baqar A. Husaini. 1985. "Stress-buffer properties of alcohol consumption: the role of urbanicity and religious identification." *Journal of Health and Social Behavior* 26:207–22.

Nisonoff, Linda, and Irving Bitman. 1979. "Spouse abuse: incidence and relationship to selected demographic variables." *Victimology* 4:131–40.

Okun, Lewis. 1986. *Women Abuse: Facts Replacing Myths*. Albany: State University of New York Press.

Owens, David M., and Murray A. Straus. 1975. "The social structure of violence in childhood and approval of violence as an adult." *Aggressive Behavior* 1:193–211.

Pernanen, Kai. 1976. "Alcohol and crimes of violence." Pp. 351–444 in Benjamin Kissin and Henri Begleiter (eds.), *The Biology of Alcoholism*. Volume 4: Social Aspects of Alcoholism. New York: Plenum.

———. 1981. "Theoretical aspects of the relationship between alcohol use and crime." Pp. 1–61 in James J. Collins, Jr. (ed.), *Drinking and Crime: Perspectives on the Relationships Between Alcohol Consumption and Criminal Behavior*. New York: Guilford Press.

Pleck, Elizabeth H. 1987. *Domestic Tyranny: The Making of American Social Policy Against Family Violence from Colonial Times to the Present*. New York: Oxford.

Polich, J. Michael. 1982. "The validity of self-reports in alcoholism research." *Addictive Behaviors* 7:123–32.

Powers, Robert J., and Irwin L. Kutash. 1982. "Alcohol, drugs, and partner abuse." Pp. 39–75 in Maria Roy (ed.), *The Abusive Partner: An Analysis of Domestic Battering*. New York: Van Nostrand Reinhold.

Rada, Richard T. 1978. *Clinical Aspects of the Rapist*. New York: Grune and Stratton.

Robinson, John P., Robert Athanasiou, and Kendra B. Head. 1969. *Measures of Occupational Attitudes and Occupational Characteristics*. University of Michigan: Survey Research Center of the Institute for Social Research.

Roizen, Judy. 1981. "Alcohol and criminal behavior among Blacks: the case for research on special populations." Pp. 207–51 in James J. Collins Jr. (ed.), *Drinking and Crime: Perspectives on the Relationships Between Alcohol Consumption and Criminal Behavior*. New York: Guilford Press.

Roizen, Judy, and Dan Schneberk. 1977. "Alcohol and crime." In Marc Aarens, Tracy Cameron, Judy Roizen, Ron Roizen, Robin Room, Dan Schneberk, and Deborah Wingard (eds.), *Alcohol, Casualties and Crime*. Berkeley, CA: Social Research Group.

Room, Robin. 1980. "Alcohol as an instrument of intimate domination." Paper presented at the annual meeting of the Society for the Study of Social Problems, New York.

Room, Robin, and Gary Collins (eds.). 1983. *Alcohol and Disinhibition: Nature and Meaning of the Link*. Washington, DC: U.S. Government Printing Office.

Rosenbaum, Alan, and K. Daniel O'Leary. 1981. "Marital violence: characteristics of abusive couples." *Journal of Consulting and Clinical Psychology* 49:63–71.

Roy, Maria. 1977. "A current survey of 150 cases." Pp. 25–44 in Maria Roy (ed.), *Battered Women*. New York: Van Nostrand Reinhold.

Saunders, Daniel G. 1986. "When battered women use violence: husband-abuse or self-defense?" *Violence and Victims* 1:47–60.

Sher, Kenneth J. 1985. "Subjective effects of alcohol: the influence of setting and individual differences in alcohol expectancies." *Journal of Studies on Alcohol* 46:137–46.

Shupe, L.M. 1954. "Alcohol and crime." *Journal of Criminal Law, Criminology and Police Science* 44:661–64.

Sobell, Linda C., and Mark B. Sobell. 1978. "Validity of self-reports in three populations of alcoholics." *Journal of Consulting and Clinical Psychology* 46:901–7.

Stark, Rodney, and James McEvoy, III. 1970. "Middle class violence." *Psychology Today* 4:52–65.

Steinglass, Peter, Donald I. Davis, and David Berenson. 1977. "Observations of conjointly hospitalized 'alcoholic couples' during sobriety and intoxication: implications for theory and therapy." *Family Process* 16:1–16.

Steinmetz, Suzanne K. 1977. *The Cycle of Violence: Assertive, Aggressive, and Abusive Family Interaction*. New York: Praeger.

Steinmetz, Suzanne K., and Murray A. Straus. 1974. "General introduction: social myth and social system in the study of intra-family violence." Pp. 3–25 in Suzanne K. Steinmetz and Murray A. Straus (eds.), *Violence in the Family*. New York: Harper and Row.

Straus, Murray A. 1979. "Measuring intrafamily conflict and violence: the conflict tactics (CT) scales." *Journal of Marriage and the Family* 41:75–88.

———. 1980. "Victims and aggressors in marital violence." *American Behavioral Scientist* 23:681–704.

Straus, Murray A., and Richard J. Gelles. 1986. "Societal chance and chance in family violence from 1975 to 1985 as revealed by two national surveys." *Journal of Marriage and the Family* 48:465–79.

Straus, Murray A., Richard J. Gelles, and Suzanne K. Steinmetz. 1980. *Behind Closed Doors: Violence in the American Family*. Garden City, NY: Anchor/Doubleday.

Taylor, Stuart P., and Kenneth E. Leonard. 1983. "Alcohol and human physical aggression." Pp. 77–101 in Russell G. Green and Edward I. Donnerstein (eds.), *Aggression: Theoretical and Empirical Reviews*, Volume 2. New York: Academic Press.

Van Hasselt, Vincent B., Randall L. Morrison, and Alan S. Bellock. 1985. "Alcohol use in wife-abusers and their spouses." *Addictive Behaviors* 10:127–35.

Vernis, J.S. 1983. "Agreement between alcoholics and relatives when reporting follow-up states." *International Journal of the Addictions* 18:891–94.

Walker, Lenore. 1979. *The Battered Woman*. New York: Harper and Row.

———. 1984. The *Battered Women Syndrome*. New York: Springer.

Wolfgang, Marvin E. 1958. *Patterns in Criminal Homicide*. Philadelphia: University of Pennsylvania Press.

Wolfgang, Marvin E., and Franco Ferracuti. 1967. *The Subculture of Violence: Toward an Integrated Theory of Criminology.* London: Tavistock.

Yllo, Kersti Alice. 1978. "Nonmarital cohabitation: beyond the college campus." *Alternative Lifestyles* 1:37–54.

Yllo, Kersti, and Murray A. Straus. 1981. "Interpersonal violence among married and cohabiting couples." *Family Relations* 30:339–47.

CHAPTER 13

Drugs-Crime Connections

ELABORATIONS FROM THE LIFE HISTORIES OF HARD-CORE HEROIN ADDICTS

Charles E. Faupel and Carl B. Klockars

The debate over the nature and extent of the relationship between heroin use and criminal activity is a long-standing one which has generated a voluminous literature. A 1980 survey (Gandossey et al., 1980) lists over 450 citations to books, articles, and research reports which directly or indirectly bear upon the heroin-crime relationship. Since 1980 the study of this relationship has continued, and several large-scale quantitative studies (Anglin and Speckart, 1984; Ball et al., 1981, 1983; Collins et al., 1984, 1985; Johnson et al., 1985) generally support the thesis that an increase in criminality commonly occurs in conjunction with increased heroin use in the United States. These studies, together with a host of others preceding them (e.g., Ball and Snarr, 1969; Chein et al., 1964; Inciardi, 1979; McGlothlin et al., 1978; Nash, 1973; Weissman et al., 1974) have moved the focus of the debate from the empirical question of whether or not there is a heroin-crime connection to empirical and theoretical questions about the dynamics of that connection.

In particular, two hypotheses, neither of which is new, currently occupy center stage in the drugs-crime controversy. The first, stated by Tappan a quarter of a century ago, maintains that the "addict of lower socio-economic class is a criminal primarily because illicit narcotics are costly and because he can secure his daily requirements only by committing crimes that will pay for them" (1960:65–66). This hypothesis maintains that heroin addict criminality is a consequence of addiction, albeit an indirect one. As physical dependence upon and tolerance for heroin increase, and the cost of progressively larger dosages of heroin increase proportionally, the addict is driven to criminal means to satisfy his or her habit. Empirically, this hypothesis predicts a linear increase in heroin consumption and a corresponding increase in criminal activity necessary to support it. In contrast, a second hypothesis maintains that the "principal explanation for the association between drug abuse and crime . . . is likely to be found in the sub-cultural attachment" (Goldman, 1981:162) comprised of the criminal associations, identifications, and activities of those persons who eventually become addicted. The basis for this hypothesis can only be understood in the context of the contemporary socio-legal milieu in which narcotics use takes place. Since the criminalization of heroin in 1914, the social world of narcotics has become increasingly intertwined with the broader criminal subculture (Musto, 1973). Consequently, would-be narcotics users inevitably associate with other criminals in the highly criminal copping areas of inner cities, and, indeed, are often recruited from delinquent and criminal networks. Through these criminal associations, therefore, the individual is introduced to heroin, and both crime and heroin use are facilitated and maintained. Empirically, this second hypothesis predicts increases in heroin use following or coinciding with periods of criminal association and activity.

A shorthand title for the first hypothesis is "Drugs cause crimes"; for the second "Crimes cause drugs." Each, as we shall see below, is subject to a number of qualifications and reservations; but each, as we shall also see below, continues to mark a rather different approach to understanding the drugs-crime connection. Furthermore, each hypothesis has quite different policy implications associated with it.

Methodology

Our contribution to understanding the dynamics of the drugs-crime connection is based upon life-history interviews with 32 hard core heroin addicts in the Wilmington, Delaware area. We purposely selected the respondents on the basis of their extensive involvement in the heroin subculture. All of the respondents had extensive contact with the criminal justice system. At the time of interview, 24 of the 32 respondents were incarcerated or under some form of correctional authority supervision (e.g., supervised custody, work release, parole, or probation). While this places certain limits on the generalizations that can be made from these data, the focus of this study is the dynamics of addiction among heavily-involved street addicts. For example, controlled users or "chippers" will not have experienced many of the dynamics reported here. Similarly, physicians, nurses, and middle class "prescription abusers" are not typically subject to many of the constraints experienced by lower-class street users. Hence, it is important to emphasize that the findings we report here are intended to describe "hard core" urban heroin addicts.

Women are slightly overrepresented, constituting 14 of the 32 respondents. Ethnically, the sample consists of 23 blacks and nine whites; Hispanics are not represented because there is not a sizable Hispanic drug-using population in the Wilmington area.

Respondents were paid five dollars per hour for their interview time, which undoubtedly contributed to the 100 percent response rate. The interviews ranged from 10 to 25 hours in length, with each interview session averaging between three and four hours. With a single exception, all of the interviews were tape recorded and transcribed. Respondents were promised confidentiality and, without exception, they spoke openly of their drug, crime, and life-history experience.

The incarcerated respondents and most of the street respondents were selected with the aid of treatment personnel who were carefully instructed regarding the goals of the research and selection criteria. This strategy proved invaluable for two reasons. First, by utilizing treatment personnel in the screening process, we were able to avoid the time-consuming task of establishing the "appropriateness" of respondents for the purposes of this research; the treatment personnel were already intimately familiar with the drug-using and criminal histories of the respondents. Second, the treatment personnel had an unusually positive relationship with Wilmington-area drug users. The treatment counselor in the prison system was regarded as an ally in the quest for better living conditions, appeals for early release, etc., and was regarded as highly trustworthy in the prison subculture. His frequent confrontations with prison authorities over prisoner rights and privileges enhanced his reputation among the inmates. Similarly, the treatment counselor who aided in the selection of street respondents was carefully selected on the basis of his positive involvement with street addicts. His relationship with area addicts is a long-standing and multifaceted one. His reputation among street addicts was firmly established when he successfully negotiated much needed reforms in one of the local treatment agencies. Because of the long-standing positive relationship they had with area addicts, this initial contact by treatment personnel greatly facilitated our establishing necessary rapport.

After a few initial interviews were completed, several broad focal areas emerged which formed the basis for future questioning. Respondents were interviewed regarding: (1) childhood and early adolescent experiences which may have served as *predisposing factors* for eventual drugs/criminal involvement; (2) *initial encounters* with various types of drugs and criminality; (3) the *evolution* of their drug and criminal careers; (4) their patterns of activity during *peak periods* of drug use and criminality, including descriptions of *typical days* during these periods; (5) their *preferences for* types of crimes and drugs; (6) the *structure of understanding* guiding drug use and criminal activity; and (7) their perceptions of the nature and effectiveness of *drug treatment*. Structuring the life-history interviews in this way insured that most relevant career phases were covered while at the same time it permitted the respondents a great deal of flexibility in interpreting their experiences.

Drugs Cause Crimes versus Crimes Cause Drugs

One of the earliest strategies for testing the Drugs-cause-crimes versus Crimes-cause-drugs hypotheses involved trying to establish a temporal sequence to drug use and criminal behavior. If it can be established that a pattern of regular or extensive criminal behavior typically precedes heroin addiction, that finding would tend to support the Crimes-cause-drugs hypothesis. Conversely, if a pattern of regular or extensive criminality tends to develop after the onset of heroin addiction, that finding would tend to support the Drugs-cause-crimes hypothesis. Previous research on this question is mixed, but mixed in a systematic way. Most of the early studies found little criminality before the onset of opiate addiction (Pescor, 1943; Terry and Pellens, 1928). Later studies, by contrast, have shown a high probability of criminality preceding heroin addiction (Ball and Chambers, 1970; Chambers, 1974; Jacoby et al., 1973; Inciardi, 1979; O'Donnell, 1966; Robins and Murphy 1967).

Our life-history interviews are consistent with the findings of the recent studies. All of our respondents reported some criminal activity prior to their first use of heroin. However, for nearly all of our respondents, both their criminal careers and their heroin-using careers began slowly. For the respondents in our study, a median of 3.5 years elapsed between their first serious criminal offense and subsequent involvement in criminal activity on a regular basis. Likewise, all of our respondents reported at least occasional use of other illicit drugs prior to their first experience with heroin. Moreover, many of our respondents indicated that they spent substantial periods of time—months and even years—using heroin on an occasional basis ("chipping" or "chippying"), either inhaling the powder ("sniffing" or "snorting"), injecting the prepared ("cooked") mixture subcutaneously ("skinpopping"), or receiving occasional intravenous injections from other users before becoming regular users themselves. Perhaps most importantly, virtually all of our respondents reported that they believed that their criminal and drug careers began independently of one another, although both careers became intimately interconnected as each evolved. In the earliest phases of their drug and crime careers, the decision to commit crimes and the decision to use drugs were choices which our respondents believe they freely chose to make and which they believe they could have discontinued before either choice became a way of life (also see Fields and Walters, 1985; Morris, 1985).

Drug and Crime Career Patterns

From our interviews it appears that two very general factors shape and influence the drug and crime careers of our respondents, not only during the early stages of each career but as each career evolves through different stages. The first of these factors is the *availability* of heroin rather than the level of physical tolerance the user has developed. "The more you had the more you did," explains "Mona" a thirty-year-old female. "And if all you had was $10 than that's all you did. . . . But if you had $200 then you did that much." Addicts are able to adjust to periods of sharply decreased availability (e.g., "panic" periods when supplies of street heroin disappear) by reducing consumption or by using alternative drugs (e.g., methadone). They are also able to manipulate availability, increasing or decreasing it in ways and for reasons we discuss below.

As we use the term, availability also means something more than access to sellers of heroin who have quantities of the drug to sell. By availability we also mean the resources and opportunities to buy heroin or obtain it in other ways as well as the skills necessary to use it. In short, availability is understood to include considerations of all of those opportunities and obstacles which may influence a heroin user's success in introducing a quantity of the drug into his or her bloodstream.

The second general factor shaping the drugs and crime careers of our life-history interviewees is *life structure*. By "life structure" we mean regularly occurring patterns of daily domestic, occupational, recreational, or criminal activity. Recent ethnographic accounts of heroin-using careers in several major cities reveal that, like their "straight" counterparts, most addicts maintain reasonably predictable daily routines (Beschner and Brower, 1985; Walters, 1985). Throughout their lives our respondents fulfilled, to one degree or another, conventional as well as criminal and other subcultural roles. In fact, during most periods of their crime and drug careers, our interviewees spent far more time engaged in conventional role activities than in criminal or deviant ones.

Many worked conventional jobs. Women with children performed routine house-keeping and child-rearing duties. Many leisure-time activities did not differ from those of non-addicts. These hard core addicts spent time grocery shopping, tinkering with cars, visiting relatives, talking with friends, listening to records, and watching television in totally unremarkable fashion.

Life structure in the hard core criminal addict's life can be also provided by some rather stable forms of criminal activity. Burglars spend time staking out business establishments. Shoplifters typically establish "runs," more or less stable sequences of targeted stores from which to "boost" during late morning, noon, and early afternoon hours, saving the later afternoon for fencing what they have stolen. Prostitutes typically keep a regular evening and night-time schedule, which runs from 7 P.M. to 3 A.M. Mornings are usually spent sleeping and afternoons are usually occupied with conventional duties.

It is within this structure of conventional and criminal roles that buying ("copping"), selling ("dealing"), and using ("shooting") heroin take place. For example, shoplifters typically structure their runs to allow times and places for all three activities. Likewise, prostitutes seek to manage their drug use so that neither withdrawal symptoms ("joneses") nor periods of heroin-induced drowsiness will interfere with their work. In order to meet the demands of criminal or conventional roles, addicts in our sample often used other drugs (e.g., marijuana, barbituates, alcohol, amphetamines, methadone) to alter their moods and motivations, saving heroin as a reward for successfully completing a job or meeting other obligations.

A TYPOLOGY OF CAREER PATTERNS

These two dimensions–*availability* and *life structure*–are critical to understanding the dynamics of addict careers. According to our respondents, differences in the ways addicts manage these functions and variations in these two dimensions that are beyond the control of addicts combine to produce fairly distinct patterns, periods, or stages in their careers. The interaction of availability and life structure may be understood to describe addict career phases that are familiar to participants or observers of the heroin scene.

In figure 13.1, we identify four such familiar career phases, each of which is marked by a different interaction of heroin availability and life structure. It is important to note that while each denotes an addict type, none of the "types" imply a single career pattern. That is, throughout their drug-crime careers, addicts typically move through periods in which they may at one time be described as one type and later as another. In our discussion of each type, we describe some of the ways in which transitions seem to occur.

The Occasional User–Low Availability/High Life Structure

Initiates into the heroin-using subculture typically begin as occasional users. For the beginning heroin user, a variety of factors typically serve to limit the availability of heroin. The initiate has usually not spent enough time in the heroin subculture to develop extensive drug connections. In addition, the beginner must be taught how and where to buy heroin, and also must learn how to use it. Moreover, the typical begin-

Availability	Life Structure	
	High	Low
High	The Stabilized Junkie	The Free-Wheeling Junkie
Low	The Occasional User	The Street Junkie

Figure 13.1.   A Typology of Heroin Use Career Phases

ning heroin user is unlikely to have sufficient income to maintain any substantial level of heroin consumption, and is most unlikely to have either the connections or the knowledge necessary to increase availability through low-level dealing or through shrewd buying and reselling as experienced addicts sometimes do.

In addition to these factors which tend to limit the availability of heroin to the beginning user and hold him or her to an occasional user role, a variety of factors related to life structure also tend to oblige the beginning heroin user to play an occasional user role, or at least to do so until that life structure can be modified to accommodate a higher level of heroin use. In many cases beginning heroin users are young, dependent, involved in school, and bear family roles and obligations which are not easily changed. Likewise, adult role obligations, such as full-time employment, housekeeping, and child rearing, can be altered so as to be compatible with occasional patterns of heroin use, but not without considerable difficulty if those patterns include high or even moderately high levels of addiction.

One of our respondents, "Belle," explained how she and her husband, "Taps" maintained a very long period of occasional use, due largely to Taps' determination to keep his full-time job:

> I know of people that does half a bag generally. Do you understand what I'm saying? That they automatically live off of half a bag and got a jones. Like I said, Taps worked–and he would shoot no more than half a bag of dope at any time he took off and wouldn't do no wrong. He would not do no wrong. He worked each and every day. And this is what I told you before—I said I don't know how he had a jones and worked, but he worked every day.

Moreover, Belle went on to explain that when the life structure Taps provided for her lapsed—and availability increased—she did not remain an occasional user:

> Taps had me limited a long, long time. I mean a long time limited to nothing but a half a bag of drugs, until he completely stopped hisself. Then when he stopped, I went "Phwee!"—because I didn't have anybody to guide me. I didn't have to take half a bag and divide it in half for him. And I went from one bag to more.

"Ron," another addict in our sample, played the role of "occasional user" without interruption for nearly eight years. During this period he consumed an average of

$10–15 in street heroin per day, while holding down a full-time job and living with his mother, who refused to allow him to use drugs in her home. Toward the end of the eight-year period he became a "tester" for a local drug dealer, a role which increased the availability of heroin. At about the same time, he also lost his job and moved out of his mother's home. Having lost the support of the stable routine imposed by his job and living arrangements at the same time heroin became more readily available to him in his role of "tester," his drug use escalated dramatically within a very short time.

Interestingly, the low availability/high life structure pattern of occasional use, which typically marks the beginning addict's entrance into the drug-using world, is characteristic of many addicts' attempts to leave it. Many formal drug rehabilitation programs impose conditions of low (or no) heroin availability combined with high life structure upon addicts enrolled in their programs (Faupel, 1985). Likewise, as Biernacki (1986) and Waldorf (1983) have extensively demonstrated, addicts who attempt to quit on their own often seek to do so by limiting or eliminating altogether their contacts with addict friends, self-medicating with "street" methodone, and devoting themselves intensively to some highly demanding routine activity such as a full-time job or caring for young children.

The Stabilized Junkie–High Availability/High Life Structure

For the occasional user to become a stabilized junkie, heroin must become increasingly available in large and regular quantities, and his or her daily structure must be modified to accommodate regular heroin use. Making heroin regularly available in sufficiently large quantities is not only a matter of gaining access to reliable sources of supply of the drug; it also involves learning new and more sophisticated techniques for using and obtaining it as well as getting enough money to be able to buy it regularly.

During the time beginning addicts play occasional user roles, they typically learn the fundamentals of copping, cooking, cutting, and spiking. These are all drug-using skills that take time to learn. It was not uncommon for the addicts in our sample to report that a sharp increase in their level of heroin use followed their learning to shoot themselves. When an occasional user learns to self-inject and no longer requires the more knowledgeable drug-using friends to "get off," this new level of skill and independence, in effect, increases the availability of heroin.

Likewise, copping skills and contacts which might have been sufficient to support occasional use require upgrading to support the needs of the stabilized junkie. The would-be stabilized junkie who must rely solely on low-quality, "street" heroin, who gets "ripped" by paying high prices for "bad dope," or who is totally dependent on what quality or quantity of heroin a single supplier happens to have available must seek to stabilize both the quantity and quality of regularly available heroin. Doing so seems to require extending and developing contacts in the drug subculture. In the words of one of our respondents:

> [Y]ou got to start associating with different people. You got to be in touch
> with different people for the simple reason that not just one person has it all

the time. You got to go from one person to the other, find out who's got the best bag and who hasn't. . . . You want to go where the best bag is for your money, and especially for the money *you're* spending. You got to mingle with so many different people.

Making, developing, and maintaining the contacts that are helpful if not absolutely necessary to stable heroin use seem to invite natural opportunities for the most common modification in the stabilized junkie's life structure: dealing. From the point of view of the would-be stabilized junkie, dealing has two major advantages over most other forms of routine daily activity. First, it can be carried on in the course of the stabilized junkie's search for his or her own supply of drugs and, second, it can be a source of money for the purchase of drugs or a source of drugs itself. Dealing can be rather easily accommodated to the needs of both availability and life structure.

All of our respondents reported that at some time in their drug-using careers they had played the role of dealer, if only occasionally. Becoming an occasional dealer is almost an inevitable consequence of becoming a competent, regular user. A stabilized junkie will not only be approached to "cop" for occasional users and addicts whose suppliers are temporarily out of stock, but the stabilized junkie will come to recognize occasions on which especially "good dope" can be purchased and resold at a profit to drug-using friends.

Because the work of dealing drugs on a small scale does not require much more time or effort than that which goes into buying drugs regularly for one's own use, dealing also has another advantage which makes it an attractive activity for the stabilized junkie. Namely, it can be carried on as a source of drugs or income without undue interference with whatever other "hustle," if any, constitutes the stabilized junkie's additional source of support. This is particularly true if, in the course of carrying on the hustle—be it theft, shoplifting, pimping, prostitution, bookmaking, or dealing in stolen property—the stabilized addict is likely to come into regular contact with other drug users.

The extent to which dealing can be carried on along with other hustles depends, of course, both on the nature of that hustle and on the extent of the dealing. The stabilized junkie will tend to divide his or her hustling efforts between dealing and other hustles with an eye toward which one delivers the highest profit. However, dividing those efforts will also involve other considerations such as the stabilized junkie's personal preference for one type of work, life style and community reputation considerations, opportunities to practice one type of hustle or another, and the physical demands each type of hustle tends to require. Among female heroin users, a rather common accommodation to the profits and opportunities of dealing and those of other hustles is a live-together arrangement with a male user. In this division of labor each tries to conduct their outside hustle during hours when the other can be at home to handle dealing transactions. An important feature of this arrangement is that, if necessary, it can be structured so as to permit the stabilized female junkie to be at home for housekeeping and child-rearing duties as well as dealing.

The Free-Wheeling Junkie–High Availability/Low Life Structure

Although most heroin users spend some portion of their drug-using careers as stabilized junkies and many manage to live for years with high heroin availability and highly structured daily routines, at least two properties of the stabilized junkie's situation tend to work against the maintenance of stability. One is the pharmacological property of heroin. It is a drug to which users tend to develop a tolerance rather rapidly, although as Zinberg (1984) has demonstrated, such tolerance is neither necessary nor universal. Moreover, as we have pointed out earlier, numerous factors in the social setting of heroin use mitigate the destabilizing effect of the drug. Work routines, household duties, and even subcultural roles all serve to structure drug consumption. However, in the absence of external structures of constraint, or when such routines are temporarily disrupted, the pharmalogical properties of heroin tend to destabilize the lifestyle of the addict further. In sum, contrary to popular belief, heroin use does not inevitably lead to a deterioration of lifestyle. Rather, the physiological dynamics of narcotics use tend to be most destabilizing under conditions where life structure is already weak and incapable of accommodating the physiological demands imposed by increased tolerance.

The other property of the stabilized junkie's life which tends to undermine stability is the hustle the junkie uses to finance his or her habit. According to our respondents, it is not hard times or difficulties in raising money through hustles which tend to destabilize the stabilized junkie's life. "You can adjust yourself to a certain amount of drugs a day," explained Belle, "that you don't have to have but just that much." In addition to reducing their drug consumption, stabilized junkies accommodate themselves to such lean periods by substituting other drugs for heroin, working longer and harder at their hustling, or changing the type of hustle they work.

On the contrary, it is the unusual success, the "big sting" or "big hit," that tends to destabilize the stabilized junkie's high degree of life structure. The "big sting" or "big hit" can come in many forms. One of our respondents—an armed robber who usually limited his robbing to street mugging, gas stations, and convenience stores—"hit" a bank, which to our respondent's surprise, produced a "take" of over $60,000. He increased his heroin consumption dramatically and, while doing so, abandoned virtually all the stabilizing routines which marked his life prior to his windfall take. In another instance, a relatively stable junkie dealer was "fronted" several thousand dollars of heroin on consignment. Instead of selling it as he had agreed to do, he absconded with it to another state, shot up most of it himself, and gave the rest away. In still another case, a relatively low-level burglar/thief came across $10,000 in cash in the course of one of his burglaries. He took the money to New York where he intended to cop a "big piece" that he could bring back to the city in which he lived and sell for a nice profit. However, instead of selling it, he kept it for his own use and his habit rapidly increased from a stable three bags per day to nearly a "bundle"—25 bags per day.

Although the "big hit" or "big sting" appears to be the most common precipitator of the transition from the status of stabilized or occasional heroin user to the status of free-wheeling junkie, many other variants of similar destabilizing patterns are common. The stabilized junkie may not be the one who makes the big sting. It may be his or her spouse, roommate, paramour, addict friend, or regular trick who receives a windfall of drugs or money and invites the stabilized junkie to share in the benefits of good fortune. "Goody," a part-time street prostitute, moved in with a big-time drug dealer who provided her with all the heroin she wanted in exchange for domestic services, sexual favors, and some modest help in cutting and packaging drugs. Although her supply of drugs was virtually limitless, she took her childraising obligations and responsibilities very seriously and they kept her to a modest level of use. However, after a year of domestic living she began to miss the "street" life and the friends she had there and to resent her total ("bag bitch") dependence on her dealer boyfriend. She returned to the street and used the money she earned from "'hoing," and "ripping" her tricks to purchase drugs in addition to what she got at home for free. This behavior not only destabilized her drug use, but it also disrupted her home life to such an extent that she parted with her dealer and returned to the street full-time. Interestingly, this return to prostitution, theft, and robbery as her sole means of support forced her to develop a new life structure and abandon the free-wheeling pattern into which she had drifted when she had a dual source of supply.

Unless heroin addicts are disciplined by a life structure to which they are so committed and obligated that it effectively prevents them from doing so, they will expand their consumption of heroin to whatever level of use the availability of drugs or funds to buy them makes possible. What marks the career stage of the free-wheeling junkie is the almost total absence of structures of restraint. In the words of "Little Italy," who described a "free-wheeling" stage of his addict career:

> I can remember, I wouldn't be sick, I wouldn't need a shot. . . . And some of the guys might come around and get a few bags [and say] "Hey man, like I don't have enough money. Why don't you come down with me?" . . . I'm saying [to myself], "Oh-oh, here I go!" and I would shoot drugs I didn't even need to shoot. So I let it get out of control.

The problem for the first free-wheeling junkie is that the binge cannot last forever and is typically fairly short-lived. After a month or two of free-wheeling heroin use—during which time the free-wheeling junkie may have no idea of how much heroin he or she is consuming daily—not only is a modest usage level unsatisfying but the life structure within which he or she might support it is likely to have been completely abandoned or at least be in severe disrepair.

The Street Junkie–Low Availability/Low Life Structure

At the point in a free-wheeling junkie's career when heroin availability drops precipitously and life structure does not provide the support necessary to stabilize heroin use, the free-wheeling junkie may manage to rebuild that life structure and accommodate to a new and lower level of availability. To the extent that this rebuilding and accommodation can be managed, the free-wheeling junkie may be able to return to the life of a stabilized junkie. However, if the rebuilding of life structure cannot be managed, the free-wheeling junkie may become a street junkie.

Street junkies most closely approximate the public stereotype of heroin addicts, if only because their way of life—both where and how they live—make them the most visible variety of heroin addict. Cut off from a stable source of quality heroin, not knowing from where his or her next "fix" or the money to pay for it will come, looking for any opportunity to make a buck, getting "sick" or "jonesing," being pathetically unkempt and unable to maintain even the most primitive routines of health or hygiene, the street junkie lives a very difficult, hand-to-mouth (or more precisely arm-to-arm) existence.

In terms of our typology, the street junkie's life may be understood as a continuous but typically unsuccessful effort to stabilize life structure and increase heroin availability. The two problems are intimately related in such a way that, unless the street junkie can solve both problems at once, neither problem will be solved at all. That is, unless the street junkie can establish a stable life structure, he or she will be unlikely to increase the availability of heroin. Likewise, unless the street junkie is able to increase the availability of heroin, he or she will be unlikely to establish a stable life structure.

To illustrate how this relationship works in less abstract terms, it is helpful to begin with a description of what low life structure means in the life of the street. Goldstein (1981:69) captures the tenor of the street junkie's situation nicely when he observes that

> [if] any single word can describe the essence of how street opiate users "get over," that word is *opportunism*. Subjects were always alert to the smallest opportunity to earn a few dollars. The notion of opportunism is equally relevant to predatory criminality, nonpredatory criminality, employment, and miscellaneous hustling activities.

The cause of the street junkie's opportunism is his or her failure to establish a stable life structure which regularly produces enough income to support an addiction. Consequently, the street junkie's life is a series of short-term crimes, jobs, and hustles. Street junkies steal or rob when opportunities arise to do so. For a price or in exchange for heroin, they will "cop" for an out-of-towner, "taste" for a dealer, "tip" for a burglar, rent their "works" to another junkie, sell their "clinic meth" and food stamps, or share their "crib" (accommodations) with a junkie who needs a place to "get off" or a "hoe" who needs a room to take her "tricks." They will do odd jobs, wash cars, paint apartments, deliver circulars, move furniture, carry baggage, or snitch to the police. The problem is not only that this opportunistic crime, hustling, or legitimate work pays very little, but that none of it is stable. While one or more of these activities may produce enough income today, none of them may be counted on to do so tomorrow. Moreover, because typical street addict crimes pay so little, because such crimes must be repeated frequently to produce any sizable income, and because they are so unpredictably opportunistic, the chance that the street addict will be arrested sooner or later is very, very high. This was the unfortunate experience of Little Italy who, after falling out with his supplier, was forced to discontinue drug sales as a major means of income and turned to armed robbery to support his use.

> I know today, I can say that if you don't have a plan you're gonna fuck up man. . . . Now those robberies weren't no plan. They didn't fit in nowhere . . . just by the spur of the moment, you know what I mean? I had to find something to take that place so that income would stand off properly, 'cause I didn't have a plan or didn't know anything about robbery.

As Little Italy's experience demonstrates, street junkies lives are further complicated by the fact that "big dealers"—vendors of quantities of good quality heroin—often refuse to sell to them. The reasons they refuse are directly related to the instability of street junkies' lives. Because street junkies can never be certain when and for how much they will "get over," they are frequently unable to afford to buy enough drugs to satisfy their "jones." In the face of such a shortage they will commonly beg drugs from anyone they know who might have them or have access to them, try to "cop short" (buy at less than the going rate), attempt to strike a deal to get drugs loaned or "fronted" (given on consignment) to them on a short-term basis, or, if necessary, engage in opportunistic hustling. Also, because street junkies are the type of addict most vulnerable to arrest they are also the most likely category of addict to be "flipped" by police into the role of an informant. Usually street junkies will be promised immunity from prosecution on the charge for which they were arrested if they "give up" somebody "big." Given the frequency with which street addicts "come up short," the relatively small amount of profit to be made in each individual transaction with them, and the higher than normal risk of police involvement, few "'big dealers" are willing to put up with all of the attendant hassles and hustles that dealing with street junkies typically involves.

While there are exceptions—the most common being big dealers who are relatives of street junkies or their friends of long standing—street addicts are mainly limited to "street dope," heroin that has been repeatedly "stepped on" (diluted) as it is passed from the highest level of dealer to the lowest. In fact, some studies (Leveson and Weiss, 1976:119) have shown that as much as 7 percent of street dope may have no heroin in it at all, while other studies (Smith, 1973) show a heroin concentration of from 3 to 10 percent in street dope as compared with an average concentration of nearly 30 percent in bags seized from "big dealers." The irony in this situation is that, as a consumer of "street dope," the street addict pays a higher per/unit price for heroin than any other person in the distribution chain. Furthermore, this very low and often unpredictable quality of heroin available to the street junkie serves to destabilize his or her life structure further.

Research and Policy Implications

The life-history data presented here have some important research and policy implications which merit brief consideration. Particularly relevant are the implications for: (1) the nature of the drugs-crime connection itself; (2) drug law enforcement; and (3) treatment policy.

THE DRUGS-CRIME CONNECTION

As we have pointed out above, early studies examining the relationship between drug use and crime have utilized the strategy of establishing the temporal priority of the onset of drug use versus criminality. While the earliest of these studies tended to find that drug use preceded the onset of criminal behavior, virtually all of the studies conducted since 1950 have found a reverse pattern, thus posing once again the perplexing question of the theoretical nature of the relationship between drug use and criminal behavior. Because the methodologies employed in these "sequence" studies are incapable of examining the dynamic nature of this relationship over time, they have succeeded in raising theoretical questions which continue to beg for explanation. More recent studies—particularly those of Ball et al. (1981, 1983) and Johnson et al. (1985)—have moved beyond the sequence issued by examining drug-using and criminal behavior on a daily or weekly basis over a period of time. These longitudinal methodologies represent a major breakthrough toward establishing the dynamic nature of the drugs-crime relationship.

This study further contributes to the emerging "post-sequence" literature by examining the drugs-crime nexus in the broader context of addict careers. Perhaps the most significant finding to emerge from our data is that the relationship between heroin use and crime is not necessarily consistent throughout the career of the addict. During the "occasional user" phase, for example, the issue is a moot one for many addicts; their limited level of drug use is quite affordable with a legitimate income, and any criminal activity that does take place is often quite spurious to drug use. During the "stabilized junkie" and "free-wheeling junkie" periods, the level of drug use seems to be largely a function of availability, typically enhanced through criminal income. Rather than *drug use causing crime,* however, it seems more accurate to suggest that *crime facilitates drug use* during these periods. Quite the reverse is the case during the "street junkie" phase, where availability through normal channels is lacking but the addict lacks the necessary structure to regulate his or her drug needs. Under these conditions the drug habit does indeed appear to "cause" crime in the manner commonly depicted.

Moreover, the life history data reveal that the relationship between drugs and crime is more dynamic than phrasing the issue in terms of "cause" typically suggests. In addition to providing necessary income for the purchase of heroin, criminal activity also serves to *structure* the drug using behavior of the addict. Crime thus provides the addict with a daily routine which for many addicts actually serves to limit or at least regulate their drug use.

In short, the respondents in this study have revealed that the relationship between drug use and criminal behavior is far more complex and dynamic than previous research has suggested. While in any given instance, it may be possible to specify a causal sequence, our data suggest that any generalizations suggesting a simple cause-effect scheme fail to capture the complexity of the drugs-crime connection throughout an addict's career.

DRUG LAW ENFORCEMENT

Since the passage of the Harrison Act in 1914, drug law enforcement in the United States has been dominated by the "criminal model" of drug use (Inciardi, 1974). While variously, articulated, this model understands drug use as primarily a *criminal* issue which should be addressed by imposing criminal sanctions on both users and dealers, and by taking steps to prevent the import and distribution of heroin. Insofar as there is a relationship between drug use and other criminal behavior, the narcotics user is understood to be a criminal, first and foremost, whose drug using behavior is an important and contributing component in an extensive pattern of related criminal behavior.

Not surprisingly, the criminalization of heroin has profoundly affected the dynamics of the drugs-crime nexus. Virtually all of the post-1950 studies have found that criminal histories preceded expensive drug-using histories of the respondents in their samples as suggested by the subculturally based "Crimes cause drugs" model. Our life-history data support and qualify the implications for the criminal model suggested by these studies. While our respondents do report criminal involvement prior to their first exposure to heroin, the drug-using histories began quite independently of their criminal involvement. Throughout their early "occasional use" phase, most of these individuals were supporting their drug use without relying on a stable income from systematic criminal activity. As their careers progressed, however, they cultivated criminal skills and associations which played an important role in facilitating a greatly expanded level of heroin use.

However, our research suggests that even if such enforcement efforts rightly characterize the drugs-crime connection, enforcement approaches may not have their intended effects of controlling or suppressing drug use or the crimes related to it. We find no reason to conclude that enforcement efforts may have an effect on very early periods in addict careers. During the period of occasional use, addicts can easily adjust to dramatic variations in the level of supply of heroin and our respondents report little need to support such occasional use through systematic criminal activity. Even in those periods of the hard-core addict's life history which we have described as characterized by a "stabilized junkie" model, our respondents report being able to adjust to periods in which heroin supplies are sharply reduced, only to return to previous levels of use when their channels of supply are restored. Moreover, our respondents report that during stabilized junkie periods in their life histories they cultivated a variety of sources of supply. Given this variety, not only could they choose vendors who appeared to offer the best quality product, but they could adjust relatively easily to the temporary or permanent loss of a supplier. Unless enforcement efforts managed a simultaneous elimination of virtually all of these sources of supply, we would not anticipate that they would have much effect on the stabilized junkie's pattern of stable use, nor on the criminal activity which the stabilized junkie typically pursues to support it. Likewise, enforcement efforts may not be expected to have much impact on hard-core addicts during "free-wheeling" phases in their life histories. Particularly insofar as these periods are precipitated by "big scores" or "big hits" and marked by short-term, unlimited availability of drugs or the money to purchase them, enforcement is already too late.

The street junkie, by contrast, faced with the lack of ready availability of adequate supplies of heroin and without the necessary life structure to constrain his or her felt need for drugs, is most vulnerable to law enforcement activity. Indeed, our data would suggest that the effectiveness of current law enforcement efforts is largely limited to this career phase. The addict in this situation is often confronted with the alternative of arrest or informing on other addicts. Either alternative almost inevitably imposes a criminal transition in the career of the addict. Arrest typically culminates either in treatment or incarceration, both of which impose a disengagement from street routine.

Even if the addict subsequently returns to the street, the conditions of availability and life structure will be profoundly altered. While informing on other addicts may buy more time on the street, this alternative will only further alienate the street junkie from the subculture. While such a strategy of "flipping" informants may be helpful in locating "big dealers," its overall impact in limiting the availability of drugs to nonstreet junkies appears negligible unless, as we have suggested, all major dealers are "hit" simultaneously. Unless our drug policies give balanced weight to educational and treatment efforts, law enforcement effectiveness appears relegated to the already vulnerable "street junkie."

TREATMENT POLICY

Narcotics treatment in the United States has also been characterized by an overriding concern with the anti-social behavior associated with heroin use. Methadone maintenance is currently the dominant model of treatment, and has generated a voluminous literature addressing its effectiveness as a deterrent to crime (see, for example, Dole et al., 1968, 1969; Gearing, 1974; Judson et al., 1980; Lukoff and Quatrone, 1973; Nash, 1973; Newman and Gates, 1973). These and other studies have reported widely varying effects of methadone treatment upon criminality ranging from a 99.9 percent reduction (Gearing, 1974) to an actual *increase* in crime following admission to treatment (Lukoff and Quatrone, 1973). Unfortunately, our understanding of the effect of methadone maintenance on criminality is severely limited because of the many methodological difficulties associated with these studies (Faupel, 1981).

However, our data suggest that to the extent that a long-term reduction in criminality is a central goal of drug treatment, treatment policy must attend to more than simply the physiological demand for heroin. Drug-free residential programs, in particular, attempt to reduce availability by imposing abstinence for a substantial period of time. Beyond simply curtailing access to heroin, however, successful treatment will require provision for an alternative life structure which facilitates and rewards conventional behavior, thus reducing demand as well. We would argue that such an agenda not only requires renunciation of past routines but also the facilitation of long-term alternative behavior patterns through a concerted effort at community reintegration (see Dembo et al., 1982; Faupel, 1985; Goldbart, 1982; Hawkins, 1979). Involvement in conventional employment, voluntary associations, and even organized leisure-time activities should tightly structure the addicts' daily routine. Just as importantly, since access to drugs is largely a function of social networks, renunciation of "street" relationships and subsequent integration into supportive conventional social networks should serve to reduce availability and demand simultaneously.

Note

This research was supported in part by DHEW Grant No. 1 ROl DA 01827 from the Division of Research, National Institute of Drug Abuse. Correspondence to Faupel: Department of Sociology, Anthropology, and Social Work, Auburn University, Auburn University, AL 36849-3501.

References

Anglin, M. Douglas and George Speckart. 1984. Narcotics Use and Crime: A Confirmatory Analysis. Unpublished Report, University of California Los Angeles.

Ball, John C. and Carl D. Chambers. 1970. The *Epidemiology of Heroin Use in the United States.* Springfield, IL: Charles C. Thomas.

Ball, John C., Lawrence Rosen, John A. Flueck and David Nurco. 1981. "The criminality of heroin addicts when addicted and when off opiates." Pp. 39–65 in James A. Inciardi (ed.), *The Drugs-Crime Connection.* Beverly Hills, CA: Sage Publications.

Ball, John C., John W. Shaffer and David Nurco. 1983. "The day to day criminality of heroin addicts in Baltimore: a study of the continuity of offense rates." *Drug and Alcohol Dependence* 12:119–42.

Ball, John C. and Richard W. Snarr. 1969. "A test of the maturation hypothesis with respect to opiate addiction." *Bulletin of Narcotics* 21:9–13.

Beschner, George M. and William Brower. 1985. "The scene." Pp. 19–29 in Bill Hanson, George Beschner, James M. Walters and Elliot Bovelle (eds.), Life *with Heroin: Voices from the Inner City.* Lexington, MA: Lexington Books.

Biernacki, Patrick. 1986. *Pathways from Heroin Addiction: Recovery without Treatment.* Philadelphia: Temple University Press.

Chambers, Carl D. 1974. "Narcotic addiction and crime: an empirical overview." Pp. 125–42 in James A. Inciardi and Carl D. Chambers (eds.), *Drugs and the Criminal Justice System.* Beverly Hills, CA: Sage Publications.

Chein, Isidor, Donald L. Gerard, Robert S. Lee and Eva Rosenfeld. 1964. *The Road to H: Narcotics, Juvenile Delinquency, and Social Policy.* New York: Basic Books.

Collins, James J., Robert L. Hubbard and J. Valley Rachal. 1984. *Heroin and Cocaine Use and Illegal Income.* Center for Social Research and Policy Analysis. Research Triangle Park, NC: Research Triangle Institute.

———. 1985. "Expensive drug use and illegal income: a test of explanatory hypotheses." *Criminology* 23:743–64.

Dembo, Richard, James A. Ciarlo and Robert W. Taylor. 1983. "A model for assessing and improving drug abuse treatment resource use in inner city areas." *International Journal of Addictions* 18:921–36.

Dole, Vincent P., Marie E. Nyswander and Alan Warner. 1968. "Successful treatment of 750 criminal addicts." *Journal of the American Medical Association* 206:2708–11.

Dole, Vincent P., J. Waymond Robinson, John Orraca, Edward Towns, Paul Searcy and Eric Caine. 1969. "Methadone treatment of randomly selected criminal addicts." *New England Journal of Medicine* 280:1372–75.

Faupel, Charles E. 1981. "Drug treatment and criminality: methodological and theoretical considerations." Pp. 183–206 in James A. Inciardi (ed.), *The Drugs-Crime Connection.* Beverly Hills, CA: Sage Publications.

———. 1985. "A theoretical model for a socially oriented drug treatment policy." *Journal of Drug Education* 15:189–203.

Fields, Allen and James M. Walters. 1985. "Hustling: supporting a heroin habit." Pp. 49–73 in Bill Hanson, George Beschner, James M. Walters and Elliot Bovelle (eds.), *Life with Heroin: Voices from the Inner City.* Lexington, MA: Lexington Books.

Gandossy, Robert P., Jay R. Williams, Jo Cohen and Hendrick J. Harwood. 1980. *Drugs and Crime: A Survey and Analysis of the Literature.* National Institute of Justice. Washington, DC: U.S. Government Printing Office.

Gearing, Frances R. 1974. "Methadone maintenance treatment five years later—where are they now?" *American Journal of Public Health* 64:44–50.

Goldbart, Stephen. 1982. "Systematic barriers to addict aftercare program implementation." *Journal of Drug Issues* 12:415–30.

Goldman, Fred. 1976. "Drug markets and addict consumption behavior." Pp. 273–96 in *Drug Use and Crime: Report of the Panel on Drug Use and Criminal Behavior.* National Technical Information Service publication number PB-259 167. Springfield, VA: U.S. Dept. of Commerce.

———. 1981. "Drug abuse, crime and economics: the dismal limits of social choice." Pp. 155–81 in James A. Inciardi (ed.), *The Drugs-Crime Connection.* Beverly Hills, CA: Sage Publications.

Goldstein, Paul. 1981. "Getting over: economic alternatives to predatory crime among street drug users." Pp. 67–84 in James A. Inciardi (ed.), *The Drugs-Crime Connection.* Beverly Hills, CA: Sage Publications.

Hanson, Bill, George Beschner, James M. Walters and Elliot Bovelle. 1985. *Life with Heroin: Voices from the Inner City.* Lexington, MA: Lexington Books.

Hawkins, J. David. 1979. "Reintegrating street drug abusers: community roles in continuing care." Pp. 25–79 in Barry S. Brown (ed.), *Addicts and Aftercare.* Beverly Hills, CA: Sage Publications.

Inciardi, James A. 1974. "The vilification of euphoria: some perspectives on an elusive issue." *Addictive Diseases* 1:241–67.

———. 1979. "Heroin use and street crime." *Crime and Delinquency* 25:335–46.

Jacoby, Joseph E., Neil A. Weiner, Terence P. Thornberry and Marvin E. Wolfgang. 1973. "Drug use in a birth cohort." Pp. 300–43 in *National Commission on Marijuana and Drug Abuse, Drug Use in America: Problem in Perspective,* Appendix I. Washington, DC: U.S. Government Printing Office.

Johnson, Bruce D., Paul J. Goldstein, Edward Preble, James Schmeidler, Douglas S. Lipton, Barry Spunt and Thomas Miller. 1985. *Taking Care of Business: The Economics of Crime by Heroin Abusers.* Lexington, MA: Lexington Books.

Judson, Barbara, Serapio Ortiz, Linda Crouse, Thomas Carney and Avram Goldstein. 1980. "A follow-up study of heroin addicts five years after admission to a methadone treatment program." *Drug and Alcohol Dependence* 6:295–313.

Leveson, Irving and Jeffrey H. Weiss. 1976. *Analysis of Urban Health Problems.* New York: Spectrum.

Lukoff, Irving and Debra Quatrone. 1973. "Heroin use and crime in a methadone maintenance program: a two year follow-up of the Addiction and Research Corporation Program: a preliminary report." Pp. 63–112 in Gil J. Hayim, Irving Lukoff and Debra Quatrone (eds.), *Heroin Use in a Methadone Maintenance Program.* Washington, DC: U.S. Department of Justice, National Institute of Law Enforcement and Criminal Justice.

McGlothlin, William H., M. Douglas Anglin and Bruce D. Wilson. 1978. "Narcotic addiction and crime." *Criminology* 16:293–315.

Morris, Richard W. 1985. "Not the cause, nor the cure: self-image and control among inner city black male heroin users." Pp. 135–53 in Bill Hanson, George Beschner, James M. Walters and Elliot Bovelle (eds.), *Life with Heroin: Voices from the Inner City.* Lexington, MA: Lexington Books.

Musto, David. 1973. *The American Disease: Origins of Narcotic Control.* New Haven, CT: Yale University Press.

Nash, George. 1973. *The impact of drug abuse treatment upon criminality: a look at 19 programs.* Upper Montclair, NJ: Montclair State College.

Newman, Robert G., Sylvia Bashkow and Margot Gates. 1973. "Arrest histories before and after admission to a methadone maintenance treatment program." *Contemporary Drug Problems* 2:417–24.

O'Donnell, John A. 1966. "Narcotic addiction and crime." *Social Problems* 13:374–85.

Pescor, Michael J. 1943. "A statistical analysis of the clinical records of hospitalized drug addicts." *Public Health Reports Supplement,* 143.

Robins, Lee N. and George E. Murphy. 1967. "Drug use in a normal population of young Negro men." *American Journal of Public Health* 570:1580–96.

Smith, Jean Paul. 1973. "Substances in illicit drugs." Pp. 13–30 in Richard H. Blum and Associates (eds.), *Drug Dealers-Taking Action.* San Francisco: Jossey Bass.

Tappan, Paul. 1960. *Crime, Justice and Correction.* New York: McGraw-Hill.

Terry, Charles E. and Mildred Pellens. 1928. *The Opium Problem.* New York: The Haddon Craftsman.

Waldorf, Dan. 1983. "Natural recovery from opiate addiction: some social-psychological processes of untreated recovery." *Journal of Drug Issues* 13:237–80.

Walters, James M. 1985. "'Taking care of business' updated: a fresh look at the daily routine of the heroin user." Pp. 31–48 in Bill Hanson, George Beschner, James M. Walters and Elliot Bovelle (eds.), *Life with Heroin: Voices from the Inner City.* Lexington, MA: Lexington Books.

Weissman, James C., Paul L. Katsampes and Thomas A. Giacienti. 1974. "Opiate use and criminality among a jail population." *Addictive Diseases* 1:269–81.

Zinberg, Norman E. 1984. *Drug Set and Setting: The Basis for Controlled Intoxicant Use.* New Haven, CT: Yale University Press.

CHAPTER 14

Social Misery and the Sanctions of Substance Abuse

CONFRONTING HIV RISK AMONG HOMELESS HEROIN ADDICTS IN SAN FRANCISCO

Philippe Bourgois, Mark Lettiere, and James Quesada

By the second decade of the AIDS epidemic, public health research has compiled a large epidemiological data base on the propagation of the HIV virus in the United States (Centers for Disease Control 1996; National Research Council 1993). HIV-prevention researchers, however, still confront major questions on how and why the epidemic spreads in different geographic and social patterns (Coates et al. 1990; Laumann et al. 1994). The precise behavioral dynamics facilitating HIV transmission among vulnerable people are inadequately understood and subject to bitter polemics. The often technical debates express deep ideological schisms regarding biology and public policy, identity politics, and cold war discourses on citizenship and individual rights (Bolton 1992, Broadhead and Margolis 1993; Caldararo 1996; Duesberg 1995; Epstein 1996; Fernando 1991; Fumento 1990; Scheper-Hughes 1993). The very methods and paradigms that the public health community relies upon to conceptualize HIV risk and treat substance abusers prevent us from understanding how AIDS is propagated. Bio-medically oriented researchers have an underdeveloped theoretical framework for addressing the prolonged everyday suffering and ecstasy of street addicts. More specifically, the power relations that constitute unsafe practices do not enter into epidemiological correlations. Following the tenets of methodological individualism and psychological behaviorism, most researchers treat unsafe practices as instances of individualized decision-making writ large, when in fact such behaviors are contradictory outcomes of politics, economics, ideology, and culture. Our critique of public health research operates on two related levels: 1) the methodological, in which we argue for participant-observation and offer concrete ethnographic descriptive analyses of risky practices; and 2) the theoretical, in which we conceptualize these everyday risky practices as intricately woven into the fabric of macro-power relations. Power refers here to the distribution of resources, the exercise of agency, and the institutionalization of social control in the production of social inequality. With respect to substance abuse, this points to the politics of social sanctioning and stigma around the uses and misuses of pleasure (Foucault 1980; Goffmann 1963). Ethnography is well situated to build on the insights provided by sociologists who problematize the relationship between insider and outsider knowledge claims and the ownership of social problems (Best 1990; Gusfield 1981; Reinarman and Levine 1989; Spector and Kitsuse 1977).

Our theoretical concerns with the centrality of power relations in propagating HIV have pushed us to link our ethnographic data on micro-level network-based hierarchies to macrostructural dynamics of constraint and resistance. In collapsing these macro-to-micro, structure-to-agency, and theory-to-method distinctions, we have found Foucault's work especially insightful—specifically his conceptualizations of 1) bio-power (1978:140–144; 1980:139–140); and 2) power/knowledge (1980). Bio-power refers to the ways historically entrenched institutionalized forms of social control discipline bodies. In the context of HIV and substance abuse a wide range of laws, medical interventions, ideologies, and even structures of feeling express bio-power (Caputo and Yount 1993; Dean 1994; Fitzpatrick 1992; Foucault 1982:208–226; Ong 1996; Williams 1977). With respect to heroin addicts, this ranges from: the prescription of methadone addiction; to such popular rhetoric and political campaigns as "just say no," and "three strikes and you're out"; the social scientific claim that "addiction is a disease"; and even more subtly, the ways taboo pleasures are pursued. Power/ knowledge refers to the emergence of academic, medical, and juridical disciplines as central components of social control through the construction of epistemological frameworks defined as legitimate science and health. The power/knowledge insight is particularly useful for our methodological/theoretical critique of public health's reaction to the HIV epidemic. It addresses how moralizing judgments define "normal" permissible behaviors and "worthy" categories of individuals, in both scientific and popular discourses.

The Power of Ethnography

One does not have to cite Foucault or privilege post-structural debates about history, the state, and discursive practices to be dissatisfied with the inadequacies of applied HIV prevention research and outreach. Even though public health researchers treat individual behavior as the crucial unit of risk analysis, they cannot explain or even document with any certainty the relative risks of specific behavioral practices. The quantitative research designs of most HIV-prevention studies do not measure accurately the intimate practices of vulnerable people. From a straightforward positivist perspective, it is naive to expect to generate valid data bases by administering questionnaires that pay addicted respondents to self-report socially stigmatizing behaviors. Indeed public health researchers have vigorously debated the limitations of self-report accuracy (Hahn et al. 1992, Haverkos and Jones 1994, Jones et al. 1994; Huang et al. 1988; McNagny and Parker 1992; Scheper-Hughes 1993; Watters et al. 1992). This is part of a larger critique of epidemiological methods and their theoretical limitations (Davey et al. 1990; Krieger and Zierler 1996; Susser 1994; Trostle and Sommerfeld 1996).

Quantitative analysis predominates in substance abuse research; there has been virtually no substantial dialogue between quantitative and qualitative researchers. The intimate practices of vulnerable populations rarely have been rigorously documented in their indigenous, natural contexts through direct observation. Although dozens of epidemiological and survey-based qualitative studies incorporate ethnographic components, none of these major research initiatives systematically collect participant-observation data (Carlson et al. 1994; Dunlap et al. 1990; Koester 1996; Wiebel 1988). Anthropology's version of ethnography, predicated upon participant-observation involving long-term, organic immersion does not appear in public health publications. Even such compromised versions of ethnography as qualitative interviewing are invariably subordinated to the primary goal of collecting statistical data in a probabilistic sampling framework (see critique by Trotter et al. 1995). Indeed ethnography is sometimes referred to as a hand-maiden for statistics (Agar 1996; Koester 1992; Singer 1996).

The marginal role that participant-observation research has played in the AIDS epidemic sharply contrasts the initially influential ethnographies of drug subcultures in the 1950s through the 1970s (Agar 1973; Becker 1953; Feldman et al. 1979; Finestone 1957; Preble and Casey, Jr. 1969; Weppner 1977). None of the old literature, of course, addresses HIV. What little recent literature exists confines itself to the descritive empiricism of structural functionalism, symbolic interactionism, and ethnomethodology (Williams 1992; Adler and Adler 1983).

Within the positivist paradigm of constructing testable hypotheses, epidemiological researchers fail to consult ethnographers to help them explain the plethora of counter-intuitive data that they sometimes publish; instead, they frequently report anomalistic statistics as puzzles, uncertainties, or "noise." Ethnographers might be able to reinterpret the information in a contextualized processual framework, to explain it as the result of predictable distortions in self-report bias, the outcome of systematic sampling discrimination, or evidence of proxy variables revealing other important social dynamics (see Bolton 1992, Elison et al. 1995). For example: 1) rinsing syringes with bleach has been described as ineffective because injectors report they have safe sex and always rinse their needles with bleach, yet they still seroconvert (Vlahov et al. 1994:765); 2) bleach use and needle sharing do not correlate with HIV status (Moss et al. 1994:226); 3) needle exchange patrons have higher seropositivity than non-exchangers (Bruneau et al. in press; Hankins in press); 4) intravenous drug-using African Americans share needles less than whites yet have significantly higher infection rates (Guydish et al. 1990; Watters et al. 1994a:118–119), including up to four-times higher seroconversion rates (Moss et al. 1994); 5) sexual- and injection-related variables are irrelevant to the HIV status of female injectors (Watters et al. 1994a); 6) studies disagree about whether crack use does (Zolopa et al. 1994) or does not (Watters et al. 1994b) correlate with HIV infection among African Americans in San Francisco; and (7) several San Francisco studies find suspiciously high rates of condom and bleach use among injectors (Watters 1994; Dorfman et al. 1992).[1]

Despite the methodological and theoretical limitations of most public health research, we do not suggest that applied research concerns be jettisoned. The positivistic questions around the who, how, and why of HIV infection are worthwhile—even urgent—for street addicts. HIV infection rates differ dramatically across the social categories that organize power in most societies and across the globe: ethnicity, class, gender, sexual orientation, age, and geographic location. Instead of limiting ourselves to a biomedical explanation of asynchronous viral introduction into demographically localized populations marked by differential individual behavior patterns, a theoretical understanding of the political economy and symbolic violence of these social markers might allow us to explain, for example, why African Americans have disproportionately high HIV infection rates, or why Latino—especially Puerto Rican—seroprevalence is spiraling upwards (Centers for Disease Control 1996). Regretfully, epidemiological researchers primarily document trends, rather than explain processes, and they do not engage central debates in social science theory. This is reflected in the types of questions they ask and the modest, descriptive explanations they usually tender.

Substance abuse literature that examines power dynamics critically is relegated to journals or edited volumes outside the purview of public health and rarely receives federal research funds. For example, a critical perspective has emerged among medical anthropologists, who address the interface between structural constraints and individual action (Farmer 1992; Singer 1994; Singer and Baer 1995). Drawing from political economy (Carlson 1996; Koester 1994), but also sensitive to social constructionism and postmodernism, these critical perspectives examine social marginalization under the broadened rubrics of "embodied social suffering," "everyday violence," and the "politics of trauma" (DiGiacomo 1992; Kleinman 1996; Quesada in press; Scheper-Hughes and Lock 1987). Critical researchers interrogate the inappropriate categories of public health and the inadequacy of conceptualizing individual risk factors for contracting HIV (Herdt and Lindenbaum 1992).

Research Site

In November 1994, the principal author (Bourgois) immersed himself in the shooting galleries and homeless encampments of a network of heroin addicts living in the bushes of a public park in downtown San Francisco.[2] In 1996, this expanded into a federally funded ethnographic team project charged with documenting risky injection practices. After two years of almost daily visits and occasional overnight stays we have developed a warm, respectful rapport with over two dozen homeless heroin addicts who run and inhabit the shooting encampments, and who sell drugs to a larger cohort of some 75–100 addicts and "chippers" (occasional injectors). We have around-the-clock access to the shooting encampments, full permission to tape record, photograph, videotape, and otherwise observe and interview the core network of addicts. This allows us to document the complex dynamics of intensive heroin addiction: from overdoses, to middle-of-the-night heroin and alcohol withdrawal symptoms, to early morning sickness and craving fits. It exposes us to the subtle interpersonal power hierarchies, hidden income-generating strategies, and the repeated mutual betrayals and everyday violence that organize their precarious lives.

During the first year most members of the core network were white, middle-aged males, although there were several Latinos, one Asian Pacific Islander, and a peripheral cohort of African Americans. Subsequently, five African Americans established themselves full-time in the core network's main shooting encampment. All primary network members have physical and emotional dependencies on heroin and most also drink large quantities of fortified wine (Cisco Berry brand). Almost all binge on crack when they have surplus cash, but their drug of choice and physical necessity is heroin. They all identify themselves as "dope fiends" (Preble and Casey 1969) and occasionally insult one another for being "wannabe dope fiends" and "winos," or, in the case of the African Americans, "crackheads" and "crack monsters." In other words, they construct their self-respect around illegal heroin addiction—not legal alcohol or illegal crack—despite often having physical or psychological addictions to all those substances simultaneously. They invariably exaggerate their levels of physical dependency on heroin. In fact, they are both proud of and aghast at being heroin addicts. They generate most of their income through a combination of day labor, panhandling, recycling, and petty survival crime (primarily shoplifting and car and warehouse burglary). As we will demonstrate, economic constraints and conceptions of self-respect influence the risks an individual is likely to take on any particular day.

Logistical Contexts for Risky Injection Practices

Network members share ancillary paraphernalia almost every time they inject heroin. Usually this takes the form of sharing water from the same cup, and a cotton filter from the same "cooker" (the bottom of a crushed aluminum can, a metal bottle top, or a spoon) in which the heroin is stirred and dissolved in water while being heated over a match or candle flame. We have seen the lowest-prestige members of the core network re-use the still-warm, blood-contaminated syringes of their companions without rinsing them with water. They sometimes sell or give as a favor to one another loaded syringes that occasionally contain visible traces of blood. When we try to stop them or warn them of the risks involved, they usually ignore us or become angry at us for interrupting them. It is noteworthy that all network members have been contacted by community-based health outreach workers who admonish them not to share any injection paraphernalia whatsoever, including cookers. They also patronize San Francisco's needle exchange program on a semi-regular basis; it is their primary source of clean syringes.

Initially, we suspected that this network of homeless users was anomalous because of the extent of their paraphernalia sharing. After further contextualizing the logic for why they share so regularly, and after consulting comparative literature, however, we found that the urgent necessities of fragile income-generating strategies mandate these risky practices (cf. Connors 1994; Koester 1996; Page et al. 1990). It is important to differentiate our power perspective on the logics and meanings of sharing from the early symbolic interactionist interpretations of needle sharing as an exotic bonding ritual (Des Jarlais 1986).

Until 1996, when prices dropped in half on San Francisco streets, heroin was sold primarily in $20 units of "Mexican black tar." The product is approximately half the size of a standard pencil eraser and is referred to as a "quarter gram" even though it inevitably weighs considerably less. The awkward consistency of black tar heroin (something between wax and tar) makes it a difficult substance to partition with a knife or razor blade as it is brittle when cold and gooey when warm. The only accurate way to divide a "bag" of black tar is to dissolve the entire portion that is being shared in a communal cooker using a measured quantity of water. The cooker is briefly heated and its contents are stirred with the tip of the plunger of a (not-necessarily-clean) syringe to ensure that the heroin is fully dissolved. The solution is then drawn into separate syringes so that the portions can be carefully calibrated and compared. Each injector receives the precise number of liquified units proportional to the amount of money he or she contributed toward the purchase of the bag. If one person draws too much heroin solution, the extra contents of his/her not-necessarily-clean syringe are dumped back into the communal cooker for others to share. Thus, accuracy, fairness, and generosity all augment risk. Homeless street injectors, especially those dependent on some form of panhandling, recycling, or petty shoplifting to generate their income, usually are unable to accumulate $10 or $20 before they are overwhelmed by physical and emotional urges to inject heroin. Consequently, many of San Francisco's street injectors pool resources with one or more "running partners" to "share a bag" several times a day. Even when running partners do not pay for their share, they incur moral debts in a complex gift-giving economy (Bourdieu 1996) obliging them to contribute a "taste" of heroin in the near future. The only other way of saving a portion of a bag is to draw the dissolved contents into a syringe, recap it, and hide it in a sock for future use. In addition to placing addicts at risk of arrest should they be stopped and searched by the police, storing heroin in ready-to-inject form is difficult when one is overwhelmed by a desire for the drug.

On a daily basis, consequently, risky needle practices are an integral part of the microstrategies that street addicts use to prevent themselves from becoming "dope sick," to minimize the risk of arrest, and to construct reliable social networks. They have to calculate how much heroin to inject at each session and at what time intervals. Ideally, they attempt to dose themselves in small enough portions to maximize the efficient absorption of heroin into their bodies without raising their habits. They frequently discuss the status of their physical addictions and criticize "greedy" network members who increase their body's physical tolerance by shooting large quantities alone. Most addicts can keep the physical and emotional pains of heroin withdrawal at bay by injecting only half or even a third of a standard street bag of heroin. By sharing, consequently, they wittingly or unwittingly ensure that four to six hours later they will still have money (or a debt obligation from a reliable partner) for another share of heroin. In contrast, when they inject an entire bag alone they often go into a heavy heroin nod for three to four hours, reducing their capacity to hustle effectively and leaving them six to eight hours later with intense cravings, but no money or debt obligations. Another dynamic in the complex pragmatics that encourage addicts to inject in social groups is the risk of overdose due to the variable quality of illegal street heroin. Only after Bourgois was forced to provide mouth-to-mouth recussitation to a peripheral network member who overdosed did we begin to understand the survival imperative of the often ignored street dictum "never fix alone."

Identity, Income Generation, and the Details of Risky Behavior

The micro determinants of risky everyday practices are not self-contained. They reflect a complex panoply of macro-power dynamics. The politics of illegal syringes and the precariousness of income-generation strategies in the underground economy affect everyday risktaking practices (Carlson et al. 1994; Koester 1994). A crucial nexus of

these micro-politics of survival defines the notions of personal respect that organize social interaction on the street. Indeed, the search for respect and economic security are
central organizing dynamics of street culture that shape the propagation of HIV (Anderson 1978; Bourgois 1995; Finestone 1957; Hughes 1977; Wacquant in press).

Ironically—but not surprisingly—street-based identity hierarchies are reflected in
popular discourses of individual worth and public health outreach modalities of behavior modification. Moralizing narratives of individual responsibility reveal themselves in the absolutist public health messages put forward by even the most sensitive,
street-based outreach programs that miscalculate the prevalence of risk-taking among
street addicts. Ethnographic immersion in shooting encampments reveals the "nor-
malcy" with which needles and paraphernalia are routinely shared in homeless street
scenes. Indeed, as participant-observers spending long hours in the shooting encampments, we found ourselves seduced by the routinization of HIV risk and often ceased
noticing potentially risky health behavior.

Pragmatic reasons and internal logics abound for why drug users who are fully
aware of the risk of AIDS and of the mechanisms for HIV transmission share ancillary
paraphernalia on a regular basis and even use dirty needles on occasion. Virtually all
the core members of our network admit that when they suffer from heroin withdrawal—or even anticipate it—they use "any old needle: hell! Even a Bic pen if it's
around" (see also Connors 1994). Sometimes up to four people must pool resources in
their desperation to ward off withdrawal symptoms, especially at early morning and
late-night injection sessions.

On the street, the standard public health outreach messages of "bleach it" or
"never share water, cookers, cottons or needles" insult addicts who cannot maintain
their dope fiend identity and "stay well" (both physiologically and emotionally) if they
do not share ancillary paraphernalia on a daily basis several times a day. These hyper-
sanitary outreach messages exemplify how the medical establishment morally rebukes
street addicts by promoting unrealistic slogans laden with symbolic violence that rele-
gate street addicts to the category of self-destructive other—hence, the utility of Foucault's concept of bio-power. In our tape recorded conversations on several occasions,
we were forced into an awareness of ourselves as agents of this no longer nebulous bio-
power, as we offended network members with the mildest outreach messages:

> Philippe: What about sharing? You know of the risks?
>
> Hogan: Ain't no dope fiend out here gonna turn down no forty units [a sy-
> ringe filled with 40 units of heroin] if he's sick. I mean, I'm serious, he just
> ain't gonna fuckin' do it.
>
> Philippe: But don't you worry about HIV?
>
> Hogan: Yeah [pause] . . . But fuck no! [Silence]. You give any motherfucker
> out here a motherfuckin' taste of forty units, and even if the man has any
> kind of knowledge about you having AIDS or something, he ain't gonna
> give a fuck. If he's sick, he's gonna fix that motherfucker. I'm sorry, that's the
> gospel fuckin' truth.
>
> Philippe [turning to Butch]: Has that happened to you?
>
> Butch: Oh, c'mon, man, you know! Don't ask me that question. [Angry] You

know damn well it has, man! Happens to everybody a million times. Okay?

Philippe: Okay, okay I'm sorry, man . . . didn't mean to offend you. We were just trying to get our AIDS prevention rap out. Sorry.

Butch [putting his hand on Philippe's shoulder and calming down]: Yeah, yeah. I'm sorry; that's cool. We know you're in the health AIDS business and all. It's okay. I mean most of us try to be careful most of the time.

Even politically committed harm reduction activists unconsciously impose what Foucault calls "normalizing judgements" on street addicts (Dreyfus and Rabinow 1982:156–158). Their well-meaning self-help messages of harm reduction resonate with middle class users, but further alienate street addicts. The extreme marginality imposed on anyone who becomes a full-time homeless "dope fiend" confines them to a social universe of mutual betrayal and auto-destruction that most middle class harm reducers do not empathize with and prefer to deny.[3] Although individual heroin addicts—like everyone else—construct complex visions of their own moral authority, they virtually all recognize that a dope fiend in withdrawal has the right to use any means necessary to obtain a dose of heroin. Running partners—even lovers—regularly rip one another off on the street. Such behavior is considered intelligent, "street-wise" prowess.

For example, when Manny stole a loaded syringe that Butch had left unattended at a shooting encampment, Butch subsequently admitted, "Hell, I might'a done the same thing if I was sick too." His first reaction had been to attempt to beat Manny with an axe handle, but he allowed the other network members to hold him back while Manny escaped. The network members considered Manny's theft legitimate because Manny suffered from two painful abscesses on his buttocks that prevented him from walking around and panhandling on the street. In fact, they considered Manny to be smart and crafty for having executed the theft successfully while dope sick, without even leaving the encampment. The fact that the syringe that Manny stole had previously been used, and may have contained traces of Butch's blood, was considered irrelevant. Dope fiends do not have the luxury of refraining from stealing carelessly waylaid syringes out of fear of HIV infection when they are suffering from full-blown heroin withdrawal pains.

Biological and emotional imperatives mandate the frequency of risk-taking. We have witnessed network members succumb to extraordinarily painful seizure-like vomiting, which they casually refer to as "fish-flopping" or "doing the tuna." Under such conditions of physical and emotional duress, it is simply impossible for them to obey the dictates of sanitary medical practices and refuse a syringe-full of heroin, no matter how obviously dirty or potentially HIV infected it may be.

Most network members take pity on running partners suffering from intense withdrawal pains and treat them for free to what is called a "cotton shot." This introduces the important dimension of the differential risks members incur during the same injecting session depending upon the effectiveness of their hustling strategy and their status within the social network. A cotton shot consists of the heroin and blood residues "pounded" out of a cotton remnant (sometimes an old cigarette filter) that was used in a previous injection session to filter heroin solution as it was drawn out of the cooker into each injector's syringe. The used cotton filter is re-wetted with water inside the same previously used cooker. The water used to re-wet the cotton and dissolve whatever heroin and blood residue still clings to the bottom of the cooker is also potentially dirty since it may have been used as rinse solution in earlier injection sessions.

Not all members engage in high-risk cotton shots with the same frequency. Only a low-prestige, economically unsuccessful member begs cotton shots regularly. Members with more successful income-generating strategies claim they never "pound cottons" and often humiliate those who regularly are reduced to "doing cottons." In fact, the lowest prestige member in our network is referred to disparagingly as "no-hustle-Hogan, the cotton bandit." He must assume a humble demeanor in front of the other network members to continue generating their gifts of dirty cottons.

Another small cohort within our network who are not necessarily low-prestige members, but who frequently engage in cotton shots, are those who establish independent shooting galleries in their encampments. Unlike New York City, where shooting gallery managers charge an officially recognized two dollar admission fee for access to the premises and paraphernalia rental (Bourgois 1992), San Francisco Bay Area shooting galleries are less formal (Waldorf et al. 1990). The standard payment is "a taste" of whatever a client happens to be injecting. This taste usually takes the form of a "watery cotton," i.e., five to ten units of heroin solution left over in the bottom of the cooker in addition to the used cotton filter. The only advantage managers of shooting galleries have over those who beg cotton shots is that they sometimes succeed in developing special relationships with outreach workers or volunteers from the city's needle exchange program, allowing them to maintain a cache of clean syringes for their personal use even when only dirty ones are available for lending to visitors. Indeed this kind of needle exchange outreach relationship with a shooting gallery manager was what facilitated our initial entry into our research site.

Shooting gallery managers often engage in and promote risky practices when visitors arrive with bonus supplies of diverse drugs and alcohol and initiate binge sessions. During binges, the gallery manager is treated to exceptionally large portions of whatever is being consumed, and this can degenerate into chaotic needle use—especially when cocaine or crack is involved. Addicts often engage in bloodier methods of injection during binges as they publicly express their companionship in their search for ecstasy. For example, individuals who normally inject intra-muscularly often will attempt to strike a vein ("direct deposit") during a binge session, thereby filling their syringes with exceptional amounts of blood as they probe for several minutes into their collapsed veins. Others with strong veins often "boot" and "jack" their injections under the appreciative eyes of their fellow bingers (i.e., draw blood in and out of the syringe upon registering in a vein) in their communal celebration of ecstasy: "Moby Dick! Thar' she blows! [as blood flows into the syringe]."

Rather than understanding binge sessions as merely pathological rituals of deviant individuals, we need to situate them within the power dynamics that produce such everyday practices. For example, binge sessions are "regulated" and promoted by state institutions. During the first few days of each month, and to a lesser extent in the middle of the month, federal and state transfer payments (General Assistance [GA], Social Security Insurance [SSI], and Food Stamps) energize the street economy.[4] Overjoyed at suddenly having cash street addicts often celebrate generously by treating one another to drugs and alcohol. This leads to a proliferation of binge sessions and gift exchange obligations where individuals engulfed in opportunistic pursuits of ecstasy often take risks that they would not routinely engage in simply because the drugs are free and immediately available. Bingeing is exacerbated during seasonal holidays when panhandling and shoplifting are facilitated. On a deeper level, the binge impulse itself can be understood as a resistance to society's disciplining the uses of pleasure—hence the outlaws' ecstatic commitment to overstimulating their bodies: "Everyday is Christmas. Get it while the gettin's good."

Race, Class, Gender, and Sexuality

Despite a superficial veneer of multi-ethnic interaction in street drug scenes, our ethnographic data reveal that addicts harbor bitter divisions across ethnic divides, especially between African Americans and other ethnic groups (Anglos, Latinos, and Asians). The core members of our social network, for example, remain largely ethnically segregated at the level of social interaction. During the first year-and-a-half of our fieldwork, African Americans rarely visited the shooting encampments, even though the immediately surrounding community is primarily African American. This quasi-apartheid organization became even more dramatic during our fieldwork's second year when an African-American customer of the main dealer moved into one of the shooting encampments. As if replaying the patterns of white flight in middle class suburban communities, within two months, the four white injectors who formerly inhabited this particular encampment moved to another site, and three new African-American injectors took their place. Two months later, the Latino dealer still residing in the original encampment also moved out and joined the white encampment, complaining matter-of-factly, "the niggers have taken over."

In contrast to the more broken down beggar/wino identity that the white dope fiends cultivate, both male and female African-American addicts in our network embrace a more oppositional outlaw identity. Their income-generating strategies are less dependent upon panhandling and involve riskier forays of burglary and shoplifting. This renders them more effective at obtaining windfall profits which they often spend on all-night speedball (heroin and cocaine) injections and crack-smoking marathons.[5]

African-American addicts in our network usually strive to make direct deposits from their syringes into their veins, rather than diffusing them intramuscularly. In contrast, most of the white injectors simply "muscle" their shots due to their collapsed veins. They do not even roll up their sleeves, instead injecting right through their clothes. One African American who has weak veins in his arms prefers to inject into the jugular vein in his neck, rather than dissipate the ecstasy by an intramuscular injection. He refuses to accept the social status of "broken down dope fiend who muscles." Direct depositing visibly increases the amount of blood in syringes, and consequently augments the potential of HIV. Furthermore, the African Americans are more likely to "jack" their speedballs, or their binge doses of heroin, i.e., draw blood in and out of their veins several times during their injection:

> Lady in red, give daddy some head . . . come back little Sheba [drawing
> blood into the syringe]; Hit the road Jack, [partially reinjecting] and don't
> you come back . . . no mo'. . . no mo'. . . . [redrawing blood into the syringe].

The white addicts, in stereotypical essentialist language, define jacking and neck injections as "something niggers do."

More subtly, the African-American addicts in our network invest more energy than the whites to portray themselves as effective and autonomous street hustlers. They are prouder of being thieves than of being beggars and they desperately attempt to prove this to themselves and to one another by taking more dramatic risks. The effective hustler occupies a particularly central symbolic place in African-American street culture (Anderson 1976, Malcolm X 1964), expressed on a daily basis in intimate and public constructions of self-respect. They invest money and energy in fashionable clothes; take pride in committing larceny ("hitting a lick"); engage in more frequent displays of violent bravado; celebrate their confrontations with the police; and triumphantly cultivate binge behavior around crack use and speedballing. Two African Americans in the core network and several additional African American addicts on the network's periphery openly claim that they are still sexually active in contrast to all of the core white network members who admit being impotent. The whites dismiss our attempts to steer conversation towards sexual activity with the trite dismissal, "my lady is heroin." When we tried to distribute condoms early in our fieldwork, we were rebuked with "What do you want us to do with them? Have a balloon party?"

The interface of the African Americans with supportive public institutions is more precarious, from GA, Food Stamps, and SSI to San Francisco's Needle Exchange Program, its Methadone detox clinics, and the local public hospital. African Americans are more frequently searched or harassed by local police patrols, rendering it more dangerous for them than for whites to carry a clean syringe. They spend more of their daylight hours inside their encampments, coming out after dark on the street, when it is most necessary to cultivate a tough outlaw demeanor. While maintaining their autonomy and dignity they refuse to succumb to police practices and to generalized social depreciation, sometimes even taunting the authorities openly and challenging the general public. For example, they drink their fortified wine without a paper bag wrapping or shout at passing motorists who do not respect their right of way at crosswalks. They are less subservient panhandlers, sometimes crossing the line into overt aggression. All these complex factors ranging from definitions of personal identity and drugs of choice, to modes of defiance and experiences with institutional racism and illegal income-generating strategies, increase African-American HIV risk in our network. It also renders them more vulnerable to institutional repression and social exclusion.

Gender is a more partial and complex boundary maintaining mechanism that accelerates HIV transmission. Women primarily enter our network as subordinated partners to men but, conversely, they strategically hustle drugs and money through their acts of subordination. Although officially they are called "girlfriends" and sometimes engage in peripheral sex work, they usually do not have sexual relations with the men in the encampments, whose heroin habits have largely incapacitated them sexually. None of the men serve as intermediaries in the women's occasional sex work. On the contrary, the women extract more drugs and economic resources from the men than vice versa. Women often strategically frequent the encampments and shooting galleries when binge episodes are most likely to occur, such as when Social Service transfer payments are received. As noted earlier, opportunistic bingers are at particularly high risk of HIV infection.

The women in our network conceal the fact that they take advantage of the men's income by symbolically exaggerating subordination to "their old man." This protects them from being sexually harassed by peripheral members of the network who might still be aggressive sexually, and legitimizes access to boyfriends' drugs during binges. Another rape resistance strategy among women on the periphery of our network is "to act crazy and be all dirty and smelly" (cf. Eighner 1993). This is especially the case for the crack addicts who fend for themselves without an "old man." All women who regularly have frequented our social network over the past two-and-a-half years symbolically reaffirm their subordination by claiming to be unable to administer their own injections. Their boyfriends, or trusted network members, have to administer their heroin injections every time they use.[6] This lack of physical control over needles and paraphernalia further increases their gender-specific risktaking. Additionally, because most of the women also engage in occasional sex-work to maintain their habits, they are already at higher risk of HIV and STD infections. Significantly, their sex work customers are largely ethnically segregated, concentrated among the crack and alcohol users in a contiguous African-American network of non-injectors that congregates in the immediate neighborhood. Yet again, ethnicity, drug-use of choice, and gender articulate in crucial ways around risky practices.

Social class is probably the most monolithic, but least understood boundary maintaining mechanism in our social scene. Virtually all the addicts, including most of the peripheral ones, come from working-class, or even lumpen family backgrounds. Because of the extraordinary growth in California's economy since World War II, several parents of the white addicts now live middle class lifestyles, but the childhoods of all the addicts were universally working class or poorer. No middle class users regularly frequent the shooting encampments, even though several dozen middle class clients occasionally purchase from network members. Significantly on the few occasions when we have observed middle-class addicts or chippers inject in the street, they were trying to conceal their substance abuse from an employer or from friends and family. In other words, they were forced into unsanitary shooting galleries not because of economic constraints, but by the sanctions of substance abuse. Once again, we see the subtleties of bio-power in action: Heroin is not merely illegal and expensive, but also taboo, thereby fostering self-destructive oppositional identities of "wannabe dope fiend."[7]

Finally, in the male-dominated, homophobic street culture adhered to by the members of our network, openly gay or lesbian identities are forbidden. Nevertheless, we have been able to document two long-term gay relationships within the network. One is camouflaged as a "running partner" relationship between a duo who sold heroin together. The other was camouflaged at first by the two male lovers "running" with a lesbian who allowed one of them to pretend he was her boyfriend. Other male members of the network have confided that they generated income as gay sex workers in their youth, even though they "hated faggots." Significantly, the "passive" members in

the male partnerships cannot inject themselves and rely on their partners to administer their doses of heroin in a re-creation of the symbolic gender subordination that pervades compulsory heterosexual relations. Despite these sometimes contradictory sexual
identities, open discussions of homosexuality precipitate physical confrontation. We
could not even begin to access data on this taboo subject until over a year into the
fieldwork. Indeed, it was not until our third year that tales and accusations of gay activities became a routine part of conversation. The standard pattern is for network
members to accuse those who have departed for long periods of time—usually due to
incarceration—of being "that way."

Demystifying the Power of Epidemiology

At the very minimum, ethnography can increase the "accuracy" of information collected in large-scale surveys of risky behavior that rely on self-reporting. Currently
many surveys are not even asking the right questions; they simply miss the central dynamics of HIV risk. For example, local epidemiological HIV-prevention projects have
interviewed a main dealer in our network several times, yet they did not address the
fact that he has a heavy "dealer's habit" with an irregular clientele at a precarious income-generating site that frequently causes him to be dope sick thereby forcing him to
pool resources desperately. Instead, embarrassed by their questions about needle sharing, the dealer soft-pedaled his risk taking. Paid self-report scientific protocols designed
to sample large numbers of street addicts are unable to document crucial social dynamics because of their single-minded pursuit of quantifiable variables. By forcing the
behavioral sciences to mimic natural science paradigms, epidemiological protocols usually elide power relations and obfuscate the most significant parameters of social
processes. Research questions become focused around discrete variables that are technocratic at best or completely arbitrary at worst. Despite an ideology of scientific neu-
trality, these analytic techniques reinforce a focus on individuals and pathology. This is
most concretely expressed in public health's applied mandate of "individual behavior
change." Public health researchers contact substance abusers through a questionnaire
interview process that reaffirms social hierarchies and value judgments between knowledge experts and aberrant individuals. Street addicts usually do not want to appear stu-
pid or offensive to a friendly interviewer. In fact they usually have at least partially in-
ternalized society's normalizing judgements and are depressed, ashamed, or ambivalent
about their marginality. No matter how resistant they may be to these bio-power dynamics, deep down inside, they know they are failures. This is exacerbated when interviewers tell them that it has been clinically proven that HIV is spread by dirty cookers and that no one should ever share any ancillary paraphernalia.

The confessional context of paid self-report interviews and well-meant outreach
messages humiliate addicts. Foucault has documented how a "discourse of science" and
medicine imposes a "millennial yoke of confession" on Western bodies and minds,
thereby marginalizing those who fail to discipline their abnormality (1978:61–64). If
street addicts listen carefully to outreach workers or answer cross-checked self-report
questionnaires honestly, they are made to appear self-destructive and irresponsible to

both themselves and the interviewer. Virtually all our network members have told us that they distort their risky behavior on questionnaires. Often their motives are straightforwardly instrumental: "When I answer 'no,' it takes care of five pages right there." More subtly, they filter outreach, messages through avoidance or cognitive dissonance. Hogan, who probably takes more injection risks than any other network member, reported to us the outcome of one of these paid, would-be confessional, intervention interviews:

> Hogan: I said, yeah, I share rigs occasionally. You know . . . only if it is somebody I know that is clean—and this and that. I said I went down and took an AIDS test with them, we came back clean: so I said I shared with them.
>
> Philippe: Why did you say that?
>
> Hogan: Well, I thought it sounded good. Which is the truth, you know. . . . But not that I could really tell if they were HIV.

In fact, of course, Hogan shares ancillary paraphernalia every day, usually several times a day, and sometimes directly shares needles. He liked the researcher administering the interview protocol, so he tried to respond in what he thought was a socially appropriate manner. He participated in the dominating confessional ritual of the self-report interview protocol precisely because of the goodwill of his street-sensitive interviewer. On another occasion Hogan was more resistant; he told an interviewer that he only shared needles with his "Old Lady." When we asked him why he bothered to make up this bizarre detail (he has not socialized intimately with a woman for over a decade), he protested: "Well it's true. I have been faithful to my Old Lady thirty years and she's heroin. I love her." Hogan was not making fun of his interviewer by fantasizing about his Old Lady Heroin. He was just trying to celebrate the dignity of his dope fiend reality by resisting the "truth imperative" of the self-report protocol (Foucault 1978:58–63).

With a fuller understanding of what takes place physically, socially, and emotionally in street-based injection scenes, we can begin to explain the actual processes that are reflected in epidemiological correlations in an effort to ascertain why, how, and when HIV is transmitted. Currently, for example, we simply do not know how risky it is to share ancillary paraphernalia, although given San Francisco's relatively low HIV infection rates among injectors (9 to 13%), we suspect that cookers, cottons, and water are not particularly effective routes for HIV transmission as compared to needle sharing without rinsing or to receptive anal sex without a condom. We will never learn the answers to these important public health questions if paid self-reporting on survey forms remains the standard methodological tool for collecting data on HIV risk-taking behavior.[8] Of course, if paraphernalia laws are reformed and syringes become legal and publicly subsidized for street addicts in all states (as they are in Canada and in almost all European countries), then the question of the potential lethality of ancillary paraphernalia or of the relative prophylactic qualities of bleach versus water rinses becomes much less important.

Many street addicts are genuinely incapable of responding accurately to self-reports on direct and indirect sharing. The reality of their practices are too overwhelmingly dangerous and self-destructive for them to admit cognitively to themselves, or to anyone else, the extent of the risks they regularly engage in to maintain identities and bodies as dope fiends. "Denial" is a crucial defense/coping mechanism that enables them to survive proudly, and self-destructively as "righteous dope fiends." Indeed, denial may represent resistance to the yoke of confession (Foucault 1978:61). In any case, denial should not be understood as a reductionist psychological construct, but rather as the deployment of agency within a socially imposed survival strategy.

The need for denial to maintain oneself on the street as a full-time "hope-to-die-with-my-boots-on" dope fiend is intricately tied with the social coercion around substance abuse. The illegality, not just of heroin, but also of syringes in the case of California—as well as the laws against public intoxication or against sleeping in public—push addicts to inject their drugs in the unhealthiest possible nooks and crannies (Lettiere 1995). Laws and moralizing judgments prevent most addicts from maintaining stable income-generating strategies. It forces them to become "beggars and thieves" and isolates them in abusive social networks (Fleisher 1995). More subtly, the social repression of drug use encourages obsessive-compulsive binge behavior and violent interpersonal relations. It promotes unsanitary injection practices on the run in dark alleys or behind bushes. Indeed, it imposes the dope fiend identity on those surviving addiction on the street. The dramatically arbitrary contrast between legal methadone and illegal heroin illustrates the pharmacologically inconsistent logic of the medical establishment: the same employed, housed individuals who are rewarded and even subsidized by the state to become physically addicted to methadone will be fired if heroin is detected in their urine, despite the fact that there is no significant difference in the coordination or cognitive abilities of an individual mildly high on methadone versus one mildly high on heroin. The Swiss public health establishment's experiments with legal heroin maintenance in the mid-1990s suggest that heroin addictions may be as relatively manageable as methadone addictions (Nadelman 1996).

Risky Business: Promoting Public Health or Private Infections

Traditional public health research methods reflect the class and cultural biases of academia, medicine, and social services. Participant-observation among socially marginal substance abusers obliges researchers to confront a wide range of uncomfortable phenomena, from distressing odors and human pain to interpersonal violence, legal dangers, and the acute sexism and racism of street culture. It is only normal for intellectuals—like most stable middle class individuals—to be unwilling or unable to engage in the non-judgmental, culturally relative interaction required for effective ethnographic data collection among addicts on the street.

Ethnographic methods in and of themselves are obviously no panacea for HIV-prevention research. Data on everyday social suffering must be viewed through a theoretical lens that privileges power. Otherwise detailed accounts of the misery of daily life merely contribute to an exotic voyeurism that becomes yet another murky reflection in a scientific hall of mirrors that demeans the socially vulnerable. Conversely, theoretical analyses of power are all too often enmeshed in tangled webs of abstraction that may appear sophisticated but have little contact with social practices. If we are to intervene effectively in the AIDS epidemic in a manner that does not reproduce social suffering and the sanctions of substance abuse, we have to confront the multiple dimensions of power examined in this chapter, being careful not to remove ourselves from concrete settings.

The challenge is not merely to access, document, and explain the dynamics of everyday suffering; but also to translate it into meaningful interventions that do not unconsciously reproduce structures of inequality and discourses of subordination. There are no technocratic quick fixes. Bleach and condoms, for example, will never definitively stem the tide of HIV infection because they are as much expressions of a repressive medical discipline as they are rationally implementable solutions. The spread and prevention of AIDS among substance abusers in the United States reaches to the heart of the collective experience of extreme social misery.

Notes

We are indebted to Steve Koester for drawing our attention to "indirect sharing" in the late 1980s. Mike Agar obtained pilot funds for this research from the Community Epidemiological Working Group (NO1DA-3-5201) directed by Nick Kozel at the National Institute on Drug Abuse (NIDA). The project subsequently was funded on an interim basis by Public Service Contract 263-MD-519210 administered by Susan Coyle in Richard Needle's office at NIDA's Community Research Branch. It received NIDA grant (R01 DA10164-01) in March 1996 when James Quesada joined the project as co-Principal Investigator and Mark Lettiere became the Principal Ethnographer. We thank Maxwell Burton, Joelle Morrow, Raul Pereira, and Jeff Schonberg for their part-time ethnographic input.

1. For example, an epidemiological, self-report study documents that bleach use rose from 3% to 89% among injectors in San Francisco between 1986 and 1992 with 52% using bleach 100% of the time in 1990 (Watters 1994). Rarely have we seen bleach used during our three years of intensive ethnographic immersion among street addicts in San Francisco, despite observing well over one thousand injections.

2. This research is protected by a Federal Certificate of Confidentiality and all identifying names and locations have been changed.

3. Despite these critiques of harm reduction, it is imperative to recognize that needle exchange in the mid-1990s was the most useful public health modality for curbing dirty needle use.

4. It is important to specify that the faltering institutional remnants of the U.S. safety net for the indigent homeless also provide avenues for reducing risk and violence. Addicts who regularly receive SSI, GA, and/or Food Stamps usually enjoy greater stability, commit less crime, and are often better able to engage in positive social interaction and personal harm reduction than those who are completely independent.

5. Because crack rather than powder cocaine is primarily available in black street scenes the African-American addicts dissolve the crack they purchase back into injectable cocaine hydrochloride form by adding lemon juice extract to their cookers.

6. The notable exception confirming the rule is Tammy who is able to inject herself intramuscularly but has a network member administer her direct deposits during binge sessions.

7. Middle-class chippers are especially susceptible to overdosing because of their inexperience in gauging street quantities and because irregular use fluctuates their physical tolerance for opiates.

8. Criminologists have elaborated graphs and equations to represent the greater disparity in crime self-report rates between African-American and white delinquent males (Hindelang

et al. 1981:171). In one study white males reported 90% of the offenses on their records while black males reported only 67% of the offenses listed on their official records, a ratio of 1.5:1 . . . (1981: 177–178)."

References

Adler, Peter, and Patricia A. Adler. 1983. "Shifts and oscillations in deviant careers: The case of upper-level drug dealers and smugglers." *Social Problems* 31:195–207.

Agar, Michael. 1973. *Ripping and Running: A Formal Ethnography of Urban Heroin Addicts.* New York: Seminar.

———. 1996. "Epnography? Ethnodemiology? Towards an epidemiology of the subject." Paper presented at conference "Integrating Anthropological Approaches in Epidemiological and Prevention Research on Drug Abuse and HIV/AIDS: Current Status and Future Prospects." National Institute on Drug Abuse and the American Anthropological Association, Washington D.C., Sept. 24–25.

Anderson, Elijah. 1978. *A Place on the Corner.* Chicago: University of Chicago Press.

Becker, Howard. 1953. "Becoming a marijuana user." *American Journal of Sociology* 59:235–242.

Best, Joel. 1990. *Threatened Children: Rhetoric and Concern about Child-Victims.* Chicago: University of Chicago Press.

Bolton, Ralph. 1992. "AIDS and promiscuity: Muddles in the model of HIV Prevention." *Medical Anthropology* 14(2/4):145–185.

Bourdieu, Pierre. 1996. "Unwrapping the gift: On interest and generosity in social life." Colloquium delivered to the Anthropology Department, University of California, Berkeley, April 8.

Bourgois, Philippe. 1992. "Une nuit dans une shooting gallery: Enquête sur le commerce de la drogue à East Harlem." *Actes de la Recherche en Sciences Sociales* 94:59–78. [English version printed as "Just Another Night in a Shooting Gallery" Occasional Paper #18, Russell Sage Foundation, New York, 1991.]

———. 1995. *In Search of Respect: Selling Crack in El Barrio.* New York: Cambridge University Press.

Broadhead, Robert, and Eric Margolis. 1993. "Drug Policy in the time of AIDS: The development of outreach in San Francisco." *The Sociological Quarterly* 34(1):3(1):497–522.

Bruneau, Julie, Edwardo Franco, François Lamothe, Nathalie Lachance, Marie Desy, and Julio Soto. 1997. "High rates of HIV infection among injection drug users participating in needle exchange programs in Montreal: Results of a cohort study." *American Journal of Epidemiology.* 146:994–1002.

Caldararo, Niccolo. 1996. "The HIV/AIDS epidemic: Its evolutionary implications for human ecology with special reference to the immune system." *The Science of the Total Environment* 191:245–269.

Caputo, John, and Mark Yount. 1993. "Institutions, normalization and power." In *Foucault and the Critique of Institutions,* John Caputo and Mark Yount (eds.), 3–26. University Park: Pennsylvania State University Press.

Carlson, Robert. 1996. "The political economy of AIDS among drug users in the United States: Beyond blaming the victim or powerful others." *American Anthropologist* 98:2:266–278.

Carlson, Robert, Harvey Siegal, and Russell Falck. 1994. "Ethnography, epidemiology, and public policy: Needle use practices and HIV risk reduction among injecting drug users in the Midwest." In *Global AIDS Policy,* Douglas Feldman (ed.), 185–214. Westport, Conn.: Bergin & Garvey.

Centers for Disease Control. 1996. HIV/AIDS Surveillance Report: Year-end Edition 1995. Atlanta, Ga.: Centers for Disease Control.

Coates, Thomas, Don Des Jarlais, Heather Miller, Lincoln Moses, Charles Turner, and Dooley Worth. 1990. "The AIDS Epidemic in the Second Decade." In *AIDS: The Second Decade.* Heather Miller, Charles Turner, and Lincoln Moses (eds.), 38–80. Washington D.C.: National Academy Press.

Connors, Margaret. 1994. "Stories of pain and the problem of AIDS prevention: Injection drug withdrawal and its effects on risk behavior." *Medical Anthropology Quarterly* 8:1:47–68.

Davey, Smith G., Mel Bartley, and David Blane. 1990. "The black report on socioeconomic inequalities in health 10 years on." *British Medical Journal* 301:373–377.

Dean, Mitchell. 1994. *Critical and Effective Histories: Foucault's Methods and Historical Sociology.* London: Routledge.

Des Jarlais, Don, Samuel Friedman, and David Strug. 1986. "AIDS and needle sharing within the IV drug use subculture." In *The Social Dimensions of AIDS: Method and Theory,* Douglas Feldman and Thomas Johnson (eds.), 111–125. New York: Praegar.

DiGiacomo, Susan M. 1992. "Metaphor as illness: Postmodern dilemmas in the representation of body, mind and disorder." *Medical Anthropology Quarterly* 14:109–137.

Dorfman, Lorie, Pamela Derish, and Judith Cohen. 1992. "Hey girlfriend: An evaluation of AIDS prevention among women in the sex industry." *Health Education Quarterly* 19(1):25.

Dreyfus, Hubert, and Paul Rabinow. 1982. *Michel Foucault: Beyond Structuralism and Hermeneutics.* Chicago: University of Chicago Press.

Duesberg, Peter. 1995. "Is HIV the cause of AIDS?" *The Lancet* (Nov. 18) 346:8986: 1371–1372.

Dunlap, Elois, Bruce Johnson, Harry Sanabria, Elbert Holliday, Vicki Lipsey, Maurice Barnett, William Hopkins, Ira Sobel, Doris Randolph, and Ko-Lin Chin. 1990. "Studying crack users and their criminal careers: The scientific and artistic aspects of locating hard-to-reach subjects and interviewing them about sensitive topics." *Contemporary Drug Problems* 17(1):121–144.

Eighner, Lars. 1993. *Travels with Lisbeth: Three Years on the Road and on the Streets.* New York: St. Martin's Press.

Ellison, B. J., A. B. Downey, and Peter Duesberg. 1995. "HIV as a surrogate marker for drug use—a re-analysis of the San Francisco men's health study." *Genetica* 95(1–3):165–171.

Epstein, Steven. 1996. *Impure Science: AIDS, Activism, and the Politics of Knowledge.* Berkeley: University of California Press.

Farmer, Paul. 1992. *AIDS and Accusation: Haiti and the Geography of Blame.* Berkeley: University of California Press.

Feldman, Harvey, Michael Agar, and George Beschner, eds. 1979. *Angel Dust: An Ethnographic Study of PCP Users.* Lexington, Mass.: Lexington Books, D.C. Heath.

Fernando, Daniel. 1991. "Fundamental limitations of needle-exchange programs as a strategy for HIV prevention among IVDUs in the U.S." *AIDS and Public Policy Journal* 6:116–120.

Finestone, Harold. 1957. "Cats, kicks, and color." *Social Problems* 5:1:3–13.

Fitzpatrick, Peter. 1992. *Sociology of Law and Crime: The Mythology of Modern Law.* London: Routledge.

Fleisher, Mark. 1995. *Beggars and Thieves: Lives of Urban Street Criminals.* Madison: University of Wisconsin Press.

Foucault, Michel. 1963. *The Birth of the Clinic: An Archaeology of Medical Perception.* New York: Random House.

———. 1978. *The History of Sexuality. Volume I: An Introduction.* New York: Pantheon Books.

———. 1980. *Power/Knowledge: Selected Interviews and Other Writings, 1972–1977.* Edited by Colin Gordon. New York: Pantheon/Random House.

———. 1982. "The subject and power." In *Michel Foucault: Beyond Structuralism and Hermeneutics,* by Hubert L. Dreyfus and Paul Rabinow, 208–226. Chicago: University of Chicago Press.

Fox, Kathryn. 1991. "The Politics of prevention: Ethnographers combat AIDS among drug users." In *Ethnography Unbound: Power and Resistance in the Modern Metropolis,* Michael Burawoy, et al. (eds.), 35–57. Berkeley: University of California Press.

Fumento, Michael. 1990. *The Myth of Heterosexual AIDS.* New York: Basic Books.

Goffmann, Erving. 1963. *Stigma: Notes on the Management of Spoiled Identity.* Englewood Cliffs, N.J.: Prentice-Hall.

Gusfield, Joseph R. 1981. The *Culture of Public Problems: Drinking-Driving and the Symbolic Order.* Chicago: University of Chicago Press.

Guydish, Joseph, Al Abramowitz, William Woods, Dennis Black, and James Sorensen. 1990. Changes in needle sharing behavior among intravenous drug users: San Francisco, 1986–88." *American Journal of Public Health* 80(8):995–997.

Hahn, Robert A., Joseph Milinare, and Steven Teutsch. 1992. "Inconsistencies in coding race and ethnicity between birth and death in U.S. Infants." *Journal of the American Medical Association* 267:259–263.

Hankins, Catherine A. In press. "Syringe exchange in Canada: Good but not enough to stem the HIV tide." *International Journal of the Addictions.*

Haverkos, Harry, and T. Stephen Jones. 1994. "HIV, drug-use paraphernalia, and bleach." *Journal of Acquired Immune Deficiency Syndromes* 7:741–746.

Herdt, Gilbert, and Shirley Lindenbaum, eds. 1992. *In the Time of AIDS: Social Analysis, Theory and Method.* London: Sage.

Hindelang, Michael, Travis Hirschi, and Joseph Weis. 1981. *Measuring Delinquency,* vol. 123. London: Sage Publications.

Huang, Karen, John Watters, and Patricia Case. 1988. "Psychological assessment and AIDS research with intravenous drug users: Challenges in measurement." *Journal of Psychoactive Drugs* 20:191–195.

Hughes, Patrick. 1977. *Behind the Wall of Respect: Community Experiments in Heroin Addiction Control.* Chicago: University of Chicago Press.

Janes, Craig, Ron Stall, and Sandra Gifford, eds. 1986. *Anthropology and Epidemiology.* Dordrecht: D. Reidel.

Jones, Stephen, Harry Haverkos, and Beny Primm. 1994. NIDA/CSAT/CDC workshop on the use of bleach for the decontamination of drug injection equipment, Special Issue of the *Journal of Acquired Immune Deficiency Syndromes* 7(7):741–776.

Kleinman, Arthur. 1995. *Writing at the Margin: Discourse Between Anthropology and Medicine.* Berkeley: University of California Press.

Koester, Steven. 1992. "Ethnographic contributions to substance abuse research." Paper presented at the 54th Annual Meetings of the College on Problems of Drug Dependence, Inc. and the International Narcotics Research Conference, Keystone, Col., June 23–27.

———. 1994. "Copping, running, and paraphernalia laws: Contextual variables and needle risk behavior among injection drug users in Denver." *Human Organization* 53:287–295.

———. 1996. "The process of drug injection: Applying ethnography to the study of HIV risk among IDUs." In *AIDS, Drugs and Prevention: Perspectives on Individual and Community Action,* Tim Rhodes and Richard Hartnoll (eds.), 133–148. London: Routledge.

Krieger, Nancy, and S. Zierler. 1996. "What explains the public's health? A call for epidemiologic theory." *Epidemiology* 7(1):107–109.

Laumann, Edward, John Gagnon, Robert Michael, and Stuart Michaels. 1994. *The Social Organization of Sexuality: Sexual Practices in the United States.* Chicago: University of Chicago Press.

Lettiere, Mark. 1995. "Is your quality of life in violation?: San Francisco's homeless and the construction of criminality." Paper presented at the 61st annual meeting of the American Society of Criminology, Boston, November.

Malcolm X. 1966. *The Autobiography of Malcolm X.* New York: Grove Press.

McNagny, S., and R. Parker. 1992. "High prevalence of recent cocaine use and the unreliability of patient self-report in an inner-city walk-in clinic." *Journal of the American Medical Association.* 267:1106–1108.

Moss, Andrew, Karen Vranizan, Robert Gorter, Peter Bacchetti, John Watters, and Dennis Osmond. 1994. "HIV seroconversion in intravenous drug users in San Francisco, 1985–1990." AIDS 8(2):223–231.

Nadelman, Ethan. 1996. "Switzerland's heroin experiment." *National Review* (July 10):46–47.

National Research Council. 1993. *The Social Impact of AIDS in the United States.* Washington, D.C.: National Academy Press.

Ong, Aihwa. 1995. "Making the biopolitical subject: Cambodian immigrants, refugee medicine and cultural citizenship in California." *Social Science and Medicine* 40:1243–1257.

Page, Bryan J., David Chitwood, Prince Smith, Normie Kane, and Duane McBride. 1990. "Intravenous drug use and HIV infection in Miami." *Medical Anthropological Quarterly.* 4(4):56–71.

Preble, Edward, and John Casey, Jr. 1969. "Taking care of business—the heroin user's life on the street." *International Journal of the Addictions* 4(1):1–24.

Quesada, James. In press. "Suffering child: An embodiment of war and its aftermath in post-Sandinista Nicaragua." *Medical Anthropology Quarterly.*

Reinarman, Craig, and Harry L. Levine. 1989. "Crack in context: Politics and media in the making of a drug scene." *Contemporary Drug Problems* 14(4):535–577.

Scheper-Hughes, Nancy. 1993. "AIDS, public health, and human rights in Cuba." *The Lancet* 342:965–967.

Scheper-Hughes, Nancy, and Margaret Lock. 1987. "The mindful body: A prolegomenon to future work in medical anthropology." *Medical Anthropology Quarterly* 1(1):6–41.

Singer, Merrill. 1994. "AIDS and the health crisis of the urban poor: The perspective of critical medical anthropology." *Social Science and Medicine* 39(7):931–948.

———. 1996. Introductory remarks at the conference: "Integrating Anthropological Approaches in Epidemiological and Prevention Research on Drug Abuse and HIV/AIDS: Current Status and Future Prospects." National Institute on Drug Abuse and the American Anthropological Association, Washington D.C., Sept. 24–25.

Singer, Merrill, and Hans Baer. 1995. *Critical Medical Anthropology.* Amityville, N.Y. : Baywood Publishing Co.

Spector, Malcolm, and John I. Kitsuse. 1977. *Constructing Social Problems.* Menlo Park, Calif.: Cummings.

Susser, Mervyn. 1994. "The logic in ecological. II. The logic of design." *American Journal of Public Health* 84:830–835.

Trostle, James A., and Johannes Sommerfeld. 1996. "Medical anthropology and epidemiology." *Annual Review of Anthropology* 25:253–274.

Trotter, Robert, Richard Rothenberg, Richard Needle, and Susan Coyle. 1995. "Drug abuse and HIV prevention research: Expanding paradigms and network contributions to risk reduction." *Connections* 18(1):29–46.

Vlahov, David, Jacqueline Astemborski, Liza Solomon, and Kenrad Nelson. 1994. "Field effectiveness of needle disinfection among injecting drug users." *Journal of Acquired Immune Deficiency Syndromes* 7(7):760–766.

Wacquant, Loic. In press. "Inside the zone: The craft of the hustler in the black American ghetto." In *The Poverty of Society,* Pierre Bourdieu (ed.). Stanford, Calif.: Stanford University Press.

Waldorf, Dan, Craig Reinarman, and Sheigla Murphy. 1990. "Needle sharing, shooting galleries, and AIDS risks among intravenous drug users in San Francisco: Criminal justice and public health policy." *Criminal Justice Policy Review* 3 (4):391–406.

Watters, John. 1994. "Trends in risk behavior and HIV seroprevalence in heterosexual injection drug users in San Francisco, 1986–1992." *Journal of Acquired Immune Deficiency Syndromes* 7:1276–1281.

Watters, John, Michelle Estilo, George Clark, and Jennifer Lorvick. 1994a. "Syringe and needle exchange as HIV/AIDS prevention for injection drug users." *Journal of the American Medical Association* 271(2):115–152.

Watters, John, Michelle Estilo, Alex Kral, and Jennifer Lorvick. 1994b. "HIV infection among female injection-drug users recruited in community settings." *Sexually Transmitted Diseases* 21(6):321–328.

Watters, John, Richard Needle, Norman Weatherby, Robert Booth, and Mark Williams. 1992. Letter to *Journal of the American Medical Association* 268(17):2374–2375.

Weppner, R. ed. 1977. *Street Ethnography: Selected Studies of Crime and Drug Use in Natural Settings.* Beverly Hills, Calif.: Sage Publications.

Wiebel, Wayne. 1988. "Combining ethnographic and epidemiological methods in targeted AIDS interventions: The Chicago model." In *Needle Sharing Among Intravenous Drug Abusers: National and International Perspectives,* Robert J. Battjes and Roy Pickens (eds.), 137–150. National Institute on Drug Abuse Research Monograph 80, Rockville, MD: National Institute on Drug Abuse.

Williams, Raymond. 1977. *Marxism and Literature.* Oxford: Oxford University Press.

Williams, Terry. 1992. *Crackhouse: Notes from the End of the Line.* New York: Addison-Wesley.

Zolopa, Andrew, Judith Hahn, Robert Gorter, Jeanne Miranda, Dan Wlodarczyk, Jacqueline Peterson, Louise Pilote, and Andrew Moss. 1994. "HIV and tuberculosis infection in San Francisco's homeless adults." *Journal of the American Medical Association* 272(6):455–461.

Index

Note: Page references in *italic type* refer to figures or tables.

About the Editors

James D. Orcutt is professor of sociology at Florida State University, where he has been the recipient of eight teaching awards. He served as editor of *Social Problems* and was elected as vice president and president of the Society for the Study of Social Problems. He has also served as chair of the Drinking and Drugs Division of SSSP and as chair of the ASA Section on Alcohol and Drugs. His previous publications include a book, *Analyzing Deviance*, as well as numerous articles on alcohol and drug problems.

David R. Rudy, professor of sociology and Dean of the Institute for Regional Analysis and Public Policy at Morehead State University, earned the PhD in sociology at Syracuse University. He has served on the board of directors of SSSP and chaired SSSP's Drinking and Drugs Division. He is author of *Becoming Alcoholic: Alcoholics Anonymous and the Reality of Alcoholism* (1986); his current research interests include regional program development and alcohol-related social movements. His published work has appeared in a range of academic journals.